"*I, Fellini* gives a good portrayal of the 'layer underneath'—the world of dream and imagination that expressed itself early in his art work and in his response to the limited instances of fantasy that entered the provincial world of his youth. . . . One of the best things about the book is that it makes clear the primary importance of Fellini's art work in his creative production, and his own awareness of that importance. . . . *I Fellini* completely fulfills its real purpose: to send us back to the movies." —*New Yorker*

"Delightful. . . . As Fellini bubbles about the work of Mae West and Laurel and Hardy, along with his own films, one thing is proved beyond a doubt: This man loved the movies." —*Entertainment Weekly*

"There are splendid moments throughout. *I, Fellini* ranges over his childhood, his career, his intensely personal approach to making films—all of them are about him, he says—his theories about men, women, and sex, and his loving fifty-year marriage to Masina." —*Los Angeles Times*

"Chandler's seemingly artless achievement is to summon up a verbal hologram of the indispensable humanity of Fellini." —*Film Comment*

"As the title suggests, *I, Fellini* captures both the legendary director's self-absorption and sense of humor. Though Charlotte Chandler is the author, it is really an as-told-to, with Federico Fellini doing the talking in plain-spoken style. Naturally, there's inside stuff about his masterpieces—*La Strada*, *La Dolce Vita*, etc.—but it's his artless little asides that stay with you. . . . The miracle is that however eccentric the orbit, Fellini manages to pull audiences along with him." —*Premiere*

CHARLOTTE CHANDLER

I, FELLINI

FOREWORD BY BILLY WILDER

Cooper Square Press

First Cooper Square Press edition 2001

This Cooper Square Press paperback edition of *I, Fellini* is an unabridged republication of the edition published in New York in 1995 (and originally published in German as *Ich, Fellini* in 1994). It is reprinted by arrangement with the author.

Verlagsbuchhandlung Gmbh, Munich, München, in 1994.
Copyright © 1994 by F. A. Herbig by Cooper Square Press
Verlagsbuchhandlung Gmbh, Munich, München

Copyright © 1995 by Charlotte Chandler

Designed by JoAnne Metsch

Published by Cooper Square Press
An Imprint of the Rowman & Littlefield Publishing Group
150 Fifth Avenue, Suite 911
New York, New York 10011

Distributed by National Book Network

Library of Congress Cataloging-in-Publication Data
Chandler, Charlotte.
    [Ich, Fellini. English]
    I, Fellini / Charlotte Chandler.
        p. cm.
    Originally published: New York : Random House, 1995.
    Includes bibliographical references and index.
    ISBN 978-0-8154-1143-7
        1. Fellini, Frederico— Interviews. 2. Motion picture producers and directors— Italy—
Interviews. I. Title.

PN1998.3.F45 A5 2001
791.43'0233'092— dc21

                                                                00-065630

⊖™ The paper used in this publication meets the minimum requirements of American National Standard for Information Sciences— Permanence of Paper for Printed Library Materials, ANSI/NISO Z39.48–1992.

TO FEDERICO

I remember walking away from Lubitsch's funeral. I was with Willy Wyler. It was hard to imagine a world without Lubitsch. I said, "No more Lubitsch." And Willy said, "Worse. No more Lubitsch pictures."

Now there won't be any more Fellini pictures.

I knew his pictures before I knew him. I discovered him as a director with *La Strada*. He was immediately noticed with that film, with his wife, who was so good. It was after *La Dolce Vita* that I discovered him as a person. I was in Rome and he took me to lunch at a restaurant about five minutes from Cinecittà. There were chickens walking on the tables.

"You see," he said, pointing at the chickens, "everything here is very fresh."

I told him I was willing to take his word for it. He had some eggs brought to the table. "Take one," he said, offering me an egg. "It's still warm."

I didn't order an omelette.

I saw him again after *8½*. We went to the same restaurant again. The chickens were still there, but I suppose they were different ones.

The author with Billy Wilder outside his Beverly Hills office.

He had a great interest in food. He was very Italian. I used to enjoy listening to him talk about women, sex, romance, passion. He could be very funny. He liked to shock. We did some spitballing, stimulating talk about things, and from one thing comes another. We were a couple of ship captains together. I'm an old ship captain. I've known the rough seas, and he did, too.

We had similar backgrounds. He was a journalist, and I was a journalist. We both began our film careers by interviewing film stars and directors. I worked on the same paper as Erich Maria Remarque. Fellini and I both became directors to watch over our scripts, just like Preston Sturges. *La Dolce Vita* isn't just about Rome, the way *Sunset Boulevard* isn't only about Hollywood.

He had collaborators, as I did. I had Charles Brackett for fifteen years and I.A.L. Diamond for twenty-five years. You have to be ready to listen to the other person and to value what he says even if you don't use it. You need someone you respect; but better that he isn't just like you, because you want to hear some different ideas, or you could talk to yourself. You try to persuade each other.

He was very interested in art, as I am, and he had an artist's eye. The difference was he had talent to draw, and I can neither draw nor paint nor sculpt, only appreciate.

One difference was I always like to use the most professional actors, and he was happy with people who had never acted; and I liked to shoot bare essentials, because the actor's energy is vanishing if you do too many takes, and he liked to have a lot of choice, even scenes he never used.

My favorite Fellini film was the wonderful *Nights of Cabiria*.

Fellini's camera is always in the right place, exactly where it should be for each shot. Most important, you are never conscious of the camera, of him showing off his directing. He never had distracting camera angles. He follows the story. I go to the movies to be entertained, as Federico did, and I never like to be conscious of the director as a performer.

If he had been working in English instead of in Italian, he would have been *more* famous. Even when he failed, he was great. It was amazing how many times his pictures failed and still he got the chance to work again. That was an advantage he had working in Italy over working in America.

He was naïve. He never stopped being naïve, even when no one wanted to put money into his films. What neither he nor I had was the luxury a Spielberg has. Imagine making films that have earned so much money you can do anything you want!

Wherever we went, people would say to each of us the same thing: "Mr. Wilder, when are you going to make the next picture?" "Mr. Fellini, when are you going to make the next picture?" And each of us could only answer: "When I can—if they let me."

In the movie theater, you always know a Fellini film. He had individual style. There are things you cannot take a course in. You are born with it. He was a first-class clown, with a unique, great concept. In life, when you were with Fellini, you always knew you weren't with anyone else. He was in his own orbit. When someone like Fellini dies, there is no way to pass on a formula, because there is no formula. What he did came out of the person, out of him. People will study and analyze and copy, and maybe someone will achieve to the point it is said of him, "His film is like Fellini."

But it can only be *like* Fellini. When you can't pass it on, it's the real stuff.

acknowledgments

With appreciation:

To Michelangelo and Enrica Antonioni, Harry Evans, Dr. Herbert Fleissner, Michael Fleissner, Brigitte Fleissner-Mikorey, Mario Longardi, Giulietta Masina, Sam Vaughan, Alberto Vitale, and Billy Wilder.

And Charles William Bush, Giorgio Campanaro, Furio Colombo, Enzo Coniglio, Mario De Vecchi, Douglas Fairbanks, Jr., Jean Firstenberg, John-Emmanuel Gartmann, Nadia Gray, Robert Guccione, Alberto Grimaldi, Dick Guttman, William A. Henry III, Richard J. L. Herson, Madeleine Lebeau, Wendy Keys, Deborah Landis, John Landis, Alberto Lattuada, Ken McCormick, Groucho Marx, Marcello Mastroianni, Paul Mazursky, Aldo Nemni, Joanna Ney, Arthur Novell, Tullio Pinelli, Richard Peña, Roman Polanski, Anthony Quinn, Joe Reece, Francesco Rosi, Roberto Rossellini, Sidney Sheldon, Alberto Sordi, Steven Spielberg, John Springer, Bernhard Struckmeyer, Giuseppe Tornatore, King Vidor, Leah Weatherspoon, Walter Weintz, Lina Wertmüller, Tennessee Williams, and Irina Woelfle.

And the Film Society of Lincoln Center, the American Film Institute, the Academy of Motion Picture Arts and Sciences, Gruppo Prospettive, the Italian Cultural Institutes of Hamburg, Los Angeles, and New York, Cinecittà, and *Der Spiegel*.

contents

F ellini was a person whose reality exceeded even his dreams. He left us those dreams on film, a rich inheritance. Fellini said that the major theme of his life was "Dreams are the only reality." He wondered, "Is the unconscious ever used up? Do dreams ever end?"

I, Fellini is Federico Fellini speaking during the fourteen years I knew him, from the spring of 1980, when we met in Rome, until a few weeks before his death in the autumn of 1993. *I, Fellini* was spoken rather than written.

Much of what he said to me was accompanied by food, in a restaurant or café; or we talked in a moving car. These situations delighted him and were conducive to bringing out his expansive, articulate nature.

"When you publish your book," he said to me, "will your publisher provide us with a car and driver?"

"I hope so," I answered.

"You must have a mountain of my words. If I wanted to know about my feelings at a certain time, I could consult you. It would be easier to look up the facts of my life than to remember how I felt at a certain time. One doesn't remember one's own life chronologically,

Fellini looking at the pressbook for *City of Women* when the film was being shown in Rome, 1980. The tape recorder is Charlotte Chandler's; it represents the beginning of the conversations for this book.

the way it happened, what was most important, or even what *seemed* most important. We are not in control of our memories. One doesn't own one's memories. One is owned by them.

"You're a good listener, and sometimes I learn something about myself from what I hear myself telling you. I have never knowingly lied to you, because you trust me. I cannot lie to a person who believes everything I say to her.

"Of course, I can lie to myself, and frequently do."

He admitted that he had achieved a reputation, not unearned, for not always being a man of his word, though my experience was that he always kept his promises. He would say to me, "I swear," to indi-cate his seriousness about anything I proposed. Whenever he agreed to do something with me **about** which he had less than perfect enthusiasm, he would **say**, "I swear"—our private joke, which meant he would do it. The **phrase became a kind** of password; when he was leaving, I would look **back and he** would **have his** right arm raised, as if to say, "I swear."

In a sense, Fellini was both the interviewer and the interviewee. I was the audience. This verbal memoir of the images in his mind is the result of conversations, rather than of formal interviews. I did not ask questions, because questions shape answers and determine subjects. He revealed the personality of the private person, as well as that of the public man. He told me that he liked these words of Billy Wilder: "Trust your instincts; then your mistakes will be your own. Instinct is a better guide to the truth than reason."

He felt that a title was a limitation. "One should never think of a title first, only last, and it should be as encompassing as possible of its subject. If you limit yourself too early with a title, you will find what you look for instead of what is really interesting; so you have to go into it with an open mind. A title does not help you, it leads you."

Fellini was an artist, and he shared his unique vision and visions with all of us. He told me, "Films are pictures that move," and he considered his own films the heirs of painting more than of literature.

Fellini's caricature of himself, which he drew for Charlotte Chandler in 1984.

Sometimes, when I look at something, I try to see what Fellini would have seen, and I hope that I see a little more and a little better—not only with my eyes but with my visual imagination—because of him.

"I have only one life, and that I have told to you," he said to me. "This is my last testament, because I have no more words to say."

I, Fellini is divided into three parts:

I. Federico—the boy and young man, influenced by the circus and profoundly impressed by the clowns, the Fulgor Cinema with its Hollywood movies, and American comic strips, from which he developed his view of the world. He took *his* Rimini with him to Rome, where his articles and caricatures led to radio writing, film writing, and then directing. In Rome he found the woman who was not only his lifetime companion but also the leading lady of his films and of his life.

II. Federico Fellini—the movie fan who became a director, discovering his purpose in life.

III. Fellini—the monomial legend in his own lifetime, who was more famous as a person than the films that had made him so famous. "Felliniesque" became a familiar word even for people who had never seen a Fellini film.

The most important character in every Fellini film was one who only rarely made an appearance in the film, yet who was always there: Fellini himself. He was the star of all his films. In life situations he was charismatic. I remember him, generous and considerate, thanking *me* for my company at a meal, for having spent my time with him, or for any gift he gave me. He told me that a person lives on as long as there are people alive who knew and cared about him. I believe that is true. He was, however, more concerned with the immortality of his films than with his own mortality.

Federico Fellini was born in Rimini, Italy, on January 20, 1920 . . .

PART I

FEDERICO

one

DREAMS ARE THE
ONLY REALITY

I cannot be somebody else. If there is anything I know, it is this.

Everyone lives in his own fantasy world, but most people don't understand that. No one perceives the *real* world. Each person simply calls his private, personal fantasies the Truth. The difference is that I *know* I live in a fantasy world. I prefer it that way and resent anything that disturbs my vision.

I was not an only child, but I was an alone child. I had a brother I liked very much who was close in age, just a little younger, and an even younger sister, but we did not really share our lives, even though we shared our parents and our house.

Some people cry on the inside. Some people laugh on the inside. Some do both. I was always a person who guarded the privacy of my emotions. I was pleased to share laughter and joy, but I could not admit to sadness or fear.

To be alone is to be all yourself, because you are free to develop, not according to others' constrictions. Being alone is a special thing, and being able to be alone is even rarer. I have always envied people who have interior resources, because they give you an independence—a freedom people say they want, but are in reality so afraid of. People are more afraid of being alone than of anything else in life. If they are left alone for even a few minutes, they look for someone, anyone, to fill the void. They are afraid of silence; the silence when you are alone with your own thoughts, with the endless interior monologue. Then, you have to like your own company very much. The advantage is you don't have to misshape yourself to conform to other people's ideas, or only to please.

I am fascinated by people who can have a life without fear of consequences, who can be passionate without caution, who hate, who love foolishly. I look with wonder at simple feeling and at behavior that doesn't fear repercussions. I myself have never learned to be irresponsible. I have always put myself on trial.

I have early memories which have always remained with me, though as I grow older, they grow fainter. Some of them predate my verbal memory and live in my mind only as images. I am not certain if they really happened or didn't. Now, with the passage of time, I cannot be certain if they are my memories or if they are someone else's memories imposed on me, as is so much of what we remember. My dreams seem so real to me that years afterwards, I wonder, "Did that really happen to me, or did I dream it?" I know only that these memories have claimed me and exist as mine as long as I exist. Those who could have testified as to their veracity are no longer alive, and if they were, they probably would not remember the incidents in the same way I do, since there is no such thing as objective memory.

two

EXPECTED AT THE CIRCUS

The puppets I knew as a child live among my strongest memories and seem closer to me now than the people who populated my young life. Perhaps the reason is that then they were closer to me than real people, so why shouldn't they now be closer as memories?

I was about nine when I began making the puppets and putting on shows. I would draw characters for my puppet theater. They were cardboard with heads of clay. There was a sculptor who lived across the street from us, and when he saw my puppets, he encouraged me. He said I had talent, and that was encouraging. There is nothing more precious than *early* encouragement, especially when it isn't just generalized approval, but for something specific. He showed me how to use plaster of paris for the heads. I gave shows and played all the parts. That was how I got used to playing all the parts and developed, I believe, the style I later used as a director, demonstrating for the actors how I saw each character. Naturally, I was the writer, too.

When I was seven years old, my parents took me to the circus. The clowns really shocked me. I didn't know if they were animals or ghosts. I didn't find them funny.

But I did have a strange sensation, a feeling that I was expected there.

That night and for nights afterwards through the years, I dreamed about the circus. During these circus dreams I had the feeling I had found the place where I belonged. There was usually an elephant in those dreams.

I didn't know yet that my future would be in the circus—the circus of the cinema.

I had two early heroes in my life. One was a heroine, my grandmother. The other was a clown.

The morning after I had been taken to the circus, I saw one of the clowns at the fountain in the square, dressed as he had been the night before. It seemed only natural to me that he would be dressed as a clown. I assumed that he *always* wore his clown suit.

He was *the* clown—Pierino. I wasn't frightened by him. I understood already that he and I were kinsmen under the skin, that he and I were one. I felt an instant affinity with his lack of respectability. There was something about his carefully planned shabbiness that went against my mother's definition of propriety. He couldn't go to school dressed like that, and he certainly couldn't go to church dressed like that.

I have always believed in omens in my life. Probably there are omens in everyone's life, and they may not recognize them. I did not speak with Pierino, perhaps because I worried that he was a dream or apparition who would disappear if I addressed him directly. I would not have known how to address a clown, anyway. One cannot say "Your Clownness," yet for me he was beyond royalty. All of this I sensed, because knowing was beyond me at that stage of my life. Years later, I could look at that place by the fountain where he stood, and I could see an aura of that symbol of my whole life, as he stood there like a herald of my future. I was moved by what I perceived, a feeling of ineffable optimism about him. He seemed to be protected by heaven.

When I first began telling my tale of how I ran away with the circus, it was a modest story. As I told the story, each time I remembered myself as being a little older than I was. I aged months in the telling, even years. What grew most was the length of my runaway absence from home. This was the story of my wishes more than of the reality of my experience. After many years of telling my embroidered version of the story, it seemed to me more true than the truth.

The exaggeration had become so familiar that it was part of my memory. Then, one day, it was taken away from me by someone who robbed me of that memory, saying that I had lied. There are people who are like that. I have always maintained that if I'm a liar, I'm an honest one.

After school, I had seen some of the circus passing through Rimini, and I followed them. I think I was probably about seven or eight. Everyone was nice to me. They were like a big family. They didn't try to send me home, probably because they didn't know where my home was.

I would like to have been with the circus for months, but it was more like an afternoon. During my runaway circus visit, I was observed by a friend of our family's who retrieved me and dragged me, squirming, home. But before I was taken away, I had made connections that would last all my life. A circus bond had been forged: I had talked with a clown, I had washed a zebra. How many people could make that claim? I suppose it's possible to find people who have talked with clowns, though I wouldn't want to have to produce one on short notice. To find someone who has helped give a zebra a bath would require a trip to a zoo. On that special day in my life, the people of the circus allowed me to help give a bath to a sick zebra who seemed very sad. I was told he wasn't feeling well because someone had fed him a chocolate bar.

From that day on, I never forgot how a zebra felt. When I touched him, it was a tactile sensation that stayed with me. And a wet zebra. I am not a sentimental person, but when I touched him, he touched me—my heart.

The clown I met was the first in a series of many sad clowns I came to know in my lifetime. One's first clown is special. All the clowns I have ever known took great pride in their work and understood that being funny is serious business. I personally, through my life, have admired totally the person who can make others laugh. That seemed to me both worthwhile and difficult.

That evening, when I was deposited at home, I was scolded for being late, but my mother didn't seem worried. I hadn't even been late enough to strongly attract her attention.

I tried to tell her about my adventure, about everything that had befallen me, about how it felt to touch a zebra, but I stopped because she wasn't listening. She never did listen to me. She was deep in her own world, listening to her own thoughts, perhaps listening to God.

She told me that I had to be punished, so I would know right from wrong and learn my lesson. I was sent to bed without supper. I went to my room, but shortly after I got into bed, the door opened, and my mother entered with a tray of food, a complete dinner. She put it down. She didn't say anything, and left. So, I learned my lesson.

Any time I ran away with the circus, I could expect to be rewarded with a tray of food in my room. I supposed that it was because she was glad I'd come back.

I've never needed to use an alarm clock. I just set myself. I have always slept very little and awakened early. As a child, I always awoke before everyone else, and I would lie in bed, afraid to move around and wake the others. I would lie there and try to remember my dreams. As I grew older, I would walk through the silent house, discovering everything about it. Because I was alone with our house, I knew it in a more intimate way than did anyone else in my family. I had the accompanying bruises dealt me in the dark by tables and chairs guarding their nocturnal privacy.

Even very early, I had a sense of drama. My mother had rebuked me for something or other. Something I did, or something I didn't do, I don't remember which. I was usually guilty of both malfeasance and nonfeasance. I decided to make her sorry. I knew she would regret scolding me if she thought I was injured.

I took one of her lipsticks, a dark red one, and I smeared most of the tube all over myself, giving, I thought, the appearance of blood. In my mind, she would return home and find me a bloody heap on the floor, and she would be sorry she had been so harsh with me.

I found a good position at the foot of the stairs. I wanted it to look as if I had been injured by my fall. It wasn't a very comfortable position, and my mother was late. My foot had gone to sleep. I switched positions. It was boring. I couldn't understand why she was taking so long.

Then I heard a door open. At last! But the footsteps were heavier than my mother's, and there was no click-clack of her high heels.

My uncle poked me. He said in a matter-of-fact tone, "Get up and go wash your face."

I was mortified. I was humiliated. I washed my face.

I never again liked that uncle. Neither of us ever referred to the incident, but I knew that both of us remembered it.

A childhood hero of mine was Little Nemo, an American comic-strip character, though at the time I didn't realize he was American. I thought he was Italian, like me. In the Italian comic strip, he spoke only Italian.

I must have been five or six, maybe younger, when I discovered Little Nemo, and I couldn't believe my eyes! What a revelation! Here was someone like me doing such fantastic things. He stirred my imagination. Sometimes he was so big, he had to step carefully over tall buildings; other times, he was small enough to be dwarfed by a flower or threatened by huge insects. He was accompanied by the most extraordinary people I've ever seen in a comic strip. A Zulu dressed like a policeman was always smoking a cigar and speaking in a strange language everyone in the comic strip understood but none of the grown-ups who read it to me could translate, or even pronounce. There were clowns inexplicably promoted to positions of great authority and responsibility, which made perfect sense to me; giants who opened their mouths so you could then slide along a gargantuan tongue and explore their cavernous insides; dinosaurs disrupting city traffic; upside-down rooms in which everyone had to walk on the ceilings; elongated people trying to get back into shape—the most amazing things you could imagine, all beautifully drawn, just the way I dreamed of drawing.

I was always trying to draw. I would copy the scenes in the comics, but I couldn't copy Little Nemo. The artistic mastery was beyond me. There was such a wealth of detail; the costumes and architecture were much too elaborate for my hand to follow, though I tried. Later I found out that the artist, Winsor McCay, had been a pioneer in movies, too. He had drawn some of the first animated cartoons, long before Walt Disney. He had actually drawn a Little Nemo animated cartoon, which I would love to see, and *Gertie the Dinosaur,* which I have seen. He also drew animated news events that couldn't be photographed, like the sinking of the *Lusitania.* There is a fantastic quality about the drawing of that ship which influenced me in *Amarcord.* I was influenced by Mussolini's ocean liner, the *Rex,* too, but even more by Winsor McCay. I don't think many people have heard about him now.

At the end of each Sunday strip, Little Nemo sat up in bed and realized he'd been dreaming. If it was a good dream, he was sorry he'd awakened, and if it was a nightmare, he was glad to be awake and wondered what he'd eaten before going to bed. As a child, I always went to sleep hoping I'd dream like Little Nemo. Sometimes it would happen. I think my dream life was influenced by Little Nemo—not that my dreams were his; I dreamed *my* dreams. But knowing of his meant there were infinite dream possibilities to explore in the lifetime ahead. Everything begins with the belief that something is possible.

I also loved Popeye and Olive Oyl, and Rube Goldberg's marvelous inventions that accomplished absolutely nothing in the most complicated way imaginable. Then there was Happy Hooligan, who wore a tin can for a hat. They don't have comic strips like these anymore. I wish I could have known their creators. If I hadn't become a film director, I would have wanted to be a comic-strip artist.

My mother liked to draw pictures, too. She did it secretly, when I was very little. She showed me how to draw, with a pencil and then with colored crayons. She said that before I knew better, I drew all over everything—the hand-embroidered tablecloth someone in her family had made, the walls. It was quite a job to clean it all off before my father saw it. She encouraged me while my father was away and when my brother was still a baby.

I never tired of drawing pictures. When my father came home, as he did on occasion, he didn't like to see me sitting and drawing for hours. My father said it was what girls do. Though he didn't say so, I know he would have preferred to see me outside practicing with a soccer ball, even when I wasn't much larger than the ball. After that, my mother stopped encouraging my drawing, and she never drew again, or at least I never saw her do it.

It happened so long ago that I'd really forgotten how I started drawing. It seemed like something I'd always done, a part of me. Then, one day, long after I was grown, when I was in Rimini for Christmas, someone said to my mother, "Federico is so artistic." And I heard her say with pride, "He got it from me. I was artistic as a girl, and I'm the one who taught him to draw." Then I remembered.

I wanted to meet Flash Gordon. When I was a boy, he was my hero, and he has remained my hero. I could never, never, quite believe that he wasn't real.

The American science-fiction writer Ray Bradbury told me that Buck Rogers was like this in his life. At one point, when he was a boy, his friends made fun of him because of his fascination with Buck Rogers, and he went home and destroyed his entire comic-strip collection. I am not personally a collector, and I try not to keep things, but I could identify with someone who felt the opposite. After he destroyed his collection, he felt lonely and lost. He decided that those "friends" who wanted him to be just like them, who wanted to take away something from him that enriched his life, were not friends at all. So he stopped knowing them and started collecting Buck Rogers again. It took a long time for him to build his collection back, but eventually it was better than ever.

I can identify with him because I remember many times caring desperately about what other children thought of me. Now I can't remember their names. But at the time, they had great power over me, the power of the peer group to make me unhappy. When you are very young, other children can be the cause of such emotional suffering.

I think I have read everything Ray Bradbury ever wrote. Ever since I read it, I have wanted to make a film of *The Martian Chronicles.* I am very fond of science fiction. Fantasy and the supernatural are what interest me. It is my religious belief.

Real life isn't what interests me. I like to observe life, but to leave my imagination unfettered. Even as a child, I drew pictures not of a person, but of the picture in my mind of the person.

In school, I was taught "No," "You cannot," "You ought to be ashamed." There were so many admonitions to remember that it was a wonder after all that I was not too incapacitated to unbutton my fly. I was filled by school and church with an overwhelming sense of guilt before I had the faintest idea what I was guilty of.

I don't remember my days in school very well. They have all blended together. It's as if each year was one day, and every day was the repetition of all the days before. My life was not in school. During classes, I always felt as if I were missing something more important, something more wonderful than anything that transpired in those classrooms.

I usually say I was a poor student, probably because that's more dramatic and interesting than saying I was an ordinary student. I've never liked to think of myself as an ordinary anything. Probably no one does. I wasn't really that bad a student. My mother would not have tolerated it. But I wasn't the student I might have been if I had applied myself, even routinely. I had no interest, no motivation, at least not for my studies.

When I was about eleven, I left Catholic school for Giulio Cesare School. There were pictures on the wall of the Pope and of Mussolini, and we studied the glories of Rome, the ancient past, and those of the future, as represented by the Black Shirts.

School offered opportunities to draw under the guise of taking notes and writing papers, and to live in my mind, fantasizing, while I pretended to listen to the words of my teachers. I drew cartoons in secret in the belief that what I was doing was undetected, and that it would be assumed I was taking copious notes. When, one day, the teacher uncovered my notebook and revealed a drawing of an exceedingly ugly monster, he took it to be a picture of him. My drawing was really much uglier than he was, but still he could only see himself in it. Luckily, he didn't see my other drawings underneath that one, which were of naked women as they existed in my own mind in those days.

I will never forget the pageantry of Easter and Christmas and the accompanying gifts of food to the teachers and principal. Not being very tall, our teachers disappeared behind a wall of food, the ritual tribute of the families of their students. It was as if the food had eaten them.

Some of the students who feared they were in danger of failing turned up with live piglets. I was a medium student, but my father, a food merchant, was in a position to facilitate my good relationships at school. He was a generous man, not only on these holiday occasions. All of my teachers received the best of his Parmesan cheese and olive oil.

My grades were adequate to get me into law school at the university in Rome, and that was important for two reasons: It got me to Rome, as the law was what my mother wanted for me, having accepted that I was lost for the priesthood. Even more important, registration at the law school guaranteed my deferment from the draft. That alone made those days in the classroom worthwhile.

I really have no regrets about what I didn't learn in school. If I had been a better student, my life might have taken a different turn, and

I could have missed the world of making films, which is what really gave meaning to my life.

Since I left Rimini, I have been trying to uneducate and free myself from the encumbering baggage with which I was weighted as a child. The intentions may have been good, but it doesn't make the baggage less heavy. Organized religion has too much of superstition and duty—that combination. Real religion should liberate man to find divinity within himself. Everyone hopes for a more meaningful existence.

I spent my life trying to cure myself of my education, which told me, "You can never measure up to the ideal; you are impure." We were affected by a pessimistic and repressive education inflicted by church, by fascism, and by parents. Sex was something not spoken of.

If I had to say what was different about the world of my boyhood and the world of now, I would say it is summed up in the former prevalence of masturbation. Not that it doesn't exist now, but the emphasis then was different. Masturbation symbolized a different kind of world. It was necessary to use your imagination. Total gratification in real life could not be instantaneous. Woman was mysterious because she was so unattainable—except, of course, for the prostitute, who would probably preside at your experience of initiation, an initiation which would be stupendous because it was hidden and forbidden, and with an emissary of the devil.

My earliest sexual memory that I think I remember was as a baby, lying on a kitchen table. There were huge distorted faces of women leaning over me, squealing with delight as they admired my little thing, and they seemed to be measuring it.

I remember my mother naked, in front of me. It was the only time I ever saw her naked. I could not yet walk. I was too young to speak, so she assumed I was too young to think, or to remember. But I saw the image, and I remember. It has been well established that we all remember more than we know. We remember, perhaps, even prenatally.

I can remember crawling around on the floor and, from my perspective under the kitchen table, checking on what the maid had up her dress. It did not look inviting. It was dark and forbidding. I was probably two and a half at the time. I don't think this had anything to do with sexual interest. It was just curiosity. It didn't really become interesting until my mother pulled me out from under the table and scolded me. Then, as soon as I understood I was doing something forbidden, it became much more interesting.

Even so early, I felt that "forbidden" and "pleasurable" were linked. At that stage, my sexual interest was more centered on myself than on anyone else.

Shortly afterwards, for the first time I consciously studied my father without his clothes. It was interesting, but I don't think I made the connection between my little thing and his well-endowed example.

My first really identifiable sexual stirrings occurred when I was four, or maybe just a little older. I didn't quite know what I was feeling, but I knew I was feeling it. It was a localized tingling sensation, and I was faint with the pleasure of it.

The inspiration for my excitement had blotchy skin and a shaven head. She was a lay sister with a religious order called the Sisters of San Vincenzo. I think she was about sixteen. I saw her as a mysterious older woman. I would follow her about, totally fascinated.

I wasn't certain if she was aware of my attention. Certainly she didn't seem to mind. She would hug me against her body. It felt wonderful. She would move me from side to side, first against one of her ample breasts and then against the other. I could feel her nipples. All the time, there was this wonderful smell to her . . .

At first I wasn't quite certain, and then I recognized it. The magical erotic scent was potato skins and old soup. Her job was peeling the potatoes for the daily soup, and after it was ready, she would wipe her hands on her apron. Heaven! Her whole body was so soft and warm, so very warm. It felt so wonderful when she hugged me that it made me feel weak. I hoped it would never stop.

At the time, I believed she was totally innocent and unaware of my motives or the effect she was having on me. Now I am certain she was enjoying herself, enjoying the effect she was having on one so young, so impressionable, and so obviously and profoundly affected.

After all these years, it's difficult to remember a smell exactly, but I think if I were to smell it now, it would have the same magical effect on me. From that time on, I searched for the repetition of that total sensation. I have smelled many of the most expensive French perfumes created to entice, but I never smelled one that was so alluring as that combination of potato skins and old soup.

My earliest sex education came from priests who warned us against "touching" ourselves, perhaps giving some less imaginative boys ideas they might not otherwise have had. I've wondered what the nuns taught girls in their schools. Catholicism makes sex obsessively interesting.

Catholicism has always had a repressive attitude toward sex when practiced for pleasure rather than procreation. It's part of a generally repressive attitude toward pleasure of any kind, toward freedom, and toward individuality.

On the other side, however, by making pleasurable sex forbidden, Catholicism does enhance the pleasure of it. Total, easy availability of sex diminishes desire. It's like food. One needs to be a little hungry once in a while in order to fully enjoy the meal.

For a time, I believed all women were aunts. I was overcome by excitement if I saw a woman in an evening dress. I discovered rather quickly that all women were not aunts. I saw Madam Dora's house where the women painted themselves, wore veils, and smoked gold-tipped cigarettes. The brothel, the house of prostitution, is an important experience.

three

GARBO'S EYELASHES

Family, Church, and school, with fascism thrown in, were supposed to be the major influences on a child of my times. Sex, circus, cinema, and spaghetti—these were *my* early influences.

Sexual feeling, I discovered all by myself. I cannot remember the time I did not have sexual feelings. I discovered the circus when it came to Rimini; movies I found at the Fulgor; and spaghetti was at our family table.

The Fulgor was older than I. The birth of this movie theater had preceded mine by about six years, but it wasn't until I was about two that I was taken there. It played a greater part in my life than any of my childhood homes. It *was* my childhood home.

I was taken there by my mother, not for my benefit but for hers. She wanted to go to the movies, and I was carried along. I have no idea what my first film was, but I remember a series of fabulous images that I loved. My mother told me I never cried or wriggled, and she found she could take me all the time. Even before I could understand what I was seeing, I knew it was something marvelous.

For the first ten years of my life, the films were silent, with musical accompaniment. When I was about ten, sound came to the Fulgor.

I went there all the time, to see mostly American films. The American movies were *our* movies. Charlie Chaplin, the Marx Brothers, Gary Cooper, Ronald Colman, Fred Astaire and Ginger Rogers—all belonged to us. I liked any film with Laurel and Hardy in it. I always liked comedy most. Then I liked detective stories and pictures about newspapermen. I liked any film in which the leading actor wore a trench coat.

My mother liked Garbo. Garbo films weren't my choice, but I saw a lot of Greta Garbo. My mother said she was the greatest actress of our time, and sometimes my mother would sit in the dark and cry. Garbo looked so white in the black-and-white pictures that I thought she might be a ghost. I didn't understand her films at all. She didn't compare with Tom Mix. I would sit and watch her eyelashes.

As a child, I used to feel very excited sitting in the Fulgor Cinema just as the movie was about to begin. There was that wonderful feeling of anticipation. I had that same feeling whenever I would walk onto Stage 5 of Cinecittà, only it was a grown-up feeling, because the control of the wonder that would be was in *my* hands. It is the kind of total emotion of sex, a nervous trembling, total concentration, total feeling, ecstasy.

When I was a boy, it seemed to me that everyone must want to be a clown. Everyone—except my mother.

As a boy, I knew very early, before I knew what I wanted to be, what I did *not* want to be. Except for being a priest, my mother's idea, I was even more unsuited for my father's plans for me—to be a salesman. I could not imagine myself following in the footsteps of my father. He traveled through Italy selling foodstuffs. I rarely saw him and was told he had to work all the time for the sake of his small family, of whom I was one, in order to keep food on the table. This made me feel quite guilty about eating, rather than grateful, as I suppose the information was intended to make me feel. At that time, I was small and extremely thin and didn't really eat all that much, so it didn't seem I should be such a burden to bear. I didn't realize that my father's absences had nothing to do with me; rather, he preferred to be away from my mother, with whom he didn't have a good relationship once the early bliss of courtship had worn off. I understood my father better later, when I myself could scarcely wait to escape my mother's oppressive ideas—her own unhappiness, which she was ready and willing to share, and her belief that excessive happiness, which she defined in practice as virtually any pleasure at all, was sinful.

My father enjoyed his work, and it was only in that respect that I eventually followed in his footsteps, though finding my own way. He was a seller of wine and Parmesan cheese. He could not imagine why his son, I, should not aspire to such a life, especially when he could introduce me to it, thus cushioning my entry into that world. I understood early that I was not cut from the cloth to be a good salesman. I could not imagine how he faced people while saying, "Please buy my cheese." I heard him explaining the merits of a wheel of his cheese over someone else's apparently identical wheel. I believed him, but the process seemed embarrassing. I was too shy to imagine myself doing anything like that.

Then, one day in my life as a film director, I was with two producers who wore gold chains and rings on their little fingers and smelled of aftershave lotion, and I realized that I had, after all, though against my will, followed in my father's footsteps. I had been forced by life to be a seller of Parmesan cheeses, just like my father, only I called them films, and the producers to whom I had to sell them did not perceive my potential works of art as receptively as my father's customers had his olive oil or his prosciutto.

I was not close to my parents. My father was a stranger to me until after his death. After his death as my father, he lived for the first time as a man, a man I could understand, one who was searching, who was not so unlike me. Annibale Ninchi, the actor who played the father to Mastroianni in *La Dolce Vita* and *8½*, reminded me of my father in the physical sense and was also an Italian movie star my father especially liked in the years before World War II.

I do not believe I was the kind of son my mother would have chosen. She was a strict and religious woman, who was bitterly unhappy with my father but who had difficulty getting along without him.

I am certain that she was a virgin when she married him. More than a virgin. I think she had had no previous experience even with touching, kissing, the feeble gropings of the normal adolescent. One might say she was repressed, only it seems to me she did not have to repress any sexual urges, because they were either unknown or repugnant to her.

My father did not get what he wanted at home, so he looked for it elsewhere. Since he was a traveling salesman, he had many opportunities. My mother would cry incessantly during the weeks he was away. I don't know if this was because she missed him or because she sensed he was being unfaithful. When he came home, she would scold him, and they would argue. Then he would depart again, seemingly with no regret. I was never the confidant of my parents, and they were certainly not mine, but I never questioned the estrangement within our family, because I assumed that was what a family was.

Whenever my father returned from a trip, he would bring gifts to my mother, but they seemed to make her even angrier. I didn't understand at the time what I suppose my mother understood. The gifts weren't so much tokens of love as tokens of guilt.

Married in his twenties, frustrated in his sex life at home, my father had an eye, and more, for the ladies, especially if they *weren't* ladies. But he did have feeling for my mother, I'm sure, and he was dedicated to the support of his home, of her, and of his children. What he did on the road was a common enough occurrence in the Italian marriage, in which the woman is more married than the man, not in the sense of commitment, but in the sense of freedom.

I think there was a certain correlation between the measure of the ecstasy he had enjoyed on the road and the size of the gift. If his outside coupling was routine, a glass vase for my mother; if memorable, a silver platter was more likely.

Once I remember he brought her, instead, a beautiful dress. My brother, Riccardo, and I were watching through the door, which was ajar, as my mother unwrapped her gift. It had a lot of paper around it and a big bow. My mother took out of the box the most beautiful dress we had ever seen. It sparkled with lights, which we were later told were hand-sewn sequins. The dress looked very expensive. My father seemed all excited, sort of aglow, as he asked her if she liked it.

My mother didn't say a word, but threw it down on the table. After what seemed to us a long silence, she said it was not at all the kind of dress *she* wore, but was more suitable for some of "his friends." At the time, my little brother and I did not understand what was meant by "his friends." Riccardo was only one year younger than I, but to me he seemed my little brother for so long, I never got out of the habit of thinking of him that way.

After that, I don't remember my father bringing any more gifts of dresses, though I think there was a hat with a feather, or perhaps the hat with the feather preceded the gift of the dress. But there were many glass vases, and my mother kept flowers in them.

Once I had a dream which I suppose said the most about my relationship with my parents, because I have always believed dreams are more true than fact.

I went to the Grand Hotel at Rimini to check in. I stopped at the desk and filled out the form I was given. The reception clerk looked at my name and said, "Fellini. There are some people staying here with the same name." He looked over toward the terrace and said, "Look, there they are." I looked. It was my mother and father. I didn't say anything. "Do you know them?" he asked. I said no and he said, "Would you like to meet them?"

Once again, I said, "No. No, thank you."

It was only after my father's death that I learned he still had the first drawings I had done, and that he had always carried them with him. That was the first time I realized that he cared about me, he was proud of me.

For both my mother and my father, marriage was all the more disappointing because they had entered into theirs romantically. They were young. Urbano Fellini, a country boy on his way back from conscription in World War I, passed through Rome. He met Ida Barbiani and so swept her away that, against the wishes of her family, she gave up everything and left Rome to marry him. He was working in a pasta factory when he met my mother, and they fell in love. My father had dazzled her, as he was to do with many women throughout his life.

Before he was twenty, my father had seen there was little work in Gambettola, where he was born, or in Rimini, the nearby big town, so he set off to find adventure and employment. He found more adventure than he craved, and not at all the kind of employment he was looking for. He went to Belgium, and with the start of World War I he was conscripted by the Germans to work in the mines. What he had to say about this time of his life, although he never told me much, made me even more certain during World War II that I wanted to forgo the "glories" of war.

What began as a romantic marriage quickly became unromantic, perhaps with the arrival of me. My mother found her life in religion and her children. My father found what he wanted on the road, but he was represented for me by a tall carafe of the finest olive oil, always present on our table.

My food genes must have come from him—or, more likely, my educated taste buds. I could pass a test on the age of a sliver of Parmesan—three years, seven years, eleven years. And as for prosciutto . . .

I couldn't understand when I was a boy why my father was home so rarely, and why the pattern was always the same. My brother, Riccardo, more than I because he was younger, would ask when was our father going to be home. My mother would answer, usually a little sharply, that he would come home as soon as he could, but that he had to be out on the road working. The implication was clear that our father was a wonderful person sacrificing for us, and that even questioning his absence showed we didn't sufficiently appreciate him.

Then he would come home, and it was different. If he was so wonderful, why was our mother so angry at him? Who were those "women" she was always going on about? Why did he always stay home such a short time? Why did he leave earlier than he had told us he would be leaving?

I didn't come to understand the answers to these questions until much later, when I was almost as old as my father had been at the time.

The more my father was away, the less my parents got along, and the more my mother talked about Rome. My mother, as a girl from a protected family, could not have imagined what it would mean to give up Rome for the farm life of Gambettola or the provincial town life of Rimini. She must have been terribly lonely.

Her Roman family had totally disowned her for eloping with my father. Her father had remained unforgiving in his lifetime, and my aunt and uncle had maintained no contact with my mother except for some sweets at Christmas, which we children devoured.

Rome was in my dreams before I could imagine what it actually was. I supposed it looked like Rimini, but bigger, or like America, but smaller. I knew it was where I wanted to go to live, and I could hardly wait to grow up so I could go there. I didn't have to wait.

When I was about ten, my uncle in Rome suffered a stroke, and my aunt wrote to my mother asking her to come to Rome to visit her brother. My mother established a reconciliation with her family, and took me there with her. Rome came to mean more than just delicious sweets at Christmas. The reality was, as rarely happened, so much greater than my imaginings had been.

We went to Rome by train. It would be exciting to take the train, my friends thought, and I did, too, but I discovered even then that I did not like traveling. What I did enjoy was looking out of the window and watching the real pictures move, just the way the scenes changed on the screen of the Fulgor. But the movement of the train made it difficult to draw pictures.

When I saw Rome, in that first moment I was filled with awe and, at the same time, I felt I had come home. I knew Rome was where I was meant to live, where I *had* to live, where I belonged. My uncle was too sick for me to know him, but he and my aunt had given me a gift much more important than their Christmas packages of nougat.

When we returned to Rimini, for the first time in my life I had a goal.

As a small child, I had a secret I never shared with anyone, not even my brother—least of all my brother. I couldn't tell him because I didn't believe he was my brother.

I had the feeling that our parents were not really my parents, rather that they had found me somewhere, taken me home, and claimed me as their own. I realized only much later that this is an archetypal feeling found in children who do not see themselves as like their parents and who do not ever establish real communication with their fathers or mothers. As I grew older, however, I couldn't help but notice that I did bear a certain physical resemblance not only to my father and mother, but to their families.

I have never been drawn to compete at that for which I have no gift. Athletics. I had no special ability in that direction. I didn't even have any interest, but being thin as a skeleton, I envied the young athletes with bulging muscles who would show off almost naked in front of everyone, as they engaged in Greco-Roman wrestling. I myself had a horror of bathing suits, of wearing one. It was part of my lifelong feeling of being ashamed of my body. I was not competitive as a child, simply resigning from competition. I secretly sympathized, empathized with the losers. When I grew up, I was afraid of beautiful women. I still felt the way I did as a boy in Rimini, watching the German and Swedish women who came to spend their summers and who were so unattainable.

As a small child, I did whistle rather well. My mother praised my whistling once, and that led, for the next months, to more whistling around the house than anyone would ever want to hear. Fortunately, it was a phase that wore off.

When I was very little, I sang in school, and the teachers said I had a very nice voice. It was quite high. They said it would drop down and be much lower, but it never did get much lower. I was encouraged to sing, and so I sang, more because I enjoyed the approbation than because I enjoyed singing. I have always responded well to praise and poorly to criticism. I sang until my younger brother, Riccardo, started school. He sang much better than I did. He had a truly beautiful singing voice. It was a gift. The teachers all exclaimed, rightfully, about how wonderful it was. I stopped singing. Through the rest of my life, I never sang. At a public gathering when there is some sort of anthem, or trapped at a friend's birthday party, I try to escape, only moving my lips. I have never missed singing.

As for Riccardo, he used his gift to sing at our friends' weddings, as he does at the wedding in *I Vitelloni*. His voice brought him pleasure, but I think because singing came so naturally to him, he didn't value it enough. He was good enough to sing professionally in the opera instead of just at the weddings of our friends, but he didn't have that kind of drive.

I believe, and I don't feel this way just because he was my brother, that he might have become a famous singer. In Italy, where so many men would like to do the same thing, one needs a balance of luck and drive, though with enough luck, you don't need as much drive. Riccardo would have needed too much luck, because he didn't have enough drive. He also needed a great deal of encouragement. If you have the luck to be successful right away, beyond what you expected, there is an energy which comes with encouragement. I had that luck.

But the person I respect most is one who is able to fail repeatedly and still has the persistence to keep trying. When you are struggling, what is most difficult is to keep respect for yourself. I don't know exactly what I would have done if it had all taken much longer and if

I hadn't been lucky. I didn't even know exactly what I wanted to do, so I had to be lucky, just to find out in time. I like to believe I would have persevered. After all, what else could I have done?

I've wanted to use the story of my first love in a film, but it never quite fit in, and I was worried that it might seem trite because the idea had been used by others. First love is a subject many people like to write about. When I was sixteen, I saw a girl of angelic beauty seated in the window of a house on the block where I lived. Though I had never before seen an angel, she was exactly how I imagined an angel should look.

She lived so near, yet somehow I had never met her, nor even seen her. Perhaps it's because my eyes weren't ready to see her until that moment. I knew I had to meet her, but I wasn't certain how to do it. It was a different time, and another code of behavior, out of the past, prevailed.

I thought of drawing a picture of her in the frost on her window along with a little message. I decided this would be too subtle. She wouldn't know who drew it, unless I signed it, and she probably wouldn't know who I was, anyway. And what would keep other people from reading my message to her? Especially her parents. And what if it melted?

I decided the best approach was to be direct. I drew a picture of her from memory. Then I walked by her window while she was sitting there, and held up my picture. She smiled and opened the window, and gracefully accepted the picture. On the back of the picture I had written a message asking her to meet me on a well-known corner in Rimini.

She arrived at the place, at the designated time. I was waiting with flowers. She was punctual, a quality I have always appreciated in a woman, or for that matter in a man. It's a kind of respect paid to the other person. When meeting a woman, I've always believed one should be early and wait for *her*. That day long ago, however, I was there so early that when she arrived promptly, I'd already been waiting a long time. I imagined that she wouldn't come, and I was already thinking about departing. Thus I would have made true any doubts I had.

From then on, we took walks together, rode our bicycles together, and we had picnics to which I brought my father's Parmesan.

In my dreams, I kissed her. My dreams were highly romantic and totally noble. I worshiped her and saved her from untold dangers and defeated all the dragons who threatened her, human and otherwise. In reality, with her being only fourteen, I hesitated to kiss her and startle away the muse. Also, at sixteen I had never kissed a girl and didn't quite know how it was done.

Our relationship was abruptly brought to an end. I had given her brother a billet-doux to carry to her, and he was to bring me one in return. At our house, he was intercepted by my mother, who offered him some of her enticing cake while he waited for me. We always had delicious food in our house. The foolish boy was so captivated by the cake that he forgot to give me the note and left it there amidst the crumbs on the table for my mother to read.

My mother immediately leaped to what was for her the most terrible possible conclusion. I am certain that in my wildest dreams I have never been able to imagine anything equal to what my mother could, because my concept of sin was not so well developed as hers. She went directly to the house of the girl and confronted my friend's parents, accusing *their* daughter of having seduced *her* son. Oh, that it had been true!

Her parents treated the accusations as hallucinatory ravings, which indeed they were, and they believed totally in their daughter's innocence. They decided, however, it was better not to have bad relations with a neighbor who lived just across the street, and though I wasn't present, I'm certain my mother presented a terrifying presence there, wearing her self-righteousness.

After that, I was too embarrassed to face my ladylove. I was not a man, but a child. All my life I've been a coward, physically and emotionally. I've never liked arguments, and have tried to avoid at all cost any sad or angry scene, especially with a woman.

Almost immediately, her family moved to Milan. I'm certain it had nothing to do with me. I had mixed feelings. I was sad that I would never see the angelic creature again, but I was grateful not to have to face the mortification of a meeting.

That was, however, not the end of it. Some years later, when I was in Rome, she wrote to me, giving me her telephone number. I called her in Milan. She invited me to come and see her. It was wonderful. She inspired some of my stories at that time. I inspired her even more.

She became a journalist, and some years later she wrote an entire novel about our relationship, which I never read, but about which I was told. Apparently, in a roman à clef, I was the male protagonist, and she was the heroine. She seemed to have remembered even more than I of what had happened, not in our childhood romance but during our meeting of 1941. It was before I met Giulietta.

What a strange feeling to have someone write about me in that way—to make public our private moments, changing them to make more dramatic and entertaining reading. Already, I was accustomed to doing that to others, but having it done to me produced an odd sensation. At the time, I didn't look at the book. Years later, I thought of looking for it, but I never did. I might have found it.

As early as when I was about eleven, I began mailing drawings and cartoons to magazines in Florence and Rome. At about twelve, I started sending them short stories and essays and anecdotes with accompanying drawings. I would have the drawing idea first, and then I would do the story to match the picture. I used the assorted names I made up so it would not seem to all be coming from one person. I don't know now why I did that. It made some sort of sense to me then. I didn't think about how it would work if one of the magazines sent a check. It didn't occur to me that the postman might be confused as to where to deliver it, because it had the wrong name. Usually, I selected a name starting with "F" that was related to my first or second name. I didn't have the problem of how to cash the check with another name, because none came until I was in my teens.

Then it happened, and as soon as I sold my first cartoon, I began to sell my work regularly. The checks didn't represent "important money," just "cake money," but it was a thrill for me to see my work in print. It looked so real.

I had supposed that when my first drawing was printed, I would rush out with the magazine to tell all my friends and show my success. Far from it. When my first cartoon was published, I hid it. It wasn't because I was ashamed; it was because I was so happy and proud that I wanted to keep my little secret, for at least a short while. I didn't want to share it with anyone. But someone saw my drawing, and quickly everyone knew without my being the one who told. I was very happy.

four

HOME OF THE HEART

In 1937, I went to Florence. I was seventeen. I really wanted to go to Rome, but Florence was closer. The weekly humor magazine *420* was located there, and I'd been sending them my writing and drawings. I got a job as a journalist. It wasn't much of a job, it wasn't much of a salary, and I wasn't much of a journalist. I was, in reality, little more than an office boy. It was my first job, my first real steady income, and I was filled with hope, even though no one at the magazine wore a trench coat like in the American movies. I was only there for about four months. I knew it was really Rome where I wanted to go.

I went back to Rimini and promised my mother I would enroll at the law school of the University of Rome. I did as I promised, but I never went to classes. I hadn't promised I would go to classes.

I had to wait until January 1938 before I could make my definitive move to Rome. As I left the train and stepped out of the Termini Station, Rome was not disappointing in any way at that moment—or ever. At the age of ten, I had a view of it only from my uncle's apartment. My mother, as a sheltered girl, probably was never more than superficially acquainted with the staggering diversity that is Rome. Rome was even greater than my ten-year-old visit had revealed.

When I arrived in Rome, I worked on a newspaper. I was eighteen.
I didn't earn enough money to buy lunch. I could have coffee and
bread for breakfast and a modest dinner, but I couldn't stretch my
money to provide lunch. But it was food I wished for, not money.
Money was an abstract. I have rarely made the direct connection
between lire and spaghetti. I have to think very consciously to remember to take money with me. Fortunately, I have good credit at the
cafés I frequent. As I had more success, I began to eat more regularly,
a mixed blessing as it later turned out.

I was influenced to become a journalist by Fred MacMurray's hat.
My picture of journalists came entirely from American movies. All I
knew was they had wonderful cars and wonderful mistresses, and I
was ready to be a journalist and have both. I had no experience with
the life led by Italian journalists. When I fulfilled my dream and went
to work as a journalist, it was not as I expected it to be. It was quite
a while before I could afford a trench coat.

I am half Roman. My mother was Roman; her family could be
traced back to the early part of the fourteenth century, and probably
further, if someone went deeply into genealogy. There was a famous,
or maybe infamous, Barbiani, my mother's maiden name, among our
ancestors. He was an apothecary who was part of the papal court and
who was imprisoned after a sensational trial in which he was found
guilty of conspiracy in poisoning. I am certain he was innocent. I don't
know anything more about it, but since he was my ancestor, I must
defend him. I feel I would know it if he had been guilty.

He was kept captive for three or four decades, I am told. It is
unimaginable how horrible it must be to be in any prison at any time.
But that was a day when living in a palace was a terrible hardship
compared to the way all of us live now in our apartments with heat-
ing and plumbing. My ancestor survived that, so he must have been
very strong, stronger than I, I'm sure. But it's good that he was so
strong, because it was important to me that the line was able to reach
until 1920—or where would *I* be? Perhaps it was that Roman blood
I felt coursing through my veins when I first visited Rome, with my
mother.

As soon as I experienced the Rome of my mother's girlhood, the
visit to my uncle's family, I thought of nothing but how to go back to
that wonderful place and never, never leave.

When as a young man I was finally able to return, I wasn't certain how I would survive there, but I knew I would. I had found my home. From then on, there really was never a minute of my life that I wanted to be out of Rome.

When I arrived in Rome, I was a virgin. I would never have admitted it to my young friends in Rimini, who had all had numerous sexual experiences—or so they said. At the time, I believed them totally, everything they told me. I, myself, had exaggerated—lied, too. I did not lie, however, in great detail, because my knowledge was so limited, all of my own experience having thus far taken place only in my imagination. I was surprised later to find out how much of sex takes place right there. The imagination is the primary erogenous zone. I had to refer to my dreams when boasting. Those were delicious and, while they lasted, totally satisfying. In my dreams, I always knew what to do. I wasn't fumbling and clumsy. I was a hero, never embarrassed or ashamed of my body.

During my adolescent years, I had my share of the kissing and gropings of youth, and there could have been more, but I was always the one who stopped, although maybe if I hadn't, the girl would have. It wasn't because I was embarrassed by my lack of experience and my not knowing what to do. I could have figured it out. What really stopped me was that all the girls were virgins, too, or they said they were, and that made the responsibility too great. I couldn't do it to them, or to myself. I didn't wish to hurt anyone, and I didn't want to do anything that would prevent my leaving Rimini.

One thing I knew was that I did not want to marry early. I didn't want to be trapped into the life my father or my mother had. I didn't know what my destiny was, but I hoped I had one, and I wanted to find it.

I longed for freedom. I could not remain with a curfew imposed by my mother, who felt she had a right, even when I was nearly a grown man, to know everything I did and to deprive me of my house key if I didn't answer her respectfully. Happiness seemed to me to be freedom.

It was in Rome that I experienced the physicality of sex, with another person, that is. I was anxious to go beyond myself, but I wanted to do it without commitment. I did not understand how people could so easily become involved in long-term commitments without even understanding that was what they were doing. The idea of choosing, saying you want something, someone for your whole life, frightened me.

The answer seemed to "lay"—the pun is deliberate—in the bordello. The attitude toward the "house" was different in those days. It was an accepted fact of life. It also had the air of the forbidden, reeking of guilt. The presence of the Devil, probably having taken the form of the madam, added the risk of putting one's very soul in jeopardy. Catholicism did a great deal to make sex more tantalizing, not that it was necessary. At that age, one's hormones scarcely need much titillating.

I was lucky, because just as I entered a house, there was only one girl free. She was young. Only a little older than me. She seemed to be a nice girl, just sitting there waiting for a friend. I was that friend.

She was not wearing black lace or red satin, as worn by the other women I saw later. Such an obvious mode of dress would probably have frightened me away. I think at that moment I was so nervous that almost anything could have frightened me away.

She had a soft voice, she didn't speak very much, and she was not intimidating. She seemed shy. Later, I realized it was naïve of me to think that a prostitute could be shy. Still later in life, I realized, Why not? I have met actors and actresses who are shy. I have known clowns who were shy when they took off their clown suits and putty noses. I know a director who is shy. When I am not directing, when I am not taken by the force that makes me forget everything, I am shy. Maybe we are all shy, and we just pretend we aren't.

I think she was very pretty. She seemed attractive to me at that moment. To tell the truth, now I don't remember exactly what she looked like. Perhaps in later years I passed her in the street and didn't even know. Maybe she recognized me. Perhaps she couldn't recognize me with all my clothes on.

I remember thinking at the time that she was the kind of girl who should have been wearing white gloves. I wondered why someone so young and lovely was sitting there all alone. Years later, I realized that it was probably because she had just finished with another client.

It was wonderful. It was everything I'd hoped it could be.

Later, I understood that there was something more, a great deal more—sex with love. But at that time, I was such a silly innocent boy, I believed I *was* in love with her, she whose name I don't remember, and that she must have been in love with me, because it felt so good.

I wanted to go on knowing her. I asked her for a date, outside of the house. I didn't understand that this probably was against the rules, and if she had been discovered going out with me, she could have lost her livelihood. For my part, I, who hadn't yet figured out how to support myself, thought perhaps I could influence her to go into another line of work. What right did *I* have to judge her?

When I asked, she said no, she couldn't, but she invited me to patronize her professionally as often as possible. She was very encouraging.

When I left, I intended to do just that, but somehow I never got around to it. I never went back. It had been so nice. I liked the memory. I didn't want to do anything to spoil it. My life took a different turn, so I no longer needed the house except to use the experience in various ways in my films. The house is a valuable experience for a writer or a director.

I've wondered about the girl and whether her feelings were hurt because I never went back.

I did have some curiosity about the world, especially about America, but whenever I left Rome, I felt I was missing something. No other place I went ever lived up to the picture I had in my mind of it. Only Rome. It was so much more than anything my imagination could produce, a reality beyond any fantasy.

When I first saw Rome, my first impression was of people eating. Everywhere people were eating with total pleasure things which looked impossibly delicious. I looked into the windows of the restaurants and watched spaghetti being wound around forks. There were more shapes of pasta than I had known existed. Resplendent cheese stores, the smell of warm bread emanating from the bakeries, the pastry shops . . .

I couldn't afford to patronize those pastry shops as I wanted to, because I didn't have enough money for even one meal a day—in addition, of course, to breakfast. So I determined that I would become rich enough to eat as many pastries as I wanted. But at that time, I, who had never been able to gain weight, I, who was too ashamed of my skinny body to wear a swimming suit, discovered the secret of gaining weight—but I discovered it *too* well. Then, when I did have the money to buy all the pastries I wanted, I gained weight eating even one. I couldn't wear a swimming suit because I was ashamed of being too fat. Finally, I learned how to gain weight from just looking in the window at the pastries, and by eating them in my dreams at night.

My parents had provided wonderful food, and there was always more than I could eat. After a big and delicious meal at home, however, I was still capable of standing in front of the bakery near our house, with my face pressed against the window, admiring some glorious cake and wishing I had the riches in my pockets to enable me to buy it. I was certainly not underfed at home, but because I was thin and undernourished-looking, especially as I grew very tall, my mother felt that I must not be getting enough to eat, no matter how much she saw me eat.

I think my skinniness may even have been a source of embarrassment to her in front of the neighbors, who, she believed, would view her as a negligent mother. It was to my father that we owed the high qualitative standard of the food we enjoyed. My brother and I, of course, didn't know it at the time. We thought that was the way everyone ate. Of course it wasn't. My father always wanted his family to have the best, even if he was never there to eat it with us. There are merchants who bring home to their families the leftovers that they couldn't sell. Not my father. Nothing but the best for *his* family. Virgin olive oil, freshly pressed. The finest coffee beans. Chocolate.

I never understood what it meant to be hungry until I left home to go to Florence. I was always ready to eat, and I thought that was what being hungry meant. Until I was in Florence, I had never spent long enough between meals to recognize the concept of real hunger. It was in Rome that I really learned about it. For breakfast, if I sold some of my writing, it meant more and better rolls, and a second or third coffee. I discovered what hunger pangs were.

I was a reserved person when I first came to Rome. I didn't know people, the people I did know couldn't afford to give parties, and I didn't get invited to parties. I thought it must be nice to go to parties, and the idea was especially attractive to me because I imagined nice, welcoming buffet tables where I could stand and eat all I wanted until I wasn't hungry anymore.

So, when someone said "party" to me in Rome, it meant "food." My experience with parties had been, up to that time, limited to familial occasions or children's birthday parties in Rimini, occasions which, except for the birthday cake, seemed more for girls.

My idea of the best way to go to a party was as an objective observer. If I could have chosen, I would have worn a cloak of invisibility—and maybe, in the early days, one with deep pockets into which I could slip some food for future reference.

It was only as I began participating in assorted social occasions, with more than a few people at a time, that I realized I didn't really enjoy this sort of thing at all. At first, I didn't feel confident that people would find me interesting, or that I could uphold my share of the conversation, since I had no interest in opera, or in sporting events, such as soccer. It was deemed more dreadful in a man not to be excited by soccer than not to be excited by a beautiful naked woman. I made an effort, not wishing to embarrass my hosts or those who had brought me to the party. It was dismal.

People said to me, "And what do *you* do?" I was struggling to make a career as a journalist or an artist. That didn't make very good telling. My friends said I should make some of my funny little drawings to entertain people, but I could never have brought myself to attract that kind of attention. Though I had to draw in front of people at the Funny Face shop just after World War II, I never had more than a few people watching me, and that was the part of it I didn't like.

As I became more established, I was invited to more parties and attended fewer. I realized that I didn't enjoy the party situation. Social occasions increasingly came to disturb me. As I became more known, besides not being good at small talk, I had to recognize and fend off the pathological liars, those individuals who felt I was responsible for their misfortunes and should contribute money, and those who were trying out because they believed they had interesting faces. They were using the party as an excuse to audition. I thought, as I got older, I would adjust; but quite the opposite.

As I felt the spotlight on *me,* I grew more shy and more troubled by the need to perform for my supper. I probably would never have gone out, except with friends or what was essential for my films, if it hadn't been for Giulietta. She was much more social than I, and loved seeing her friends. I didn't like to embarrass her by always sending her out alone.

When I was a child, I was part of an educational system that exalted heroes of war. We were told that uniforms and medals made people special and those who had them were to be particularly venerated. We were taught that there was nothing more glorious than to die for others in a noble cause, but I wasn't a very good student. Personally, I never understood the fascination with Mussolini. He was very boring in black and white in the newsreels at the Fulgor Cinema. I mostly remember his boots.

Fascism and I were born about the same time. With the growth of fascism, war was represented as something to look forward to, a sort of party which everyone would want to attend. I must say, however, I personally was not sold on the glory of being a modern Roman soldier and marching off to battle, and did everything I could to avoid being invited to the party. I was particularly anxious to escape my father's fate in World War I. Now it is considered perfectly acceptable, even clever, that I avoided being a fascist soldier in the service of Mussolini, thus an ally of Hitler and the Nazis. But at the time, there were some who perceived my hiding in alcoves as an act of cowardice.

I bribed doctors and acted out any number of rare illnesses. I became a master of symptoms. Shortness of breath was one of my specialties. Sometimes before an examination, I ran up and down several flights of stairs as fast as I could. I was so convincing in acting out my symptoms that sometimes I convinced myself and didn't feel at all well. I felt even worse when the Italian doctors were replaced by German doctors. That was serious.

It became apparent that Italian doctors in Rome were no longer going to be able to give out medical deferments, except to those who couldn't walk. Someone from Bologna suggested that I go to the hospital in Bologna, where there was less scrutiny, to get my medical deferment. He said it had worked for him.

I made the appointment there and arrived early. I wanted to engage in my ritual of running up and down the stairs before being examined, hoping to alter my heartbeat, or my pulse rate, or my blood pressure. At the appointed time, I was told to go into a room and undress. The

Italian doctors seemed stern, uncharacteristically unfriendly. There were German inspectors.

As I stood in the cubicle assigned to me, I mentally reviewed my symptoms. It was a wonder I was still alive. No army in the world could want someone in my condition—I hoped.

Then it happened. The bomb hit.

It wasn't a direct hit, as I learned later, but it felt direct enough for me. There was total panic. People were running around and the ceilings were collapsing. I found myself in the street in my shorts. I had grabbed one shoe as I ran out to escape the collapsing roof. I was covered with dust and ceiling plaster. The shoes were together, so I don't know why my reaction was to pick up only one.

I knew people in Bologna, but I had to walk a long way from the hospital. No one seemed to notice me as I walked through the streets in my shorts. It reminds me of a René Clair picture I had seen. I can't remember the title, only the image of a man in his underwear, wearing a bowler hat, entering a police station to lodge some kind of complaint. No policeman stopped me, as they did the man in the film, because the policemen were all busy during the bombing. I never saw a single one.

When I finally arrived at the home of friends, they were not surprised that I was almost naked. Those were strange and difficult times. I have always assumed that my records were lost in the bombing, because I was never again asked to appear for a military physical. But still I didn't have a medical deferment.

As a boy in Rimini, I drew some caricatures of film stars from their photos displayed outside the Fulgor. A friend of mine colored the pictures. I signed the sketches "Fellas," and they were put up at the theater. Then the two of us were given free admissions. We didn't get paid. We exchanged our work for seeing movies, some of which we watched several times.

Some time later, in Rome, I had a similar arrangement. One of the first people I met there was Rinaldo Geleng, who was an artist, and we became friends. Geleng was very talented, especially with color. He knew how to use watercolors and oils. We would go around to restaurants and cafés and draw pictures of the customers. I did the drawings and he colored the pictures. I earned enough money to get by, but occasionally someone who was very pleased treated us to cake and coffee, or even a dinner.

Business would have been better if Geleng had done the drawings, too, because he did more flattering pictures than I did. I drew what I saw. People at the other tables would watch what I was drawing, and when they saw it was not a portrait but a caricature, they didn't buy one. Sometimes, the people I drew didn't even want to pay when they saw the way I had drawn them, and sometimes they *didn't* pay. The worst was when someone paid and I saw them later making a little ball of the picture and throwing it away. Of course, it hurt, but I couldn't work differently. I couldn't draw except what *I* saw. So, I suppose it was the same as the movies. I had to do what I felt and believed.

Geleng and I also found some work doing art for shop windows. I drew pictures and he colored them, until business was so good that each of us had his own shop windows to decorate. We were supposed to "catch" customers with our work. Often, we were called on to promote a sale the shop was having. I usually attracted a big crowd of onlookers while I was drawing, but that didn't necessarily translate into sales for the store.

My specialty was drawings of abundantly endowed, unrealistically curvaceous female creatures. They would beckon people into the store, for the markdowns. These drawings weren't especially appropriate when the store was selling ladies' shoes. Most of the people who stopped to look at my drawings were men, so my voluptuous ladies weren't very successful as "selling" pictures for whatever they were supposed to sell. I suppose I was already demonstrating that I didn't have a highly developed commercial sense, or that I couldn't set myself to work just for money. I wasn't willing to reshape whatever talent I had. As long as I could live doing what I wanted to do, I hoped someone would like it enough to pay me, so I could survive. Money in itself did not seem an interesting goal.

Our business really ended when I tried doing oil painting on the windows. That was Geleng's specialty, but we had two store assignments at once. People watching me draw always made me feel somewhat nervous, but I had accustomed myself to it; however, when I used the oils, I couldn't erase. I couldn't change anything, and the crowd watching saw the trouble I was having. I was so embarrassed. People laughed. The proprietor came out, brandishing a high-heeled lady's shoe. I thought he was planning to hit me. I ran, leaving my paints there. The worst was that as I ran, I heard the people in the crowd laughing. Running was a lifelong pattern: I knew I was a coward.

I moved frequently, from boardinghouse to boardinghouse, for various reasons. I lived in rented rooms, and I couldn't pay much, so I was always looking for something better, to move up in my standard of living. Sometimes, however, I couldn't pay the rent and had to look for a cheaper room and move down in my standard of living. I had an allowance from my parents, but I didn't want to tell them it wasn't enough. Rome was more expensive than Rimini, but I didn't ask for more because I wasn't following their dreams for me in Rome. I was following my own.

A few times I had landladies who wanted more than the rent from me, and their ardor embarrassed me. I had to move on. I found one place I did like, but I had to leave that one because I wasn't ready for a romantic attachment. The landlady there was older than I, but quite sexually attractive. I wasn't twenty yet, and I was probably sexually retarded, not in fervent interest, but in experience. She seemed to like me, and I didn't want to hurt anyone, so it seemed best to leave, even though I couldn't find another sunny room.

Whenever I'm not in Rome, I worry about the city, afraid that something will happen to it while I am away—as if, by being there, I could protect it, save it. When I return, I am always surprised to see that nothing has changed at all. Rosati is the same, and so is their coffee. No matter how many times I leave and return, every time I go back to Rome, it seems to me more wonderful than I remembered.

I've always liked living in ancient places. If you live in a new place, it ages and makes you feel old. If you live in antique surroundings, you cannot see any sign of its getting old. The centuries have given it its look, and the alterations produced by a few decades cannot be discerned.

Rome became my home as soon as I saw it. I was born that moment. That was my *real* birthday. If I remembered the date, it is the one I would celebrate. It is often like that in life. When the most important times are occurring, we don't even recognize them or notice. We are just busy living our lives. Only looking back do we know what was a great moment in our lives.

When I had just arrived and didn't know people or how I would earn my way or what my life would be, I was not afraid or lonely. I wasn't afraid, not just because I was young, but because Rome was magic for me. I knew I had found my place and would never want to be anywhere else. I wasn't lonely, because the city was my friend, and I knew *it* would take care of me.

Rome was even where I planned to die, although I didn't really plan to ever die.

five

HER BEST DIRECTOR, BUT NOT HER BEST HUSBAND

I got a job as a cartoonist and writer at *Marc' Aurelio,* a humor magazine in the spirit of *Punch.* I began writing for radio. I wrote jokes and bits for movies.

Then I met Giulietta Masina and she became my Rome family. I met her in 1943 when she won the part of Pallina in a Sunday-night radio serial, *Cico e Pallina,* which I had written. I heard her voice before I saw her.

I called and invited her to have lunch. I chose a very good restaurant which was in fashion at the time. I could not imagine doing less. It was an act of respect. She told me later that she had been surprised, because as a student at the University of Rome, she was used to being asked for coffee dates. She confessed she had brought along extra money in case I didn't have enough to pay the bill. She was very sweet, protesting that she wasn't hungry and trying to order the lightest, cheapest dishes. I encouraged her to order all the wonderful things on the menu, but she kept her eye on the prices. I was somewhat disappointed, because it meant that I couldn't order all of the wonderful things *I* had planned to try. How could I order the expensive things while she ordered only the inexpensive things? Giulietta didn't know that I had gone by the restaurant and looked at the menu *before* I invited her, to be certain I could afford it. It was a restaurant I had been looking forward to trying. Later I found out that her aunt, with whom she was living in Rome, hadn't wanted her to go to meet a stranger, even one who had written the show on which she was performing. She had relented when she heard the name of the restaurant I had selected, assuming, I suppose, that nothing too bad could happen to her niece in so chic a setting.

I don't know what Giulietta's aunt thought when, after a courtship of only a few months, we married. When you marry in your early twenties, you grow up together—although Giulietta has told me a few times during the years that I didn't grow up at all. You are not just lovers, husband and wife, but brother and sister. Sometimes I was a father to Giulietta, and sometimes she was a mother to me.

I am always a little embarrassed to talk about Giulietta as an actress because I've never really been able to talk about her professionally without thinking of her personally. We have shared our lives for so long, and yet I realize when I speak with interviewers that if I were to put into words for them exactly what part she has played in the creation of my films, I would be telling them something I never told her.

Not only did she inspire me in the creation of *La Strada* and *The Nights of Cabiria,* but she has been a little good fairy in my life. With her, I entered a landscape in life which *became* my life, territory which without her I might not have discovered. I met her when she was chosen to be the star of the radio show I had written, and she became the star of my life.

Men and women have a different attitude toward sex outside marriage. Women think when you have sex with another, you are parting with your soul instead of your prick. A man knows you are not parting with it, you are just lending it a little. But you cannot explain to your wife that it was just that someone else borrowed your prick for the night.

The idea of being married forever is romantic for a woman, frightening for a man. Masculine premarital sex is important, but unfortunately you can't store it up.

Giulietta and I were young together. Together, we discovered life. I introduced her to sex.

Neither of us had had much experience in life, in sex. I had more than she. She was a very sheltered girl.

She was so tiny and needed my protection. She was innocent, trusting, sweet, good. I towered over her. She looked up to me in every way, not only physically. I had never impressed anyone else that much before. I suppose partly I fell in love with my own reflection that I saw in her eyes. Her favorite photographs of us together are those which show us embracing, and I tower over her.

In terms of sex, at that time I was not very experienced except in my mind, and there my experience was amazing. Sex had been my predominant thought since before I had language to verbalize, when I had to rely only on images. My ambition was to be *very* sexually experienced before I married. Giulietta was a virgin.

Monogamy does not come naturally to man. Physically, man is not a monogamous animal. No matter how hard he may try, to be so represents a tyranny over his natural instincts. He must unnaturally suppress the stirrings within him, which takes more energy than to give in to the drive.

Relationships between the sexes have always been difficult for me. It's strange when you meet a woman you were in bed with a few times, twenty or thirty or forty years ago. She feels you owe her something. Perhaps I owe her remembering the occasion, and sometimes I don't remember it.

Giulietta has a more precise memory about these things than I do. Sometimes, she even remembers something that didn't happen. I think a man looks at the whole, the entirety, the big picture, and a woman looks most at the smallest part.

Once, I remember I was away and I called Giulietta at home. She didn't answer the phone, even very late. I didn't know where to find her. I imagined everything that might have happened to her. I promised myself—and God, too—that if only I found her well and safe, I would be a perfect husband. She arrived home and answered the phone.

After that, I still was not a perfect husband. But I do believe I was a good one.

The myth is that when people marry, two people become one. It is not so. They are more likely to become two and a half, or three, or five, or more.

The disappointment is especially great because the reality is *so* different from our indoctrination.

"They lived happily ever after" is for fairy tales. No one talks about the "ever after" when Cinderella becomes a nag. They do not say what happened when Prince Charming felt that eternal sexual twitch and a sudden sexual longing for someone who was not Cinderella.

I did not really want to get married when I did. I loved Giulietta, but I was too young. The war made everything seem more urgent. Everything was accelerated, and the future was less certain.

Though I did not want to get married so early, I never regretted being married to her. Through the years, I never wanted *not* to be married to her, though I think that she regretted many times being married to me.

Giulietta and I had a very romantic courtship. We married for love. It was the happy meeting of mind and body. Giulietta always had her feet on the ground, and I always had my head in the clouds.

Much later in our marriage, I was a Sunday husband. Reading the papers. It was disappointing for Giulietta, and especially so because nothing in our courtship or the early years had prepared her for the change in me, while she did not change.

For Giulietta, our marriage was not what she envisioned. It did not fulfill her dreams of personal life. Children were an essential part of her dream. She wanted a house. She expected a faithful husband. She was disappointed by me. I was not disappointed by her. I do not believe I could have found a better wife for me.

Something I have always loved about Giulietta is her unending hopefulness. She never loses it. Sometimes, she lives in Fairy Tale Land, but she will fight like a knight, not like a damsel in distress, to defend the walls of Fairy Tale Land against the assaults of the marauders. Her hopefulness got us into trouble many times because she was always hopeful of changing me. She never resigned herself to my wayward ways.

For faith, I didn't need to go anywhere but to Giulietta. Perhaps that is why I didn't need formal religion. In my life, Giulietta took its place.

Once when Giulietta was very angry at me for one of my transgressions, which I no longer remember, she said to me, "We'll divide the apartment. You will get this part, and I will get that part," and she started to plan its division so that neither of us would cross into the other's territory, but each of us would have a path in and out of the door. She was really in a rage.

I said to her, "What a good idea," and she looked shocked. "I mean for a movie," I said quickly. "I think I'll use this in a film."

She wasn't pleased, and got even angrier. It wasn't really at me she was angry, but at nature.

It was inconvenient to have Giulietta be jealous of other women with whom she believed I was having affairs, but I suppose I would have disliked it more if she hadn't been jealous at all.

Being a woman, she naturally gravitates toward one man, who becomes her universe. Because the human male, on the other hand, is not monogamous by nature, marriage is an unnatural state of being for him. It is a tyranny he tolerates because he has been conditioned from birth to accept it, along with other malfunctioning ideologies we accept as natural law, but which are really only the mandates of men who ceased to exist eons ago.

I have tried for years to explain all this to Giulietta, but she has her own views on the subject, quite contrary to mine and equally implacable.

I heard about a plan to have renewable marriage contracts. Each year you take your vow again. Giulietta didn't like that idea, and I know the Catholic Church would not approve.

If we had that system, each year I would marry Giulietta again, but maybe she wouldn't marry *me* again. I think she would. She would first probably exact from me, against my will, some promises which would have to be lies, and then she would agree, and each year we would have our ritual.

It is very important to have memories in common. I think the most terrible thing that could happen would be to live so long that I outlived everyone who shared my memories.

Giulietta always worried about me. She made sure my socks matched, wondered if my feet were wet so I wouldn't catch a cold. It's really the countless *little* things that make or break a marriage. Even when we quarreled, I knew she cared about me.

No one else meant so much in my life. But the wrong education she had, that I had, did not equip us for marriage, for the fairy-tale fantasy which has nothing to do with human nature. The word that should be talked about is not marriage, but *rapport*. When I talk about Giulietta, that is the word I think of for our relationship.

I'm not as good a friend as I should be. I'm not as good a husband as I should be. Giulietta deserved better. I was probably her best director, but not her best husband.

Early in my relationship with Giulietta, I experienced new pleasure and my first great pain.

When I am asked if I have children, I always answer quickly and simply, "No, my films are my children." That way, I finish with the question and with a subject I never like to talk about. Even after all these years, to talk about it is to relive that time which is so painful.

Before we married, I knew that Giulietta wanted children. It was a part of her thinking. I had never given any special thought to the subject, but I suppose if anyone had asked me if I planned to have a family, I would have responded, "Of course. Someday."

We did not talk much about it. We never said, for instance, a specific number. We were in agreement that there would be children, though she was more concerned with the subject than I was. I thought we should wait till the war was over. I could have been taken away at any moment, even when I had a deferment, and certainly after I lost it. I spent a lot of my time hiding in the apartment with Giulietta, as walking in the street was dangerous for any young Italian man who wasn't in Mussolini's army and didn't want to be. We didn't have money, and the opportunities for work were very limited then.

I was twenty-three and Giulietta was twenty-two. Though she was a year younger than I, Giulietta was really older, because she was more mature and better educated. She came from a more sophisticated background. She had lived in Bologna, Milan, and Rome, and had studied at the university in Rome. Also, I believe, up to a certain age girls are ahead of boys in many things.

It was wartime. Half of my time was spent trying to hide, not to exist, to be nobody. The other half was spent foolishly out in the streets trying to be somebody.

The order of everything—records and administration—had broken down disastrously. Patrols were searching with ever-increasing diligence to round up young men of the right age who were not in uniform, and the simple answer was just to stay out of sight. But that was not an easy answer for me. I was young and full of energy and, I have to admit, foolish. I was still at that stage in my life where I believed bad things were what happened to other people. I was in Rome, and I couldn't just hide forever in Giulietta's aunt's apartment. I had the desire to achieve, to be a success—and, more immediately, to be able to buy some food to put on the table. If I'd been wise, the thing to do would have been to stay in the apartment and not venture out. But one day, I did go out.

Of all places to choose, I took a walk across the Piazza di Spagna. After all, it was one of my favorite places to walk. If I had been paying attention, I would have seen the worried looks on the faces of those around. No one warned me, because they were afraid. The military had blocked off the area, and they were checking the papers of all young men who weren't in uniform. As soon as I understood what was happening, I tried to go back the way I had come, but I saw the street had been closed.

There was no way out. I was trapped. I determined not to panic. I would use my verbal skill. I would talk myself out of this predicament.

We were herded toward the Spanish Steps. Some of the interrogating soldiers were Germans. Their Italian was limited to asking for our papers, our deferment papers.

The next thing I knew, I was in a truck with other young Italian men, all of us doomed. I knew that I had to do something, but I didn't know what.

I thought to myself, What if this were a story I was writing? What would I do?

I saw a young German officer standing alone in the street. He was holding a package which looked like a panettone from the pastry shop in the Via della Croce. He was probably a person of taste, because it was the best panettone in all of Rome.

I leaped off the truck and ran toward him, calling, "Fritz! Fritz!" I threw my arms around him with all the warmth reserved for a long-lost, beloved brother. The truck just continued on, and I wasn't shot, another scenario which I hadn't thought of until afterwards. My scenario, limited though it was, had given me the confidence to act.

The German officer was so surprised, he dropped his panettone. I picked it up and handed it to him. He spoke to me in what sounded like very refined German. I didn't understand a word. I suppose he was explaining that his name wasn't Fritz. It wasn't likely that it was, but at the time, I knew only two names in German, and the other was Adolf.

I made as quick a departure from the scene as possible, while resisting the impulse to run. I tried not to look suspicious, which probably made me look even more suspicious. At the Via Margutta, I took a furtive glance back, saw a few Italian civilians who seemed to be watching me, though not unsympathetically, and ran.

I entered a shop where I pretended I was looking, and stayed for what seemed like an hour. Then I left and went back to meet Giulietta at her aunt's apartment. The Via Margutta had been a lucky street for me. I think what happened that day influenced me, much later, to move there.

The card Federico drew for Giulietta on the occasion of their wedding day, October 30, 1943. The two streets in Rome they lived on, Lutezia and Nicolera, were to become one, like the joined hearts. Cherubs play on the clouds, as the baby in the couple's near future leaves heaven, headed straight for their new life together.

•   •   •

The experience was a great shock. Suddenly life seemed shorter and potentially tragic. Giulietta wanted me to marry her. She felt an urgency I didn't feel, but I loved her, and all of a sudden the taken-for-granted infinite future didn't seem such a perfect certainty.

We were married on October 30, 1943. On the wedding card I made for her, I drew a picture of a baby coming from heaven in our future.

We were married in her aunt's apartment. Conveniently, a priest lived in the building who was permitted to perform the ceremony. Only a few relatives and close friends were present. Our parents didn't even know, because they were in other parts of Italy, and the phones weren't working well. Because of the war, it was difficult to communicate outside of Rome.

Our good friend Alberto Sordi couldn't be at our wedding because he was doing a show in a nearby theater, so after we were married, we went to see him. We entered while he was onstage. He saw us and turned up the lights, announcing to the audience, "My dear friend just got married, and I know he has a lifetime of applause ahead of him, but let's give him his first big hand." The spotlight was turned on Giulietta and me. I never was very good at being in hiding.

The baby happened more quickly than I might have wished, but Giulietta was so happy, and I was, too. I was very concerned with Giulietta's happiness, and at that time it seemed her happiness and my happiness were one and the same. It was a little frightening, this change in our lives, but we were both looking forward to it.

Then, something terrible happened. Giulietta fell on some stairs, and she lost the baby. She didn't want to know if it was a boy or a girl. Perhaps it would have made the baby more real for her to know. They told me it was a boy. We had planned to call the baby Federico, if we had a boy. Giulietta was inconsolable about the miscarriage, but she was also resilient. She was so young.

The only way to cure the pain for her was to quickly have another baby.

I don't remember consciously making a plan to have another baby so quickly, but it happened. I do remember that when Giulietta told me, we were both very happy.

We didn't think about the war that was getting worse, or about what I was going to do in life to earn a living that would support three of us. We thought only about the baby.

Giulietta and I believed we knew each other perfectly. I think we did. We knew each other better than we did twenty years later. We were still almost children ourselves in wartime Italy.

The baby was a boy. We named him Federico. Our son lived only two weeks.

Giulietta was told she couldn't have any more children. Our son had lived long enough for us to know him and believe in his existence. This was even more terrible for her, because she had always thought about being a mother. When you are told it can never be, it all takes on a significance you cannot imagine.

Perhaps if there had been better hospital care . . . if there had been medicine available . . . At the time, I didn't realize that maybe the lack of drugs in the hospital, as well as the shortage of doctors, made a difference for our baby. If there hadn't been a war when Giulietta had the baby, perhaps baby Federico could have been saved. Maybe they could have helped Giulietta, and there would have been more children.

Our child who didn't live was a stronger bond in some ways than the children we might have had. We didn't talk about it. Painful. But his presence, or lack of it, was always there with us. We did not talk about it because it would have made it more constantly sad. Shared tragedy, especially when you are so young, forges a strong bond. When people without children stay together, it is because the bond is truly strong. They have only each other.

Establishing contact with another human being is the most precious thing in life.

I never liked to talk about the baby Federico and the unborn child before, because people say, "I'm sorry." What else can they say? But receiving sympathy is terrible. It only forces you to relive the sadness each time. And you can't say to the people who are talking to you about it, "Be quiet!"

Regrets are the worst things. They are the past crippling you in the present.

People ask me if I have had a happy life. I always say "a full life." Happiness cannot be a constant. There is no way to hold on to it tightly. In fact, when we clutch too tightly, it seems more likely to disappear. We can be perfectly happy only if we can take happiness for granted, and since that can never be, one element of happiness has to be lacking—security.

The full life has its sorrows, too.

If my son had lived, I don't know what I would have taught him. I know I would have learned a lot from him.

I would have talked with him to see what was attracting his attention. I would have encouraged him to pursue the interests that attracted him. Above all, I would have encouraged him to observe. Drawing helped me to observe. I had to know something very well to be able to draw it.

I would have said to him, "Put yourself into life and never lose your openness, your childish enthusiasm throughout the journey that is life, and things will come your way."

What I would have tried *not* to do would have been to impart my own fears or disappointments to him. I believe children, in their innocence and openness to life, have the capability of foreseeing what their lives can be. It happens like this:

The child has an experience in which he recognizes an atmosphere, an occurrence that has been, until that moment, unknown to him, only it seems very familiar, for no reason at all; he feels an intense sense of belonging, warm and comfortable, and at home. It was what I felt when I discovered the circus.

A trusted adult confidant can help a child to recognize this direction, so he finds his way early and doesn't get lost. I would have liked to have filled that role for my son, that of a trusted adult confidant.

So now, looking back at Giulietta and me after so many years together, it is strange that most of our life is in the past, not in the future. I realize now that what happened made finding fulfillment in our work more important for both of us, so in the end it seems that what I answered was true—our films, especially the ones we made together, have been our children.

I have spent my life trying to separate myself from possessions of which I would think myself master, but which would in their subtle way take me hostage and condition the way I lived. I have always sought to unencumber myself.

I never wanted to have too much space for things, because I knew I would fill it up. I suppose if I had to always make the effort to suppress my spirit of acquisition, it was an unnatural act. I could easily have been the opposite, one of those who cannot throw away even a menu, a matchbook, a piece of paper with scribbles, a photograph of a schoolmate whose name you can't even remember.

I think my lack of belief in possessions was born when I had to leave my puppet theater behind in Rimini. Or perhaps it was when I saw the bombed buildings of Italy during World War II. It is a terrible thing to see people who have lost all of their possessions. Anyone who lives through this cannot help but be marked by a wartime psychology which pervades your being, though if you are young when it happens, you may not realize it is there. Perhaps I found it easier not to have possessions, to throw things away myself, rather than to have them taken away.

My personal dream of the most luxurious existence was a suite in a hotel with room service, the Grand Hotel in Rome if I could, a room with those wonderful silk lampshades with beige fringe, a little like spaghetti.

This would have not been fair to Giulietta. She wanted a house. In fact, she wanted two homes—one in Rome and one for the weekend and for summer. We always lived in an apartment, but for a while we did have a weekend house, too, in Fregene.

I know that I have always wanted to live life fully in the present, and that is best done for me without too many dust-collecting souvenirs. I prefer the memories in my head because they don't need dusting—or, if they do, I don't know about it.

Even when a lot of crimes started taking place in Rome, I felt safe everywhere because people had always greeted me in the street, in cafés, with such good-hearted warmth. Walking on summer nights, the streets of Rome—the whole of the city—had seemed to me like an extension of my own apartment. Then in the early eighties, it changed.

Women were warned not to carry the type of purses which are worn over their shoulders, to hold on tightly to purses, whatever kind they had. Or better yet, it was advised that they not carry a handbag at all. It was suggested in the newspaper that women carry only a little money, a powder puff, and lipstick in a paper bag, so it would look like they were just carrying home a few oranges, even going so far as to carry two oranges to put in the top of the bag. This didn't seem to be a very practical idea, because the purse snatchers might read the article, too, and especially watch for women with paper bags of oranges.

I would tell Giulietta that she should not go out with her purse swinging jauntily over her shoulder. I would get angry at her, but she would say it was the only one she had that would hold everything and that she had no other way of carrying everything she needed. Then she would go out with that oblivious, unaware look on her face that would just invite trouble. Usually she didn't carry much money, so if something happened, the worst would be the loss of her purse, and of course the trauma.

One day, Giulietta was taking some things to the jeweler to be repaired: some rings of hers and my best pair of cuff links. We were just leaving the Via Margutta, and Giulietta was talking with me, looking up at me as she always does, totally preoccupied in her way of innocent enthusiasm, when a Lambretta whizzed past us. There were two boys on it, and one of them leaned forward, snatching the bag from her shoulder. Then they shot off into the distance.

Giulietta screamed and I took off after them, probably looking like a kangaroo. I was shouting in the street, I, who never like to make a public scene or attract undue attention to myself, screaming, "Stop, thief!" The thieves, who were obviously not new to the business, began mimicking me, shouting, "Stop, thief!" as though they, too, were chasing the robbers, rather than themselves being the criminals.

I saw a policeman, and as well as I could talk while gasping for air, quite out of breath, since apparently I was much out of condition for giving chase to a Lambretta, I told what had happened. He was sitting on a motorcycle, but he made no move to give chase. "They've stolen my wife's bag," I said, still shocked by the invasive experience.

"What can I do about it?" he said, not interested at all. "Do you know how many purses are stolen in Rome every day?"

No, I didn't, and I assume he didn't, either.

We spent the next day feeling very foolish, as well as violated. We thought of Cabiria, who had twice lost her purse in the film.

The next afternoon when I returned home, there was a character who looked like he should have been in an Antonioni movie leaning against the wall and apparently reading a newspaper, except I noticed he was holding it upside down. That immediately made me suspicious.

"Federico," he said, implying an intimacy I certainly did not remember, "I hear Giulietta has lost her purse."

I said, "How do you know?" and he said, in what seemed at the moment to be rather an ominous tone:

"Giulietta should not have called the police."

"Why not?" I asked bravely.

He looked me in the eye and said, "You want the stuff back or not?" I said we did. He said, "Give me your phone number." Just as almost everyone in Rome knew our address, almost no one knew our phone number. When asked for my home number, I would always say, "The number is being changed," or "It's out of order," or "We don't have a phone." I thought a minute.

I wanted to get Giulietta's purse for her. Besides, this was interesting!

I gave him our phone number.

The next day, the phone rang. I answered. A man's voice asked to speak with Giulietta. She took the phone, and he told her that a boy had brought him a package and had told him to call her at this number and say the package was there, at a bar in Trastevere.

I went right there, to Trastevere, and the bartender had Giulietta's purse. I offered him a reward, but it wasn't accepted.

I took home Giulietta's purse. She was pleased. Everything was there, and she was sentimental about the rings. And she liked that particular purse. We thought that was the end of it.

But the next day, a letter arrived addressed to Giulietta. A story worthy of Dickens. Inside was a note which said:

"Excuse us, Gelsomina."

One of the saddest moments for me in any of my films is when I show the family that has bought Cabiria's house, just as she is leaving, she believes, to get married. For her, these people are invaders. It is she who has sold the house to them, but she is like a child who has said yes and then has changed her mind.

When I wrote the scene, I had to resist the urge to warn her, to stop her from making a mistake. Then, after it was too late, and she had sold her house, I had the impulse to undo it for her; but I could not, because the film had a life of its own. Once a character has gone as far as Cabiria had gone in her development, I had to let her live out her destiny.

Later, this happened in real life to Giulietta when we had to give up our house in Fregene. She had always wanted a house. With the money from *La Dolce Vita,* I was able to buy her one. Then, when I became a target for the tax people—unfairly—and we had to give up the house, I saw that look on Giulietta's face, years after she had acted it in *The Nights of Cabiria.* I understood that, as Cabiria had, she was imagining strangers who did not belong there, living in *her* house.

six

FUNNY FACES
TO NEOREALISM

In June of 1944, the Americans had occupied Rome. There were shortages of everything—food, power—and the black market was king. There was no work in the film business. The Cinecittà studios had been bombed, and people who had lost their homes in the bombings were living there along with other displaced persons and Italians who had been prisoners of war and were on their way home. The system had broken down, and there were people who didn't have a place to live or enough to eat. Giulietta was going to have a baby, and I had to figure out a way to support the three of us. There wasn't any film, radio drama, or even magazine work. So, I turned back to my boyhood career, when I drew pictures for the lobby of the Fulgor in order to have free admission to the movies.

Together with a few friends, we opened the Funny Face shop in Rome. We chose the Via Nazionale because we wanted a busy location with a lot of off-the-street business. We did cartoon portraits of GIs. That particular place was exceptionally secure because it was right across the street from the American military police. They would come racing out if they sensed any sign of a disturbance. They often did so, though their rough arrival on the scene usually created more of a disturbance than any they prevented.

The Funny Face shop was like I imagined the western saloon in Hollywood films. It became a kind of GI meeting place. I made a sign in English, or English as spoken by me at that time, that said, "Watch Out! The Most Ferocious and Amusing Caricaturists Are Eyeing You! Sit Down, If You Dare, and Tremble!"

The GIs understood.

Our business was entirely American soldiers, and it was from them that I learned to speak English. That is how it happens I speak GI English.

We had cardboard blowups of famous Rome landmarks—the Fountain of Trevi, the Coliseum, the Pantheon, among others. We had scenes with cutouts for faces. There were also joke cutouts, like one of a fisherman catching a mermaid. The soldier would be drawn in as the fisherman.

A GI could put his head into a cut-out circle and send back to his family or girlfriend a caricature or a photograph of himself as Nero playing a lyre while Rome burned. He could, instead, choose to be Spartacus the gladiator fighting the lions inside the Coliseum, portrayed kicking the lion into defeat. There was also the possibility to be Ben-Hur in a chariot, or Tiberius surrounded by sexy slaves. All the captions were in American English, or as close as we could come to it.

It was a particularly profitable enterprise because the Americans were so very happy. They had survived. These were the ones who had lived through combat, not wounded, and now they felt rich, and they were very generous.

I think running the Funny Face shop was the richest I ever was in terms of buying power. Not only was the business extremely successful, but the GIs were just the way they were in the American movies. They paid for their pictures, left generous tips, and also left tips of canned beef, vegetables, and cigarettes.

The cigarettes were a revelation. We'd never smoked cigarettes like that. If we'd smoked those American cigarettes, in those wonderful packages, before the war, everyone would have known that no one could defeat America.

I don't remember what we charged for the caricatures. It was the beginning of my long history of not paying attention to how much was paid. The number I remember is either too little or too much. My concentration was always on what I was doing, on doing what I liked to do. I paid a price for that, but I could never manage to equate success with money. I didn't understand exchanging money for some poor animal's skin which Giulietta might wear, or for a diamond when I couldn't see with my eye the difference in beauty between a diamond, a rhinestone, or a piece of faceted glass.

One day, I was drawing a caricature when a man entered who looked gaunt, as if he might be a displaced person or maybe someone who had been a prisoner of war. I recognized him even with his hat pulled down and his overcoat collar turned up and only a little bit of his face showing. He was Roberto Rossellini.

I knew he hadn't come to have me draw his picture. He indicated that he wanted to talk with me, and he sat down to wait for me to finish. The soldier I was sketching didn't like the picture I had drawn of him. He found it unflattering. He was about to make a scene. He had been drinking. His friends subdued him, and we said he didn't have to pay. But he insisted on paying, and then he left a tip that was more than the price of the picture.

When the commotion subsided, I went into the back of the shop with Rossellini. I couldn't imagine why Roberto Rossellini would have come to the Funny Face shop. We didn't have any Italian customers. Italians were buying food on the black market, not sketches, and Rossellini was a sophisticated and privileged Roman. It occurred to me that he might want to buy an interest in the Funny Face shop. Rossellini was a shrewd businessman. Actually, he would have been too shrewd to be interested in a shop with as limited a future as ours, one probably doomed at the end of the American occupation of Rome.

I did not realize that he had come to change my life, to offer me everything I wanted in life—before I even knew what it was I wanted. What if I had been out? I suppose he would have waited, or come back. I suppose . . .

Rossellini had come to ask me to write a scenario for a film which would become *Open City*. He told me about a script he had from the writer Sergio Amidei about a priest who had been executed by the Germans. He said he had backing from a rich countess. Women loved Rossellini. I tried to understand why, because I was interested in being loved by women. I didn't understand then what this fascination he had was, but now I *think* I do. It was because he was fascinated by *them*.

Women like a man who is interested in them. He would think it was he who was spinning a web, then *he* would be caught in it. Love affairs and films, films and love affairs were his life.

Rossellini had worked on the script, but he said he needed me. I was tremendously flattered. Then he added, "By the way," a phrase that makes one immediately wary. His postscript was, as he was almost out the door, that moment when the most important part of the conversation frequently occurs, could I persuade Aldo Fabrizi, a friend of mine, to play the priest? Things were not so different then from now. The value of a box-office name. It was disappointing, not to be wanted just for myself alone, but I swallowed the lump in my throat and said, "No problem."

Well, it *was* a problem. Fabrizi didn't like the idea. He preferred being a comedic actor. The story was too grim and painful, and in his opinion not what people wanted to see while they were living through their own real-life grim and painful experiences, just like what Rossellini was planning to put on the screen. Besides, what if the Germans came back? And the money wasn't good.

One of the important meetings of my life had been with Aldo Fabrizi. He was a character who, if I hadn't known him, I should have made him up. I met him first by chance in a café. We had both been going there alone. Because it was our neighborhood café, we noticed each other and began to speak.

Fabrizi invited me to a restaurant. I think it was because I was so thin that he thought I must be hungry. He was right. I *was* hungry, but not because I wasn't earning enough money at the time, but because I was always hungry. I had a good appetite, but no matter how much I ate, people felt the need to feed me.

We went for night walks, which we both liked to do. He was good company. He had a comic gift and had toured through Italy as a vaudeville performer. It was from him I learned all about live theater in the provinces, and later he would be the one to win the opportunity for me to work on *Avanti c'è posto,* my first real screenwriting credit. Although my name didn't appear on the screen, it did appear on the film's registration documents, and I was suddenly perceived as a screenwriter. I had worked on films since 1939, but as a gag contributor and rewrite man. All of these are "lost" films—I hope. *Avanti c'è posto* was a big success, and I had a lot of offers to write material for film comedies. Since I met him as a journalist, or perhaps I should say a *trying*-to-be journalist, I should be more sympathetic to those who make their living with a pad and pencil.

I went back to Robertino with a shortened version of my conversation with Fabrizi. I said simply, He wants more money. It turned out to be the truth. Rossellini sold some of his own antique furniture to give Fabrizi more money, and I was part of the project, even if it wasn't totally out of recognition for my brilliance as a screenwriter. Now I was part of neorealism.

Something I learned from Rossellini was that directing could be done by someone who is just a human being. This is not to diminish Rossellini, who *was* a special person. It is only to say that if there is something you want to do, it is good to take a look at the people who are doing it, because when you see that they are, after all, human beings, you realize that what they do is attainable. It is like meeting Fellini and saying, "Well, he's not so special! If *he* does it, *I* can make films." What Rossellini did convey to me was a feeling, his love for directing films, which helped me to realize my own love of directing.

When I first was on movie sets, to do interviews as a journalist, and then after I had worked on scripts, I did not immediately recognize the film set as the place where I would find my greatest fulfillment and happiness, what Tennessee Williams called "the home of the heart." It wasn't until I worked with Roberto Rossellini in the 1940s that I found the meaning in life for me.

I understood very early that I was different from other people. I realized I would either be considered crazy or a film director. The luxury of being a director is that you are allowed to give life to your fantasies.

Our dreams are our real life. My fantasies and obsessions are not only my reality, but the stuff of which my films are made.

I have often been called mad. Madness is an abnormality, so I don't take that as an insult. Madmen are individuals. Each is obsessed by an individual obsession. It seems to me that sanity is learning to tolerate the intolerable, to go on without screaming.

I have always been fascinated by the idea of the insane asylum. I have visited several and found that there is a kind of individuality in

insanity that is rare in the so-called sane world. The collective con-
formity that we call sanity discourages individuality.

What had stopped me from making a film about insanity, until
Voices of the Moon, was my research into it, which made it seem all too
real. I became so sad and depressed. I couldn't hold on to my sense
of fantasy. I was interested in the individuality of eccentricity and the
adjustment of the happily, mildly retarded, but I didn't find it in the
real world of insanity.

I had the opportunity to observe an asylum. I saw people who had
no happiness in their madness, but were endlessly trapped in their
own nightmares. It was not as I had imagined it. These were prisoners of the torment of their own minds, an even more terrifying
prison than that of the walls which confined them. I would never
have been able to endure the months of staying with a project such
as this, nor was it what I did. Perhaps Antonioni or Bergman might
have done it.

What really stopped me was one incident, one little person. One
can somehow escape a generalization more easily, such as "Thousands
died in a war," than the loss of one specific person you knew who was
alive and then dead.

I was taken into a dim, small room. At first I didn't see anyone.
But in there was a child, a little girl. I was told that she was a Down's
syndrome baby and was deaf and blind. She was like a little heap, yet,
sensing my presence, she made sounds like a puppy. When I touched
her, it was clear that she wanted tender attention, warmth, humanity.
For the moment, as I held her, I thought of the unborn child Giulietta had lost. What if . . . ?

The little girl has haunted me since. I wondered what future could
she have had, but I never tried to find out because I suppose I really
knew the answer.

It was only later, many years later, that I was able to touch on the
subject of insanity, but only because what I treated was poetic lunacy
rather than actual insanity.

I was a kitchen writer during World War II and during the period just
after. There was no heat, and I worked in the kitchen by the cooking
stove. This may have had an influence on my writing of that time, but
if it did, I will leave it for those who like to ponder the past. I would

not like to see a student waste his young life writing a thesis on "The Kitchen Writings of Fellini."

Open City was written in a week, one of the kitchen-table collaborations. I was credited for writing and as assistant director. I deserved it, but everyone doesn't give what you deserve. Robertino was never stingy with anything.

As a boy, through his father, who was an important builder—he had built some of the major cinemas in Rome—Roberto and his brother, Renzo, had free movie privileges at some of the biggest and best movie theaters. Robertino always took a crowd of boys in with him.

We made *Open City* and *Paisan* just after the liberation of Italy by the U.S. military forces. We did *Open City* for less than $20,000, so you can imagine what kind of salaries we had. I, personally, have no idea what I was paid back then. The money was of absolutely no interest to me as long as I could survive. I was doing what I wanted to do with people I wanted to work with.

These films had a documentary style, some of which was a deliberate roughness. The style was called neorealism. It developed out of necessity because of film shortages and shortages of virtually everything in Italy at that time. There was fluttering electricity, when there *was* electricity. Neorealism was melodrama perceived as truth because events like the ones that happened in the film had just shortly before been happening right before everyone's eyes in the streets.

Neorealism was the natural way in Italy in 1945. There was no possibility of anything else. With Cinecittà in shambles, you had to shoot at the real location, with natural light, if you were lucky enough to have film. It was an art form invented by necessity. A neorealist was in reality any practical person who wanted to work.

Paisan is an episodic tale of the American advance into Italy during World War II. It represented a very important moment in my life. I had the chance to continue my association with Rossellini, who certainly influenced my life, I learned a lot about filmmaking, and I saw Italy, places I'd never seen before. I met Italians I had never known. I saw the ruins and disasters of World War II, and the war seemed more immediate for me than when it was happening. These images became part of me.

It was traveling with Rossellini through Italy that I grew up in the political sense and understood the extent to which the fascist regime

Roberto Rossellini (left) and the twenty-six-year-old Fellini (right) while they were shooting *Paisan* in 1947. The unidentified man in monk's habit, not a professional actor, appeared in one of the film's segments. The use of nonprofessional actors was typical of Italian neorealism.

had blindfolded us. The full extent of the horrors of World War II was more apparent in places other than Rome. I was amazed by the upbeat, optimistic spirit of people who had suffered, but who were constructively rebuilding their lives. I also became familiar with the existence of so many dialects, of so many ways of speaking that existed throughout Italy. I began to make notes of lines, phrases, words. The experience was like filling my lungs with oxygen.

There are people who come into your life who, for one reason or another, play an important part. We were just finishing *Open City* when an American soldier tripped over the cable we had in the street. He followed the cable, found us, and said he was an American film producer. We accepted what he said and totally believed him. We showed him the film. The young soldier, whose name was Rodney Geiger, loved it. He said it was great, and he said he could show it in America. Rossellini, who was very trusting, gave him a print. I was very trusting, too, in those days. As it turned out, it's lucky we were so naïve.

He wasn't really a producer, but from our innocent trust came our success.

This soldier, Geiger, took the print back to New York and showed it to the Mayer-Burstyn company, which was distributing foreign films. Despite the poor quality of our print, they bought it right away.

Rodney Geiger made money on the deal and contacted Rossellini, telling him that he would finance his next film and that he could get him American stars. I think Rossellini asked for Lana Turner.

Geiger did come back to Italy, with some unknown actors and, more valuable, some fresh film stock.

If someone had approached us on the street some years later, I certainly would have been more suspicious and probably would not have trusted a total stranger. I would have been closed to my own good luck and would have defeated my guardian angel. There are probably times in later years when I did.

Rossellini was a charismatic personality. Working with him, I realized making films was exactly what I wanted to do, and he encouraged me in the belief that it was an art form I could master. He was older than I, ahead of me in so many ways.

Having always loved the circus, I saw the resemblance between movies and the circus. As a boy, my greatest dream would have been to be the director of a circus. I love the fantasy and the sense of improvisation in both.

The Miracle was based on a story I remembered from my childhood. Rossellini had just made a film based on Cocteau's *La voix humaine,* and he needed another short film to go with it. I didn't think they would be captured by the tale if they knew I had made it up, based on a real story that happened in Gambettola, in Romagna, where, as a child, I had spent my summer holidays with my grandmother.

I said that the story was by a great Russian writer, whose name I made up, and that it was based on something that had happened in Russia. No one wanted to admit to not knowing this great writer's name, which I have since forgotten. I forgot it right after I said it. Russia was more mysterious and glamorous then than it is now, and I easily caught the attention of the group.

They all liked the story and immediately decided to do it. But then, they liked the story *too* much. They wanted to know the name they had missed of the Russian novelist, and I couldn't remember what I had said. They asked me about his other works, thinking where there was one good story, there would be more. So, finally, I had to confess that I had made up the story, but they liked it just as much.

The story on which *The Miracle* is based involved a character who may or may not have been a Gypsy. Gambettola was a village with woods, and I loved it because I loved my grandmother more than anyone else in the world. At that time, she was the most important person in the world to me. I could not imagine life without her. I felt she understood me and would love me no matter what. Many of the happiest times of my childhood were spent with her in Gambettola during those summer holidays. It was there that I used to talk with the animals. I would talk with horses, goats, dogs, owls, bats. I wished they would answer me, but they never did.

My grandmother always wore a black head scarf. I don't know why. It never occurred to me to ask. I thought it was part of her. She carried a cane and shook it at the men who worked the land for her. They always treated her with great respect.

My grandmother told me a story she invented. It's like the story of the Frog Prince, only in this case it was a Chicken Prince. I was very, very little. Yet today, if I eat chicken, I am worried that I have eaten a prince, and that either I have destroyed him or that he will come to life inside me. Just after my grandmother told me the story, I ate chicken for dinner. I had the most terrible stomachache. My mother put me to bed and told me that I should go to sleep, and my stomachache would pass. But I didn't believe her. I couldn't tell her what I was really worried about. I thought that the chicken had turned into a prince inside my stomach.

Every animal was personified. My grandmother humanized them. She would say, "Sophia is in love," Sophia being one of the pigs. Or she would say, "Look, Giuseppe is jealous." Giuseppe was a goat. When she pointed it out, it was obvious that she was right. She had special powers. She could predict the weather, and she could see into the heart of the small boy who was me.

Gypsies used to come to the woods in the summer. There appeared one tall, handsome man, with dark curly hair, not only on his head, but on his chest. He had knives hanging from his belt. All the pigs in the neighborhood squealed when he came near. All of the women squealed too. They were afraid but totally fascinated by him.

He was diabolically attractive. Everyone believed he was infinitely menacing, the Devil incarnate. I was warned to stay away from him, or something terrible would happen to me. I imagined him spearing me with one of those sharp knives, spinning me in the air over his head, and then roasting me on a spit for dinner. Once I found a dark hair in some sausage my grandmother served, and I thought it was the hair of a child who had fallen into the hands of this menacing Gypsy.

In the village, there was a simpleminded woman. She was not young at all, but she fell madly, obsessively in love with this charismatic figure. She was pitiful, but the villagers regarded her with scorn, or at best ignored her. She gave herself to this man and had his son. She claimed it had happened without sexual intercourse between them, and that it was some kind of miracle. Nobody believed her.

When I went back two years later, I saw the little boy playing by himself. He was already large for his age, a beautiful child, with long eyelashes and piercing eyes. The villagers called him the son of the Devil.

Rossellini's imagination was captured by my story idea for *The Miracle,* and he had the idea that I could play the part of the young man whom the simpleminded peasant woman, to be played by Anna Magnani, believes is St. Joseph. Rossellini imagined that the young man who would seem a saint ought to have light golden hair. I had at that time very thick, dark hair. The only answer, he said, was to dye it. When he asked me if I would like to play the part, I didn't hesitate a second. When he asked me if I would be willing to dye my hair, I hesitated; but then I agreed to do it.

Rossellini made the appointment for me at a women's beauty shop, not my favorite beginning. It was agreed that he and I would meet at a coffeehouse a few blocks from the beauty salon after "the dye was cast" and I was a blond.

Rossellini waited. And he waited. He couldn't drink any more coffee. He had read his newspaper more than once. He left the café and went to see what had happened to me. Robertino found me hiding inside the hairdresser's, my hair a perfectly hideous shade of golden blond. The dye job was so obvious that when I had ventured forth, some young men in the street called after me mockingly, "Rita—it's *you!*" referring to Rita Hayworth.

I rushed back into the salon, followed by jeers and more calls of "Rita, dear, aren't you coming out to see us?"

As it turned out, the hair photographed well enough in black and white. Afterwards, Rossellini would from time to time greet me as "Rita," enjoying it all the more because he believed I never saw the humor in it. For my participation in *The Miracle,* Robertino surprised me with my first car, a little Fiat.

The Miracle gave me a chance to know how an actor feels, even a star, which for my brief scene I was. It is wonderful to have the world focused on you. *You* are everything, all-important. Everyone caters to your every whim. They watch the flicker of your eyelashes, the barely perceptible movement of your hand.

It's like being a great voice at La Scala, or the president of the Republic. Others think for you, cosset you. You are totally taken care of. I never had more fun. It's no wonder the Fox in *Pinocchio* sang "Hi-diddle-dee-dee, an actor's life for me." Actors are spoiled children because we spoil them, at least for their moment in the spotlight. I couldn't believe it. I could sit down without looking and there would be a chair under me. My every desire was anticipated. I had only to look like I wanted a cigarette, and it would be lit for me. I felt I had but to clap my hands, and slaves would be summoned, even slave girls. I was hesitant to test this. I felt like an emperor or a pharaoh.

I first met Magnani when I worked as a writer on *Campo dei fiori* (*The Peddler and the Lady*), in 1943. I noticed her, but she didn't pay much attention to me. I was very skinny then. It was hard to see me. People looked past me or through me. She was involved with Rossellini at the time, and I was nobody. Everyone was nobody when they were next to Robertino.

Magnani had a reputation for wanting and getting a lot of sex, but I don't know if that is true. I never saw her offer herself to anyone. She talked about sex often and in a vulgar way, but because it suited her persona, it didn't seem startling that she had a man's sense of humor. I found it funny and not in bad taste. If someone is deliberately trying to shock you, it can't seem very shocking. She had started out as a singer of bawdy songs, and she was a total performer, ready to do anything to get attention. She had a little dance she did privately in which she played she was a man with an erection, done with anything handy that served the purpose stuffed under her dress or pants. This may be a little surprising the first time. After you have seen it a few times, you hardly notice. It's even boring. But she never seemed vulgar to me.

With me, she was natural, though once in a while she did a little act for me. That meant she had heard I was casting a new film, and it was her way of letting me know she was available, but for a part in my film. People said that when she talked about sex, it was meant to be a turn-on, though I never took it that way. It was said she did the propositioning with men, like a man, taking the initiative to get whom and what she wanted. It was said she knew *how* to ask and was prepared to take the rejection a man has to be prepared to accept. All I know is she never asked me. Maybe she understood that at the time there was no room in my life for any other woman but Giulietta.

I like to feel protective with a woman. I never felt strong enough to protect Magnani, except at the end when she was sick.

She was extraordinary. When she died, all of the stray cats in Rome mourned her. She was their best friend. Late at night, she would bring them food from the great restaurants of Rome.

Her last performance was for me in *Roma*. I knew she was sick. She knew she was sick. But we didn't talk of it. She was an actress and happiest when working. When she was gone, I sometimes gave food to the cats in the Margutta, and I would say to them, "For Magnani." Of course, they were another generation of cats who hadn't even known Magnani's cats and Magnani, but it didn't matter.

In 1949 Rossellini handed me a twenty-eight-page script to look at. It had been written by two priests who knew nothing at all about dramaturgy, not to mention screenplay writing, but who knew a great

Restaurants became a frequent setting for conversations between Charlotte Chandler and Federico Fellini as this book developed.

deal about Church history. The subject was St. Francis of Assisi and his followers. Roberto told me that he would like to make a short film based on the script, but that it needed some rewriting. Obviously it needed a great deal of work. Would I like to do it?

After reading the script, I said no. Absolutely no. He said, Would you like to be assistant director? I said yes.

Then he gave me the script to rewrite. It was to be called *The Flowers of St. Francis.*

Why did he choose this subject? His view of religion is clearly evidenced in *Open City, Paisan,* and *The Miracle.* He respected sincerely religious individuals while questioning the sincerity of organized religion. He especially admired the devout religiosity of the early Christians, which is possibly a reason he wanted to make this film. He may also have been trying to placate the Catholic censors, who were incensed by his open affair with Ingrid Bergman.

Why did *I* participate in such a venture? I *could* say that I looked upon it as a challenge and an opportunity.

The truth is I wanted to work, especially as an assistant director and especially with Rossellini. He was a great talent, and I liked him as a person.

And it wasn't as if I received so many offers. There was no line around the block, and had there been, there would have been no one like Rossellini standing in it, because there was no one like Rossellini.

The story is static, the characters are unconvincing, the subject is too remote to be believable for modern-day audiences, but I knew even at that youthful moment in my life that there is an advantage to receiving a script *that* bad. Obviously, one can only make it better.

I talked Aldo Fabrizi into appearing in the small role of the Tyrant, a barbarian conqueror, a scene I created especially for him. I really worked hard to make it a fine scene—so we could remain friends. The rest of the cast was mostly nonprofessional and, sometimes, I have to admit, *un*professional. It was neorealism in an unlikely guise.

My favorite scenes are those with Brother Juniper and John the Simple, who try even the patience of St. Francis. This is not easily accomplished. In spite of St. Francis's admonitions to Brother Juniper not to take his teachings too literally, the overzealous monk comes back to the monastery in his underwear, having given his cloak to a beggar who seemed to need it more than he.

I still remember being pleased with my scene in the barbarian camp, which seemed to me rather realistic, though in a fantastic, almost Kurosawa-like way, in terms of what we might imagine happening in the thirteenth century. I remembered that scene while I was making *Satyricon,* even though it's not set in the same period. The actor who played the priest in this scene also played the priestlike detective in *Juliet of the Spirits* some fifteen years later.

I never really liked doing scripts from other people's ideas, though I admit that perhaps because of this prejudice, later in my career I missed some good stories that I was offered. My own ideas were more than I could ever carry out. It was self-centered of me, I suppose, not only that my own ideas seemed more attractive to me, as our own ideas seem attractive to all of us, but I believed I could carry them out with greater feeling, I could stay with them and give them a unity because they were born of me, and I could achieve the greatest understanding and intimacy with my characters. I stayed with them absolutely, every step of the way, until they were ready to fulfill whatever their destiny might be in their encounter with audiences. That was when I abandoned them to their fate, like sending your child to school. I had done what I could do. I was their first audience. When they went into the movie theaters, I couldn't help them in the popcorn competition, in the world of the crumpled chocolate-bar wrapper.

I remember a moment that I know was a turning point in my career, in my life. Rossellini was working in a small dark room, peering intently at the Moviola. He didn't even hear me enter. His intensity was so great that he was living on that screen.

The images on the screen were silent. I thought, What a wonderful way to see your film—silent—so that the visual is everything.

He felt my presence and wordlessly beckoned to me to come closer and share the experience with him. I think that was a moment that shaped my life.

seven

THE GOOSE AND
THE DIRECTOR

After World War II, I thought I could make a living as a writer, while Giulietta worked as a radio and stage actress. Screenwriters didn't make much money in those days, so it was necessary to keep busy. Besides working with Rossellini, I wrote for Pietro Germi and Alberto Lattuada, whom I had met through Aldo Fabrizi.

Tullio Pinelli was also writing for Lattuada, but we had never met, though we knew about each other. One day, I saw him at a newsstand and said, "You Pinelli, me Fellini," imitating Tarzan, though I didn't beat my chest. He was older than I and had more experience, but we got along right away. We talked about all the ideas we had for films. An idea I remember telling him about was the story of a man who could fly, just like in "The Voyage of G. Mastorna," an idea that would stay with me for all of my creative life.

The first picture I worked on with Lattuada was *The Crime of Giovanni Episcopo* [also known as *Flesh Will Surrender*]. I think something I wrote appeared on screen, but I'm not sure. Lattuada liked what I did and suggested I try something else. He gave me an idea to work on. It became *Without Pity*, Giulietta's first film. She wasn't the star, but she won a Silver Ribbon at Venice for her performance.

Giulietta and I got along well with Lattuada and his wife, Carla Del Poggio, a popular actress in Italian films. I went to see *The Magnificent Ambersons* with Lattuada. I was overwhelmed, but I had no idea that I was seeing only part of the film. Now I can understand how Welles felt when so much of his picture was cut. It's happened to me many times.

Lattuada wanted to form his own production company, and Giulietta and I were invited to participate. We wanted to be free of producers, so this was an opportunity to become our own producer. We formed Capitolium Film. Our first—and last—film was *Variety Lights*. Pinelli was involved, and so was Ennio Flaiano, whom I knew from *Marc' Aurelio*. It was the beginning of an important collaboration.

Since my contribution to *Variety Lights* was to be more than that of just a screenwriter, Lattuada suggested we share credit as directors. While this was an exceptionally generous gesture on the part of an established director, I feel that I earned my co-directorial credit. I have been asked many, many times about who really directed *Variety Lights*. Should it be counted as one of my films or as one of his? He counts it as one of his, I count it as one of mine. We are both right. And we are both proud of it.

I was important in the writing. Much of it was based on my own observations of the Italian variety theater. I always loved live theater of this sort, the provincial performers. I was also important in the casting and rehearsal of the actors. Lattuada had a great deal of experience in cinematic staging and direction, so he was important in these respects. He was extremely precise in his planning. I am not. I prefer a great deal of spontaneity. In spite of this difference in temperament, we produced what I think was a very good picture, although no one went to see it.

I am very sympathetic to the characters of *Variety Lights* because they wanted to be show people. The level on which one competes is not what is important. I feel a bond with everyone who has the aspiration to make a show. The people of the little troupe are dreaming of the glory, but they have no qualifications for it. The performing goose symbolizes it. He performs with heart. The ones in the film were like us, the ones who made the film. We thought we had the artistic qualifications. So did they. Our business qualifications weren't any better than theirs. We lost all our money. Lattuada had put in more than we, so he lost more, but what we lost was more important to us, as we didn't have much money and couldn't afford to lose any.

I approached *The White Sheik* with great trepidation, though in retrospect its filming seems tranquil compared to what I would face on and off the sets of my following pictures. But at the time I didn't know what the future held. I have never been good at looking to the future. I am not even good at looking into the present.

After *Variety Lights,* I was confident I could direct a whole picture by myself, but until I actually had assumed the responsibility, had committed myself, I didn't know how it would really feel. When I aspired to it, it was a mental process, but when it came time to do it, I felt it in the pit of my stomach. I had trouble going to sleep, and I would

Melina Amour (Giulietta Masina) contemplates an uncertain future in small-time Italian vaudeville with her unfaithful lover, in *Variety Lights* (1950).

wake up several times during the night. As the first days of shooting drew closer, I couldn't sleep at all. I ate more—and enjoyed it less.

I felt alone. Now it was I who was totally responsible, with no place to hide, as previously had been the situation with the collective anonymity of scriptwriting, with the shared responsibility of being a co-director. What if I failed? I would let down all these people who believed in me.

I couldn't let them know that I didn't believe in myself. I had to be the leader—infallible, or nearly infallible—so they would put themselves into my hands. It would not be good for *The White Sheik* for people in it to feel they were supposed to have confidence in someone who didn't have confidence in himself. I couldn't share my self-doubts with anyone, even Giulietta, although I couldn't totally hide my nervousness from her. When I left home for the first day of shooting, she stood in the doorway to kiss me good-bye. It was not a token kiss, but one given with the passion before a departure on an adventure from which I might never return.

I felt like the moment in battle when you first come into direct contact with the enemy. Where could I go if I failed? I would have to leave Rome. For me, that would have been a fate worse than death.

Panic. I felt the sensation of falling.

To add to the regular difficulties of directing a first film, I had insisted on Alberto Sordi as the White Sheik and Leopoldo Trieste as the bridegroom. Sordi was considered a character actor with no charisma, who could not bring people into the theater, and Trieste was a writer, unknown to the public. At the time, no one imagined that Sordi would become such a big star. The rest of the cast, including Giulietta, was considered not sufficiently attractive, not at all "box office," but I had been stubborn, even on this first fragile solo venture. I had to follow what I believed. It has always been that way for me.

Sordi was the person who dubbed Oliver Hardy's voice in the Italian versions of Laurel and Hardy films. He had won a contest to do that. As far as I was concerned, that was a good omen. When I met him it was as close as I believed I could come to Oliver Hardy, although there wasn't really any resemblance. But for me, he was Hardy's voice. In later years I wondered, What did Hardy really sound like? When I finally heard him speak, he sounded to me like an impostor. I said, "Where's Sordi? I want Sordi." We live much more in a world of appearances than of reality, in the cocoon of that to which we are accustomed. To have said no to Alberto Sordi for the parts in *The White Sheik* or *I Vitelloni* would have been for me like saying no to Oliver Hardy.

Sordi was at that time a skilled performer in the live shows in Rome that preceded the showing of the movies. There is a feeling for the audience that the performer develops from being live in front of them, and he brings it with him, a special sense. When he is in films, he has this sensitivity to an audience reaction. It's one thing to perform for the camera; that is much more of a learned skill, and a director can control that. The ability to reach out to the people who at a later stage will be the audience for whom the film is being made, that is an art. It showed in the way Sordi could reach out to the people on the set while we were filming him.

When I feel something strongly, I must do it my way. I approach the situation, go into the meeting, and say to myself, "Fellini, you will compromise. You will do some of what you want and give the others something of what they want. You will be rational, reasonable. You will choose what is most important to you, and on those points you will concede nothing. But as to other mere details, not the basic ones, you will be gracious. You will recognize that it is *their* money."

Then, at the meeting, someone says, "I don't think the character should have a handkerchief in his pocket," and I am once again a willful two-year-old. My mother told me, more than once, that I have never changed.

The concept of *The White Sheik* requires some explanation. At the time, adult comic strips using photographs instead of cartoons were popular in Italy. They were known as *fumetti,* and a movie about them was considered to have "commercial" potential.

The idea for a feature film about the *fumetti* had been suggested by Antonioni, who had himself made a fine short on this subject a few years earlier. But when Antonioni was approached to be the director of a feature film about the *fumetti,* he declined. Lattuada also did.

Since Pinelli and I had already started on a script, I approached some producers with the idea that I could direct it. I started with the producers who had originally agreed to do it, but they rejected investing in a young director with only half a credit. They were so unreceptive that it was as if one half a credit was less than no credit at all.

It was that thing of How do you get started if you aren't already started? I had had a taste of directing, and I was certain that I had found what I wanted to do. Finally, Luigi Rovere, who had produced for Pietro Germi, agreed to give me a chance. He had liked *Variety Lights* and believed I could become another Germi. Thus, my pattern of starting a picture with one producer and finishing with another began, and it wouldn't end until *8½*, when I became associated with Angelo Rizzoli, for whom I made more than one film.

Rovere was supposed to have produced my following film, which was to have been *La Strada,* but he dropped out because he didn't think the idea for *La Strada* would make a commercial movie. The producer who did like it, Lorenzo Pegoraro, encouraged me to make *I Vitelloni* first while I looked around for a "younger, more attractive" actress than Giulietta to play Gelsomina. He wasn't diplomatic at all in telling me that. The drama behind the lens was often more intense than that in front of it.

Pinelli and I went to work creating a situation in which real people became involved with the characters of the *fumetti* and the models who play them. He suggested a provincial couple coming to Rome for their honeymoon. Immediately I was inspired. As soon as we began, I was able to see virtually the rest of the film in my mind. The woman would be secretly infatuated with a hero in the *fumetti,* while the husband has arranged for his family to meet his bride and to take them for an audience with the Pope. The idea of bourgeois provincials in Rome immediately appealed to me. I instantly identified with them. I knew that was the way some people saw me—as a provincial. To some extent, they were right.

No matter how well an Italian from the provinces thinks he is prepared for Rome, the reality that meets him upon arrival in the big city is overwhelming. All my life, my mother had told Riccardo and me about the Rome she remembered as a girl, so I grew up knowing the Rome of my imagination and of her memory. My mother's memories became my expectations.

Working from my own recollections, I set to the task of providing a story for my newlyweds arriving in Rome, just as I had arrived on that day I'll never forget. My own first day always seems to me as if it were only yesterday. For the bride, it's her first time. The bridegroom has relatives in Rome he wants her to meet. An audience with the Pope has been arranged by the husband's uncle, who is obviously an influential person. I remembered that such a meeting was the dream of my mother when she was in Rome, so I gave her dream to my characters. The story, as I envisioned it, would be limited to only one day. Contrary to what many people think, limitations, especially in cinema, often stimulate the imagination more than total freedom.

During these twenty-four hours, the marriage would face its first crisis. Wanda, the bride, is grateful to be married, but she could imagine a more romantic hero than her husband. Leopoldo Trieste had the perfect comedic face to play Ivan, the husband she appreciates but does not yet cherish. Ivan is stable, prosperous, and respectable, but certainly not dashing. He is characterized by his need to always be near his hat. At the beginning, on the train platform as they arrive in Rome, he becomes disoriented when he almost loses the hat in the confusion of unloading their suitcases. Throughout, he is never entirely secure without this symbol of his middle-class respectability. Even alone with his bride in their hotel room, he has to know where his hat is or he isn't comfortable.

The idea for Ivan and his hat came to me when Leopoldo asked me about the character of Ivan. Being a writer himself, he was interested in a different way than an actor would be. At the time, he was wearing a very nice hat. I noticed it and said, "Ivan is the kind of man who is so proper, he even takes his hat to the bathroom with him in case there is an emergency, so he won't ever be caught without it." The hat became a delineator of Ivan's character.

Wanda, like many Italian women of the period, is secretly addicted to *fumetti*. The romantic stories she reads there are what she has come to expect from love and marriage. She is, in fact, secretly enamored of a particular *fumetti* model, who poses as the White Sheik. He's a sort of Valentino type, perfectly played by Alberto Sordi, whose enormous talents had gone relatively unnoticed up to that time. Wanda's secret hope in Rome is to meet the White Sheik. In answer to her fan letters, he has sent her a letter inviting her to visit him if she ever gets to Rome. She takes it seriously, not realizing that it's a form letter. Without telling her husband, she goes to meet the White Sheik, and gets separated from Ivan for a whole day. Ivan is then too proper to tell his uncle that he doesn't know where his wife is, so he offers the feeble explanation that she's sick and confined to her hotel room.

Wanda (Brunella Bovo) meets her romantic idol, Fernando Rivoli (Alberto Sordi), in *The White Sheik* (1952).

Meanwhile, Wanda gets stranded on a beach shooting location with the White Sheik. Like Ivan, he turns out to be his head apparel. As soon as the White Sheik takes off his hood, he turns into an ordinary man. Less than ordinary, in fact. Instead of being larger than life, he is smaller than life.

Hats can be a good indicator of character. Mastroianni becomes a movie director in *8½* by wearing one like mine. I wear hats. It's not to give myself character, however; only to hide my thinning hair. Marcellino took to wearing one himself after I convinced him he needed thinner hair for *Ginger and Fred*. When his hair didn't grow back immediately, I think he wore the hat to bed.

For the script, I also drew on impressions from stories I'd written for *Marc' Aurelio,* reflecting my own thoughts on the doomed nature of romance, young love confronting bittersweet reality, the spoiled honeymoon, the disappointments inherent in early marriage, and the impossibility of preserving one's early romantic dreams.

An image that remains fixed in my mind from my early years in Rome is that of being interrogated by a figure of authority. It was one

A disenchanted Wanda looks on as the White Sheik is exposed by his wife, played by Gina Mascetti.

of the many attempts to induct me into military service during World War II. I was asked questions by a man in uniform, and as I answered, a secretary beside him would rapidly type out what I said on a big, noisy typewriter. It sounded like machine-gun fire. I felt as if my words were being put up before a firing squad and executed almost before I could get them out. That image inspired the scene in the police station when Ivan goes to find out about missing persons without revealing that his wife is among them. His reaction, that of feeling persecuted by uniformed figures once he has exposed himself to their authority, was exactly mine. I gave it to Ivan. During the war, I imagined people were following me.

Uniformity and regimentation are my enemies. I never liked doing the same thing everyone else was doing at the same time. Saturday-night lovemaking never appealed to me. Well, there have been exceptions.

I didn't want to believe that others had control over me, especially over my mind. I don't like to see any movement toward our becoming a society of ants. I remember in my youth seeing young people moving in organized, regimented groups, like schools of fish. Even when they weren't wearing uniforms, they conformed to the prevailing dress code, which amounted to uniformity. I remember especially the orphans of Rimini. Poor little things. Whenever a group was needed for any event—a funeral procession, a parade, whatever—they were turned out en masse in their little black uniforms. They wouldn't have the vaguest idea why they were there, just that they had been ordered to do so and they had no alternative but to obey. Not only had they lost their parents, but they were depersonalized, de-personed.

The brief appearance of Giulietta as Cabiria, the good-hearted little prostitute who tries to cheer up Ivan when he thinks he's lost his wife, is important to Giulietta's career as an actress, and to mine as a director. She was so wonderful, the producer could no longer say she wasn't capable of playing Gelsomina, and of course *Nights of Cabiria* was inspired by this scene. Cabiria was, so to speak, Gelsomina's poor, lost sister.

The White Sheik was the first time Nino Rota wrote the musical score for one of my films. Our long and serendipitous relationship began outside Cinecittà before we knew each other. I noticed a funny little man waiting in the wrong place for the tram. He seemed so happily oblivious to everything, I felt compelled to stand and wait with him to see what would happen. I was certain the tram would stop in its regular place and we would have to run for it, and he was equally certain it would stop wherever he was standing. I think we often make true what we believe. To my surprise, the tram did stop right in front of us, and we boarded together. We remained together until his death in 1979. There will never be another one like him. He was a natural.

I showed a print of *The White Sheik* to Rossellini before I had finished editing it. Robertino was very encouraging. It meant a great deal to me. I respected him as a director, and his praise at this crucial, early moment in my career was important to me. Shortly afterwards, I told him that someday I hoped I would be able to repay him for his generosity. He said that I could repay him by encouraging someone else. Someday when I was in the position of being one of the most important Italian directors, which I surely would be, he said that I should remember him and help someone younger than myself.

With *Paisan*, I knew that I *wanted* to be a film director. I thought maybe this was where my future was, not as a journalist. It was with *The White Sheik* that I *knew* I was a film director.

PART II

FEDERICO FELLINI

eight

MAKING FILMS IS
MAKING LOVE

Much has been made of the autobiographical nature of my work, and my willingness to tell everything. I use my experiences as a framework, not as exact reportage. I don't mind speaking autobiographically because I reveal less of myself talking about my real life than I do if I talk about the layer underneath, the one of my fantasies, dreams, and imagination. That is the real person, naked. It's easy to wear clothes over your outer self, but it isn't easy to cloak your inner self. I believe even if I made a film about a dog or about a chair, it would have to be somewhat autobiographical. To know me most deeply and personally is to know my films, because they come from the deepest part of me, and I am totally exposed, even to myself. Through my films, I find myself having ideas for a film, thoughts I didn't know I had. In what comes from my imagination, that is the revelation, the deep truth of my inner self. Maybe it's my kind of psychiatry. It's something like interviewing myself, when I make films.

If you see a dog run and catch a ball in his mouth in midair and proudly bring it back, you understand all there is to know about dog nature, and people nature, too. The dog is happy and proud because he has a trick he can do that is special, in demand, appreciated. This will result in love and high-quality dog biscuits. Each of us looks for our special trick in life, the one that will be applauded. The ones among us who find it are fortunate. *I* am a film director.

I cannot imagine working without a good feeling and a congenial environment around me. I don't like to work alone, and I need to work with people I like. Sometimes I can have someone I don't like, as long as it's an individual with a strong personality. Any real relationship is better than no relationship. The bearded lady has her own beauty. I am, after all, a man of the circus, so I need to create a little family. We all need a positive atmosphere, and we need to believe in ourselves and the creature we are about to bring forth. The atmosphere of shooting a film makes everything immediately familiar, and on the set, everyone becomes part of a family.

I feel at home as soon as I have a crew. I feel like Christopher Columbus with my crew, going forth to discover the New World. In our case, we are going to create a New World. Sometimes my crew needs encouragement, and sometimes I have to be strong to force them to continue on the voyage.

I have always wanted to make a picture about America. The way I would like to do it is to reconstruct America at Cinecittà. I have already fantasized such a project cinematically in *Intervista,* in which I'm planning the elaborate sets of an early-twentieth-century New York City in a film to be based on Franz Kafka's *Amerika.* I have many reasons for wanting to work in Italy, really in Rome and especially at Cinecittà, aside from the ten thousand details I wouldn't know if I worked elsewhere. The most important reason for me is that familial atmosphere I find at the emotional center of Cinecittà which allows my inspiration to flourish.

The people on the film set are my *real* family. I was always a little uncomfortable as a child with my parents, even with my brother. My sister was so far from me in age, almost another generation, that I didn't really know her except as an adult. I believe the film world must be analogous to the world of the circus, where the bond between the bearded lady, the Lilliputians, the trapeze artists, the clowns, is greater than the one they have with their more normal brothers and sisters who live "civilian" lives away from the circus.

I have been criticized for making my films only to please myself. The criticism is well-founded, because it's true. It's the only way I can work. If you make the picture to please each person, you don't please anybody. I believe you have to please yourself first. If you make what pleases you, that's the best you can do, all you can do. If what pleases me pleases other people, enough of them, I can go on working. Then, I am lucky. If it doesn't please me, I am tortured and can barely go on.

Steven Spielberg is fortunate that what he loves is then loved by so many people in the world. He is both successful and sincere. An artist must express himself doing what he loves in his own style, without compromise. Those who only want to please cannot aspire to being artists. A little compromise here, a little compromise there, and at what point is the soul lost? Chip, chip. Crack.

Being an artist, to my way of thinking, has less to do with external judgments of whether what you do is good or bad than whether you did it to please yourself or only to please others.

I tell myself, when it seems so difficult to make a movie—to be a director, to raise money—that I am glad it *is* difficult to do this work I have chosen. After all, *everyone* must want to be a director, and if it were easy, there would be so much more competition. I tell it to myself, but I am not persuaded. I'm lazy, especially about doing what I don't want to do at all. I really wish I could have a patron, like in olden days, one who would say to me only, "Do what you wish, do the best that you can." Money has so many strings to it that I can identify with Pinocchio, who didn't wish to be a marionette and wanted to be a "real boy"—that is to say, his own self.

Every day that I'm not making a movie is for me a day lost. In that way, for me making movies is like making love.

When I'm making a film, it's my happiest moment. Though all of me is taken by it, though it consumes all of my time, thoughts, energy, I also feel freer than I do at any other time. I feel in better health, even if I don't get any sleep. Everything I ordinarily enjoy in life, I enjoy more, because I am in a state of heightened perception. Everything I eat tastes better. Sex feels better.

When I'm directing, that's when I'm most fully alive. It's my most virile moment. A special energy comes upon me, and I can do all the parts, participate in every aspect of the film, and am never tired. No matter how late it is when we stop shooting at night, I can hardly wait for the next day.

Energy, extremely high energy, is essential for a film director. I never thought of myself as that kind of person. I saw myself as having below-average energy, even being a little lazy. I have never needed much sleep, nor have I ever been able to sleep much, only a few hours a night. It may be because my mind is always working.

I have so many thoughts that it's hard for me to go to sleep. After a few hours, I wake up thinking. My mind is always more active at night. I don't know if it's because of the silence and freedom from distraction or if it's because of a clock within me, and I'm on a different time from everyone else.

In my sleep I have some of my best thoughts, because they are images rather than words. When I wake up, I try to draw them without waiting too long, before they become faint or disappear. Then sometimes they recur, but usually not in exactly the same form.

When I'm directing, it's an advantage that I need so little sleep, no more than a few good hours, and that I am such an early riser, no matter how late I go to bed. I try to be conscious of the fact that everyone else working on the film needs more turnaround time in order to rest.

Directing my first film, I worried about whether I would have the physical capability, but I no longer worry. That adrenaline is always there when I am directing.

The ideal for me would be to have some pauses after my film has started shooting: to work many weeks, and then to be able to go away from the set for a few days—not to escape what I am doing, but to be free to absorb what has happened, to assimilate it all, and let it become part of me, without the pressure of the set. That would be quite a luxury. I used to try to get some little breaks provided for in my contracts, but I couldn't make the producers understand. They sneered: "Fellini needs a little vacation." They didn't understand. I wanted to work harder, but my way. I could not ever make them understand that I didn't want time off to play. Giving me time to play, a vacation away from my film, would have been the most terrible punishment anyone could have inflicted on me.

The thought of professional impotence must, I think, threaten every creative person—the fear that one day the well will run dry. I've dealt with this preoccupation of Guido's in *8½*. Thus far, I myself have never felt any sign of it. Usually ideas are coming too fast for me to make use of them. Yet I could imagine being empty. It's like sexual impotence. I don't feel it near, but if I live that long, it would be the same as with professional impotence. I would hope to have the humility to retire from the scene. Meanwhile, I have the energy, the enthusiasm, the urge to do as much as I can.

Because so many of my ideas came to me in my dreams at night, and I didn't know how or why they came, my creative forces were left dependent on something over which I had no control. A mysterious gift is a great treasure, but there is always the fear that as it came, mysteriously, it could thus be taken away, just as mysteriously.

I dreamed once that I was directing a film and was shouting, only my voice didn't make any sound. I was shouting and nothing came out. Everyone—actors, technicians—they were all waiting for my instructions. There were even elephants, trunks poised, waiting for direction, so the movie set had a certain resemblance to a circus ring. I couldn't make anyone hear me. Then I woke up. I was very glad to find out it was a dream. Usually I enjoy my dreams, but I was glad to leave this one.

When I go to see a film, someone else's film, what interests me now is the story. I want to escape. I want to experience the drama. I have no interest in the camera. If I'm aware of it, that's wrong, though when I'm making a picture, I constantly look through the camera viewfinder. I also feel compelled to act out all the parts for the actors. I'm even a very good nymphomaniac. For me, the set is life. I think nothing personal happens to me anymore.

I find "improvisation," a word used frequently in connection with my films, an offensive term. Some people say I improvise and mean it as a criticism. Others mean it as a compliment. It's true that I am not rigid. I am open to possibilities. I admit I change quite a lot, and I must be free to do this. But I prepare everything, even more than is necessary, because that gives me the freedom to be flexible. I have removed the pressure because I am prepared, in case the adrenaline doesn't flow. In case there is no sudden inspiration, then there is preparation. But the juices always flow—thus far.

My films are not made like Swiss watches. I could not work with that kind of precision. They are not like Hitchcock's scripts.

Hitchcock could work with so precise a script; not only every word, but every gesture was preplanned. He saw the film in his head before he made it. I see the film in my head *after* I have completed it. I know he worked from drawings, as I do, but he used his drawings in a totally different way than I do. He used them like architectural drawings. Mine are for creating and exploring character, so the story can come from character. I see many movies in my head, but the final one is different from all of them. After a certain point, any film of mine has a life of its own, even apart from me. Made by me at a different time in my life, it would be a different *La Dolce Vita* or a different *8½*.

My film characters live on for me. Once they have been created in a film, even for a film I never was able to do, each has a life of his own, and I go on imagining stories for them and thinking about them. Like the puppets of my childhood, they are more real to me than real people.

I come to the set of my pictures with a clear idea of what I want, carefully written out, everything planned. And then I put it aside.

In this way, I am like a piece of paper that has been typed on one side and is blank on the other. Even though I may have worked for days on the written side, when I arrive on the set, the blank side of the script is more important. I will keep referring back to the written side, but it is only a suggestion of what the completed film will be like. For this reason, I like actors who don't come too well prepared, because I am going to make changes according to what I find there. In this respect, Mastroianni is a joy. He doesn't care ahead of time what will happen. He just steps into the character without asking any questions. He doesn't even have to have read his dialogue. He makes everything a playful experience.

I work in the way I do because it's the only way I can. If I could do a first draft of a script that was perfect, I suppose I would use that, and it would save a lot of money, but I cannot believe it would make a good film. It certainly wouldn't be fun. I think the film of mine that emerged from such a process would be a dead thing. The magic for me can come only when everyone is gathered and the actors are breathing life into the characters. The printed page for me cannot go directly to the screen.

An example of how I was inspired to change things, in what was a carefully written out screenplay, is *Juliet of the Spirits*. The character of Lynx-Eyes, the private detective Juliet employs, is quite different in the actual film from the one originally conceived on paper. The reason in this case was the actor himself. I had used him before for small parts in *Il Bidone* and *La Dolce Vita,* but he was especially good in *The Flowers of St. Francis.* In it, he played a priest who saves Brother Juniper from being executed by the barbarians. When I remembered that the actor had played a very understanding priest at a difficult moment, I got the idea to rewrite Lynx-Eyes as a sort of priest instead of the character I had originally envisioned. I even had him wear a clerical collar, a disguise Lynx-Eyes uses on some of his cases, and I have him appear in this disguise in some of Juliet's fantasies, one of them even before she has ever met him. I suppose certain priests have seemed to me to be sort of private eyes. As a child, I never liked going to confession. I didn't want *anyone* to know everything about me. I didn't have anything interesting to tell, unless I made it up, which I sometimes did, especially when I believed the priest who was my confessor had fallen asleep. I wasn't very interesting until I was pretty certain he was asleep. Then I confessed to having killed a school chum with an ax on the way to church, adding that there was a lot of blood. His snores never missed a beat.

I never try to totally change an actor to fit a part, because it's not possible. It's better not to try to change the actor, but to change the part to fit the actor.

Even though I change the script many times, a series of transformations, I could not imagine going to the set without it. If it's only a crutch, it's a necessary one. Total commedia dell'arte, and I would feel panic. Creating a work of art cannot be a committee project. Committee art would be more unthinkable for me even than commedia dell'arte. Producers can never force me to do what I feel is wrong. Their power over me is in limiting me, by not letting me have enough money to do everything I want to do.

My idea of casting goes far beyond what is called typecasting. I search for the flesh-and-blood incarnation of my fantasy characters. It doesn't matter to me whether they are professional actors or actresses or whether they have never acted before. It certainly doesn't matter whether they speak Italian or not. If necessary, they can recite numbers in their own languages. We can take care of that part in the dubbing. My job is to bring out the best in each. I try to relax the actors, experienced or not, so they lose their inhibitions, and if they are professionals, so they lose their technique. Frequently the professional actors are the most difficult to work with because they have learned the wrong lessons, which are so strongly ingrained that they cannot shake them off.

When I choose someone to be an emperor, I select someone who looks and seems like the emperor I have in my mind. I am not concerned with whether he *feels* like an emperor. If I am successful, I am able to transport actors into my environment, where they can be natural—laugh, cry, and react spontaneously. Everyone can be assisted to express his own emotions, his own joys or sorrows, to turn inward rather than outward. It's my goal as a director to open up each character, not to limit. Each character has to find his own truth, but he has to be selective in his self-revelation. The actor must find not his own truth, but the truth of the character he is portraying. When he finds this truth, he achieves the mastery of the illusion. No one has ever achieved the mastery of truth and mystery of illusion more for his or her character than Anita Ekberg in *La Dolce Vita* or Mastroianni in *8½* or Giulietta in *La Strada* and *Nights of Cabiria*.

I'm asked how I get an idea. It's not a question I'm fond of.

There are the things that happen to you, and the things you make happen. If you respond only to what happens to you, you feel dependent on what you scarcely know: Luck. An accident. A whim of the gods. My inspiration often comes from things I have observed in life.

A famous writer used to come to the café Rosati, and he would have coffee with a lady who was his constant companion. They would order and then they would sit and quarrel. They looked angry and unhappy, but no one ever heard exactly what it was they quarreled about. This went on for years. They never married. Perhaps that was what they quarreled about.

Then they didn't come for a while. When the man returned, he came alone. The lady had died.

He always came alone after that. He seemed so sad. He never smiled. He never talked with anyone. He never brought anyone else. He just sat alone and looked into space, or read the newspaper, or wrote.

Once he left what he was writing on the table, and the waiters looked at it. They were love poems, odes to the woman who had died. They put the poems into an envelope and gave the man the envelope when he came the next day. He said only thank you. Nothing more.

Giulietta Masina, Anthony Quinn, and Aldo Silvani as they appeared in *La Strada* (1954).

I meant to put the vignette into one of my films, but producers always want explanations. What did the woman die of? What happened then? What were they really quarreling about? When all the questions have been answered for the audience, and they have no questions left that they want to ask, the film has become very dull.

I like to go to Cinecittà even when I'm not working on a film. I need to be alone in that special setting for inspiration.

I need to be in contact with my memory of emotions.

For me, having an office apart from what I have at Cinecittà is also important. It must be separate from the producer's control. I think a great deal at home, and Giulietta is used to that; but I do not like to have strangers coming to my house, so I need a place in which to see actors. It's not for other people that I go to an office, but for me. This office offers space and gives me the illusion that I am working. And then, suddenly, I *am*.

The jottings and drawings are my first step toward inspiration. That first step is made when the board is put up and I begin mounting faces on it, photographs of faces to stimulate my imagination.

Faces first. As soon as they are on the board of my office, each photograph says to me, "I am here!"—waiting to catch my attention and shove the others out of my consciousness. I am searching for the film, and this is the first essential part of the ritual. I am not worried, because I am here, and I know the film will arrive. There will be a knock on the door. An idea is a door into the courtyard.

When I think back to the days of loving movies at the **Fulgor**, I remember being particularly fascinated, not only by the **films, but by**

Fellini taking a break and **amusing** everyone during the filming of *I Vitelloni* (1953).

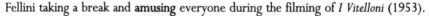

the posters outside. **Sometimes** they had wonderful drawings, which I tried to copy, and **they had pictures** of **the American** stars. There were the stills of the scene **from the films, and the publicity** photographs of the stars. What caught **my attention** particularly were the stills of the faces. I looked at those faces and imagined the stories in which they might star. I imagined Gary Cooper acting in a movie in my mind. I suppose at that early age, without knowing what I was doing, I was casting.

As a boy, when I made my puppets, I would make two or three heads for each one, sometimes each one with a different face, or sometimes the same face but with a different expression or a different nose. Faces were so important to me, before I even understood it myself.

When I am working on a film, that's the time I am bombarded by the greatest number of outside ideas, ideas not for the film on which I am working. That would be natural, to have ideas for the film in which I'm involved, but the ideas that come knocking are for other stories, entirely different ones. These ideas are actually competing for my time and attention, diverting my concentration. There is a kind of energy, actually a synergy of ideas. The creative forces are let loose, but the creative spirits do not know anything about discipline.

In life and in making films, it's really important to keep your innocence. Pull a little tail, and maybe there is an elephant at the end.

The important thing is that you have to be open to life. If you are, the possibilities are infinite. It's important to preserve your innocence and your optimism, *especially* when it's not easy.

It's wonderful, the look in the eyes of some dogs. Such innocence. Such sincerity. A dog does not know how to wag his tail insincerely. Such wonder. Such admiration for us, because we are bigger and seem to know what we are doing. It's an openness which I could almost envy if it did not involve such dependence. It's what I would not like about being an actor.

Dependence is a dreadful state for a person. Perhaps it's not the best for a dog or a cat either, but what can they do? We have a responsibility toward them.

People ask me, "Do you like dogs?" "Do you like cats?" I answer yes. It's simpler that way. They are not looking for a complex answer. But more correctly, I would say I like some dogs, some cats.

Once, I prepared minestrone for fifty starving cats in Fregene. I do not cook, never, but on this occasion they approved my culinary talent and ate it all. Since they were starving, they were not exactly the most discerning judges.

Success is supposed to bring a lot of friends. People think I have so many friends. There is so much they do not understand. I am surrounded by people who want something—to work in my films or to interview me. It is a crowd that makes me feel more alone.

Fame is not what it might seem to be. People who aren't famous think they would like it because it's supposed to bring happiness. What is happiness? There is no doubt that success has brought me certain pleasures. When I was young, it seemed success would be wonderful, it would open the doors of the world, make my parents proud, show my schoolteachers—most of whom had found me worthless and would never have thought I was the kind of person who could have fame—how wrong they were.

Fame. How? For what? My drawings weren't good enough. I didn't think my puppet theater had that kind of promise. Certainly not. Perhaps as a journalist I could uncover great stories, and I would have a byline. That was my highest aspiration, since I had no idea where my destiny was taking me, except that I felt very early it was to Rome. Fame for me meant being on the screen of the Fulgor Cinema, and there was no way *I* could do that. I was not Gary Cooper. Later, I realized that the screen of the Fulgor did not exactly represent the ultimate dream of a director.

All of us have a desire to impress our parents, not only when we are children. Perhaps in that way we never grow up. We want to show them our success, and see pride in us reflected back. It was truly important to me that my parents had the chance to see me as a famous film director.

I assumed that fame was somehow involved with money. I have never had any interest in money except when I didn't have what I needed. The artist needs reassurance more than he needs food. In the early days, what I needed was money for a coffee, for a sandwich, or for my room in a Rome boardinghouse, as near to the center of town as possible. Later, what I needed was millions to make films.

It was only after fame came to me that I realized that fame didn't buy money. Since I was recognized by every taxicab driver, it meant

I had to give bigger tips, or they might spread the word that Fellini is stingy.

I am expected to **entertain**. Visitors come through to meet me. Since Rome is my city, **it seems** I should entertain them, and the person I invite is often not **alone**. Sometimes I would be making a film, and one of my many producers had the honor of receiving the bill, but usually the honor was mine.

As a successful person, I am expected to live in a certain way. Now, it doesn't matter to me what people think, except if you don't have the appearance and appurtenances of success, you are perceived as a failure, and you can't get money for your next picture.

There is also a tendency on the part of the world to confuse the real person and the work of the person. The work of the person is his extended self, a concept I didn't make up, but which I like. As the actor is confused with the characters he plays, the director is thought to be like his pictures. Because I sometimes make opulent, lavish films which look expensive, I am assumed to be rich.

I am assumed to be so rich that sometimes when I suddenly find I'm compelled to entertain a large group for a business dinner at the Grand Hotel, I have to hide at home. The promises are theirs, and the gamble is mine. I am easy to fool because I have to be hopeful for my next film, or I cannot live, but the bill has to be paid in the present. I do not like to charge things into the future or to have debts. I have the enjoyment of the meal now, so I believe I should pay for it now.

One's fame seems to give others rights they would otherwise never feel they had—to look through your garbage, to try to overhear your personal conversations. It gives them a license for speculation. I told Giulietta that we must never, absolutely never, quarrel in public. We had quite an argument at a crowded restaurant over this.

Whenever I am seen with another woman in public, having a glass of wine, taking a coffee, walking on the Via Condotti, it is reported like news, and Giulietta and I have to deny publicly that we are getting a divorce. Giulietta is embarrassed and, worse, she wonders what is true. Worse yet, often she believes what she sees in print.

During the shooting of *Il Bidone*, gossip circulated that there was a romance between Giulietta and the American actor Richard Basehart. I told Giulietta I thought it was a foolish story. I laughed. She said, quite

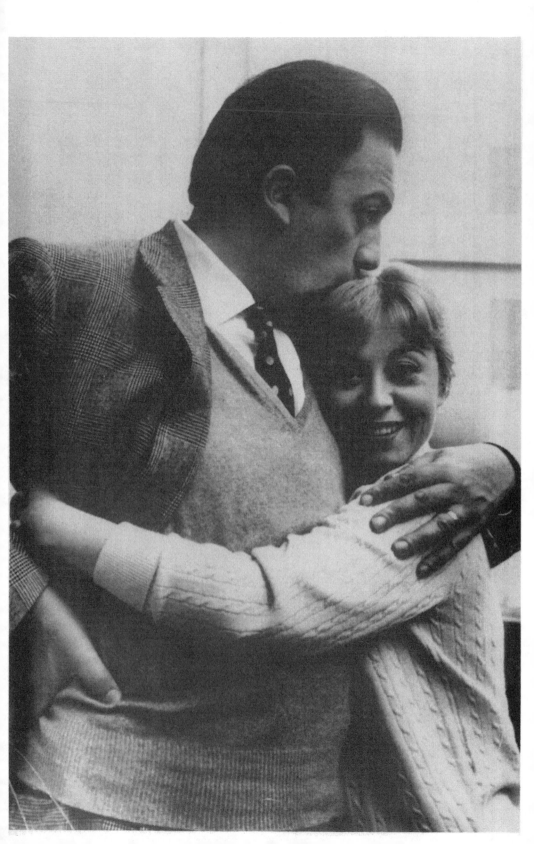

annoyed, "Why are you laughing? Don't you believe it could be true? Aren't you jealous at all?" I said of **course not. Then** she got *really* angry.

Success takes you away from life. **It robs you** of the contact that gave you the success. What you create that pleases people comes out of you—the extension of your own imagination. But that imagination did not grow in a vacuum. It found its individuality through contact with others. Then came success, and the greater it is, the greater your capacity to disassociate yourself. Your aura of success becomes a ring around you to keep out the others—those who originally inspired your imagination. What you created to protect you becomes a prison, which shuts you in. You're more and more special, until you're all alone. Your perspective from the high tower is greatly distorted, but you adjust to it, and you begin to think that's the way everyone sees things. Cut off from what sustained the artist in your life, that part of you withers and dies in the tower of the castle where you fled.

Taxi drivers are always asking me, "Fefe, why don't you make pictures we can understand?"

"Fefe" is a nickname used by a few of my intimates, a detail which has frequently been reported in the newspaper, so now it is a favorite way some taxi drivers have of addressing me.

I answer them that it is because I tell the truth, and the truth is never clear, while lies are quickly understood by everyone.

I stop at that, but what I'm saying is not sophistry. It's true. An honest man is contradictory, and contradictions are more difficult to understand. I have never wanted everything to be explained, wrapped neatly in a package, complete at the end of my films. I hope the audience will remember the characters and think about them and go on wondering about them.

Whenever I have my next film all set, the contract signed with the producer, I am the happiest. I consider myself very lucky because I do exactly the work I want to do. It's difficult for me to understand how I became so lucky, and certainly it would be difficult for me to advise on how to become lucky.

I think that one can have luck if one tries to create an atmosphere of spontaneity. You have to live spherically—in many directions. To

---

Giulietta's favorite picture of herself with Federico. She particularly wanted this photograph to be included in this book.

accept yourself for what you are without inhibitions, to be open. I think that if you tried to understand why one man is so lucky and another is so unlucky, and you conducted a real research without prejudice, one reason must be that probably the man who is lucky doesn't put too much confidence in his rationality. He accepts, has faith. He is not afraid to trust his intuition and act on it. It is a kind of religious feeling to believe in things, to believe in life, I think.

In my work, I have to leave a part of myself without responsibility—more infantile. I leave that part of myself free. Another part, the intellectual, rational part, is against this and makes a bad judgment about what I am doing. When I do things without any explanation, but just with spontaneity, even if my rational part is against it, I can be sure that I am right. Perhaps it's because the feeling, the intuition, is really me, and the other is the voices of other people telling me what I *should* do.

Equilibrium is difficult. Usually one part pretends to be more right, more important, and that stronger, louder voice is my rational part, which is always wrong.

Work is the same as making love, if you are lucky enough to work at what you would do anyway, even if you didn't get paid for it, even if you had to pay to do it. It's like lovemaking, because it's total feeling. You lose yourself in it.

When I work, each film is a jealous mistress. She says, "Me! Me! Don't remember the past. Those other films never really existed in your life. They couldn't have meant to you what I do. I will stand for no unfaithfulness! You must perform only for me. I am the one." And so it is. The film now is my total passion, but one day that film will be finished. I will have put everything I have into it, and the affair will be over. It will pass into memory, and I will search for or find my new mistress—my next film. And there will be room in my life only for her.

Once a picture exists complete, I've fallen out of love. But each of my films has a sort of echo, which remains after the filming, even after the cutting. Only when the new film draws close does the other depart, so I'm never alone, because my old characters keep me company until the new ones win me over to them.

A picture says many little good-byes to you. It is in that way like a love affair. At a certain point, it begins to say its small good-byes in oh so many ways.

After you have finished cutting, there is the dubbing. Then the music, so you are leaving your creature in a very soft way. There is not an ending—just an interruption. You know that your feature is going out from you, day by day, operation by operation. After the good-bye from the mixing, there is the first projection, the first running. So you never have the feeling that you are leaving in an abrupt way. When you are finally separated from your picture, you are practically in a new one. Or that is the ideal. As in a love affair where both parties have enjoyed themselves and there is not a confrontation with tragic overtones at the end.

When my picture is finished, I don't like to live in the shade of that picture—the ritual of going around the world to talk about what I have done. I don't want to be on exhibition, because people expect me to be like my work. I don't want to disappoint them by not being abnormal enough.

nine

FROM THE STREET CORNERS
OF RIMINI TO
THE VIA VENETO

I avoid reseeing my films because it can be such a frustrating experience. Viewing them even many years afterwards, I get new ideas, or I get depressed remembering scenes that had to be cut. In my mind the scenes are still there, so I run my memory of the film in my mind. Sometimes I have been tempted by the chance to see *I Vitelloni* again. It came at an important point in my life. Its unexpected success made everything that happened afterwards possible.

In my early teens, I would stand with my young friends and we would study the women and speculate on who wore a brassiere and who didn't. We would position ourselves at the bicycle stand in the late afternoon, when the women came for their bicycles, so we could watch from behind with the best view as they sat down on their bicycles.

I left Rimini when I was seventeen. I really didn't know the young men who hung around the street corners, the "lady-killers" I portray in *I Vitelloni,* but I would observe them. They were older than I, so they weren't my friends, but I wrote about what I saw of them and their lives, and about what I imagined. For a young man in Rimini, the life was inert, provincial, opaque, dull, without cultural stimulation of any kind. Every night was the same night.

These overgrown calves, which is what the title means literally, haven't been weaned yet, but they are already wonderfully able to get into trouble. Fausto is capable of fathering a child, but not capable of being a father to the child. Alberto states it: "We're all nobodies." But he does absolutely nothing to become somebody, willingly accepting his sister's sacrifice to preserve his own status quo, and not liking it at all when she departs in search of her own happiness. It could mean his having to *think* about going to work. Riccardo wants to be an operatic singer, but he never practices except when he's performing at parties, like my brother, Riccardo. Leopoldo thinks he wants to be a writer, but he is easily distracted by his friends and the girl upstairs. Only Moraldo, the observer, does something about his somnolent existence. He makes the only choice possible for him. He leaves, with the unanswered question he has just been asked still in his ears—"Weren't you happy here?"—as his early-morning train seems to pass through the bedrooms of the people he leaves behind. With his departure, he will no longer be a part of their lives, as they will no longer be a part of his. They continue sleeping as Moraldo wakes up to life.

When I left Rimini, I thought my friends would be envious because I was leaving, but far from it. They were perplexed. They didn't feel the drive to leave that I did. They were content to live in Rimini and were surprised I didn't feel as they did.

When *I Vitelloni* won the Silver Lion at Venice, it made possible the continuation of my career. After the failure of *Variety Lights* and *The White Sheik,* if *I Vitelloni* hadn't been successful, I believe my career as a director would have ended there, and I would have had to go back to being a collaborator on scripts for other people. My number of films would have remained two and a half. Perhaps I would have, one day, been given another opportunity. Perhaps not.

Although I was initially associated with some of the neorealists, I have never embraced movements that have names. Rossellini was a great talent who could transcend dogma and the expectations of politically motivated critics. Others found neorealism a convenient excuse for being creatively lazy, spending very little money and even masking incompetence.

I was offered the possibility of directing a segment for Cesare Zavattini's *Love in the City* in 1953. I had known Zavattini since my

Marc' Aurelio days. He had become a producer. Zavattini told me he wanted something in the journalistic style of certain American pictures of the time. They purported to be documentary dramas while really being pure fiction. Often they employed the device of a narrator who sounded like an authoritative newsreel voice. In those days, newsreels in theaters were taken as seriously as TV news is today.

I Vitelloni had been criticized by the neorealist press. They accused me of being "sentimental," and I resented it. Given this opportunity by Zavattini, I set out to make a short film in the most neorealistic style I could achieve, with a story that could not under any circumstances be true, or even neo-true. I thought, "What would James Whale or Tod Browning do if they had to make *Frankenstein* or *Dracula* in the neorealist style?" That is how *A Matrimonial Agency* happened.

As I recall, the script, such as it was, evolved during the shooting schedule, so that the scenes were shot in the approximate order in which they appear on screen. This was easy to do on such a short film, although how it was done on a complicated production like *Casablanca*—which is how I heard they did it—is beyond me. Contrary to what some people think, I like to be totally prepared, and then to make changes. Carelessness means lack of caring, and there hasn't been a minute when I haven't cared.

Pinelli and I had a great deal of fun making up or changing what was going to happen next, sometimes even while the actors and technicians were setting up for the next shot. Our challenge was to do the unbelievable in a straightforward, almost prosaic, way.

The only professional actor I used was Antonio Cifariello, a young leading-man type of the period. Otherwise, the rest of the cast was nonprofessional, a neorealist practice employed as much for economic reasons as artistic.

One night, not so long ago, I had the strange experience of entering a bar to use the phone, when suddenly I heard a familiar voice from the past. It was that of Cifariello, speaking from the TV set in *A Matrimonial Agency*. I stopped and was tempted to go in and watch, but someone switched the channel.

I caught a glimpse of the girl in the film, who is so eager to get married that she is willing to adapt to the vagaries of a victim of lycanthropy—that is, a man who is a werewolf, or who at least believes he is one—and to marry him. She is appealingly pathetic, trying to escape the overcrowded conditions of her family, convinced she can accommodate even the extraordinary needs of a wolf-man because she tends to become "fond" of people, no matter what their problems or defects.

I wonder what became of the character afterwards? I hope she found someone. Her low expectations gave her a chance for happiness. I feel sorry at the end of the episode that the reporter can't bring himself to go on with his interview, but he is uneasy because he has probed too deeply into a human psyche, and besides he already *has* his story. Maybe he has a date, or another story to cover. Unintentionally, *A Matrimonial Agency* became a sort of horror film.

My "neorealist" intentions are established in the opening sequence. The reporter is led by children along the corridors of the rundown tenement building where the matrimonial agency has its offices, passing open doors where the intimacies of family life go on, virtually in public. Later, to make the story seem more realistic, I told the press that the matrimonial agency was located in my own apartment building.

The reporter hides his true identity from the marriage agency counselor while explaining to us apologetically, in the American-style voice-over narration, that on the spur of the moment he couldn't think of anything better to tell the interrogator than he has a friend who is a werewolf, and can they arrange to find him a wife? The woman accepts this request in a calm, matter-of-fact way, as if it happens every day, and sets about searching through her files for a suitable mate for a werewolf.

For me, the interrogation situation is always disturbing, the interrogator being someone who represents authority. I suppose this comes from being brought up under Catholicism, with confession, and during the fascist regime, living through the German occupation of Italy, when interrogators had so much power over an individual's future. They could, in fact, determine if the person even *had* a future.

When the film was released, the critics accepted it as an example of neorealism.

La Strada is about loneliness and how solitude can be ended when one person makes a profound link to another. The man and woman who find this bond may sometimes be the least likely, on the surface, and yet the bond is in the depth of their souls.

I cannot remember exactly the moment when the idea for *La Strada* was first conceived, but for me it became real when I drew the circle on paper that was Gelsomina's head. Of all of my films in which Giulietta appears, the character of Gelsomina is the one I most based on the actual character of Giulietta. I utilized the real Giulietta, but as I saw her. I was influenced by her childhood photographs, so elements of Gelsomina reflect a ten-year-old Giulietta. I remembered the look of that little closed-mouth smile of her childhood pictures. I encouraged her not to act, but to be herself, that self *I* saw.

Gelsomina personified innocence betrayed, so Giulietta was the perfect actress to be Gelsomina. As a person, she was still that sheltered girl who looked with awe at the mysteries of life. Because she was open to finding delights, her own nature remained young, innocent, trusting. She was always hopeful of a good surprise, and when the surprise was not so good, she seemed to have an internal mechanism that kept her from being deeply wounded. Her body could be injured, but not her soul.

It was Giulietta who introduced me to Anthony Quinn. She had a part in a picture with him, and she presented the idea of *La Strada* to him. Richard Basehart was in the same film, and Giulietta introduced me to him, too.

Rossellini and Ingrid Bergman wanted to persuade Tony Quinn to do my film, so Ingrid invited him to a wonderful dinner and afterwards they screened *I Vitelloni,* so he could see my work. The dinner or my film must have impressed him. Robertino was very persuasive and he always got what he wanted, but he told me the dinner and showing my film was Ingrid's idea. At the time, I believed he was just saying that, but later I thought about it, and I remembered that Ingrid liked Giulietta very much.

The French critics gave *La Strada* wonderful reviews. It made money in Italy, in France, in many places. Nino Rota's theme sold millions of records. They wanted to make Gelsomina candy bars. There was even a Gelsomina club, formed by women who wrote to Giulietta about how badly their husbands treated them. These letters came especially from the south of Italy.

I had given up any participation in the financial returns, as I was to continue to be forced to do, for the usual reason—to get the film done. I made other people rich, but I was the richest, not in money, but in pride. I was so proud.

So was Giulietta. Her performance as Gelsomina was compared to the best of Chaplin, to Jacques Tati.

I cannot say it pleases me, however, when the critics continue to praise *La Strada,* which I made so long ago, and do not say the same about my current work. I don't enjoy talking about *La Strada,* because it exists to speak for itself. It is complete. Since the world has accepted it, I don't feel obligated in the same way I feel toward one of my orphan films. *Voices of the Moon* was not loved by anyone else, so it needs some love from me. In the case of *Voices of the Moon,* I don't care what the world says as long as they don't say it's Fellini's last film.

There was another benefit, a bonus of making *La Strada.* Giulietta and I moved out of her aunt's apartment and bought our own apartment in Parioli, a lovely neighborhood of Rome.

And when it was nominated for an Oscar, *La Strada* gave me my first trip to the fabled America, which I had dreamed of as a boy. America was the place where you could grow up to be president without speaking Latin or Greek. Going to America, I did not believe I was going to a strange place. I knew it intimately from the screen at the Fulgor Cinema. Giulietta, Dino de Laurentiis, and I went to Hollywood. *La Strada* received the Oscar. We were celebrities.

By the time I left America, I felt I knew it less than before I had made the trip. There was too much to know, and I knew then that I would never know it. The place I was in love with was the past of America, which didn't exist anymore. I understood that the innocent, open, trusting childhood of America was over.

I was booked for an interview on American television in which I was supposed to demonstrate how to kiss a hand. I would have had to take lessons, since I had never kissed anyone's hand. I had to tell them I didn't feel well, so I couldn't do the show. It was true in a way, because I wouldn't have felt well if I had done the show.

Among my films, none was more poorly received than *Il Bidone,* which literally means a large empty can, like an empty oil drum. In this case, it's meant to imply empty promises made by people who sell worthless, empty things to unsuspecting, though not always innocent, people. It's about small-time con men who are smart enough to make an honest living but don't want to do that. They enjoy the thrill of fooling people and getting away with it. Perhaps the subject interested me because the film director should be a magician and master of illusion, though it's not his intention to cheat people.

I was inspired to make *Il Bidone* after *La Strada* by a number of encounters I had had with con men, though I personally was never the victim of one. In Rimini there was one who preyed on the tourists, but who was admired locally because he was very amusing and entertaining, especially if you plied him with enough wine to get him drunk. He would "sell" real estate, like land belonging to the church, to foreign tourists, especially to Scandinavians and Germans visiting Rimini in the summer. They seemed to regard us Italians as South Sea island natives or as characters in a Jack London novel. They saw in our gullibility the opportunity to buy land at bargain prices. This particular con man was reputed to have sold the stretch of beach belonging to the Grand Hotel to one of the tourists, although I suspect he himself started the rumor in order to get us to buy him more wine. Perhaps he sold us the story in the same way he sold the land he didn't own to the tourists. Maybe the story of the sale of the land wasn't true at all, and we were the ones being conned. Or perhaps the con man believed everything and was really conning himself.

When I first came to Rome and was working as a reporter on a newspaper, I was approached by a con man who invited me to offer bargain diamonds to the movie stars I was interviewing. I didn't realize that the diamonds, far from being bargains, were excessively expensive, since they were fake. I was saved by my understanding of my own ineptitude as a salesman, especially then, when I was so painfully shy and withdrawn, and I declined. It was unimaginable for me to contemplate trying to sell a diamond, in the same way my father sold Parmesan cheese, to one of the people I was interviewing. I had enough difficulty selling myself and trying to ask my pitiful list of questions. Another journalist with whom I worked was not so fortunate. He sold one of the "diamonds," lost his job, and nearly went to jail.

Of course, in wartime Rome it was absolutely essential to be something of a con man in order to survive. The person who could talk himself out of the army or into a supply of hard-to-get food was greatly admired at that time. Thus, the dividing line between the ordinary person and the con man was not so clear-cut.

After the success of *I Vitelloni* and especially that of *La Strada,* I received many offers to do more films—as long as they were just like what had already been successful. I had already said everything I wanted to say about Gelsomina and Zampanò, and my thoughts about what would happen to Moraldo in the big city were not yet formulated, so I decided to do something totally different. A sort of con man had appeared briefly in *La Strada,* selling cheap cloth as if it were expensive wool, and I was reminded of him by the con man who wanted to engage me to sell his fake diamonds. We happened to meet in a café, and I tried to learn, as I always do, more about human nature, even about inhuman nature, from him.

He called himself Lupaccio, and he *was* actually wolflike. Strange. Far from being repentant or even apologetic for what he did, he was proud and seemed to enjoy bragging about how he cheated people. He treated it as his great accomplishment in life, like an explorer who has discovered a new civilization or a businessman who has created a financial empire. Or a film director who has just made a great picture.

I encouraged him by seeming to approve of what he did, but he didn't need a great deal of encouragement. I remembered what W. C. Fields said: "You can't cheat an honest man." This con man believed everyone has a larcenous side to his nature, which is what makes the person a natural and deserving victim for the con artist. And he *did* regard himself as a *sort* of artist. Those who want something for nothing are the best "marks," he told me.

As he outlined in detail his various dishonest transactions, I wondered how he knew he could trust me. I supposed that in order to be a successful con man, you must also have a perceptiveness about human nature, or at least *think* you have. Or maybe he just had a compulsion to talk and to see the appreciation of his cleverness reflected in the eyes of his small audience.

My conversation with Lupaccio inspired me to get to work with Pinelli and Flaiano on a script about con men. The idea, however, was not well received by the same producers who were begging me for my next picture—*any* picture, just so long as it was about Gelsomina. They couldn't imagine who would want to pay to see such a movie as I proposed, let alone pay to produce it. The more they didn't like the idea, the more stubbornly certain I became that it would be a success. The more my project is attacked, the more stubbornly I defend it. If people praise my project, I question whether they are correct, whether they are just being polite. The negative, which I do not enjoy, makes me more staunch in my defense, to the point of willful foolishness. It's my personality.

I finally persuaded Goffredo Lombardo of Titanus Films, but only on condition that he have the option on my next film, too. He exacted that from me. He saw that as a bonus, or as a protection, but after the financial failure of *Il Bidone,* he would find an excuse to decline the role as producer of *Nights of Cabiria.*

The original scenario of *Il Bidone* was a sort of picaresque comedy, reminiscent, I thought, of Lubitsch—three rogues traveling the provincial countryside, conning the villagers, who were then too ashamed of their own gullibility and inherent greed to report that they had been swindled. That was the best situation for the con man. I had been told that the idea was to find people who wouldn't want anyone to know they had been made fools of, so they would never tell the police.

Further inquiries and investigation of this subculture revealed to me little humor in their activities. In reality, they didn't seem at all even like antiheroes, but more like sordid, mean-spirited misfits. I decided I could not work with characters I didn't like, and resolved to abandon the project; but then something happened to change my mind.

A number of actors had been suggested for the lead, everyone from Pierre Fresnay to Humphrey Bogart, but none of them was quite right for my visualization of Augusto, who was like Lupaccio. Personally, I never enjoyed the acting of Humphrey Bogart, nor did I ever like his look. He seemed like someone who would be angry even when making love, which I imagined him doing while still wearing his trench coat. Then, one windswept evening in the Piazza Mazzini, I saw my Lupaccio.

Weathered, torn posters have always attracted my attention. They are infinitely more interesting than those just put up. They reveal their own story, the story not just of what they are supposed to tell, but of the posters themselves. They add the dimensions of depth and time to an otherwise flat, temporary surface. The poster I saw that evening had been there so long, only part of it was still intact on the wall, though in shreds. I could see half of the face, half of the title of the movie it was advertising: *All the . . .* The eye above a puffy jowl reflected a rapacious, cynical mind, much like that of Lupaccio—a wolflike animal of prey, incarnated as a human being. Here was the actor I needed, Broderick Crawford, who had been the star of *All the King's Men*.

Much has been made of his alcoholism, but he was mostly sober during the shooting. Mostly. And conveniently, when he wasn't, it turned out to be appropriate for the particular scene. It's always good to be lucky.

From him I wanted a certain bored detachment from his work as a petty swindler. He's tired of his life and wants to change it, but not by reforming. He really wants to retire after one big final swindle, so he can live like other successful con men he's observed and also so he can put his daughter through school. This appealing young woman is the humanizing factor, which Lupaccio and other con men I talked with lacked. His simpleminded colleague, Picasso, also has the redeeming factor in his wife and child, whom he supports with his dishonest profits. Otherwise these people are totally unsympathetic, without humor, and unworthy of a film.

I was fortunate that Richard Basehart was still in Rome after *La Strada*. He had exactly the right saintly expression for the sympathetic con man who barely understands the moral implications of what he is doing. He has a conscience, but it's well hidden.

Franco Fabrizi, after his excellent portrayal of the womanizing Fausto in *I Vitelloni*, was ideal for the same kind of character in *Il Bidone*. I even visualized the possibility that Fausto might have left his wife and child to follow his brother-in-law, Moraldo, the character who is more or less me, to the big city. There, he slides into the life of a con man like Roberto. Later, in another screenplay treatment, I explored a different possibility: having Moraldo receive the news that Fausto and Sandra have had two more children. This screenplay, which would have been called "Moraldo in the City," never had its life as a film. Parts of it, however, found their way into other films I did.

When Giulietta read the part of Iris, Picasso's distressed wife in *Il Bidone*, she informed me that she had to have it. She had never played this kind of character before. Truthfully, I had envisioned another actress for the role and personally didn't see it as an interesting part for Giulietta—I thought it was less interesting than others she was being offered at the time with other directors—but she persisted. I think what she really wanted was to look more glamorous and to have audiences realize that she wasn't *only* Gelsomina and wasn't typecast. I took it as a compliment that she preferred working with me, even in a smaller part, rather than working as the lead in another director's film.

The choice of a girl to play the crippled daughter of the last farmer being swindled came in a special way. I was auditioning various candidates as they stood on crutches, but I could not make up my mind. They all seemed good. That happens to me sometimes. Then I don't know what to do. But then something always happens that gives me the sign I have been waiting for, and I know.

One of the girls stumbled and fell. Her reaction was exactly what I wanted, and she became the girl. It was also important that she resembled Augusto's daughter, Patrizia, so that his dormant conscience is touched when he understands he's taking the money that insures her future.

I shot the ending of the picture several different ways, finally settling on the least depressing, most poetic view of Augusto's death. At the end, I leave certain ambiguities about his character for the spectator to ponder. Was he cheating his colleagues because he intended returning the stolen money to the crippled girl who desperately needed it, or was he going to give it to his own daughter for her schooling, or was he simply going to keep it for himself? If the sequence with the English chorus girl hadn't been cut out of the final version, the money would have allowed a renewal of Augusto's affair with her, if he made the choice to be selfish. I'm afraid the actress who played her is still crying! I believe it is essential that an audience wonders at the end, and that everything isn't answered for them. I have failed if they don't want to know what happened to the characters after the film has ended, not only for *Il Bidone,* but for any film I make.

As it turned out, the whole picture was too ambiguous for audiences, according to my producer, who said I had to cut the original two-and-a-half-hour version, which did not make it less ambiguous. I was told it was necessary so it would have a better chance at the Venice Film Festival of that year. That was not an argument of consequence for me, but producers seem to love film festivals. Parties. Girls. When it was ignored there—worse than ignored—I was forced to cut it some more, down to 112 minutes, and then 104, finally even shorter for its belated American appearance. It showed there only after the successes of *Nights of Cabiria, La Dolce Vita,* and *8½.* Cutting *Il Bidone* was a sad experience for me, and certainly hurt the film. I didn't want to cut it. When I completed *Il Bidone,* it was my film, the film I had made. Forced to cut more, I wasn't certain at all about what to cut. At any other time, I might have cut different parts. Whatever I had to cut, I knew I would have regrets. I had the "final cut" of my film, but it didn't matter. Orson Welles told me later how he had felt about what was done to *The Magnificent Ambersons.* Sad. I thought it was such a great film; I didn't realize what they had done. It is not imaginable what his film would have been if we could have seen it as he intended it to be.

A great many meaningful scenes were cut from *Il Bidone* and, along with them, important strands of the story which develop the characters. I couldn't save my favorite scenes because I had to concentrate on the story making sense after the loss of so much footage. One scene I tried to save, but couldn't, was the one in which Iris, who has left Picasso, confronts Augusto, blaming him for her husband's life of crime, and he defends himself with his own warped, but deeply ingrained, logic.

In this scene, Augusto encourages her to take her husband back. Once he has his freedom, he warns her, Picasso won't be coming back to her and their child, because "freedom is too beautiful." His theory is that Iris wouldn't have left Picasso, even though he was supporting her in a dishonest way, if he'd been more successful. He tells her that a man who has money *has* everything and a man who doesn't have it *is* nothing. As he extols the beauty of money, Iris stands up to him.

Originally, this was a key scene, but as I cut the film, this scene along with others disappeared. Story lines and character development ended abruptly without explanation, creating in the minds of some critics a deliberate stylistic intention that never existed. Professionally, I knew I would be unable to face the finished *Il Bidone.* Personally, it was hard for me to cut so much of Giulietta's fine performance. She was *so* good, especially in the parts I cut. I hoped she would be understanding, because she is my wife. But she was not understanding, because she is also an actress. I believe I made it up to her in my next film, *Nights of Cabiria.*

When a film is completed, it exists forever in that form. It seems that it's the only way it could have ever been, because then it's the only way it *can* ever be. But far from it! Any film I made could have, *would* have, been a different film if I had, for example, made the same picture at a different time. I could have made the same film three or four different ways. In fact, I did. One reason I never want to see my films after I've completed them is they exist in my memory as I shot them, with all the footage I wanted to include. In my memory, my films exist in a different running time than the exhibitor's version. Many times, I had to cut fast, under duress by the producer, who always wanted less, to save money. If I were to see my films as the audiences are seeing them in theaters around the world, I would be sitting there and saying, "Where is the scene about this?" and "Where is the scene about that?" and I would feel destroyed for the sake of my poor creature, as *it* has been destroyed. When the film is complete, I must cut the bond. Or I must try to.

The subject of loneliness and the observation of the isolated person has always interested me. Even as a child, I couldn't help but notice those who didn't fit in for one reason or another—myself included. In life, and for my films, I have always been interested in the out-of-step. Curiously, it's usually those who are either too smart or those who are too stupid who are left out. The difference is, the smart ones often isolate themselves, while the less intelligent ones are usually isolated by the others. In *Nights of Cabiria,* I explore the pride of one of those who has been excluded.

The brief appearance of the Cabiria character near the end of *The White Sheik* revealed Giulietta's acting abilities. As well as being an excellent dramatic actress in *Without Pity* and *Variety Lights,* she revealed herself capable of being a tragicomic mime in the tradition of Chaplin, Keaton, and Toto. In *La Strada,* she emphatically reinforced this impression. Gelsomina grew out of her original brief Cabiria portrayal, and at the time I sensed that Cabiria had the potential for an entire picture based on her character, starring, of course, Giulietta.

During the shooting of *Il Bidone,* I met a real-life Cabiria. She was living in a little hovel near the ruins of the Roman aqueduct. At first, she was indignant at my disruption of her daytime routine. When I offered her a lunch box from our food truck, she came closer, like a small homeless female cat, an orphan, a waif, maltreated and living in the streets, but still very hungry, hungry enough to overcome her fears with the offer of food.

Her name was Wanda, a name I might have made up for her if it hadn't already been hers. After a few days, she communicated with me, though in her inarticulate way, some of the circumstances of being a streetwalker in Rome.

Goffredo Lombardo had the option for my next picture. He was appalled by the idea of a story about a prostitute, an unsympathetic character as far as he was concerned, and he found his excuse to back out of the deal. He wasn't unique. Quite a few producers didn't like the idea, especially after the box-office failure of *Il Bidone*. There is a story which is often quoted about something I said when I offered the script of *Nights of Cabiria* to a producer. Sometimes the same story is told, but a different film is substituted.

The producer says, "We have to talk about this. You made pictures about homosexuals"—and I suppose he is referring to the Sordi character in *I Vitelloni,* though it is not a point I made specifically—"you had a script about an insane asylum"—he is referring to one of many scripts that was never filmed—"and now you have prostitutes. Whatever will your next film be about?" As the anecdote goes, I respond angrily, "My next film will be about producers."

I can't imagine how that story got started, unless I started it myself, but I don't remember doing that. I don't remember saying it, but I wish I had. More often, I'm the kind of person who thinks of what I wish I'd said after the occasion has passed, and it's a little embarrassing to call back a day late with one's quick retort.

Finally, Dino de Laurentiis stepped forward with a five-picture contract which would allow me to make *Nights of Cabiria*. Giulietta thought I should receive more money, but I just wanted to make more films.

Throughout my life as a director, I have persisted in this pattern. Giulietta has always had a better sense of the future than I have. Perhaps if I had asked for more money, producers would have thought I was worth more, and then I would have been able to work more. Who knows? I still don't care about having more money, but I would like to have more films.

Some previous ideas I had for films found their way into the story, such as the incident of Cabiria being pushed into the Tiber by her current lover. This was based on a newspaper report of a similar event, in which the prostitute was not saved. The entire opening sequence, in which Cabiria romps through the countryside with her lover, was filmed entirely on a long shot. I cast Franco Fabrizi as the man, though you never clearly see his face. He had played more important roles in *I Vitelloni* and *Il Bidone,* but he told me he would enjoy being in this film in any part. In this instance, I didn't cast an actor for his face.

The casting of François Périer as Oscar was at first prompted by the need for a French member of the cast, a stipulation of De Laurentiis's French co-producer. The plot behind the screen is often more tangled than anything the writers could create. Critics have complained that Périer isn't sinister enough, but that was exactly what I wanted. I think he is perfect in the role, especially at the end, where he becomes too frightened to carry out the murder of Cabiria. Perhaps there is also some other human emotion, less selfish, which stops him, and he feels remorse. We don't know, but we hope for the best. I would be curious to know what he does with the money, all of Cabiria's savings, and whether he goes on to do the same thing again with someone else. Even among the outcasts of *Il Bidone,* he would have been an outcast, like the Peter Lorre character in *M,* so heinous is his crime.

There is no connection between my *Nights of Cabiria* and an early silent Italian film called *Cabiria,* which was based on a story by Gabriele D'Annunzio. If there was any influence on me, it was Chaplin's *City Lights,* one of my favorite films. Giulietta's portrayal of Cabiria reminds me, as it has many people, of Chaplin's tramp, even more so than her Gelsomina. Her exaggerated dance in the nightclub is reminiscent of Chaplin, and her encounter with the movie star is similar to that of the tramp's encounter with the millionaire, who recognizes Charlie only when he's drunk. I leave Cabiria looking at the camera with a glimmer of new hope at the end, just as Chaplin does with his tramp in *City Lights.* It is possible for Cabiria to yet again have hope because she is so basically optimistic, and her expectations are so low. The French critics referred to her as the feminine Charlot, their affectionate name for Chaplin. That made her very happy when she heard it. I was happy, too.

For Giulietta's wardrobe, we went to a street market to shop for the clothes Cabiria would wear. Afterwards, because she wasn't going to have pretty clothes to wear in the film, I took her to an expensive boutique to buy a new dress for herself.

The relationship between Cabiria and Gelsomina is that Cabiria is Gelsomina's fallen sister. Not so obvious is how *Nights of Cabiria* anticipates *Juliet of the Spirits.* In both, the protagonist is a mature woman trying to cope, through religion, mysticism, and love, with the downward trend in her life. What both really seek is love, but seeking love doesn't guarantee finding it, as giving love doesn't guarantee receiving it. Everything outside these women fails them. In the end, both characters must find whatever salvation they can from resources within themselves.

The miracle scene in *Nights of Cabiria* is repeated to some extent in my next film, *La Dolce Vita,* but only as an afterthought when another segment had to be cut from that script. In the first film, I follow Cabiria in tight close shots with some other people not only to give a claustrophobic sensation, but also to save money on an otherwise costly scene with many extras and a big set. In *La Dolce Vita,* I had a more generous budget, so I could concentrate on the spectacle of the occasion itself with wide shots, appropriate for the new wide-screen lens. *Cabiria* was, in fact, my last feature made in black and white on a conventional-ratio screen.

Incidentally, the "man with a sack" sequence, which only the audience at Cannes saw, still exists and could be restored in future versions, as could a great many of the cuts I was forced to make in my films. After so many years, however, I don't know how I would feel about it. I think the scene is especially good, but with or without it, the film stands on its own, so I feel lucky that it was the only part about Cabiria which the Church found unacceptable for Italian audiences. The man with a sack had food in his pack, and he went around feeding the homeless of Rome who were hungry. This was based on a real-life character I actually saw. There were those in the Church who objected, saying that it was the role of the Church to feed the homeless and hungry, and that I had made it seem the Church wasn't doing a good job with its responsibility. I could have responded that the man with a sack was a Catholic, a very good example of a Catholic who was taking individual responsibility, but I didn't know to whom I should tell this.

I understand that the term *auteur* to describe a cinema director was first used in talking about me, by the French critic André Bazin in a review of *Cabiria.* The American Broadway musical comedy and Hollywood picture *Sweet Charity* was inspired by *Nights of Cabiria,* and my name is on the credits, but I disagreed with Bob Fosse's way of doing it on so many points, I prefer that the film be regarded as his creation.

The positive nature of Cabiria is so noble and wonderful. Cabiria offers herself to the lowest bidder and hears truth in lies. Though she is a prostitute, her basic instinct is to search for happiness as best she can, as one who has not been dealt a good hand. She wants to change, but she has been typecast in life as a loser. Yet she is a loser who always goes on to look again for some happiness.

At the end, she has made herself as close to beautiful as she can, because she is feeling more glamorous with her approaching marriage. To go away with Oscar, she sells her beloved little house, all that she has in the world, the result of years of sacrifices, and she takes all her savings from the bank. Then she discovers the man she thinks loves her for herself alone wants *only* her money. Her face is mascara- and tear-stained. Has she has lost everything, including hope? No. She can manage a little smile, so there is still hope.

Cabiria is a victim, and any of us can be a victim at one time or another. Cabiria is, however, more of a victim personality than most. Yet even so, there is also the survivor in her. This film doesn't have a resolution in the sense that there is a final scene in which the story reaches a conclusion so definitive that you no longer have to worry about Cabiria. I myself have worried about her fate ever since.

La Dolce Vita was the first picture on which I worked with Marcello Mastroianni. I knew him, of course, because he was already well established in Italy as a stage and film actor. Giulietta knew him better. They had been students at the University of Rome, and had acted together in the theater. We would see each other sometimes in restaurants. He was always eating a lot. I noticed that because I have a natural affinity with people who like to eat. You can always recognize a person who likes to eat not because of the quantity he consumes, but because of a sort of gusto, a person experiencing true pleasure. So first I noticed Marcello because I felt this restaurant rapport with him.

I am asked frequently if Marcello is my alter ego. Marcello Mastroianni is many things to many people. For me, he is *not* my alter ego. He is Marcello, an actor who conforms perfectly to what I want from him, like a contortionist who can do anything. As a friend, he is perfect, the kind of friend found in British fiction, where for noble reasons men who are like brothers give their lives for each other. Our friendship is like that, or like anything else you can imagine—because you have to imagine it, since in our real lives, except when we are working together, we almost never, practically never, see each other outside of our work. That is perhaps one reason it's the perfect friendship, and each of us can imagine that the other is always there for him. It is never tested. I believe more in him than I believe in me, because I know I am not a really reliable friend. Possibly Marcellino has more faith in me because he knows himself better. There is never any falseness between us. We play, but without pretense. Genuine play has its own truth.

We don't have to say anything to each other. We can hear the unspoken. Sometimes, we are in such accord I cannot separate what we said from what we thought.

Ever since I gave up smoking, it has irritated me for anyone to be smoking nearby, and Marcellino never does anything *but* smoke. I think he smokes three packs a day, a prodigious feat of which he's actually proud. He wouldn't think of quitting. But when I ask him to please stop smoking that cigarette, he does so immediately. Then, reflexively, he lights up another one.

He's so natural. He's never nervous when he acts. The only times he's ever nervous is when he has to go on television and talk about acting. Sometimes I think he's less nervous with the camera than without it.

So I knew of his talent, and I knew I wanted to work with him. For *La Dolce Vita* I thought he would be perfect.

It was more difficult finding the producer. I changed producers something like twelve times before I found the right one who really wanted to do it and did it.

As soon as I knew I was making *La Dolce Vita,* I phoned Marcello. I always call people myself, because things work better that way. Generally, I don't like to deal through lawyers and agents. I asked Marcello to meet me at my house in Fregene. He didn't come alone as expected, but he brought along his lawyer.

When I explained why I had chosen him for the part, he was probably shocked because I was very indelicate. He reminds me now that I said to him, "I called you because I need a very normal face, a face with no personality, a face with no expression, a banal face—a face like yours." I meant it well. I didn't intend to be offensive.

I explained to him that I had refused a big American star whom the producers wished to impose on me. Marcello sat there, a little bit astonished, when I told him that I had refused someone as famous as Paul Newman. I have a lot of admiration for Paul Newman, especially in the last ten years. He's grown into a great actor. But *La Dolce Vita* was the story of a young provincial newspaperman who would regard such a star with great admiration. I could not cast a great star to play this role. For that reason, I explained to Marcello, "I have chosen you because you have an everyday face."

It wasn't uncomplimentary to Marcello. Robert Redford has had a successful picture called *Ordinary People,* so it means that there is a certain romantic appeal about being very normal. Very normal in a movie-star way, I mean. Marcello also represents a kind of ideal man. He is the man every woman would want. It's an enviable way to be.

He didn't like my explanation at all, but he was still ready to look at the script. He wanted me to tell him how I saw the role. I said I could show him.

I gave him a thick manuscript, every page blank except the first. On it was a picture I had drawn showing his character as I saw him. He was alone in a little boat in the middle of the ocean with a prick that reached all the way down to the bottom of the ocean, and there were beautiful lady sea sirens swimming all around it. Marcello looked at the picture and said, "It's an interesting part. I'll do it."

I work very well with Marcello, especially in the kind of picture where the protagonist, the leading character, has to be in an ambiguous position. He is *in* the picture—and, at the same time, he is *out* of the picture. In all of the pictures I've made with Marcello, the character is an echo, always the same. He is supposed to be an intellectual. It is difficult to represent an intellectual in movies or on the stage, even in a book, because an intellectual is someone who has an interior life. He thinks, but he does not act very much. Marcello has these particular qualities. He is believable as someone who does not react to events, but watches them. Sometimes, of course, he is a person of action. Thus, he is in the ambiguous position of someone who is living the story, yet at times is apart, observing.

With Marcello, credibility is no problem. He is so believable. His talent as an actor is being sensitive, yet very assertive. He really helps the director in a delicate and precious way. Though his talent is natural, he also really tries.

Once I read such a nice, intelligent answer of Marcello's during an interview. Some newspaperman asked him, "Is it true, Mastroianni, that when you are working with Fellini you don't read the script?" And Marcello answered, "Yes, I know what Federico is going to do. In a general way, I know the story. But I prefer not to know too much, because I have to try to maintain the same curiosity as to what will happen tomorrow, the day after tomorrow, all during the story, throughout the shooting, the same curiosity that the leading character has to have. I don't want to know too much."

I find this an intelligent attitude—to be in the picture, detached and available, like a child. When we were children, we played gangsters and police. One of us says, "I'm a gangster, you're a policeman. Let's go." Everything happens naturally. I tell Marcello what he has to say, and he says it. The only important thing to know exactly is the character. It is essential that he becomes the character. Then the character, policeman or gangster, can say what he wants, reacting naturally. The character takes the actor by the hand and leads him. That is really how I see the role of the director, not as helping the actor to find the character, but helping the character to find the actor.

During a film, Marcello and I never disagree. I fight to try to have him get thinner, more anguished, more fascinating. If he's playing a character who is suffering inside, I want to read in his face this kind of misery, instead of the look of a big cat who has just enjoyed fish and cream.

At the beginning of one picture, I told him to go on some kind of diet. I didn't care what kind of diet, just so it worked. He told me he knew of a place in the north of Germany at which in only three days he could lose weight, ten kilos. When I heard that, I said, "Marcello, leave! Go to that place, but only for three days." And he went for three days. When he came back, he was the same. I was lucky he didn't *gain* weight.

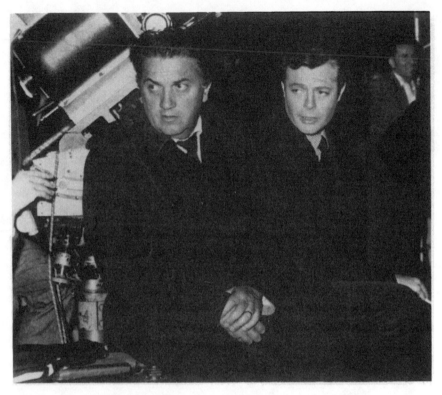

Fellini and Marcello Mastroianni on the set of *La Dolce Vita* (1959).

When I first saw a newspaper picture of Anita Ekberg, it was like seeing one of my drawings come to life. I had no idea in mind who could be Sylvia, but when I saw Anitona's picture just as I needed her, it was like an omen. I knew I had to have her for the film, and I had my assistant contact her for a meeting. Her agent said she never worked without seeing a script first. The agent was speaking for himself, I think, saying he didn't work unless *he* saw a script first. My assistant told her agent that there was no script. So, Ekberg signed.

When I met her, she was even more the character than ever I could have believed. "You are my imagination come to life," I told her.

"I do not go to bed with you," she answered.

She was understandably suspicious. She thought every man wanted to go to bed with her, just because every man *did* want to. She didn't trust me because she couldn't see a script and hold it in her hands.

I told Marcellino I had met our Sylvia, and she was "unbelievable." He was anxious to see her with his own eyes. I invited them both to dinner, but it was far from instant attraction. Most women found Mastroianni attractive and sexy, but **Ekberg did not,** or if she did, it didn't show. She was cold to him. There **was** no rapport. He didn't speak his few words of English. She didn't speak her little bit of Italian. Afterwards, she told me she didn't find Mastroianni attractive. He told me he didn't find her attractive. It made no difference. I had found *my* Sylvia.

The way they felt in life about each other made no difference for the film. On the screen, they both radiated sexuality.

In life, they weren't suited because she was accustomed to having men pursue her. She did not have to do the pursuing. Marcello was used to having women pursue *him.* Besides, he liked thin women.

La Dolce Vita changed Anita Ekberg's life. After that, she could never go too far away from the Fountain of Trevi. She had found the place where she truly existed, and Rome became her home.

For *La Dolce Vita* I drew some sketches of Walter Santesso, who played the press photographer, Paparazzo, as I visualized him—naked except for his camera and his shoes, which he needed to get around and take pictures.

I have best been able to conceptualize the characters for my films by drawing them. When I have to commit them to paper, I learn things about them I didn't know. They reveal their little secrets to me. As I draw, they take on a life of their own. Then I take these pictures, and in my films I make them moving pictures, having found the actors to give them life.

When we came up with the name in 1959, I had no idea "paparazzo," or "paparazzi," would become a word in many languages. It's from an opera libretto with a character named Paparazzo. Someone told it to me, and it sounded just right for our soulless photographer, who is more of a camera than a man. It's really his camera that observes. He sees the world through the lens of a camera, the reason I go in close on the camera he is holding in his last appearance in the film.

My intention in the title of *La Dolce Vita* was not understood. It was taken more ironically than I meant it. I was thinking of "the sweetness of life" rather than "the sweet life." It's a strange phenomenon, because usually my problem has been in the other direction. I would say something, intending it ironically, and it would be taken literally.

Then, I would forever be quoted as having said the opposite of what I believed and intended. These supposed quotations from me were always coming back to haunt me.

When people ask me what *La Dolce Vita* is really about, I like to answer that it's about Rome, the Internal City as well as the Eternal City. *La Dolce Vita* didn't have to take place in Rome. It could have been in New York, Tokyo, Bangkok, Sodom, or Gomorrah, anywhere, but Rome is what I know.

For truly seeing a place, the marriage of experience and innocence is the best. The ideal way to see Rome, I have discovered, is through two pairs of eyes, one pair that knows it exceedingly well, every nook and cranny, and one that sees it for the first time, wide-eyed, open to life.

The innocent person can obviously learn from the other, but what is most startling is how much the knowing one has ceased to observe. The jaded glance is jolted, awakened to a new sensibility, revealing what you see every day without really seeing it at all.

This is what Marcello throws away at the end of *La Dolce Vita*. He fails to notice when Paola tries to communicate to him that she would like to accept his offer to teach her typing—and there is the implication of more. He doesn't understand that her innocence and openness to life could offer him the freshness that could turn his cynicism into constructive sophistication. She is Marcello's nostalgia and his romanticism.

I don't believe in villains, just in people. The good can behave quite villainously. And a villain can be a victim of extenuating circumstances, or he can be a black-hearted fiend who may be touched by a kitten's meow.

In *La Dolce Vita,* Steiner starts out as heroic and ends up as the worst villain in any of my pictures, like Magda Goebbels, the person who can kill his or her own children. The Steiner incident bothered a lot of people, including producers and critics, who thought I'd gone too far, but it's based on a real event.

Some of the critics writing about the Steiner character said he was secretly a homosexual. His character never told me that. Some of the critics said that I admired and respected his intellectuality. I was not in any way sympathetic to him. He was a false intellectual. He did not care how much he damaged lives.

I thought Henry Fonda would be the perfect actor to be Steiner—intellectual, seemingly happy, having everything, but in reality so deeply troubled that he makes tragedy a self-fulfilling prophecy. I could not imagine anyone else so perfect for the part. A wonderful actor. Word reached me that Fonda wanted to do the part, even though it wasn't a starring part. I was very happy.

Negotiations began with his agents. Then, we never heard anything. I chose Alain Cuny for the part.

A long time afterwards, when the film had been shown in America, I received a letter from Fonda saying what a great film it was, and what a fine part. It was polite of him, but it was all over. Too late. There was someone with me when the letter arrived who was excited about a letter received from Henry Fonda. So, since I do not keep old letters, I gave it to him.

In my life, I've had several meetings with my father in which he and I had excellent communication, but all those meetings were only in my mind. When we were actually together, we were worse than strangers with each other. As adults together, we were both inarticulate, and spoke only about what was meaningless. Several years after he died, while I was doing research on supernatural phenomena for *Juliet of the Spirits,* I tried to reach my father through a medium. I wanted to talk with him, to tell him, "I understand."

In *La Dolce Vita* and *8½,* I talk with my father in my mind. I hardly knew him. My main memory of him is a non-memory. I remember his absence rather than his presence. Though I didn't like to admit it even to myself, as a boy I felt abandoned by him, unable to win his attention and approval. I believed he didn't care about me, that I was a disappointment to him, that he wasn't proud about me. If I had only known that he carried my first drawings around with him on those trips, I would have been able to talk with him. Everything could have been different. Now I have only a framed picture of him. I keep it where I can see it.

I had feeling for my mother, but it was the best when I was in Rome and she was in Rimini. That is not meant sarcastically. It's just that when we were together, we never had good communication. With my father, I had too little communication, and with my mother, too much. With my mother, it was one-sided communication. She had the conviction that she knew best for me, and she wasn't much interested in my opinion. We didn't argue because I don't like to argue, but she wanted me to be someone else. Yet I know she was proud of me. I think she was proud of me without actually enjoying my films. I believe she enjoyed being "the mother of Fellini," but she couldn't understand why I didn't make films she understood.

A woman in Rimini told my mother she thought my films were vulgar. My mother immediately believed her, though I don't think my mother had seen all of my films. She was more embarrassed by what she could imagine than by what I could imagine. Her own feeling for religion and her guilt about anything sexual magnified the sex act beyond any mere man's imaginings.

Vulgarity is in the eye of the beholder, a way of looking at things. Many people who find certain private functions offensive will not be offended by brutal killing depicted graphically on the screen, and they laugh when something painful happens to Laurel or Hardy. I read recently that certain tribes in New Guinea or Borneo or somewhere consider it bad manners to defecate alone. They look upon the entire nourishment process, from one end of the alimentary canal to the other, with equal pleasure, so defecating is only a part of eating. It's a viewpoint.

I suppose if one thought too much about the slaughtering of animals for our food, the civilized eating process could become vulgar. I personally do not want to know about how a chicken dies. I certainly couldn't strangle one. I don't want to imagine a fish gasping for air. And lobsters being boiled alive! Too terrible. I even wonder about the feelings of fruit and vegetables. . . .

In *Roma,* I show a child peeing in the aisle of a crowded variety theater. When members of the audience protest, the mother says, "But he's only a child!" I actually saw this happen in 1939. The audience in the theater didn't think it was funny, but the audience for *Roma* laughed. I suppose it has something to do with aesthetic distance from the puddle.

My impression is that generally men find sex funny and women take it more seriously. For obvious reasons, I think, since women bear the children, and there seems no humor possible in childbearing. The difference in the sexes' perception of sexuality may also stem from the fact that woman has been seen through history by many as either the embodiment of virtue or the personification of carnal vice. A man can participate in the sex act outside of marriage without contaminating himself morally, though he may receive a physical punishment, while the punishment of the woman is moral—in the eyes of most, she becomes a whore. This is particularly so for us Catholics, although I, personally, do not believe I am affected by a double standard. I try not to be. All of us are affected by early education or mal-education, the inculcation of attitudes before we are aware we are taking them in. It is like a mother cat with her kittens, imparting her values.

In *La Dolce Vita,* Marcello overlooks his father's dalliance with the chorus girl, even encourages it, while the father perfunctorily rebukes the son on the hazards of living with a woman not his wife. In Italy, the straitjacket of hypocrisy is loosely worn.

I believe that in the beginning we were neither male nor female, but androgynous, like angels or certain reptiles. Then came the division, and symbolically Eve was taken from Adam, though it could have been the other way around. Our problem is to reunite the two, thus man is always looking for his other half, the part that has been taken from him eons ago. If he is lucky, he finds that mirror of himself. He can't be complete or wholly free until he has found *his* woman. I know this will make me sound like a male chauvinist, but I believe it's his responsibility, not hers. In carrying this out, he must make her his sexual companion, not just an object of lust or an untouchable saint, but an equal. Otherwise, he can never achieve his completeness and be whole again.

This is a great problem for the protagonists in *La Dolce Vita* and *8½*. Both Marcello and Guido are surrounded by women, but neither can find *his* woman. On the other hand, each of the women believes he is *her* man. A man has much longer in life to make his decision, while a woman must make her decision more quickly. The man has the opportunity for greater freedom to experiment and should have gained more experience and understanding before he marries. All of this is unfair, but it is nature's unfairness.

I cast the same actress as the whore in *La Dolce Vita* and the good woman in *8½*, both in relationship to the embodiments of the same man, Marcello and Guido, who are actually extensions of Moraldo in *I Vitelloni*. Anouk Aimée is an actress who can embody both extremes while giving some clue as to the real person who is between these extremes. This would be impossible to do with Anita Ekberg, who so strongly incarnates one side of woman's nature, although she, too revealed another side in *La Dolce Vita,* that of the child within the mature female. There is a child within each of us, of course, but Anitona's child is nearer to the surface. The wanton side of her nature is a matter of viewpoint. What's wrong with a woman being so magnificently endowed? Nothing. Obviously, I could not have cast Anouk Aimée to play this part, although both are capable of playing whores. Those fantasy breasts of Ekberg's also evoke the image of the mother. I needed someone who was almost a caricature of Venus, who could bring out the humor of the situation between the sexes, as Mae West had done so brilliantly. Mae West was the supreme mistress of humorous relations between the sexes in life as shown on the screen. She was one of the people I would most like to have known.

For the aristocrats' party, I used real aristocrats in a castle, and I was able to take blood from them—figuratively speaking, that is.

For the striptease in *La Dolce Vita,* I didn't know exactly who I wanted for it, but I did know I wanted someone ladylike. She had to be someone who had never before taken off her clothes in that kind of situation, someone who would *never* participate in an orgy, but someone who was attractive enough to be welcome at such an event. There were a lot of women who wanted to take off their clothes onscreen or to try out for me *en déshabillé.* The very fact that they liked the idea, wanted to do it, disqualified them. It had to be shocking, and it could be shocking only if done by someone ladylike.

Sometimes I learn from an actor, and I am persuaded that the actor knows better for his or her character, and I have to admit I am wrong. For the character of Nadia, I saw her in a chic dark cocktail dress, not too tight, but showing that there was a shapely figure underneath. I selected Nadia Gray not only because she had a good figure and was the right age, but because she was extremely sensual without being blatantly sexual. There was something hidden, something mysterious behind that enigmatic, provocative Eastern European smile.

She had been married to a Romanian prince when she was very young, and I could easily imagine meeting her on the Orient Express, but going westward. She had made some British films in which she

Marcello Mastroianni and Nadia Gray in *La Dolce Vita.*

was a proper foreign lady. I could see her clinging to Victorian values while secretly responding to more primitive urges. She would be ideal for the ex-wife of the producer whose home the party has invaded, where she performs her dance.

I had decided that the Nadia character should wear a white brassiere and white panties under her dark dress. I thought the contrast would be striking and sexy, but Nadia Gray refused. She said that no woman who knew anything about clothes would ever be caught wearing a white brassiere and white panties under a dark dress. It might show through. And she would certainly never be confident taking off a dark dress and revealing white underwear. She said she couldn't do it. It was absolutely contrary to the character. She was so convincing, I believed her. She persuaded me. We got her a black brassiere and black panties.

I had faith in my ability to judge what is sexy for a man. The color of the brassiere and panties made no difference. But it was Nadia who could judge best what made a woman *feel* sexy.

She also refused to be the girl Marcello rides around on like a horse while he pelts her with pillow feathers. That was the way I had originally planned the scene, but Nadia quite correctly pointed out that her character wouldn't behave like that, so I gave that part to another actress. Nadia was that rare actress who was willing to make her own part smaller rather than compromise the character.

I won on at least one of the things I'd envisioned for Nadia to do. I wanted her to finish the dance lying on the floor, without a brassiere, but covered by a fur piece, wriggling out of it as her ex-husband appears. Since the brassiere had to be taken off, but not as the climactic moment in the striptease, I asked her to take it off from inside her blouse. This didn't make sense to her. She said it was impossible, but I knew from personal experience that it could be done. When I showed her how, she was a quick learner and deft indeed. It was as if she had been doing it that way all her life.

What I cared about was the look on her face, her subjective reaction to what she was doing. I wanted to convey more what she was thinking, and especially feeling, than how the others perceived it. The reactions of her current lover and her husband, as well as of the others, create a synergistic effect between performer and audience that was greater than the sum of the separate reactions. I remember during the striptease, I took off my own tie.

If you want to show sensuality in a film, it's better to be personally aroused, but unsatisfied. Your own desire and frustration will be projected onto your characters, and will enhance the sexual intensity of their needs and desires, which they so urgently wish to fulfill.

Now when *La Dolce Vita* is mentioned, they talk about the striptease as much as of Anita Ekberg's part. No one ever mentions Yvonne Furneaux, who was so good as Marcello's mistress. It's because her character was complete, with so little room for further speculation, while the other two, who remained mysterious, were thus more intriguing. They were incomplete, which is comparable in life to people who are not open books.

I am often asked what happened to Anita. I am asked what happened to Nadia. They don't mean the actresses, because when I start to say that Anita Ekberg lives in Rome and Nadia Gray in New York, they protest. "No! No! What happened to their *characters?*" They thought if I did "La Dolce Vita, Part II," they would be satisfied. Not true. The opposite. They would have had all their questions answered. That would have left them unsatisfied, not only by "La Dolce Vita, Part II," but with their memory of *La Dolce Vita,* "Part I."

Sometimes it happens in life that you meet a person who has mystery and you have a wonderful time and you want to continue the experience. But you take it too far; you learn everything. There is nothing left then but the emptiness, the vague disappointment.

Nadia Gray near the climax of her striptease in *La Dolce Vita.*

Nadia Gray and Fellini on the set of *La Dolce Vita*.

La Dolce Vita was the first Italian film to last three and a half hours. I was told no audience could watch a film that long. In truth, I hadn't realized that so many people in Italy would find my picture as shocking as they did. I said publicly I didn't care, but I must say, all alone by myself, I was a little shocked when I saw on a church door a poster with my name on it that had a black border. Had I died and didn't know it? It was a situation I later wanted to use for my film about Mastorna, a man who dies and doesn't know it, during the time he hovers between life and death. The poster said, "Let us pray for the salvation of the soul of Federico Fellini, public sinner." It was a shock. It made me shiver.

I would never put anything in a movie just to shock that wasn't true to the story I was telling. I would not betray my characters, who are as real in my life as any real people I know.

But *La Dolce Vita* was perceived by many as scandalous. It achieved instant notoriety. I didn't make it to be scandalous, I didn't view it as scandalous. I didn't understand the reaction, but I know it helped to make the picture so financially successful and to give it such big international attention. For me, personally, it was disturbing to be accused of being a sinner and an exploiter, but after people saw the picture, for the most part they were pleased and did not find it so shocking, although some did.

It was because of *La Dolce Vita* that I met Georges Simenon, who was one of my favorite writers when I was a boy growing up in Rimini. His books were so wonderful that I really didn't think of them as being written by a person. Years later, when I met him in Cannes, I was thrilled. Then he said that he was thrilled to meet me. Simenon, it turned out, was the chairman of the jury of the Cannes Film Festival that gave the Golden Palm, the first prize, to *La Dolce Vita*. It would have been a thrill to meet him at any time, but to meet him in *that* way was more than I can describe. Giulietta was so happy that she kissed him, leaving an impression of red lips on his cheek just as he stepped out onstage.

What surprised me about Simenon was that he considered himself a failure. He never felt like a real success. He told me how much he admired what I did—I, who had so admired his work! I asked him why he felt the way he did about his wonderful stories, and he said it was because he dealt only with a pedestrian reality.

Someone told me that a popular and respected American dictionary lists "dolce vita" as an English phrase since 1961, after *La Dolce Vita* premiered. The movie isn't mentioned, but the derivation is given as Italian and the phrase defined as "a life of indolence and self-indulgence." I was amused to find "paparazzo" is also in that dictionary. What astounded me was that "Felliniesque" is listed as an adjective after my name in the biographical section. I assume, however, that American producers don't use that dictionary. Italian producers evidently don't use dictionaries much, either.

I discovered I had to reconstruct the Via Veneto, because the real one wasn't real enough, and because I wanted heightened reality and couldn't control the environment on the real street. In order to do this, the producer, Angelo Rizzoli, told me I would have to give up the percentage of profits I had in my contract. I had a profit participation clause which, as it turned out, would have made me rich. It was my choice. Well, it was no choice at all. I had to do what was good for my film. Without a second's hesitation, I surrendered all future rights to any monetary benefits from *La Dolce Vita*. Worse yet, if I had to do it over again, in the light of and with full knowledge of what I gave up, I would have to do the same as I did.

I received fifty thousand dollars to make the film. That was it.

The film took in millions. It made many people rich, but I wasn't one of them. Angelo Rizzoli gave me a gift—a gold watch.

ten

JUNG AS AN OLDER BROTHER

After *La Dolce Vita* was my moment in life to make a lot of money, if that was what I wanted, or to make a lot of films, if that was what I wanted. The only problem was that I couldn't make the film I wanted at any price, and I would not compromise.

It didn't bother me that producers wouldn't pay me much money unless I accepted their projects, but the terrible part was that the financing was too difficult for what *I* wanted to do. The producers didn't want to make a Fellini film, they only wanted a film done by Fellini. It was not that producers said no. It was that they didn't say yes. Hope was held out. I was too patient. I wanted to make *my* movie, not *theirs.* And I had no idea that my moment had arrived, that it would not come again, nor that it would last only such a brief time.

I wasted time being resentful because I had been paid so little for *La Dolce Vita,* and resentment saps energy. Then I regretted being resentful, and regret saps energy.

At the time, I hadn't known it was going to be the financial success that it was destined to be, nor did I know the future—that no film I made would ever have that kind of commercial success again. If I had known, I don't know what I could have done about it. I truly cared only about making the film. As usual, I had had difficulty finding a producer, and I could never again achieve the situation where two or more were fighting over the next Fellini film. With only one offer on the table, the bargaining position isn't good. One buyer doesn't make for a very profitable auction. Giulietta never could understand why I couldn't get better paid for my work.

The press was asking me what I planned to do after *La Dolce Vita*. I was receiving offers. That is an unaccustomed pleasurable sensation, not to be selling one's wares, but to be pursued. Oh, courtship! It didn't take any time at all to adjust to being wanted. It doesn't take time to come to like a more pleasing situation. Like a beautiful young girl, I assumed the way it was was the way it would always be. I didn't know how little time it would last, but I can say I savored the sensation in its moment.

Not knowing that I would never again have that moment in time had two disadvantages: I did not use it sufficiently, nor did I enjoy it enough. But it had one advantage: I enjoyed it in the carefree way that is best, when life is eternal and death is for other people. When what is precious is too tightly held, it is strangled.

I've never been able to understand the American producers. When they come to Rome, they stay at the Grand Hotel. They come to make deals, like at that wonderful hotel in Beverly Hills where everyone goes, the Beverly Hills Hotel, and they make deals in the Polo Lounge. In Rome, they spend their days sitting in their underpants in the biggest suites making long-distance calls. Why would they come so far only to call back to where they came from? They always have a bottle of mineral water on the table. And when they receive you, they seem totally unaware that they are wearing their underpants, and they make no effort to put on anything more. I thought they did it to make me feel ill at ease.

They spend most of your time speaking long-distance on the phone with someone else, to their people back in the United States or to Japan, or anywhere far away. Maybe it's to demonstrate for you how important they are, or maybe it's just to demonstrate it for themselves. They shout because they don't trust the Italian telephone, the way they don't trust the water. When they do talk with you, they talk a long time about irrelevant things, everything in the world that is unrelated to what you came for. Then, casually, they throw in the important part, supposedly the reason you are there, during the last few minutes you are together. Why do American businessmen spend hours making small talk, telling jokes, avoiding only the reason for which you are there, then mentioning it in the last few minutes? Are they afraid of something?

If you say no to anything, they believe you are only bargaining. They never think you really mean no. Then they want you to go on television to sell what you do, like soap. In the United States, they wanted me to do a TV show demonstrating how to cook spaghetti. I never cooked spaghetti, even at home. I never had the patience to wait for the water to boil. In effect, my answer was no. I would not repeat to a lady, to children, or in print exactly what I told them.

I was nominated for the Academy Award as best director for *La Dolce Vita,* the first time a foreign-language filmmaker was chosen to compete as best director.

Because of *La Dolce Vita,* I was given the opportunity of which I had dreamed since I first became a director, for which I had hoped when Lattuada and I made our own company. I was offered a partnership in a company to be called Federiz. It even incorporated my name. I would own twenty-five percent of the company. Little did I know that it meant one hundred percent of the responsibility and twenty-five percent of the profits after the others' accountants had determined there weren't any. If I had understood that, which I didn't, I still would have done it.

Power. I thought I had it. I thought I had the possibility to finance my own pictures. Also, I could help young directors to get their work done, and I could even influence Italian cinema.

The opportunity was a show of appreciation for all the money Rizzoli had made from *La Dolce Vita* and also for the acclaim and attention. He really hoped I would make "La Dolce Vita, Part II" and assign young directors to make a lot of little *La Dolce Vitas.* He told me I could do "anything," but he didn't mean it. I had only apparent power.

My brother, Riccardo, came to me for the financing of a film. I had to say no, and I don't think he ever understood or accepted my saying it. We were not truly close, but before that, there had never been any source of resentment or friction. Though he did not talk about it, I wonder if he forgave me.

Because the sound—including the dialogue—in his pictures was dubbed in post-production, Fellini was able to talk to his actors while filming scenes.

Worse, Giulietta wanted me to do a film about Mother Cabrini, in which she was intent on playing the title role. It was her dream. She could hardly wait to begin. She wanted me to direct. She was certain it could only be a success. I remember the hurt look on her face when I said no.

I saw the new office opened for Federiz as a kind of workshop or salon where we could all drink coffee and exchange ideas. I selected a very nice office on Via della Croce. It had everything we needed, including being near a wonderful bakery. I always say I don't care about possessions, but maybe it's partly because I couldn't ever afford to buy the antiques I admired in the elegant shops around the Margutta. I found an antique table on which I could spread out my photographs for casting. The set designer who did *La Dolce Vita* decorated the offices. We used the couches from *La Dolce Vita*. It seemed lucky, in addition to being a good economy, and they were so comfortable. There were also Grand Hotel influences, as I had always admired that style. My personal office would be separated, so I could always retreat into the privacy of my own world. That was important to me.

It was a medieval court with a despotic monarch. But I would be benevolent, dispensing money for movies, instead of being a beggar.

All of my director friends appeared, each with a film project. All of my would-be friends appeared. Suddenly, there were friends I didn't know I had. *They* remembered how close we had been. I was almost buried in an avalanche of paper. I never answered my phone. I couldn't find an idea that appealed. All this was interfering with my own work, which required an unfettered imagination.

La Dolce Vita had changed the standard for what producers expected from me. They expected less, as long as it said "Fellini's" before the title. But my standard for myself had also changed. It was a nice warm feeling to have success. I wanted to repeat it, and I knew success was a key to working all the time.

Meanwhile, I was losing my friends. Each time I said no, one less. It never failed. I was losing people here and there. I didn't really mind. It was like a test. Except with Giulietta. She was furious with me. That *was* terrible. But I could not do what I didn't like. I felt a responsibility toward the producers' money, not to lose it. I was not a good gambler with their money.

As it was given, so it was taken away. Rizzoli was dissatisfied because I hadn't found a film to produce. When I accepted doing one of the four stories for *Boccaccio '70,* being produced by Carlo Ponti, Rizzoli thought it disloyal of me. He did accept a co-producing role, but he had lost faith that I would produce any films other than my own. I think he may have been losing faith that I would even produce any of my own. When the office was closed, I was disappointed, but though I didn't tell anyone how I felt about it, not even Giulietta, I was also relieved.

I now could return to doing what I *really* wanted to do. Already *8½* was germinating in my mind.

Giulietta was not able to understand why I hadn't produced her Mother Cabrini project before "losing" my Federiz company. It was not a subject I wanted to do, but I knew the others would never have

Federico and Giulietta at a premiere in Rome during the mid-1960s.

accepted the project as having commercial possibilities even if it had appealed to me. I tried to persuade her of that, but I wasn't sufficiently persuasive. The only answer was for us to mutually agree that since my power to produce was over, at least for the time being, we would not mention the subject of Mother Cabrini, the film. But Giulietta sometimes forgot.

Thus, from *La Dolce Vita* had come what I believed was a major opportunity, one of which I had dreamed. It was like getting my three wishes, because all of my three wishes were really the same wish: to be able to work without wasting time begging for money, and to have control over what I did. To be able to help others and influence Italian films, not to be limited to what I could do myself, was the extra dollop of whipped cream.

As it turned out, it ended just like the fairy tale: badly.

I lost friends. I lost time. I missed making a film I could have made during that time. Federiz spoiled my home life. At night, Giulietta's wonderful spaghetti sauce and Mother Cabrini. It was bad for digestion.

If a person aspires to be a so-called auteur, he should be able to initiate his own projects, but the creative person and the business person are rarely found in the same body. The business person needs money to buy food, and then more money, even when he can no longer eat all the food his money can buy. The artist, however, needs reassurance even more than he needs food.

I always believed I wanted to do it all, but Federiz showed me that being called producer was not the perfect answer to what I desired, which was actually artistic control.

When Carlo Ponti had approached me with the suggestion that I contribute an episode to a composite film to be directed by Rossellini, Antonioni, Vittorio de Sica, Luchino Visconti, Mario Monicelli, and myself, I was tempted. I would be back doing what I was meant to do in life. That was why I'd said yes. Rossellini and Antonioni dropped out. The theme was to be a reply by each director to oppressive censorship. I had not gotten over hearing that one Jesuit publication had gone so far as to recommend that I be jailed for *La Dolce Vita.*

Boccaccio '70 had no discernible relationship to the *Decameron* and was being made in 1961. In it, I treat the effect of our religious training, as well as other factors, on one repressed little man. Dr. Antonio hides his passion for a woman, played by Anita Ekberg, even from himself, under the armor of self-righteous indignation against her unavoidable erotic display. The Church is not the only factor that has contributed to his attitude. He is incensed by her big, utterly desirable tits, which are enlarged on an enormous billboard appropriately advertising milk. Actually, she is the embodiment of his exaggerated image of female sexuality, though he is deterred by his complexes from taking pleasure in looking at her. He has been deformed by a distortion of theological thinking.

When he imagines that she has come to life and is pursuing him, the impulse he feels is to defend himself. He kills her with a lance to the right breast. In doing so, he kills everything in himself except his own pitifully stifled libido, which can only cry out, "Anita!" He must now go on living without her—his greatest punishment, since he has not killed his own desire.

In this short segment, my intention was to show how man's repressed appetites can finally break their bonds and swell into a gigantic erotic fantasy that comes to life, taking over his reason and finally overwhelming him. Again, as in *La Dolce Vita,* Anita has some understanding of her sexuality, enjoys using it, but feels it isn't her fault and shouldn't be held against her—symbolically, I mean.

I often wonder what happened to that billboard. I must go to Cinecittà one of these days and look for it. It was a great billboard.

The character of Dr. Antonio was against every modern trend which would lift the veil of mystery and obscurity around sex, a veil

In *The Temptation of Dr. Antonio,* an episode of *Boccaccio '70* (1962), Peppino De Filippo crusades against Anita Ekberg for revealing her charms on a billboard advertising milk.

that deforms it, making it seem clandestine and impure. The human body, hidden, can be erotic or go unnoticed. Nude, it can hardly go unnoticed, and it's just as likely to be humorous as erotic. What people like Dr. Antonio don't understand is that the totally undraped woman loses only her visual mystery, but she continues to possess those unfathomable secrets which remain invisible to the eye.

I do not believe that I, personally, will ever come to understand women. I hope not. Total knowledge would work against the tingle that exists between man and woman—when it exists.

In my films, I find my female characters more exciting to create, probably because woman is more intriguing than man—more erotic, more elusive, more stimulating to my creative impulse. I like to have women in my films who are sexually attractive because I believe not only men, but women, too, enjoy looking at them.

As I see it, the creative person is a medium. In his creative activities he is possessed by many different personalities. As a film director, I have had the opportunity to live many lives and in different periods of time. One can become a Kafka-like beetle in his metamorphosis even though he has never lived that life. Kafka was one of the most exaggerated examples of a person whose imagination may have been too strong for him as a person. It was good for the world, but not for him. Kafka, in my opinion, was completely autobiographical. At his best, the artist becomes both Dr. Frankenstein and monster, or a vampire without really having been one. I would have liked to have done a vampire sequence in one of my films, even though, personally, I cannot even look at blood, let alone drink it. I had the idea when I was working on *The Temptation of Dr. Antonio.* But the vampire is a concept too strong for fantasy.

Moraldo was looking for the meaning of life as I, myself, was doing. Moraldo became Guido [in *8½*] about the time that I understood that perhaps I wasn't going to find life's meaning after all. It was then that the Moraldo in me disappeared, or at least hid himself, embarrassed by his naïveté.

I never felt the need to go to a psychiatrist as a patient, but I did have as a friend Dr. Ernst Bernhard, a leading Jungian analyst who helped to open the world of Jung to me. He encouraged keeping records of my dreams and of dreamlike occurrences. These play an important part in certain of my films.

The discovery of Jung helped me to be bolder in my trust of fantasy over realism. I even made a trip to Switzerland to see where Jung lived, and to buy chocolate. The effects of Jung, as well as the chocolate, have remained with me all my life.

My discovery of Jung was important, very important, not in changing what I did, but in helping me understand what I do. Jung confirmed in an intellectual way what I had always felt, that being in touch with your imagination was a gift to be nurtured. He articulated what had previously been emotional for me. I met Dr. Bernhard at the moment of *8½*. I believe my interest in psychotherapy is reflected in *8½* and of course in *Juliet of the Spirits*.

For a brief time, I spent many hours with him, visiting him regularly, not in a professional way as a psychotherapist, but as a stimulating social friend. I went to see him because I wanted to discover a world of the unknown which had fascinated me; but what I discovered was myself.

It was as if Jung had written especially for me. I thought of him as my big brother. As a little boy, I remember wishing I had an older brother to lead me by the hand into the great world. I was a naïve child, and at one point I know I hoped my mother would go to the hospital and bring home an older brother for me. When she finally did go to the hospital, what she brought home was a tiny baby girl, who, at the time, didn't seem to me to have been worth the trip. My younger brother, Riccardo, when we were small children, seemed to understand even less about life than I did. I wanted someone older than I who could tell me answers, or at least pose questions. As a young man, I tended to have friends older than I. It seemed to me that Jung would have been exactly the confidant I would have wanted.

For Jung, the symbol represents the inexpressible, and for Freud, the symbol represents the hidden—because it is shameful. The difference between Freud and Jung, I believe, is that Freud represents rational thinking, and Jung imaginative thinking.

What was most important in my reading of Jung was that I was able to personally apply what I found there to my own way of being and to shake off feelings of inferiority or guilt left over in my head from my early days, the recriminations of parents, of schoolteachers, and sometimes the taunts of children, who felt that to be different was to be inferior. Though I had friends, I was a solitary child in the sense that my interior life was my more important life, far more important than my exterior life. For the other children, throwing snowballs was more real than imagining, dreaming. Being an alone child, alone in a crowd, meant I was the most alone you can be.

I have created my own family on the movie set, bonding with people whose interests and feelings were more like my own. I was fascinated by the idea of delving into my interior space, one reason that Carlos Castaneda and his writings interested me so much. Jung did not seem to me to be pretentious or to expound the unattainable. I found his work friendly. He was like that older brother I had wanted to find, because he said to me, "Here—come this way." Since I respected his leadership, an essential element, and since it happened to be the direction in which I was going anyway, it was easy for me to follow him through the open door. He seems to me the perfect sage for those who respect creative imagination and symbolic expression.

Our dreams and nightmares are the same as those that people had three thousand years ago. They are the same basic fears we enjoy in our houses that people had in caves. I used the word "enjoy" because I believe there is a certain enjoyment in fear. If not, why would people seek out the roller coaster? Fear gives an edge to life, as long as it's only in small doses. It has always been considered unmanly to admit fear. Fear and cowardice are not the same thing. The greatest bravery is that which man accomplishes in conquering his own fear. The totally fearless are lunatics or mercenary soldiers or both. These "fearless" are not responsible or trustworthy, and they have to be isolated, so their fearlessness does not endanger other people.

I don't know if my discovery of Jung affected my work, but it affected me, and I think what affects me and becomes part of me has to become part of my work. I know that I found with him a kinship and a reaffirmation of the same sense of fantasy that is basic to my being, an extra sense. Jung shared with me the exaltation of the imagination. He saw dreams as archetypal images which were the result of the common experiences of man. I could scarcely believe that someone else had so perfectly articulated my feelings about creative dreams. Jung dealt with the coincidences, the omens, which I felt had always been important in my own life.

Juliet of the Spirits offered not only the occasion for an adventurous exploration of Jungian psychology but also of astrology, the séance, mysticism of every sort. My films offered me an excuse to take the time to pursue what were really my own interests. Of course, *City of Women* represents the total discovery of the dream experience, which began in *The Temptation of Dr. Antonio.*

Someone introduced me to Luise Rainer when she was in Rome. I knew she had won two Oscars in a row in the thirties. I didn't know at the time that she had been married to Clifford Odets. When I saw her face, I realized that she would be perfect in *La Dolce Vita.* She was tiny, very slender, wearing a little cap in the style of the twenties, with a fringe of wisps of hair, and large piercing eyes. Perfect.

I immediately offered her a part. She asked me to tell her about the plot, the character, the other characters. This is not something I usually do. I could not be rude, however, not to so great an actress. So I started to tell her, but she began to tell *me* about the character. She had not said yes to my question, but I assumed this meant she had accepted my offer of the part. I had another appointment, but she didn't stop to breathe. She was so full of ideas. It reminded me of me. Too much. Finally, I had to interrupt her to say that I had to leave. At the time, she was on her way to New York and she said that she would write and send me her notes on the character. I did not expect anything, because people are always saying they will write, and don't. But she wrote. And wrote. And wrote.

The character was a minor character, a small but nice part. She began to rewrite the part. Her part was growing. Then she began to rewrite the film. She was deeply interested in psychiatry. She called me from New York and wanted to discuss the psychological nature of her character and her disturbances. She said she liked Rome and was ready to come and stay for a long time.

For Miss Rainer, I had even agreed, reluctantly, on some changes. It's *not* what I do. Even Giulietta knows how difficult it would be to persuade me to agree, in advance, to script changes involving a character. On the set, yes, perhaps. But I did this totally out of respect for Miss Rainer.

Every time I gave in, conceded, she asked for something more.

I cannot say that I was exactly heartbroken when I had to break the "sad" news to Miss Rainer that her part had been cut from the script.

That was how it happened that Luise Rainer did *not* appear in *La Dolce Vita*. But she did inspire a character in *8½*, which was played by Madeleine Lebeau, who was Humphrey Bogart's French girlfriend in *Casablanca*. This changed Madeleine's life more than Miss Rainer's. Luise Rainer returned to London, where she lived a full life. Her husband was an important publisher. Madeleine stayed in Rome and eventually married Tullio Pinelli. I was the witness at the wedding, as I deserved to be.

Sometimes people ask me why I often use the actor's real name for the character. I don't know. Perhaps it's simply because I'm lazy. I started doing it with my brother, Riccardo, Alberto Sordi, and Leopoldo Trieste in *I Vitelloni,* and never got out of the habit. I was never good at remembering names, just as I never forget a face. I know I have an excellent memory, but it is one which is excessively visual. Sometimes the actor is chosen before the character has been named, and I can't think of him or her any other way. That was the case with Nadia Gray, but with Anita Ekberg, her character already had a name. In *8½,* I didn't call the protagonist Marcello because I didn't want him confused with the character in *La Dolce Vita*. Also, Guido appears earlier in an unrealized screenplay I wrote, "Journey with Anita." At the time, I had Sophia Loren in mind as Anita, not Anita Ekberg, whom I hadn't met yet. The name was a coincidence. I believe that coincidences are more than coincidences. They are something we don't understand, something of the mystical world of infinite possibilities.

When I wrote "Journey with Anita," I not only didn't know Anita Ekberg, I didn't even know *of* her. I have been denying for years that I wrote with her in mind. It was one of the few times I chose a name at random. I was always told that using real people's names would be a problem. But it was "Anita" which got me into trouble, especially with Giulietta. I told her there was no one in my life named Anita. "Then what *is* her name?" she asked.

When Sophia Loren wasn't available to play the part, Carlo Ponti lost interest in producing "Journey with Anita," but I might have found someone else. Actually, I let her unavailability stop me because of the autobiographical nature of the story, although it wasn't one hundred percent autobiographical. I felt a little embarrassed when I realized I would be standing out there naked, and I didn't want to cause Giulietta any pain. "Moraldo in the City" is also to some extent autobiographical, but it's about a part of my life before I knew Giulietta.

"Journey with Anita" is the story of a married man who uses his father's illness as an excuse to take a trip with his mistress to his hometown so he can visit his father. Then, while he is there, the father dies, and he feels guilty because he has never really established communication with him, and suddenly it is too late. It can never happen.

My own father had died recently, and I was regretting my failure to tell him that I no longer resented his infidelities. As a child, I had assumed my mother's attitude. As a grown man, I understood my father's point of view. In the screenplay, I expressed the feeling I had on seeing my father's dead body lying there. Then, in a dream, I saw myself, an older version of myself lying there in my father's place.

The Anita character loves to eat, to roll around naked in the grass, to feel deeply, and to show her emotions. It is everything a man wants—and fears. By the end of the trip, Guido's relationship with Anita is over.

At a certain point, the script no longer clamored in my mind to be made. It had used me up. So I sold it for a film which was made with Goldie Hawn. Alberto Grimaldi bought the screenplay, and Mario Monicelli directed it, and Giancarlo Giannini, who does not resemble me physically or in any way, played the Guido character. The picture retained its title in Italy, *Viaggio con Anita,* and it was called *Lovers and Liars* in English, which is scarcely a title at all, because it could have fit dozens of films and didn't fit any. I never went to see the film, but I did cash my check.

Our minds can shape the way a thing will be, because we act according to our expectations.

The hard thing is beginning. Whatever it is you want to do in life, you must begin it. The point of departure for the journey I must begin for each film is generally something that really happened to me, but which I believe also is part of the experience of others. The audience should be able to say, "Oh, something like that happened to me once, or to someone I know," or "I wish it had happened to me," or "I'm glad it didn't happen to me." They should identify, sympathize, empathize. They should be able to enter the movie and get into my shoes and the shoes of at least some of the characters. I first try to express my own emotions, what I personally feel, and then I look for the link of truth that will be of significance to people like me.

The picture I make is never exactly the one I started out to make, but that is of no importance. I am very flexible on the set. The script provides the starting point, as well as offering security. After the first weeks, the picture takes on a life of its own. The film grows as you are making it, like relationships with a person.

I must keep a closed set, though I make many exceptions and welcome good spirits, as long as there aren't too many of them. But if I become conscious of one wrong person watching me, my creativity dries up. I feel it physically. My throat becomes dry. It's insidiously destructive to work when there are long faces.

Understanding what makes a thing difficult doesn't make it less difficult, and understanding *how* difficult it is can make it more difficult to attempt. Pictures do not get easier for me to make, but more difficult. With each one, I learn more of what can go wrong, and I am thus more threatened. It's always satisfying when you can turn something that goes wrong into something that is even better. If I saw that an actor like Broderick Crawford was a little drunk on the set, I tried to make it part of the story. If someone has just had an argument with his wife, I try to use his upset state as part of his character. When I cannot correct the problem, I incorporate it. I realize that the dream cannot be touched, that the picture in my mind will never quite be the one on the screen. One must learn to live with the acceptance of that.

Finding the right project is the most difficult. I need a raison d'être to set off on a journey. For me, it is the contract. So many people say, "I'm going to write a book," but knowing you have a publisher and a contract makes all the difference, or *almost* all the difference. You need a combination of purpose and encouragement. It's difficult to write if you don't know you're going to be published, or for me to direct a film no one will produce. I need a contract in order to go through the discipline, and the studio means a great deal to me. The studio provides shelter and control.

In the case of *8½*, something happened to me which I had feared could happen, but when it did, it was more terrible than I could ever have imagined. I suffered director's block, like writer's block. I had a producer, a contract. I was at Cinecittà, and everybody was ready and waiting for me to make a film. What they didn't know was that the film I was going to make had fled from me. There were sets already up, but I couldn't find my sentimental feeling.

People were asking me about the film. Now, I never answer those questions because I think talking about the film before you do it weakens it, destroys it. The energy goes into the talking. Also, I have to be free to change. Sometimes with the press, as with strangers, I would simply tell them the same lie as to what the film was about— just to stop the questions and to protect my film. Even if I had told them the truth, it would probably have changed so much in the finished film that they would say, "Fellini lied to us." But this was different. This time, I was stammering and saying nonsensical things when Mastroianni asked me about his part. He was so trusting. They all trusted me.

I sat down and started to write a letter to Angelo Rizzoli, admitting the state I was in. I said to him, "Please accept my state of confusion. I can't go on."

Before I could send the letter one of the grips came to fetch me. He said, "You must come to our party." The grips and electricians were having a birthday party for one of them. I wasn't in the mood for anything, but I couldn't say no.

They were serving spumante in paper cups, and I was given one. Then there was a toast, and everyone raised his paper cup. I thought they were going to toast the person having the birthday, but instead they toasted me and my "masterpiece." Of course they had no idea what I was going to do, but they had perfect faith in me. I left to return to my office, stunned.

I was about to cost all of these people their jobs. They called me the Magician. Where was my "magic"?

Now what do I do? I asked myself.

But myself didn't answer. I listened to a fountain and the sound of the water, and tried to hear my own inner voice. Then, I heard the small voice of creativity within me. I knew. The story I would tell was of a writer who doesn't know what he wants to write.

I tore up my letter to Rizzoli.

Later, I changed the profession of Guido to that of film director. He became a film director who didn't know what he wanted to direct.

It's difficult to portray a writer on the screen, doing what he does in an interesting way. There isn't much action to show in writing. The world of the film director opened up limitless possibilities.

The relationship between Guido and Luisa has to show what once was there between them and what is left over in their relationship. It is still very much a relationship, though it has undergone changes from the days of courtship and the honeymoon. It's difficult to show the bond between a husband and wife who married because of romance and passion, but who have now been married a long time. A friendship largely replaces what was there before, but not totally. It's a friendship for a lifetime, but when feelings of betrayal enter into it . . .

Guido (Marcello Mastroianni) and his wife, Luisa (Anouk Aimée), spend a rare moment together in *8½* (1963). As usual, he's not paying attention to her.

Marcello and Anouk are excellent actors who could pretend. I cannot say, however, that I minded that the two of them found each other *so* attractive. I think some of that was caught on the screen. Of course, Mastroianni and Anita Ekberg *didn't* find each other so attractive in real life, and certainly there wasn't anything going on between them, yet *La Dolce Vita* worked.

I had a different ending in mind for *8½*, but I was required to film something for a trailer. For this trailer, I brought back two hundred actors and photographed them as they paraded before seven cameras. When I saw the footage, I was impressed. The rushes were so good, I changed the original ending, which took place in a railroad dining car where Guido and Luisa establish a rapprochement. So, sometimes even a producer's request can have a beneficial effect. I was able to use some of the discarded material in *City of Women*. The segment in which Snaporaz thinks he sees the women from his dream sitting in his railway compartment was inspired by a segment of Guido thinking he sees all the women from his life sitting in the dining car, which was to have been the end of *8½*.

I had wanted to see *Nine,* the Broadway musical inspired by *8½*, but I was never in New York at the right time. The film I have most wanted to see made into a Broadway show is *Juliet of the Spirits*. I have several good reasons for it that are not financial. I would like to see my show on Broadway. I would like to go back to my original conception and some of the ideas that were not used because, at the time, they didn't struggle hard enough to be born. The ideas that won out did not win because they were best, just stronger. Giulietta loved this film, but she was unhappy with what I did. She had her own, different ideas, and I would like to try them in the play, because I would like to please Giulietta, and because I now think she was right. I have been working with Charlotte Chandler for some years on the idea, and Marvin Hamlisch wants to do the music. I hope it runs as long as *A Chorus Line*. That will give me enough time to see it.

I have never needed drugs and I was never attracted to them. Truly, I never felt need of them, though I admit I was curious. I saw the "stoned" hippies on the Spanish Steps.

When I make a film, I certainly don't need to take a drug. Besides my film, and some food, I'm happy and I don't need anything else— except sex. I'm so full of the life force. Some directors have told me that when they are directing a film, they give up sex or reduce the amount of sex in their lives, because the energy needed for directing and for sex is the same energy. I, personally, feel more alive when I'm directing than at any other time. A greater energy comes upon me—directing energy, sexual energy. Making films is intensely exciting in *every* way.

I wouldn't have taken a risk while I was making *8½*, but once I had completed the film, the crisis began, as it always did for me—the in-between-films crisis. Just as I am in perfect control on the set, I've never felt in control that way in real life.

I decided that I wanted to experience LSD, just once, but I wanted to do so in a controlled environment. Since there had been a history of heart problems in my family, I had my heart checked first. I passed the test. It was suggested that I have a cardiologist present at the scene. I couldn't imagine what he would do if I had a heart attack. I did the experiment with a stenographer present, because I wished to record everything. There are people who say that Fellini always has to make a "production" of everything.

I have to admit that Carlos Castaneda's books had influenced me to try LSD. I wanted to meet him, and I thought we might even share some drug experience as well as speak to each other. It would give us a reference point in common. As a creative person, I thought I should know what people were talking about and doing, even though I was timid about it. I had always wanted to be in total control of myself, and this seemed like a total surrender of control. I feared permanent damage, not so much physical as to my dream powers. Yet I was curious about the much-talked-about hallucinatory effects of LSD and of the mescaline of Castaneda, too.

The truth of the matter was that after I said I would do it, I didn't really want to go through with it. I didn't like resigning myself to a situation in which I saw myself losing my own will, and I wasn't certain that there couldn't be permanent damage. I contemplated a disturbance of the delicate balance. I never wanted to change myself mentally, only physically. Could I lose my dreams? But I had said I wanted to do it. I had agreed, the arrangements were made, and I didn't want to seem a coward.

Afterwards I remembered nothing of the experience. I couldn't imagine what all the fuss was about. Castaneda certainly must have had access to better drugs, perhaps because they were derived from natural sources by Indians, who used them in their religious ceremonies. I didn't feel better, transported . . . anything.

I did have a slight headache. I felt very tired.

I was told that for hours I never stopped talking and I never stopped pacing. It was no wonder I felt tired. It was explained to me that since I was a person whose mind was always in motion, under the influence of the drug my body had acted out the activity of my mind. I didn't need anyone to tell me that my mind was always in motion.

I considered it a wasted Sunday, but I tried not to waste time regretting how I had wasted time. Making films is the only stimulus I crave, but my "drug" is very expensive.

I have never been exactly a true believer in astrology either, but I have always been interested in the subject. In my life, it has been more true than the factor of mere chance would explain. Perhaps I should have paid more attention to it. I am interested in any area where there is more than I can understand and everything is not explained. I try to keep an open mind. I have met with astrologers and have listened with interest to what they said to a person whose sign was neither clearly Aquarius nor Capricorn. I was born on January 20. I have never been certain how these signs influence me. I know I have never liked goat meat, and I never learned to swim, which seems inappropriate for a water sign, for whatever meaning such facts have. There were times, however, when I spoke with astrologers who did make some uncanny predictions. I believe that there is more out there than we know, and I think that there is definitely something to the study of astrology.

Meditation fascinated me, the idea of clearing my mind totally. My thoughts come fast, and I cannot control what Castaneda called the interior dialogue. I spoke with an Indian guru about it, but it was something I couldn't master. I got bored meditating. Also, perhaps I was afraid if I ever turned off my images, my waking dreams, they might be startled away and never come back, and I would be left alone without them.

Being a film director, you cannot always do exactly what you want to do. You have to be flexible. You can't count too much on any one thing. When I was making *Juliet of the Spirits,* I was counting on filming a wonderful tree that was about one hundred years old. The night before we were to shoot the scene, there was a storm. No tree.

When Giulietta saw me drawing a little circle on a piece of paper, she caught her breath, knowing *it* had begun. She didn't need to look closely to know that the circle was her face. She knew that I would begin with her character which I knew best, and she recognized *her* circle. Giulietta gets very quiet when she first sees her head go on paper, because she knows a part is coming. Thus began *Juliet of the Spirits*.

eleven

MY GUARDIAN ANGEL
COULD ONLY BE A WOMAN

I worked a great deal with Giulietta on the set, and at home, too. Finally, one night she said to me, "Why are you so much harder on me than on the others? You're nice to them."

I hadn't realized it, but it was true. She was right. Because I began with her character, it was the one on which everything depended, and it was the one of which I had the clearest conception. Thus, I was the most disappointed if the character Giulietta was playing didn't do exactly what I expected her to do.

Juliet of the Spirits was created especially for Giulietta because she wanted to act again, and I wanted to do a picture for her. There had been many ideas, and it is difficult to say exactly why it was this one that became a film. Again, I suppose this idea fought harder to be born than the others.

One of the ideas discarded was for her to be the richest woman in the world; another was the story of a nun, but it was too simple a story and too religious, though it was the one Giulietta liked best. I liked an idea about a famous psychic, but it was what they call in America a bio-pic, and I feel my hands are tied if I have to be faithful to a story that is real, especially about a person in modern times.

Instead, I made up this story, which was really parts of several stories, and Giulietta liked it. For the first time, I asked her specifically what she would say or do at a certain moment, and I used some of her suggestions.

For Gelsomina and Cabiria, I drew from what I knew of Giulietta's character, and she added silent bits with her genius for mimicry and pantomime. In those days she was very docile, accepting everything I said and always looking up to me. By the time of *Juliet of the Spirits,* it was different. On the set, I had the same docile acceptance, good nature, respectful deference Giulietta had always given me. She always had tried the hardest she could, putting everything she had into each role. But with *Juliet of the Spirits,* while she apparently agreed with me on everything, it was only that way publicly, on the set. When we went home at night, Giulietta had saved up everything she'd thought during the day, especially about what was wrong, to tell to me. It was always about her own part. Giulietta is ever the actress, never the writer. She had many different ideas about what the character would be feeling and how she should be acting. She had many criticisms pertaining to the character of Juliet, and I think they made me stubborn in defense of my creation. I wanted to protect *my* concept of character. She wanted to protect *her* character. I believe now that she was right in much of what she said, and I think I should have listened more to her.

Juliet of the title is an example of the Italian woman who, because of her religious education and what she has been taught about the institution of marriage, believes that getting married brings happiness. Whenever she finds it's not true, she can't understand or face it. She escapes into her private world of memory and myth. Such a woman, when her husband betrays her, is left with the reality that the television set is her company in life.

This is where Giulietta and I disagreed in our interpretation of her character's future. I had asked her, because of my respect for her ability to delineate a character, for advice; but at the point where Juliet's husband leaves her, we completely differed. Though I stubbornly adhered to my way, with the passage of time I've come to think she was more right than I was. Maybe I sensed something of that at the time. Though she tried not to show any discontent on the set, some of her attitude did seep through even there. She had never before so determinedly differed with me.

I believed, and still do to some extent, that when Juliet's husband left her, the world was opened up to her. She had been given her freedom to find herself. She could now develop on her own—her interior life as well as her exterior life.

Giulietta differed. "What could Juliet do at that point in her life?" she asked me. "It's too late. It's different for women than it is for men." Juliet, in the opinion of Giulietta, was not on her way to finding herself, but to being lost. She said I was imposing the thoughts, values, ideas, and ideals of a male on a female character. She complained not in front of the others, but at home, all the while we were doing the film. Then, when it was all over, and the picture wasn't especially successful, she never complained. She never once said, "I told you so."

Giulietta, the actress, also wanted to be more glamorous. As the character developed, Juliet, the character, had her own life and had to go her own way. I had done the drawing of the character, who really came to life through those little pictures; so in a way, I had created not only her look from the Juliet I saw in my mind's eye, but her very being.

I drew her clothes, appropriate to revealing the betrayed little wife who was wearing them. On paper, Giulietta seemed to find the clothes acceptable. Then, when the clothes were made, she decided they were unbecoming. "Becoming" was not the point. My drawings are always funny little caricatures, never meant to be becoming. I endeavor to draw what I see inside as well as what I see outside. What was important was, Did the clothes help the audience to perceive the character, and did they help Giulietta to better feel her role?

She said no, the clothes did not help her perform. Personally, I think the problem really came from her seeing the rushes and not seeing herself as glamorous, not being happy about the way she looked. The younger an actress is, the more desperate she is to play a hundred-year-old woman. When she herself is in middle age, she hopes to look younger.

Part of being pretty for a woman is to feel pretty. When she feels pretty, she looks prettier to herself and to men. It's a man's responsibility to help a woman to feel pretty.

When we were making *Juliet of the Spirits,* I told Sandra Milo, "You must believe in your own prettiness. You have to stand in front of a mirror, full-length, all alone, preferably naked, and say to yourself out loud, 'I am pretty. I am the prettiest woman in the world.' " She was rather put out because, after that, I told her she would have to have her eyebrows removed. I'd assured her they would grow back, more beautiful than ever, but she wasn't happy. She said she would look like a monster. Still, she did what I asked. Fortunately, her eyebrows did grow back.

All my life I am pursued by an angel-like presence shaking her finger at me. I know her. She is the angel of my childhood. She is my guardian angel, always somewhere around. I could not imagine having a guardian angel who was not a woman. This one has never been pleased with me, like all of the other women in my life. Frequently, she has appeared to me as a presence shaking her finger at me as if to say I am not living up to her ideals. I have never quite seen her face . . .

One of the most important things a film director must be is author-itative, and it was something I could never imagine being. When I was a young man, I felt shy, and I could not envision myself speaking with power and authority to anyone, especially to a beautiful woman. Now I am still shy, but not when I am the director.

I was always shy with women. I didn't want a woman who had great lovers and who would be comparing me to all of them, even just in her mind. I was not a competitor in bed. I like shy women, except it is awkward when two shy people get together.

Sometimes I may say to one of the women on my set, "Did you make love last night?" Embarrassed, she will usually answer no—maybe even if she did. And I will say something like, "Then it was a wasted night."

If one of them is bold and says yes, then I may say, "Good. And how was your orgasm?"

Women were always throwing themselves at Marcello. I told him, "You are lucky."

He said to me, "They throw themselves at you, but you don't catch them. You don't even see it, and you let them fall down."

I like innocence in a woman. I like the innocence in myself, and that part of me responds openly when I sense no need to be guarded. I like innocence in anyone who has it.

I've always been rather afraid of women. It has been said that I frequently put them down in my films. Far from it. I raise them to the heights of goddesses from which they sometimes put themselves down. They fall off their pedestals. I do this because I still have my vision of them from the vantage point of a pre-puberty or slightly post-puberty boy. Someone wrote that I see them "in an adolescent way." That is not true. I totally deny it. In my understanding of women and my relations with women, I never got far enough along to be called adolescent. I exalt them.

Man frequently invests woman with the essence of being almost a divinity, because if he doesn't, his relentless pursuit of her makes him a fool, even in his own eyes. Women are infinitely more complex than men, just as sex is so much more complex for them. I am always showing what simple beings men are. But men never seem to take offense at my characterization of them. Women are so much more sensitive. They often complain about the way I show them in my films.

After almost fifty years of marriage to Giulietta, I've never felt I quite understood her. I always believe I understand her as an actress, as my working partner. I can predict what she will think and do. I can fathom even her pout, her sulk, her tantrum. I can manipulate her performance, for good or for bad. In the interest of what I, as director, determine is best for the film, I can overcome any resistance I feel in her toward the interpretation of the character. Or better yet, I can learn, as a writer and a director, from her as an actress, and I can adjust the character I have conceived to her portrayal. She thinks I do it to please her or sometimes to pacify her. I do it only when she is right, which is not always, but often. She is a professional, but even more important, she has wondrous innocent intuition. She can still allow her emotions to rule, and when the source deep within her is touched, she draws on a wellspring which touches all of us. No one could just write that part on paper.

As a man with a woman, I feel sometimes like putty in her hands. In our home, Giulietta can easily direct me. She is almost as unpredictable and mysterious for me as she was the day I met her.

A nude Sandra Milo slides down to her indoor swimming pool in *Juliet of the Spirits* (1965).

The man who likes women remains young. And the man who remains young likes women. Both are true. The liking keeps you young. It's the same as with youth. The old who have the possibility of being with the young remain younger—they get a transfusion. But it's rather vampirizing for the young.

King Vidor told me that he envied director George Cukor, who, being a homosexual, never found himself overwhelmed by sexual attraction to his leading ladies. He could remain cool and in command. Vidor was so personally affected by the attraction he felt for many of his actresses that he had to fight his own male instinct in order not to permit it to distract him from his work; and also not to lead him to succumb to the actresses' seductive devices employed to get him to give them what they wanted—often something against the best interests of the film, sometimes even against their own best interests.

I found myself so engrossed in my work that, for the most part, I could be almost oblivious to the near nudity of some of my actresses. Almost.

I would have liked to meet Mae West. I admired her enormously. She was wonderful. She always seemed to be anti-sex because she made a joke of sex and made you laugh, and that is anti-erotic. I think work was really her sex. It seems to me that her career was everything, and that she cared so much about "I," she probably had no time for sex. A person cannot do everything in life. If a woman chooses to have sex in her life, she must spend her time in that, with *la toilette,* making herself attractive. If she chooses the career, the investment of time and energy is there. Personally, I have always been attracted by women who didn't seem to spend a great deal of time and effort on their looks.

I wrote Mae West a letter once when I was going to be in the United States, telling her I wanted to meet her. I rewrote the letter several times, but then I never mailed it. So it was no surprise when she didn't answer. It's difficult to know what to say to someone who has been a part of your life, but who doesn't know you exist. Writing to her, I felt like I was still the little boy in the movie theater in Rimini. She looked so big on the screen, but I heard that she was really very tiny, wearing extremely high-heeled platform shoes. It would have been strange for me to be standing with her, looking down at her. So much of life is illusion. I wonder if she really had a mirror on the ceiling over her bed . . . ?

I wanted to offer her a part in one of my films. I would have written a part especially for her. I would have written a *film* especially for her!

I have always been moved by the beautiful sight of a woman who loves to eat. Sexually moved. For me, there is a close correlation between the woman who loves to eat and the woman who loves sex. For a man, a woman who loves sex is exciting. Maybe it's why I have had so much interest in fat women. The dieting woman who rations food will be, it seems to me, abstemious and stingy in all things. The woman who truly enjoys eating cannot pretend.

Sometimes you have to warm up your imagination, the way an athlete warms up muscles he hasn't been using when he suddenly wants to call on them to be at their best. It's like doing mental calisthenics.

I do it by drawing. Drawing helps me to see the world. Of necessity, it heightens one's powers of observation, especially when you know that you will be reproducing something you have seen when you no longer have the subject present. Drawing releases my imagination.

I've heard that Henry Moore believed he saw more, observed more when he was drawing. My drawings are like that for me. That's not to say I think I'm a Henry Moore, but I can develop a character by drawing that character. The drawing is my first key step. Finding the actor to fit the drawing is more difficult. I look until I find someone who makes me think, "You, *you* are my drawing!" This is probably true for every part, except Giulietta's. I have such a firm grasp on her character that if she ever gets out of character—rather, out of the character I have imagined for her—I get angry at her. I never get angry at any other actor in that same way.

Film is an art. I speak with no condescension and with certainty. Cinema is equal to any of the arts. It *is* one of them. For me, it is not like literature, but like painting, because it is made of pictures that move.

I believe that for many directors the spoken word is more important than the picture, and they are literary directors. For me, the film is the child of painting.

The painter translates *his* vision for the rest of us. It is a look at someone's personal reality, and this is what I consider absolute reality, which can be the truest reality. This translation of my vision is what I try to do on the screen, which is *my* canvas. I admire Van Gogh. The wheat field with the black sun is his because only he saw it. Now it is ours because he made it possible for all of us to see it.

I make a film only for myself, like a painter. I don't know how to do anything else. Then I have to hope that people want my vision, but it's an expensive vision. I have used the producers' money to pay for the film, and the one who takes the money from the other must prove he is not a thief.

Sometimes I have envied the painter. When Balthus came to visit me, he said he envied me, making art that moved. But I envied him because he could work every day of his life. He needed only paint and canvas and some soup.

When people show me drawings I've done over the years, often I don't remember having done them, although I can always recognize my work. I know I did it, even if I don't remember doing it. The difference is usually in whether it's something on which I worked very deliberately, with purpose, or just one of my warm-up jottings.

Sometimes when I am casting, or in pre-production, or writing, my hand seems to draw without me. In those moments, I am most likely to do enormous female breasts. My second most frequent doodle is excessively large women's behinds. Tits and asses. In my sketchbooks, most of the women I draw look like they are bursting out of their clothes—if they are wearing any.

I don't know what a psychiatrist would say about this, but I am certain he would have something to say, because they always do on everything, especially about sex. I do not believe there is anything deep in my interest, just the obvious one. I became aware of women at an extremely early age, well before I could talk, and I was curious about their difference from me.

I enjoyed the images of women's bodies even before I had the words in mind to describe what I was seeing. Little boys have the advantage of seeing female nudity in their formative period because some women tend to equate inability to verbalize with inability to see and inability to have sexual feelings. After that, there is a time when it's difficult to catch even a glimpse of a naked female body.

Whenever I could get out alone with my friends, we would go to the beach and see the summer people, the blond German and Scandinavian women who had come for the sun. One could see quite a lot right there on the beach, but the best was if one could look through a space in the boards of one of the cabanas used for changing . . .

I believe there is more to life than we yet know or will ever know. The religious; the mystical, the psychic, the miraculous; fate, destiny, coincidence. The land called the Unknown. I know I have been laughed at and ridiculed sometimes for my openness to everything from A to Z, astrology to Zen, from Jung to Ouija boards and crystal balls, but the promise of marvels fascinates me. I am not stopped by snickerers or scoffers. Let them live planted in the mundane, those who believe everything has to have a pragmatic scientific explanation. I don't wish to know people who can't say, "Imagine that!" in response to some awe-inspiring, unexplained phenomenon. Wishful thinking is the most important kind of thinking. The advances of man are made in the belief as to where he can go without regard to what is already known.

When I was preparing *Juliet of the Spirits,* I seized the opportunity to go to séances, to visit mediums, to consult tarot card readers. Some of the tarot cards were so beautiful. I collected a few. I could tell people I was doing research. So it seems whatever I may say to the contrary, I do care what people think. I needed to make some study of the subject of psychic phenomena, but it was also an excuse to devote time to something I had always wanted to do. My research was thus more thorough, and it did not stop when the film was completed. It was an interest in witches, sorcerers, magic that began when I was a child in Rimini and has persisted all through my life.

I believe that there are people who are "sensitives," who can perceive and even communicate with dimensions beyond our known senses. I'm not one, I don't think, although when I was a child, I had some remarkable experiences or fantasies. At night, just before I fell asleep, I could turn my bedroom upside down in my mind, just as Little Nemo did in the comic strip, so that I had to hold on to the mattress for fear of falling down to the ceiling. Or I could make the room seem to spin as if the house were in a tornado. I worried that once I'd imagined these things, they wouldn't stop, but still I couldn't resist the excitement of trying again.

I've never told this to anyone. I was afraid I would be thought crazy. As a boy in Rimini and Gambettola, I had seen what happened to children who didn't have all their wits, and I didn't want to be shut away somewhere. I was afraid to ask other children if they had similar experiences. Children can be crueler than adults. I wouldn't like it if one of them noticed the Emperor Fellini has no clothes.

Because one encounters fakes doesn't mean there isn't reality in unreality. It's like not being able to believe in your religion because you know a priest or nun who is unworthy of your respect. My involvement with the inexplicable unknown was an exploration I had to make, not because I believed I would find answers. I was looking for questions. What is exciting in life is what cannot be explained.

A film I would like to make would be based on the autobiography of Benvenuto Cellini. Not only was he a fabulous character, but he experienced a miraculous supernatural encounter in which he saw frightening spectral visions in the Coliseum, conjured up by a mystic at night. What a wonderful scene this could be in a film! It would be even more convincing because Cellini was a skeptic until this happened to him.

After *Juliet of the Spirits,* I estimated my income, after expenses, at about $15,000 for 1965 tax purposes. I thought I was justified because of the years I had to work to develop projects without earning any money from them. Maybe I hadn't been correct, but the subsequent ruling that I owed almost $200,000 was terribly unfair. It made me seem like a criminal. With the film successes of the past years, I suppose it seemed to the world that I was rich, and to the tax collector in Rome it appeared that I had made a fortune. They confused the opulence, the lavishness of some of my productions with my personal life. In *Juliet of the Spirits,* people thought the house I used as the home of the affluent was *our* home. I tried, but our house did not serve the purpose, and having a house that was so right it wasn't noticed was essential. Rather than accept that I had put everything into owning our house, that I had struggled for years to reach that point, that we had to live for years with Giulietta's aunt, it was easier to assume that it represented only a fraction of my worth. It was speculated in the press that I had millions put away in some numbered account in Switzerland. I was presumed guilty. Unnamed sources can be quoted in the press, making any kind of irresponsible accusation. There is no way to prove you do *not* have accounts in Switzerland. For some reason, there are many people who enjoy your failure. Rumor travels on longer legs than truth.

The taxes are set up to punish those who make all their money in one year and don't make any in other years because in other years they have to prepare what they will do, and then to somehow sell it to the producers of money. It's not a fair system at all for the artist who may in many years have only one good economic year. He may have only one good year in his life. I didn't even know to whom I could protest.

The protests I made were useless. I was punished unfairly, and Giulietta was punished, too. She was so proud of that first apartment of our own, and we were forced to sell the Parioli apartment. We moved to a smaller apartment on Via Margutta. It was a mortifying experience which was shared with the world. Giulietta didn't want to go out. Newspapers and magazines printed the story of Fellini's tax evasion. It was printed in other countries, including America—especially America. I didn't feel like going out of my apartment either, but I had to. I had to work out my next film. Also, I knew I had to go out, right away, and face the bad jokes and the expressions of sympathy or I would never be able to do it. I had to behave like it had reached me only financially and not seem humiliated. To avoid this kind of thing, some famous Italians in the cinema had found it easier just to give up their Italian citizenship and pay no taxes at all in Italy. That was all right; but I could never have done that. Never.

I am Italian. I am a citizen of Rome or I am a man without a country. This was not Italy which persecuted me, but one or a few people who worked in the tax department and resented me, who saw me as a target. Maybe they didn't like my films. They said, "Let's get Fellini!"

Well, they did.

"The Voyage of G. Mastorna" was to be my next project. For a long time, I had hoped I would be able to make the film. It's become famous as a film that never was.

The idea first came to me about 1964 in an airplane as we were about to land. It was winter in New York, and I had a sudden vision of our crashing in snow. Fortunately, it was only that, a vision, and we landed uneventfully.

In late 1965, I wrote to Dino de Laurentiis an outline I had worked out for a new film. The lead character, G. Mastorna, is a cellist. During a flight to a concert performance, the plane on which he is flying has to make an emergency landing in a snowstorm. The plane lands safely near a Gothic cathedral, inspired by the cathedral in Cologne, which Tullio Pinelli once had insisted on showing me. Mastorna goes by train through what looks like a German city—again inspired by Cologne—to a motel. There is a cabaret in the motel, with odd acts and a Gothic festival in the street. Mastorna feels lost in the crowd. He can't read the street signs because they are all in strange languages. He finds the railway station, but either the trains have grown or he has shrunk, because the trains are the size of office buildings. Then, Mastorna sees a friend, and he is, for a few seconds, happy. But he remembers that the friend he has just seen alive had died a few years before. It comes to him that perhaps the plane crashed after all. Is he himself dead?

When he has to accept that he has died, Mastorna does not feel terrible, as he thought he would. Everything is resolved. There is no more struggle. No more agony or tension or dilemma. He feels a kind of relief. The worst is over, and it wasn't so bad.

Mastorna explores alternate universes, such as those in science fiction stories. He is able not only to see his parents and his grandmother again, but he meets the grandfather he never knew, and his great-grandparents, who died long before he was born. He likes them very much.

He also visits, invisibly, his wife, Luisa.

That I give her the same name as Guido's wife in *8½* is not because I'm too lazy to think of another name. It's how I think of the character, so it's more natural, and it's easier.

Luisa is very happy with a new man. She seems to have totally gotten over her loss of Mastorna. She and the new man are in bed together. Mastorna is not shocked by that. He does not mind at all. But he is shocked by his own not minding.

An important factor in the film's never being made was my own sickness in 1966. Perhaps I got sick because I was afraid of the task, or felt I wasn't up to it. Sets had been built, people had been hired, money had been spent, but I was unable to proceed. I suffered from an acute neurasthenia, aggravated not only by my own need to exceed what I had done before, but also by the usual, always debilitating, arguments with producers. I considered the possibility that the film itself was killing me because it didn't want to get made. Whatever caused it, I found myself in a hospital room in early 1967, convinced I was deathly ill.

It began in our apartment on the Margutta. I was alone. Giulietta had gone out. I remember feeling so sick that I put a note on the door for her, warning her not to enter. I was, despite my desperate misery, rational enough to keep my head and think of Giulietta and how horrified, frightened, sad she would be, how terrible it would be for her, if she were the one, all alone, who discovered my body. There were many things I had not been able to spare her, but this was something I could save her from. I imagined her grief-stricken horror at finding my dead body. It could be an image from which she would never recover. I've always thought of Giulietta as like a little sparrow: fragile, not at all prepared for the hardships of this world—and yet, in many ways, strong, a survivor of the winter.

In the hospital I truly believed I was dying. I had severe pains in my chest—and worse, I had lost all my dreams and fantasies. One is left only with the terror of reality.

I tried to call upon imagination to transport me to another, more congenial locale, but the reality was too strong, and my own fear, from which I wished to escape, imprisoned me with its all-encompassing grip on my mind. I knew I was not ready to die. I had so many films left to make. I tried fitfully to make one in my mind. Even in the best of moments, I had never been able to visualize the whole of one of my films as it would eventually be before I began shooting. This time, I could not even create a part of my film. I was unable to entertain even myself. Thus deprived of my refuge, my sanctuary of waking dreams, I felt naked, vulnerable, alone. When I began receiving sentimental letters, even visits, from people who had been angry at me when I was in good health, I became even more certain that the end had come.

Being in a hospital reduces you to the status of being a thing, not for yourself, of course, but for the others. They talk about you in the third person, referring to you as "he" while they're in your presence.

When you are sick, no matter how many people visit, no matter how many people take care of you, you are alone. It is this kind of moment when you are forced to discover whether you are good company or not.

The endlessly repetitive nature of the days is excruciating, yet boredom is what you hope for, and that another boring day will be yours.
Too much drama is what you fear. Your mind is obsessed with
thoughts of death—yours, not a character in one of your films, and you
cannot get control of your own thoughts. You are the victim of your
own mind, and no one can torture us as we can torture ourselves.

The depersonalization of illness is the most terrible thing. The
healthy don't know what to do in the presence of illness. They bring
biscuits and fruit. They send flowers, enough flowers to fill the room,
so you cannot breathe. And who will water all those flowers?

When I was in the hospital, they brought balloons to a man who
had had a massive heart attack. The image has stayed in my mind. He
was lying there, and one was not certain if he was wondering why
they brought the balloons, or even if he knew they had brought them.
It's because they didn't know what to do, and felt the need to do
something. And they met a balloon seller.

When you arrive in that world between dreams and reality, to
which you have been transported not by jet but by injection, in that
state the nuns ministering to you seem like black apparitions in the
night, more like assassins or bats, coming for your blood at worst,
your urine sample at best. I imagined giving a urine sample to be
dragged away in gallon containers by teams of workmen. One's world
becomes simplified and one's horizon narrows. The great world out
there becomes of little importance as compared to the walls of your
tiny room. Your interests become fewer in your shriveling world.
Suddenly you are the excuse for a great social occasion as your
acquaintances, with their forced and uneasy cheer, gather to catch the
last glimpse of you. In their eyes, you are suddenly free of all wrong-
doing. The perishable fruit for which you have no appetite comes
unceasingly and spoils as the flowers wilt and die. In the face of the
dying flowers, you see your own future.

Then I saw in my mind a fleeting parade of the films I had wanted
to make but hadn't gotten around to. In my mind, they were born
suddenly complete, without struggle. They seemed perfect, better
than anything I had ever done—babies as yet unborn, waiting to be
conceived and have their life. Everything was of vast, epic proportions
and the most splendid colors. It was like dreams you have that you
feel lasted hours, but they were really only a few minutes long.

I knew that if only I recovered I would do everything I had ever intended to do, and more. But as soon as I recovered, I allowed all the mundane matters of living to intrude.

After you have been in a hospital with a serious illness, or in a crisis situation, you are never quite the same again. You have been forced to confront your mortality. You are both more afraid of death, and less afraid, but you are changed. Life has more value, but you have lost the spirit of carefree. Extreme illness from which you recover really does take away some of the fear of death, because death represents the fearful unknown. When you have been that close, death is no longer a total stranger.

One thing a brush with death showed me was how much I wanted to live.

twelve

COMIC STRIPS, CLOWNS, AND CLASSICS

Limitations can be exceedingly useful. For example, the limitation of not having everything brings out ingenuity and imagination, which tap the resources of you as a person, rather than you as a budget director. I have never envied the resources of the Americans, because whatever we didn't have was what stimulated our ingenuity.

I remember in this respect the puppet theater I was given as a boy. It seemed to me the most incredible gift in the world, the most wonderful puppet theater. Of course, it could have been a more expensive one. It might have come complete—with a set of wonderful costumed puppets—and I could have stopped there, just making up stories that fit those characters. Instead, I had to make my own costumes, leaving me the freedom to create those characters that suited the fantasies of my own imaginings. When I learned how to make these puppet costumes, I also learned that I had some small artistic gift. I didn't have enough puppets to act out the stories I had for them, so I learned how to make more puppets. From the puppet faces, I realized the importance of faces, which I later incorporated into my films.

My puppets and I inhabited a special and total world together, which was only ours and of which the only limits were those of imagination.

Part of my world of imagination came from reading. I loved the popular comic strips of my youth, *Bringing Up Father* and good old *Felix the Cat,* but I read books, too. A favorite of mine was the *Satyricon* by Titus Petronius, a nobleman of the time of Nero. It has only come down to us in fragments. Some of the stories have no endings, some no beginnings. Some have neither, only a middle, but all of this only intrigued me more. I was even more fascinated by what wasn't there than by what was there. Stimulated by the fragments, my imagination could roam.

I contemplate the image of our own descendants in the year 4000 coming upon a hidden vault which contains a long-lost twentieth-century film and the facilities for screening it. "What a pity," an archaeologist laments, upon viewing something called *Fellini Satyricon.* "It seems to be missing its beginning, middle, and end. It is so strange. What kind of man could this Fellini have been? Perhaps he was mad."

When you choose a subject like Petronius' *Satyricon* for a film, it's like doing science fiction. Instead of projecting into the future, it projects into the past. The time that far back is almost as strange to us as is the unknown future.

There was a great advantage for me in making historical films or fables relating solely to imagination. It allowed me to explore the realm of fantasy without being bound by the present and having to adhere to the rules of the present. Portrayal of action in the present day prevents one from transforming the atmosphere, the setting, the costumes, the mannerisms, as well as the faces of the actors. I am interested in plot structure and reality only as they serve imagination. But reality, or rather the illusion of reality, is necessary even in the imagination, or the viewer cannot sympathize or empathize.

In *Satyricon,* I show a time so remote from our own that we can't even imagine it. Though it's our heritage, it's impossible to know what life was really like in ancient Rome. As a boy, I used to fill in the missing pieces of the *Satyricon* with my own stories. When I was in the hospital, I returned to reading Petronius, which offered escape from my drab and depressing surroundings, and I speculated more. I was like an archaeologist piecing together fragments of ancient vases, trying to guess what the missing parts looked like. Rome itself is an ancient broken vase, constantly being mended to hold it together, but retaining hints of its original secrets. It thrills me to think about the layers of my city and what may be buried under my footsteps.

Petronius wrote about the people of his time in terms we can understand now, and I wanted to replace those pieces of his mosaic that had fallen out and been lost. What wasn't there appealed to me most because it created the opportunity for me to fill it in using my imagination, and I could actually become a part of the story. It enabled me to go there and to live in that time. It was like speculating about life on Mars, but with the help of a Martian, so *Satyricon* satisfied in me some of my desire to make a science-fiction film. It also made me even more anxious to one day do one.

With the section that has come down to us almost intact, "Trimalchio's Feast," I believed that I would be held to a more literal standard. Scholars all over the world would be comparing Fellini with Petronius. Being too imaginative can be a greater fault in the eyes of critics than being too prosaic. I can work only to please myself and share my dreams, so I have to shut out the critics, as best I can.

Many of the situations in *Satyricon* are analogous to the present. The tenement that collapses is not so different from the tenement in *A Matrimonial Agency,* and the protagonists are not so different from those in *I Vitelloni*—young men trying to prolong their adolescence indefinitely, whose families are willing and able to indulge them in this. These boys don't want to grow up and be forced to accept the responsibilities of adulthood. Sometimes parents don't want to lose their children, and so they continue to support them like children. Grown children mean their parents have grown older, too.

Because of the picture's open, nonjudgmental portrayal of homosexuality, some journalists seized upon the tempting notion that I must myself be a homosexual or at least a bisexual, just as in *La Dolce Vita* they were quick to assume I must actually be living that jet-set life. Anyone who knew me then knows I did not live in the world of celebrities and the rich, and the Via Veneto was not my street. Indeed, I chose to have it reconstructed at great cost in Cinecittà rather than attempt to control it for a film. An occasional coffee at Doney's, by the Excelsior Hotel, does not constitute a sellout of integrity, as some implied. It was essential for purposes of observation. Even fantasy has to be drawn from real-life observation. You don't have *be* something to imagine the characters. If I write about a blind man, I don't have to be blind to portray him. I would need only to close my eyes to feel lost and helpless. If I want to portray a lunatic, as in *Voices of the Moon,* I don't have to be mad—although in my profession it might be an advantage, and some also have suggested that I am that, too.

Life at the time of *Satyricon* is unimaginable for us. Surgery without anesthesia. There was no penicillin, there were no antibiotics. Twenty-seven years was considered optimum as a life span. Now we believe at that age we have barely begun to live. What is now youth was then middle age, even old age. Superstition was as authoritative as was primitive medical science. The belches of Trimalchio after his feast are taken seriously as prognostications. We can look back at that time from our lofty pinnacle of hindsight, but perhaps we also have our belch interpreters.

The vulgarity of Trimalchio's funeral rehearsal is not so different from what could happen today. And what of sex? People say that we're going too far these days in our treatment of sex in films. But look at Aristophanes in the fifth century B.C. The actors wore false pricks that hung down to their feet and dragged along the ground as part of their costumes, and the practice continued into the Roman era. I thought it was very funny, though I was certain it would be shocking to many people if I used it, and that once again my mother wouldn't be able to face her friends in Rimini.

Petronius himself appears in *Satyricon.* He is the wealthy freedman who commits suicide with his wife after he has freed his slaves. The actress who plays his wife is Lucia Bosé, the beautiful star of Antonioni's early films. When I first saw her in those pictures, I fell madly in love with her, as did, I understand, many other males. She deserted us for the Spanish bullfighter Luis-Miguel Dominguin. It was a great mistake, because her career ended, and some years later, she and the bullfighter separated.

The beautiful widow is a sequence I considered leaving out. She is so inconsolable in her mourning for her dead husband that she wants to die there with him. Then, given the chance to live on with a new lover, she succumbs to the young Roman soldier, allowing herself to be seduced beside the bier of her husband. We realize she wasn't really in mourning for her husband, but for herself. When she offers the body of her dead husband in exchange for the life of her new lover, she goes from being the extreme romantic to being the extreme pragmatist. This is natural, because the extreme person is extreme in everything.

In *Satyricon,* I was influenced by the look of the frescoes. At the end, these people, whose lives once were so real to them, are now only crumbling frescoes.

I am not so interested in the history of man as I am in the history of man's imagination. I would describe myself as a storyteller. Simply stated, I love to invent stories. From the caves to Titus Petronius to the troubadours to Charles Perrault and Hans Christian Andersen, I would like to be in this tradition with films that are neither fiction nor nonfiction, but approximate autobiography, archetypal tales of heightened life, told with some inspiration. This is what I try to do. Sometimes I fail, sometimes I succeed, but I rarely want to see my finished film because I don't think I can ever put what I feel totally on a screen. If what I were to see disappointed me too much, perhaps it would inhibit my trying again with my whole heart, and only what one can do with a whole heart is worth doing.

Becoming a director and making the *The Clowns* was my opportunity to live vicariously.

I have always been attracted to comedy, but I don't know why we laugh. I used to think about it. I theorized that laughter was a release of tensions built up in us by a repressive and illogical social system. Then I saw a chimpanzee laughing in the zoo. I think he was laughing at my theory. Apparently monkeys have a very good sense of humor.

Now I'm inclined to think we sometimes laugh for the wrong reasons. Some of our humor is a little sadistic. The most I've ever heard an audience laughing was at the end of a Laurel and Hardy picture. It had a medieval setting, and the two were taken to a torture chamber. The fat one was put on a rack and the thin one in a press, and the torture began. When they were finally released, they were reversed— Laurel was now short and fat, Hardy tall and thin. The thin one had been squashed and the fat one stretched, and they walked away pathetically deformed as the picture ended.

It was so sad and pitiful. Laurel and Hardy were so well-meaning and innocent, yet this terrible thing had happened to them. I can still hear in my mind the laughter in the Fulgor Cinema, but I was puzzled. It didn't seem funny to me. I was worried about them. The next time I saw them on the screen, I was relieved to see that they were all right.

Why was the audience laughing so hard? Was it because it had happened to Laurel and Hardy and not to them? I will have to ask that chimpanzee.

When I was a boy, I believed being a clown was one of the ideal existences to which anyone might aspire. I knew it was something for which I could never hope because I was too shy.

I was shy inside, but it didn't show for other people. I suppose my self-consciousness was really being overly self-aware, which is a kind of egotism. I attributed it to a lack of self-confidence, particularly about my appearance. The strangest part about it is that I realized only very much later that generally people had found me an attractive person. It's too bad I didn't understand it then. I could have enjoyed it. I'm never shy when I'm a director, but in the rest of my life I have always felt as if I have a pimple on my nose.

When I approached making *The Clowns,* I wondered, Could clowns still make people laugh? Had people changed? I remember people laughing at simpler things in my childhood. Many things we laughed at, like the village idiots, would not be proper objects of ridicule today, while other things we took quite seriously now seem hilarious. One dared not laugh at the fascist officer who proudly wore an overcoat so big it dragged along the ground, as depicted in *The Clowns.*

You never clearly see the face of the child in *The Clowns* because the child is inside me. I was totally inspired by Little Nemo. The child's point of view is like that of Little Nemo, and while we were shooting, I kept a Winsor McCay book by the side of my bed. When I studied Latin in school, I was surprised to learn that "Nemo" means "No One."

Among the old clowns I interviewed for *The Clowns,* I found that some were happy remembering what they had been able to do, while others were unhappy remembering what they had lost.

When the clown escapes from the old people's home, he is a character I identify with very much. He died laughing. I would choose that. It's a good way to go, to die from laughing too hard at the clowns in a circus.

I was surprised that some clowns didn't like what I did, because they saw what I considered my realism instead as a pessimistic view, predicting the decline both of the circus and the clown. They were right, except that I wasn't predicting it. I believed it had already happened. I, who was the most sympathetic person in the world to the circus and to the clown! It shows that in life you never know what reaction you will elicit in someone else.

In *Roma,* I wanted to get across the idea that underneath Rome today is ancient Rome. So close. I am always conscious of that, and it thrills me. Imagine being in a traffic jam at the Coliseum! Rome is the most wonderful movie set in the world.

Any kind of **digging** in Rome is likely to turn into an archaeological excavation. Tunneling for the subway, they actually did come across relics of the past that held up construction while archaeologists tried to preserve what they could. Of course, nothing as perfectly preserved as the household unearthed in *Roma* was ever found. As was the case with many of my film ideas, it was inspired by a dream.

I dreamed I was imprisoned in an oubliette deep under Rome. I heard unearthly voices coming through the walls. They said, "We are the ancient Romans. We are still here."

When I awoke, I remembered a Hollywood movie I'd seen as a boy, *She,* from the book by H. Rider Haggard. I was so impressed by it, I read the novel. I speculated on the possibility that somewhere under Rome a similar preservation had taken place, perhaps a family's domestic chambers in perfect condition because they had been hermetically sealed for centuries. Even the best-preserved of archaeological discoveries look so remote from us that it's not easy to imagine how it must have seemed to the people of those times. It's difficult enough for me to put myself into the turn-of-the-century Rome my mother knew.

I envisioned walking into a perfectly preserved Roman apartment of the first century A.D., just as if I were one of its original inhabitants. The trouble is, as soon as I opened the hermetically sealed chambers, the delayed erosion of centuries would commence before my despairing eyes. Statues and frescoes would crumble to dust in a compressed two-thousand-year minute.

Rome's subway seemed the perfect setting. It's not only the most likely place, but also mysterious and forbidding.

The live variety theater scene in *Roma* illustrates my belief that the audience is often more interesting than the show. The whole world is right there in the theater. That is the way of theater. It takes you so completely that when you leave the theater, it seems you are going out into a strange world, and it's the outside which isn't real.

In the World War II sequences of *Roma,* people believe Rome will never be bombed just as Rome at that moment *is* being bombed. Their belief has little to do with reality.

Near the end of the film, there is a scene where a woman is running off in the background. In my mind, I imagine her rushing for help because her children are in a building that has just been bombed and is burning. The men who were standing around and didn't seem heroic run to help her. They hadn't appeared to be the sort who lived useful, productive lives. They were more accustomed to hanging about heckling and being minor bullies, with no veneer of sophistication and showing no promise for the future. Then, suddenly, when there is an emergency, they risk their lives to run into a burning building to save children. Without a second's thought, that's what my characters would do. They act spontaneously, without hesitation, as a reflex, doing it as naturally as they stood on the street corners ogling the young women. They didn't seem heroic until there was a situation that called for heroism. A hero cannot be a hero without the right moment. He doesn't know himself what it is that he will do. He only hopes.

Meanwhile in the foreground, the characters in this moment of crisis have not forgotten about sex. Emerging from the bomb shelter early in the morning, the character who represents the young Fellini is invited to the home of the lonely German singer whose husband is on the Russian front. Under the circumstances, it seems almost innocent, like children playing adult games they don't understand.

When I was directing *Roma,* I asked Anna Magnani if she would like to make a vignette appearance. I knew she was very sick, but I also knew she loved to work. "Who is going to play opposite me?" she asked.

"Your part is only going to be about a minute long," I explained.

"Who is going to play opposite me?" she repeated. "I never accept a part without knowing that."

"I am," I replied, thinking quickly. I assumed her silence was assent, since she was never silent if she disagreed.

At the end of the film, we have a nocturnal encounter outside her front door. Magnani was a creature of the night who slept half the day and prowled half the night. She was a kindred spirit to the hungry Roman stray cats she would feed in the early hours, just before dawn. Off camera, I made a little fun of myself.

"May I ask you a question?" I say, concluding my lines, and she says, "Ciao, go to sleep," and then goes inside.

The "Ciao" she speaks to me is the last line she ever spoke on the screen. She died just after that.

thirteen

THE FRAGILITY OF LIFE

People who live in several towns, cities, countries and have feelings for all of them always have a small piece of themselves in some other place. All of me is in one place, Rome. It could be said that there is something of me in Rimini, but I don't think so. I took Rimini away with me, and now it's the Rimini I remember, a place people who live there now wouldn't recognize if they could look into my mind. *Amarcord* is the look into the world of my memory.

I don't like to go back to Rimini. Whenever I do go back, I am assailed by ghosts. The reality goes to war with the world of my imagination. For me, the real Rimini is the one in my head. I could have gone back there to film for *Amarcord,* but it wasn't what I wanted to do. The Rimini I could re-create was closer to the reality of my memory. What could I have had, if I had made the trip with all of my troupe to the real place? Memory is not exact. I discovered that the life I've told about has become more real for me than the life I really lived.

There was also a pragmatic reason for me not to admit that *Amarcord* was autobiographical. If I did, real people who still lived in Rimini would be recognizing themselves or others in my characters. They would even be recognizing what wasn't true. Often, I exaggerated the characters, emphasizing their foibles, poking some fun at them, tacking on to them characteristics blended from someone else's personality, real or imagined. Then I would create situations in which the characters would be true to their identities as I had created them, but doing things the real people would never have done. I would have been needlessly hurting the feelings of the real people of my childhood, something I never wanted to do.

For the part of Gradisca, who represents for that period an ideal of mature femininity and sensuality, I originally wanted Sandra Milo, but she had decided to retire—it was not the first time. I had persuaded her to return for *8½*, but this time I wasn't successful, so I chose Magali Noël.

Magali was glad to be working with me again. She is one of the most cooperative actresses I have ever known. She would do anything I asked. Anything. For a scene that was later cut, I asked her to bare her chest, which she did without hesitation.

I had to cut her favorite scene as Gradisca, and I'm not sure she has ever forgiven me. I hope she has. The scene is in front of the local cinema at night with the camera moving in slowly until it reaches Gradisca standing beside a poster of Gary Cooper. She is gazing up worshipfully at her hero as she files her nails. He was a man any woman would love. I had to cut the scene. It would have made Gradisca the central character, and this was not a picture about Gradisca.

When I asked Magali if she liked the picture, she bit her lip and bravely tried to smile, but her eyes were still red from crying.

Over the years, from time to time, I had wondered about the real Gradisca and her fate. I remembered that look on her face, all glowing, the day she left Rimini with her new husband for her new life. She was so happy to finally have caught someone.

One day, driving through Italy, I recognized the name of the place someone had told me Gradisca had gone to live. I couldn't remember her husband's name, so I didn't think I had much chance to find her, but the temptation was too great.

I saw an old woman hanging out the wash. I got out of my car and told her I was looking for Gradisca.

The woman looked at me in a funny way and in a suspicious tone asked, "Why?"

Gradisca (Magali Noël) passes the local cinema in *Amarcord* (1973). Fellini said he was influenced throughout his life by Hollywood posters, such as the ones shown here of Gary Cooper.

I said, "I'm looking for her because I was a friend of Gradisca's."

"I am Gradisca," said the old woman.

When I returned to Rimini in 1945, after World War II, it was terrible. Houses I had lived in were gone. Rimini had been bombed many times. I felt rage. I also felt a little ashamed that I had lived so apart from the war and was so little touched by it.

Rimini has grown. It was rebuilt after the bombing, but differently. The medieval could not be put back. It is more like an American city. The rebuilding began with U.S. aid, but the Americans are not responsible for the bad pizza. Rimini has changed without my permission.

When the Oriental potentate arrives at the Grand Hotel in *Amarcord,* he is short and very fat. His fatness indicates that he is prosperous and successful, that he lives well, and that he is comfortable with himself. It's a happy cultural difference. In the part of the world I inhabit, it's a sign of weakness to be fat.

I always feel good in the atmosphere of grand hotels, especially the Grand Hotel in Rome. Perhaps it's because my idea of luxury was born as I looked in from the outside of Rimini's Grand Hotel. When I was a boy, that magnificent habitat of the inconceivably rich seemed unapproachable, surrounded by the barrier of inhibition I had built in my own mind, and confirmed by the doorman who chased me away. He really didn't need to chase me, because I was too timid to enter.

I don't know what the source of my childhood fascination with the Grand Hotel of Rimini was. Maybe it's because I lived in a grand hotel somewhere in an earlier life—perhaps as a mouse. I think it's probably because the atmosphere of beauty is a transfusion, and because such hotels wrap you in total comfort and irresponsibility. The high bed is made for you with cold sheets and warm down comforter, delicious food is served while the used dishes disappear magically, and I am left free to imagine.

I've always liked riding in a car, especially in Rome, whether I was the one driving or not. I like to watch the world moving by, all those images of the city moving by, like films. I find it very stimulating to watch everything in motion as I'm sitting in the car, especially if I'm not driving.

But riding in a car around Rome is not without dangers. Many Italian men choose to prove their masculinity through driving. If that is how they choose to do it, perhaps it is the *only* way they can.

There is so much to see and experience right now in Rome. I no longer feel the need to go anywhere else. In my youth, I had the desire to see more of the world, but the need went away. What I saw satisfied me, even when it disappointed me. My earliest interest in travel had been to see America. I did that many times. Now, the longest trip I wish to make is by car.

At one time, driving was one of my passions. When I learned how, the first time I drove was one of the great sensations of my life. I loved cars. I loved owning one. I enjoyed driving. I believe I was a skillful driver.

As a boy, I looked forward to the day when I would learn to drive, but the possibility of owning a car hardly seemed within my reach. Owning a car was rarer in that time, and I didn't know yet how I was going to earn my way in life. A car was the only possession I ever deeply desired, and as soon as I could have one, I did. I think my first dreams of cars were born at the Fulgor Cinema, and they were of American cars.

It was in an American film I first saw a Duesenberg. It wasn't what I wanted for myself, but I never forgot it. It could pass anything on the road, except a gas station. There were those wonderful open Packard touring cars, and the police and bootleggers in them shooting at each other. I could scarcely believe the Pierce-Arrow really existed, with its headlights built into the fenders. Someone told me you could see a Pierce-Arrow coming, but you couldn't hear it. That seemed remarkable to me when I was a boy. It still does.

I remember Charlie Chaplin riding around in a Rolls-Royce Silver Ghost in *City Lights*. The Model T Ford was a great comedy car. When I think of a Model T, it makes me laugh, because it was in so many comedies. When the Keystone Kops, Laurel and Hardy, and W. C. Fields got into Model T's, you always knew something funny was going to happen. I remember one that was squashed flat between two trams, but no one got hurt, only embarrassed. It wouldn't have been funny if anyone got hurt, but I didn't find it funny because of what happened to that marvelous car.

Mastroianni loved cars, too, and for a while we used to have a friendly competition over who would own the best car. I had a splendid Jaguar. Once I had a Chevrolet convertible. I had an Alfa-Romeo. Each car I owned gave me a thrill. Sometimes I had cars so wonderful that people tipped their hats as I rode by. From time to time, someone would bow, paying tribute to one of my impressive cars. I was especially proud of excelling at driving, perhaps because there were many physical activities at which I wasn't good, including nearly all sports.

When I first began to drive, it was a much more enjoyable experience to drive a car in and around Rome. It was before the terrible traffic jams took over in the streets. What was once a luxury became tedious. There were crazy people driving, so one had to be alert every second, and it was very tense. More and more, one had to go outside of Rome to be able to enjoy driving. I enjoyed driving through Italy, not so much to see the places—though I did enjoy that, too—but to study the people and take notes on customs and dialogue.

One day in the early seventies, I was driving along and something hit my car. I felt the impact before I saw it. A boy on a bicycle had come the wrong way on a one-way street and gone through a light. He rode into my car. Later, witnesses verified that.

I got out of the car. A boy, about thirteen years old, was lying in the street next to his bicycle. My heart stopped beating. It was a terrible, terrible, terrible moment for me.

Fortunately, he got right up. He wasn't hurt. Even his bicycle didn't seem damaged. Well, he was a little shocked, but not as much as I.

Cars had stopped. A small crowd had gathered. The people who had been sitting at the café in front of where the accident took place had left their coffees to get cold so they could come to watch.

Then, I heard it. One of the bystanders said, "Look! That's Fellini. He almost killed that boy."

I wanted to say something, to defend myself. It hadn't been my fault, but sometimes people don't see what really happens, and they think they saw something different. Witnesses see different things. I'd thought once about a story I'd read involving a trial in which all of the witnesses had different truths. At the time, it had seemed a good possible subject for a film. Standing there in the street, that idea no longer seemed entertaining.

My life, past, present, and future, passed before me. I saw Giulietta mortified by the headlines and stories in the newspapers, collapsing in shock and grief. I imagined the most unflattering photographs of myself in the newspapers. They like to use only the worst pictures. Then, people could say, "See how terrible Fellini looks. He must be guilty." It would be easy to find unflattering photos of me. Photographs of me are nearly always unflattering. I have wondered why that is. I suppose it's because that is the way I really look.

I saw myself on trial, in prison. Worse: I thought I might not be able to make films.

The police arrived. The boy said he was fine, and that he had ridden into me. The police looked at my license, talked with me for a few minutes, and then said we could all go.

A German tourist who had witnessed the accident had heard me give my name to the police. Just as I was about to get into my car to leave, he approached me and said he would like to buy my car as a gift for his wife in Germany. If I ever considered selling it, would I contact him? Not only was it a great car, but it was the car of the famous director of *La Dolce Vita*. I said, "Yes, I would consider it. Now."

We made the arrangements right there with the crowd of bystanders looking on. We exchanged cards. I set the price. I did everything but take his check and give him the keys. I wanted to sell him the car right then, that very minute. I was so anxious.

But I thought, What would Giulietta think if I just took a check for all that money from a total stranger?

The car was never more valuable than at that moment. It had ACV, added celebrity value, like VAT, value-added tax. But consistent with being the poor businessman I have always been, I wanted to get rid of the car so badly at that very moment that I asked for an amount much too low. It was as though my handsome car had been to blame, and I asked less than I paid for it, much less than it was worth on the market, as though *it* had done something of which to be ashamed.

It seemed right that the car should go home, to Germany. The next day, the German met me with the money, and I gave him the keys, and I never drove again. I took the event as a sign. I never touched a steering wheel again.

I was a good bicycle rider, so in Fregene, I did that. No one could understand why I never drove again. People said I was superstitious. After a while, they forgot, and it was assumed that I'd never learned to drive. In Rome, there are many more people who have never learned to drive than there are in the United States—people who couldn't afford a car, those who grew up during the war, and some who didn't need to drive in a city like Rome. I think it must be the same in New York, where it is easy to get around without a car and a problem to own and park one. You don't have to watch out for car thieves if you don't have one for them to steal. I realized that it was *riding* in a car that I enjoyed, not driving.

I like having my mind free. As I grow older, my mind wanders more, and I like not having to concentrate on driving. I can live in the world of my imagination, where there are no traffic jams.

Now that I don't drive, I can talk, seated in the back with a friend. If I'm alone, I always ride up front next to the driver. I enjoy taxis. They are my favorite luxury. Taxi drivers are very interesting. I learn a lot from them. They tell me how to make films.

There is always someone around to drive me. If I am caught in the rain, unable to get a taxi, not finding a bus, I go into the middle of the street and look at someone in a car who appears kindly and who makes eye contact with me. Then I pretend to know the person. Once in a while, I do. Often they know me. When the driver stops for me, I pretend I've made a mistake, but first I make certain to introduce myself and say my name clearly. I am almost always given a ride. Sometimes the people go far out of their way, even in the opposite direction from the one in which they are going, to deliver me right to my door. Maybe it's because Romans have tender hearts. I believe it is one of the many benefits of being a film director.

For long trips, I get a car with a driver. In my life since that day of the accident, I have never once had the desire to drive again. That experience changed me. I realized how fragile everything in life is.

PART III

FELLINI

A LEGEND AND
THE SMALL SCREEN

Fame and legend are not the same thing. Fame makes it easier to work, and legend makes it impossible.

Since I first discovered the work that gives my life meaning, the only thing I have wanted to do is work, and being a legend, it seems, is not a help but a handicap to being a working director.

Becoming a legend is a gradual process, like growing old. You don't become a legend in a day or a year, and you don't know when that moment arrives, just as you don't know when you have made your last film, and *they* have retired you.

People talked about the great films of Fellini they had seen in the past, but they were not going to the movies I was making in the present. They talked about Fellini's films, even those who had never seen one. I began to identify with the statues whose toes I used to tickle when I passed them in the street.

A famous director is permitted some less-than-successful efforts. A legend is overanalyzed.

I make a big thing of saying that I do not make message films. Of course, that is not to say that my films are devoid of saying anything. Even *I* receive messages, which my characters reveal to me—not in advance, but as we go.

I learned from Casanova, "Absence of love is the greatest pain."

Donald Sutherland wasn't the stereotype of Casanova. I liked that. I knew I didn't want a Latin-lover type. I had studied portraits of Casanova. I read his writings. I wanted to know, but not to be too much influenced away from my own conception. I gave Donald a fake nose and a false chin, and shaved off half of his hair. He was very good about putting up with the hours of makeup, but when his hair had to be shaved off, he flinched visibly, though he uttered not a word of complaint.

Casanova is a puppet. A real man would have had to have some concern for how the woman felt. He is so engrossed in his own sex act that, really, he is a mechanical man, like the mechanical bird he carries about.

Since my vision of Casanova was as a puppet, it is perfectly natural that he should fall in love with a mechanical doll, his ideal woman. My early influence and experience as a puppetmaster in boyhood is, I think, more apparent in *Casanova* than in any of my other films.

I myself was enchanted to be "at court" with Casanova. I have always wanted to be as much "in" each film as I could be. I've had, through my films, experiences I could never otherwise have had. I was constantly being asked, "Why don't you make another *Dolce Vita*? I did. *Casanova* was *La Dolce Vita* of the 1800s, but no one noticed.

Television has infinite possibilities. The faults are not with the technological creation, but with the people who make the programs and those who watch them. I've seen programs on television I've respected. I was very impressed by the Muppets—wonderful puppets, wonderful characters. They remind me of some of the puppets I made as a boy. They are the successors to the great screen comedians of the past—the Marx Brothers, Mae West, Laurel and Hardy. Miss Piggy is the heir to Mae West, and Kermit to Stan Laurel or Harry Langdon. The Muppets would be nice to work with. I am always looking for faces, and they have unforgettable faces, and they are a sympathetic troupe of players with congeniality. I would have liked to have known them when I had my puppet theater, but the Muppets were not born yet, and they don't even know where Rimini is.

Television offers you the chance to do something you might not have the chance to do on film, and you can do it faster. Sometimes I

Fellini directing Anita Ekberg on the set of *The Temptation of Dr. Antonio*. In the background is a Rome apartment complex specially reconstructed at the Cinecittà studios.

like to direct a program for Italian television because I can do something different and get a more immediate satisfaction. That can be very nourishing. Immediate satisfaction may be better than something bigger that is too slow in coming. It confirms your sense of self-image and strengthens you for the ongoing battles.

It is a different experience for me. When people gather in a theater, there is the sacred aspect of the spectacle. Television comes and gets you in your house, where you are off guard. When your film enters people's houses on the TV set, it is in a position of weakness, having lost respect or reverence. The audience is undressed and eating.

I do not feel exactly the same way about discussing my television films that I feel when asked to talk about my theatrical movies. Being made for the small screen, they do not necessitate a strong viewer decision to leave home to go out and see them. The works for television cannot have the magic of the movie theater. I am proud of them because they represent my best efforts for a medium which is now so important that I feel an obligation to work in it. Television is playing such a role in shaping the way people are thinking that it cannot be ignored. I can't say, however, that the television films I did are an extension of me in the way that my other films are. My films for the theater are my children. My TV films are more like my nieces and nephews.

Orchestra Rehearsal is not just about an orchestra rehearsal, though of course that is what is specifically treated. It represents a situation which is the same for any group that arrives on the scene with a unified purpose, but brings separate identities that must be submerged and merged, such as on an athletic field or in an operating room, or even on a film set. I have carried to this forum some of my experiences as a director.

For the rehearsal, the musicians arrive at the studio not only with their diverse instruments, but also with their individual temperaments, their personal problems, their bad humors, their illnesses, the scolding voices of their wives or mistresses still ringing in their ears, or just the frustration and nervous exhaustion of Rome traffic whirling in their minds. Some of them have brought only their bodies and their instruments, while others have brought their professional pride, and a few have brought their souls.

The various instruments of the orchestra look incompatible, from the tall, awkward double bassoon and the slender, sylphlike flute—who often have to sit next to each other—to the graceful harp, standing alone on the side like a weeping willow tree, or the sinister tuba, coiled in the background like a lethargic reptile, or the womanly cello.

Until it actually happens, I can never believe that this inharmonious mass of people, hardware, and carpentry is going to be fused into the unique abstract essence of music. I was so strongly moved by this creation of harmony out of chaos and discord that it struck me that this situation could apply, metaphorically, to a society where individual expression can be compatible within a group.

I had wanted for a long time to make a little documentary which would express my own feeling of wonderment at this phenomenon and give an audience the comforting impression that it is possible to do something together while retaining one's individuality. The orchestra situation seemed to me to be the perfect setting.

We set to work on it in 1978, when other projects, "The Voyage of G. Mastorna" and *City of Women,* had to be delayed while I engaged in the endless tedium and noncreative work of searching for financial backing.

I admit that my own relationship with music is a purely defensive one. I always seek to protect myself from music. I am not someone who willingly goes to concerts or the opera. If you told me Pavarotti was singing in *Osso Bucco* instead of *Nabucco,* I would probably believe you, though in recent years I must admit that I have come to realize the greatness of Verdi and of the Italian opera.

Since music has the power to condition subliminally, I prefer to avoid it whenever I am not listening consciously, as with my work. Music is too important to be relegated to the status of background noise. If I enter a restaurant or an apartment where recorded music is being played, as politely as I can, I request that it be turned off, much as I

Marcello Mastroianni, Giulietta Massina, and Fellini in 1962, on the set of *8½*

would ask someone to please stop smoking in close quarters. I resent being a captive listener, a captive inhaler, a captive anything. I don't understand how people can eat, drink, talk, drive, read, even make love while listening to music. Imagine having to chew faster to keep up with the beat. And the situation is getting ever worse. Unwanted music is becoming as pervasive as pollution. In New York, I heard music on the telephone, music in the elevators, music even in the toilets, where the ultimate captive audience is to be found.

The opportunity to make this little documentary was offered by Italian television, provided it could be fitted into a television format. It had to be crammed into a little box. The budget was $700,000, half of which I was told would be provided by a German company. I was to be given total artistic control. That was my temptation.

There were limitations, of course. I was told that the film should contain no nudity, be no longer than eighty minutes, and have a lot of close-ups. What more could a director need to know?

In TV, the director's projected audience is narrowed down to one or just a few individuals watching a set. Their reactions are not conditioned by the shared, more formal situation of the theater audience. It is more of a one-sided conversation than a speech.

For me, however, the decision to work on the small screen went beyond a question of morals, technical limitations, or aesthetics. I had done television twice before, *A Director's Notebook* and *The Clowns,* but each time it meant walking into a fog of blurred, confused images. I felt ambivalent about contributing again to the jumble of images with which TV fills our minds every second of the day and night. Insidiously, it seduces us, obliterating every vestige of discernment, substituting an alternative, synthetic world to which we must adjust. Worse yet, we *want* to adjust to it. I see TV and its viewer as two mirrors facing each other, reflecting between themselves an infinite void, endlessly monotonous. The question we must keep asking ourselves is, Do we believe what we see or do we see what we believe?

I wonder how I would explain the phenomenon of television to a time traveler from the past. It is a diplomatic post I would reject.

Fellini demonstrating for British actor Martin Potter how he imagined an ancient Roman might have behaved, on the set of *Satyricon* in 1969.

What is wrong with television is not the medium but the mediocrity. The invention is a marvel, full of potential, but the exploitation of it is a disaster.

I plunged into the project convinced that at least I could do no worse than what was already being done. Besides, my intuitive voice said to me, "This could be an interesting opportunity." It certainly was not the Dante's *Inferno* I feared. I made *Orchestra Rehearsal* with the great advantage of flexibility. For television, I had at my disposal a production machine that was more supple, easier, and less laborious to run, less gargantuan than for theatrical films.

Surprisingly, in the milieu of television I felt less burdened by responsibility. I was therefore able to see the project through with a renewed freshness and spontaneity that was totally unexpected. Also, because of the very limitations, I was better able to envision the whole from beginning to end, as I could never have done with one of my theatrical films. Apart from this, I am not conscious of having done anything different from what I did before or after. That is, with the limitations imposed and the few lire at my disposal, I told my story; I followed my natural inclination toward the miraculous, the exaggerated, the fantastic; and I expressed, as I always had, what seemed to be a disturbing or mysterious vision of life.

We set to work by talking with musicians at my favorite restaurant, Cesarina; thus the adventure could not be a total loss. If I got no great food for thought, I would at least get great food. As it turned out, the most remarkable contribution the musicians made was to make me aware of the practical jokes orchestral musicians play on each other. They feel the need to lighten the intensity of what they are doing, to be apparently more casual about their commitment. I didn't get the opportunity to use many of these, but one I couldn't resist was the condom stuck like a child's balloon in the trumpeter's bell.

For this film, I asked Nino Rota to write music beforehand, an unusual but necessary procedure under the circumstances. I also requested that he write something professional but undistinguished, and as always he understood exactly what I needed. Of course, I didn't mean that it should not be good, but here the music is just a prop. It's like the piano Laurel and Hardy have to carry up that long flight of steps. That is one of the most unforgettable scenes in any film.

At about the same time I was to do *Orchestra Rehearsal,* a nightmare happened in reality: Aldo Moro, the prime minister and a friend of mine, was kidnapped and murdered by the self-styled Red Brigade. Terrorism is an unacceptable reality I cannot understand. There is no easy answer. How can anyone shoot someone he doesn't know and then live with that crime afterwards for the rest of his life? What devils possessed him? In wartime, a collective insanity holds most of us in its grasp. I think that all my grown life, I have been vaguely influenced by my own small experience with war. The word "war" became not just a word, but a reality, something I could not just say, but something I felt deeply in the pit of my stomach.

An old musician asks the conductor, "How did it happen, Maestro?" and he answers, "When we weren't paying attention." This is because of the terrorist murder of Aldo Moro.

I am reminded of workers tearing up a city sidewalk and finding beneath the pavement of civilization exactly the same soil one might expect to find in a jungle. Is the layer of our civilization that thin? Do the same kind of primeval thoughts lurk beneath the surface of the civilized brain, allowing mankind to revert whenever expedient? Dark thoughts like these clouded my mind as I planned my little documentary. Not until after it was completed did I realize how much they had affected both me and the film. When I am making a film, I like to separate myself personally from the news and from other people as much as I can. The repetition of the same depressing event on television, over and over again, makes one feel that whatever it is, it is happening over and over again. My mood influences my films, and the moods of others can influence me. I always wonder how a surgeon or a pilot who has responsibility in his hands for life manages to separate himself from the frowning faces or bad moods of those around him.

I make it a point not to see my films once they are completed, because I look upon each film as a love affair, and encounters with one's ex-mistresses can be embarrassing, even dangerous. Thus, I can tell you only what I remember about *Orchestra Rehearsal.* It is an active memory of what happened while I was involved in the doing of it, which is different from the more passive kind of memory one has from only viewing it. I cannot remember it as a critic remembers it, because I never saw it as a critic sees it.

Isabella Rossellini, the daughter of Fellini's friend and mentor Roberto Rossellini, and director Martin Scorsese on a visit to Fellini at Cinecittà in the mid-1970s.

The setting itself of *Orchestra Rehearsal* is already a comment on the twentieth century. After the titles have been shown on a darkened screen, with the cacophony of Rome traffic in the background, I fade to a chapel, lit by candles. The old copyist who is distributing the orchestral parts is dressed as if he is from another century. He tells me, for I am the camera, that this chapel was built in the thirteenth century and is where three popes and seven bishops are buried. Because of its excellent acoustical properties, it has been revived for use as an orchestral rehearsal hall. In Rome, where *everything* is old, or even ancient, this is not unusual.

Into this sacrosanct setting file the musicians, many of whom look as if they are there to witness a soccer match instead of to play music. One of them, in fact, has a small transistor radio so that he can keep up with scores and relay them to his fellow woodwind players during the rehearsal. Not everyone is so unfeeling. Some of the older players, notably the copyist and a ninety-three-year-old music professor, can remember a time when musicians took their calling more seriously and consequently played better.

I interview some of the players, who tell me about their relationships with their instruments. The degree of attachment ranges from the bassoonist, who hates the sounds his **woodwind** produces, to the harpist, who doesn't have any friends *except* her harp. She looks a little like Oliver Hardy, so when she **enters, the sports-minded** woodwind players make fun of her by **playing the Laurel** and Hardy theme. The harpist is my favorite character. I **identify** best with her. She too much likes to eat and she eats too much. She **loves** her work. She is not willing to change herself to please the others. The lady flautist, who looks like a flute herself, is so overeager to please, she does an impromptu cartwheel to impress me.

The musicians speak in every Italian dialect, and there are even a few foreign accents, noticeably a German conductor, who when he gets too excited lapses into his native tongue. His approach to music is almost religious, and he is perhaps a little irritated about having to conduct a second-rate Italian orchestra instead of the Berlin Philharmonic. The actor is actually Dutch, and I remembered seeing his photo for something else, but it stuck in my mind. I have a very strong visual memory, especially for faces.

The rehearsal proceeds like the Rome traffic heard at the beginning. Most of the players want to get it over with so they can be somewhere else. *Anywhere* else. For them, it's just a job, like at the Fiat factory. It's an attitude about work, even creative work, all too prevalent nowadays.

The orchestra members play jokes on each other, listen to the soccer scores on the radio, chase a mouse, have a union dispute, and are easily distracted by other diversions, such as an attractive lady pianist who is willingly pulled under her instrument and seduced. As she is making love during the rehearsal, she also eats, displaying little passion for either sensual pursuit, not to mention an indifference to her art.

Because the orchestra is playing with such total lack of interest and purpose, the conductor becomes abusive, provoking a union dispute, followed by a disruptive revolt in which posters of famous German composers are pelted with dung. A huge metronome is finally set up in place of the deposed conductor, and then, in turn, it is displaced.

This childish chaos is interrupted by a wrecker's ball, which comes crashing unexpectedly through a wall, killing poor fat Clara, our sympathetic harpist. Thus, order is restored through chaos, a recurring universal human process. But as in every upheaval, something precious is destroyed, and the music must now go on without its harp part. A treasure has been lost, perhaps forever. That is what is most significant.

The wrecker's ball is the enemy of human values. It is merciless. It is mercenary. Like those who control it, it moves without heart in its business of destruction. The real tragedy is that its damage is soon forgotten. A world that has been impoverished is in an instant ready to accept that this is the way it has always been. The unthinkable is taken for granted.

At the end, after the contrite musicians realize they need a leader, the conductor returns to the podium and says, *"Da capo, signori."* The orchestra starts playing again, from the beginning, and the petty bickering also resumes, with the conductor lapsing into a long tirade in German over a darkened screen. The more things change, the more they remain the same. Human nature is only human.

The conductor's final outburst has been interpreted in many ways, but I did not consciously intend for it to be any more than an expression of his frustration, even perhaps expressing some of mine, as a conductor in my own field. Earlier, when I interview him in his dressing room, he says, "We play together, but are united only in a common hatred, like a destroyed family." Sometimes, when things aren't going right on the film set, I feel exactly that same way.

One critic suggested that the opening traffic jam and the tirade in German at the end, both on darkened screens, have deep significance. As for the "deeper meanings" in my pictures, all I can say is that I have provided employment for many critics, even if unintentionally.

Communication is not a science, but an art, in that what one wishes to communicate may not be what is communicated. In drama, the audience plays an important part, interpreting what they hear and see. They see through their own eyes and hear through their own ears. I must not tell them what to think, or I am a pedant limiting them. I am often—usually—surprised by what people tell me they saw in my work. The creative role is to open up the world for your audience, not to close it. But sometimes it's like a parlor game where one person whispers something to another, and the other to the next one, and

When Fellini rebuilt Venice at Cinecittà, there were those people who said he was throwing money away. Fellini, however, said that such sets gave him "the control you cannot have on location." Still, this set was not an exact replica; it was "Fellini's Venice."

Fellini enjoying lunch during the early 1970s with director Paul Mazursky (seated, left) and actor Robin Williams (seated, right) in Rome. Fellini's long-time publicist and friend Mario Longardi is standing.

by the time the message comes back to the person who spoke it first, he doesn't recognize it.

No drama is complete until it has been witnessed by an audience. In the case of cinema, the audience is the only character that can vary its role from performance to performance. I am sometimes amazed, though not often amused, by the meanings that come back to me which people have taken from my films.

I am reminded of the time someone in a men's room whispered something in my ear. He had just seen *Orchestra Rehearsal*. He said, "You're perfectly right. We *do* need Uncle Adolf again." I zipped up my fly and left as quickly as possible.

The first public showing of *Orchestra Rehearsal* occurred under unusual circumstances. Before he became president, Alessandro Pertini had requested a private showing of my next picture. The unofficial premiere took place, therefore, at the presidential palace in October of 1978 before an invited audience of politicians. It was an honor I really would have preferred to avoid, but since I had agreed *before* President Pertini had been elected to let him screen the film, I was trapped.

The politicians were ominously polite. Some of them were distressed by the language, but the president defended me. He could not defend me, however, against some of the other criticisms. Everyone took the film personally, or at least politically. Wherever a negative interpretation could be imputed to something, it was. The leader of the Communist Party, who was from Sardinia, was sure he was being ridiculed in the character of the obstreperous Sardinian union representative. The truth is, the actor who played the part was Sardinian, an unintentional coincidence.

RAI–TV, upset by the press notices, postponed their announced TV premiere indefinitely, and the film appeared first in theaters. By the time it reached television, everyone had forgotten why they should be outraged by it.

fifteen

DAYMARES AND NIGHTDREAMS

My dreams seem so real to me that years afterwards, I wonder, Did that really happen to me, or did I dream it? Dreams are a language made up of images. There is nothing more true than a dream, because dreams resist obvious interpretation—dreams use symbols instead of concepts. Everything means something in a dream—each color, each detail . . .

I have a wonderful life at night in my dreams. My dreams are so interesting that I have always looked forward to going to sleep. Sometimes I dream the same dream more than once. Sometimes it is an old dream with different nuances and slight variations. Of course, I don't always have these dreams, but often enough. I have worried that one day—or rather, one night—they might stop. Thus far, they have not; but I must say that as I have grown older, I have slept more nights without them, and they have grown shorter. I suppose that is natural, since so many of the dreams are sexual.

They are not always sleeping dreams. It's my mind playing at night. These are really visions more than dreams. A man's subconscious creates the dream, but his vision is a conscious idealization. Some of the dreams are very old dreams, with Laurel and Hardy dressed like two little boys, playing near a swing.

I can create a dream with open eyes, imagining something. It's not quite sleeping. Some people consider this a kind of escape because I don't like to face the everyday problems. When I don't know how to settle something, it's true. My way of solving problems is to try to get rid of the thought. I hope someone else will settle it. I'm like the heroine of *Gone With the Wind*—I'll worry about it tomorrow. I'm like that with everything except a film, and then I assume total responsibility. I believe, however, that no one is more realistic than the person who has dream visions, because he intensifies the most profound reality, which is *his* reality.

Though I was born by the sea in a place to which people came from all over Europe to swim, I never learned to swim. In one of my earliest dreams, a recurring dream, I was drowning. But I was always saved by a giant woman whose enormous breasts were huge even in light of her statuesque size. At first, when I had this dream, I was quite terrified, but after a while I came to expect the giantess, who would scoop me out of the water and cuddle me between her breasts. There was no place in the world I would rather have been than right there, squeezed between those huge breasts. As the dream persisted, I came not to mind almost drowning, because I was confident I would be rescued in time, and the erotic thrill of being between her breasts would again be mine.

I am never sexually impotent in my dreams. Dreams are so superior to reality. In my dreams I can make love twenty-five times a night.

In my dreams, I am quite often naked, thin and naked—and I never get fat. I eat delicious food in my dreams, especially sweets. A rich chocolate cake regularly appears. I dream a great deal about women. Man is like the male spider—lost, the victim of his own libido. Sex is dangerous.

In 1934, when I was fourteen, there were stories about a sea monster who had been caught in a net, and I saw a drawing of it in a newspaper. It was an incredible image for me. I had many dreams about this sea monster. The sea was always a powerful force in my life. My entire early life was not dominated by the sea, but rather the sea was a taken-for-granted part of life, like an arm or a leg, or like one of the walls of our home.

In my mind, the monster was a woman, a giant woman. In my life, a woman was the authority figure, my mother. She was very strict, though I don't think she was fully aware of this. She was the authority figure because my father was away most of the time. My father wanted us to love him, so when he was home, he gave us gifts, took us to buy cakes, and told us funny stories we didn't understand too well.

My mother didn't feel she had to win our love, because we owed it to her. After all, she *was* our mother. I'm certain she believed she was a perfect mother, and she was dedicated to that role in life; but as we grew up, she didn't recognize the change in us. Perhaps it was because she didn't want to recognize the change in herself, that she was growing older. Also, I think, consciously or unconsciously, she wanted us not to be like our father. She wanted to save us for her religion, Catholicism. For her, goodness was equated with not eating meat on Friday.

In my dreams, I am made unhappy when I am confronted by figures of authority, and often I am afraid of women. This is true in real life, too.

In the first of my sea-monster dreams, I was there with my mother. I wanted to go forward and get as close to the monster as possible. I wanted to see every detail, so I could go home later and draw a picture of the sea monster. My mother was trying to hold me back. She was telling me it was for my own good, but I didn't believe her. She was saying something about how the sea monster would eat me. That sounded foolish to me, because somehow I knew that boys were too tough to eat and not at all the diet of any self-respecting sea monster worth its weight in kelp.

As the giant sea monster was lifted out of the water, I saw that it was actually a huge woman. She was both beautiful and ugly at the same time, which did not seem at all a contradiction to me. Then, as now, I have always felt that female beauty comes in all shapes and sizes. I could not help but notice that she had huge thighs. Even in relation to her gargantuan proportions, her thighs were abnormally large.

I heard a voice of authority speak. It didn't seem to be attached to any particular body, but to come out of the air, which is consistent with the way authority usually is. The voice knew my name and singled me out, and everyone looked at me. I was afraid I was blushing like a girl. I felt dizzy and worried that I would faint. The voice told me I would have to leave unless I instantly dismissed my mother.

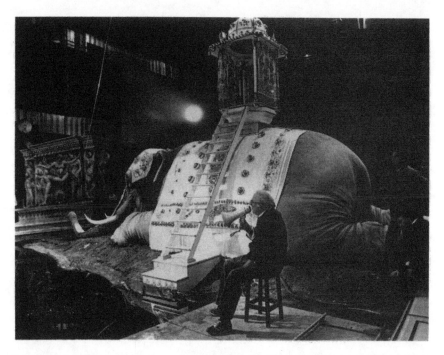

Fellini had always wanted to direct elephants, but this one took very little direction.

Mothers were not permitted, and besides, the sea monster did not like my mother.

I found my control and clapped my hands together. The sound was like a thunderbolt. I commanded my mother to go. She disappeared. I don't mean that she left. I mean that she just disappeared.

The giant female sea monster beckoned to me. She wanted me to come closer. It was what I wanted, too.

I remember, not without fear, my mother's warning that the sea monster would swallow me whole. Somehow, that seemed very inviting, as well as frightening. I thought it must be very warm inside of her.

I moved forward.

Then, I woke up. After that, I was not a boy anymore.

A dream has recurred to me over the years. As a young man, I had the dream very often. It's a sex dream. The dream persisted through my middle years. Recently, I have had it less often, only sporadically, and I suppose the reason is obvious. It's one of the vivid sensual memories of my early life. It is based on something that really happened, and I used it in *8½*.

I'm a child in a tub being bathed by women. It's an old-fashioned wooden tub, like the one that was outdoors at my grandmother's farm, the kind we children used to mash the grapes for wine with our bare feet. Before mashing the grapes, we had to wash our feet. Afterwards you could still smell the residue of fermenting grapes when you took a bath in the tub. It could almost make you feel drunk.

Sometimes I bathed with several children, little boys and girls, all of us naked. The water was deep, over my head, which was my definition of deep. All of the other children could swim. I was the only one who couldn't. Once I nearly drowned. I had to be pulled out by my hair. Fortunately I had more then than I do now, or I *would* have drowned.

In my dream, as I get out of the tub, my naked, wet little body is wrapped in big towels by several women with huge breasts. Women in my dreams never wear brassieres, nor do I think brassieres that large ever existed. They wrap me in the towels. They hold me against their breasts, rolling me back and forth to dry me. The towel brushes against my little thing, which flips merrily from side to side. It's such a lovely feeling, I hope it never stops. Sometimes the women fight over me, which I enjoy, too.

I've spent my life looking for the women of childhood who wrap you in towels. Now, when I have the dream, I need stronger women. In real life, Giulietta does it for me, but the towels make a big mess in the bathroom.

I had a dream thirty years ago which sums up the meaning of my whole life. I've never told this to anyone before.

I was the chief of an airport. It was night, a night full of stars. I was behind my desk in a big room there. Through the window I saw all the planes landing at the airport. A great plane had landed, and as chief of the airport, I was proceeding to passport control.

All the passengers from the plane were in front of me, waiting with their passports. Suddenly I saw a strange figure—an old Chinese man, looking antique, dressed in rags, yet regal, and he had a terrible smell. He was waiting there to come in.

He stood in front of me but spoke not a single word. He didn't even look at me. He was totally absorbed in himself.

I looked down at the little plaque on my desk, which said my name and gave me the title, showing I was chief. But I didn't know what to do. I was afraid to let him in because he was so different, and I didn't understand him. I was tremendously afraid that if I let him in, he would disrupt my conventional life. So I fell back on an excuse that was a lie that exposed my own weakness.

I lied as a child lies. I couldn't bring myself to take the responsibility. I said, "I don't have the power, you see. I'm not really in charge here. I have to ask the others."

I hung my head in shame. I said, "Wait here, I'll be right back." I left to make my decision, which I didn't make. I am still making it and all the while I wonder if he will still be there when I go back. But the real terror is I don't know if I am more afraid that he will be there or that he will no longer be there. I have thought about it constantly through the thirty years that have passed. I understand full well that there was something wrong with my nose, not with his smell; yet I still have not been able to bring myself to go back and let him in, or to find out if he is still waiting.

I've been asked how can one dream stories, visions, fantasies. How can one free one's mind in this way, so it can create characters, worlds?

I don't know. I don't even know how to tell myself how to do it.

When I make a film, what I strive for is to allow myself to be mesmerized like a dreamer, even though I am the one who made the dream.

I have always taken great pleasure in going to bed, in lying there and savoring the moment. I like a big, high bed, cold sheets, a down comforter. I enjoy the quiet of the night, and I am anxious for dreams. Lying there waiting for my dreams is like sitting in the movie theater waiting for the film to begin.

I always enjoy waking up. I am instantly awake. I open my eyes, fully ready for the life of the day. But before I forget them, I try to put down my dreams of the night before. I do this with drawings rather than words, although I remember dream dialogue. I usually put that over the character's head in a balloon, like a comic strip. I am always the main subject of my dream, the dream protagonist. I suppose someone might say it's because I am so self-centered that I always dream about myself. I believe everyone has the right to dream in a self-centered way.

Waking up totally, without needing to have coffee or breakfast first, is an advantage, because I don't lose any part of the day.

Color is very important in dreams. Color in a dream is like it is in painting, an integral part of the mood—a pink horse, a purple dog, a green elephant. None of these is foolish in a dream.

Faces have always inspired my imagination. I never tire of looking at faces till I find the right one for the part. For the smallest part, I could and often do look at a thousand faces to find the perfect one for what I want to express. Face is the first thing of which we have understanding.

As babies, we see a face as one of our points of focus. Though we don't consciously remember it, we look at our mother's face as our security. Then, we look at other faces.

Our face typecasts us. I have observed actors who are affected by parts they play. They find a part in which they are particularly successful, so they come to play that part in life. I knew an actor who played the fool so long that now he is one all the time. He got those parts because he was something of a fool to start with. But then, playing those parts brought out that side of him and reinforced it.

There is a common misunderstanding about what I look for when I search through my gallery of photographs for faces. Usually, I am not looking for unforgettable faces. Unforgettable faces are easy to find. The difficult thing is to find forgettable faces.

Though I have always been interested in dreams, of all my films only *City of Women* was almost entirely a dream. Everything in the picture has a hidden subjective meaning, as in a dream, except the beginning and end, in which Snaporaz is awake in the railway coach. It's the nightmare aspect of Guido's dream in *8½.*

Snaporaz dreams of bringing together all of the women in his life—past, present, and future—to live in harmony. It's a male fantasy, a man's dream that the women in his life would love him so much that they would be willing to share him, to understand that they each represent a different stage of his life, different feelings, and that he could even be a bond between them. Instead, they would prefer to tear him apart. One gets an arm, one gets a leg, one a toenail. They would rather preside over a corpse than have someone else get him.

I had the idea for *City of Women* one night walking in Rome with Ingmar Bergman. Liv Ullmann was with him. He and I had just met, and we found that we had an instant rapport.

We would collaborate, two directors, one film. Each of us would do half. Maybe each of us would provide a producer who had half the money. Each of us would do his own story, and there would be some vague link. "Like love," one of us said. I don't remember which one of us said it. It might have been Liv Ullmann. It sounded good to us, since both of us believed in the search for love as a dignifier of man. Also, it was a very beautiful night in Rome, and on a night like that, all ideas sound good. I like very much walking around Rome at night. These were very special visitors, and I learned a lot about *my* city seeing it through their touristic eyes. Bergman and I knew that both of us would have to have a certain amount of self-discipline, though not the discipline imposed by producers. We were both justifiably known for our tendency to want to make films that were too long.

Usually films born in such a moment of outpouring of emotion never make it to the screen. In fact, very few ideas for films make it to the screen. In this case, both of ours did, but not in a collaborative effort. They became two films—his and mine.

Having decided that we should make a film together, we had the problem of geography. I wanted to be in Rome. He wanted to be in Sweden. But who knows—if our geographic proximity had been achieved, would our rapport have held up? We had the greatest respect for each other's bodies of work, and it was really our bodies of work that met. His celebrity met my celebrity.

My idea became *City of Women,* more than a decade later. Like the Bergman film *The Touch*, it underwent many transformations along the way. Like Bergman's, it did not have anything like the successful reception by the public which I thought it would enjoy. There are some who would say we both would have been better off not to have met that night.

My first producer for *City of Women* was an American with an Italian name, Bob Guccione, a famous American magazine publisher. I found him a congenial companion. As a young man, he even drew little caricatures of people in restaurants, as I did. People said I preferred to have a different producer each time because it gave me the greater freedom to do what I want, but I believe quite the opposite. Breaking in a new producer is like breaking in a pair of new shoes, patent leather. It is hard on the feet. What I would really have liked is a patron such as artists had in the days of Michelangelo. The accountant's balance sheet has never been my friend, nor have the accountants who make and interpret them been my friends.

Guccione did not finish the film as its producer because it was going over budget, and he had problems with another film he was producing. Also, he wanted me to use American or English actors to speak for themselves, actors with "box office" names. Another problem was the conception each of us had of how sex should be portrayed on the screen. He thought I was a prude. I *was*, by his definition. He wanted to show much more sex than I like to show, and in close-up. It seems to me that other people's sex is funny. Our own, no; but others', yes.

It was his idea to do "Fellini's Catherine the Great," which appealed very much to me. We talked about many ideas for it, but it never happened.

In *City of Women*, the world is seen through the eyes of Snaporaz. It's the viewpoint of a man who has always looked at woman as a total mystery, not only as the object of his fantasies, but as mother, wife, lady in the drawing room, whore in the bedroom, Dante's Beatrice, his own personal muse, brothel enticer—and more. He projects onto her all of his own fantasies. Through the ages, from the beginning of time, I'm certain man has covered woman's face with masks. They are, however, his masks, not hers. They are the masks of the viewer, not of the woman, and what they hide is not what they seem to cover. The masks come from the man's own subconscious and they represent that unknown part of himself.

I don't remember when I first thought of the name "Snaporaz." It came to me as a funny name for Mastroianni. I thought of him that way, and I started to call him Snaporaz. When I was planning *City of Women*, it seemed to me just right as the name for the character Mastroianni was going to play. It attracted a lot of questions. I was asked, "What kind of name is that? What does it mean?"

When this happens, I like to make suggestive faces to imply it's something naughty, too terrible to say, so some of the questioners won't even want me to go on. Actually, it's just a word I made up.

Fellini shows Bernice Stegers how he wants her to treat Marcello Mastroianni in *City of Women* (1980).

When I called him Old Snaporaz, he didn't seem to like it that much, but maybe it was the part about being old, rather than the Snaporaz part, he didn't like.

When Mastroianni arrived on the set, he had to pass through the crowds of women who were appearing in the picture, as well as the ones waiting near Cinecittà to catch a glimpse of him. It seemed he would enjoy the adulation, women throwing flowers at him, but he looked worried and said to me, "Going past all those women throwing flowers at me scares me."

There was a lot of criticism of me after *City of Women,* especially by women. It was said that I was anti-women. I would never have believed that this was a possible interpretation. It reaffirmed for me that you can never really know in advance what people will see in what you do. I considered my film impudent, honest, and humorous.

Women have been some of my best friends. I have always needed to bask in the warmth of the company of women. Having women around on the set brings out the best in my work. They are great admirers and encouragers. I am stimulated by them and perhaps, showing off for them, I do my best work. I am like the foolish, preening male peacock who must get up his tail for the female. I could never be happy making a picture about soldiers or cowboys without women.

Fellini was accused of being anti-feminist in *City of Women.* He said that what he was really portraying was a womanizer's nightmare.

I have spent most of my life with one woman, Giulietta. Often I have women assistants on the set. Some of my favorite characters in my films are women. I never understand it when a critic writes that my films are about men and for men. Gelsomina, Cabiria, Juliet, all of them are as real for me as any real people I have ever known.

Ten thousand women! Perhaps the realization of this could be a little tedious, but not in the fantasy. And the fantasy is what's important. The cake with which Dr. Katzone celebrates his ten thousandth woman in *City of Women* is supposed to have ten thousand candles on it, but of course it doesn't really. In pictures, illusion is more important than reality. Real things don't seem real. To capture the illusion of reality, it may be necessary to film something many times.

The character of Dr. Katzone was based on Georges Simenon, who became a good friend after *La Dolce Vita*. He told me that since the age of thirteen and a half he had seduced exactly ten thousand women. Evidently, he keeps better records than I do.

I am always being asked by people—usually students, professors, and critics—what is my aim in doing a film, what is my message. In other words, they want to know *why* I make films. They have to believe there is some reason beyond creative necessity. You might as well ask a hen why she lays eggs. She is fulfilling the only purpose in life of which she is capable, except to be eaten. Laying eggs is decidedly preferable. I am like the ballerina in *The Red Shoes* who, when asked why she dances, answers, "Because I must."

If I tell them the truth, they are disappointed and don't like it. So sometimes, if I'm in the mood, I make the effort to invent reasons I don't have, but could have had, for doing this or that. I start out wanting to be polite, to please them, but I always end up becoming angry. They do not let the encounter end well. My reward for answering their questions is always the same—to be asked yet another.

At one point in my life, I had thought owning a restaurant would be a nice investment. Then I realized it would mean responsibility, and that what I really enjoyed was eating in a restaurant, not owning one.

For me, everything is emotional and intuitive. I am like a chef in a kitchen with a lot of ingredients, some strange and some familiar, who says, "What shall I cook today?" Then I get inspired and start mixing and stirring, and a new dish is created. This is only an analogy. I can-

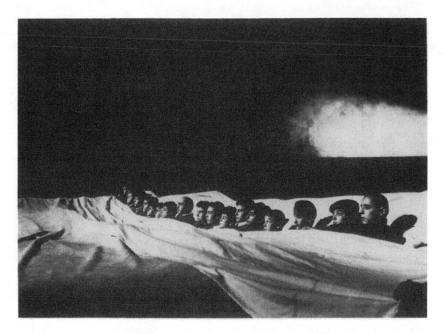

Fantasy bedtime in *City of Women*.

not cook at all. When I was very young, a long time ago, I thought I might have some interest in learning to cook, but it turned out my only interest in cooking was in the eating of what was cooked.

A journalist might come up to me and say, "What was your intention in creating Spaghetti à la Fellini?" and I can't just answer, "I was hungry." He will think I'm being disrespectful to the press and, antagonized, he will go away and write something that will keep people away from my restaurant. So I invent an elaborate fiction about Escoffier appearing to me in a visitation, in which I am saved by a soup pot coming down over my head, just as in *The Clowns* I was saved by a bucket.

The truth is, I can't explain why I make films. I just like to create images. There is no other reason. It's congenial to my nature. That seems enough of an explanation.

Until I was about twenty-five, I didn't know what I wanted to do. I had no idea I would like to be a director. If I'd had the idea, I would have had no faith that I could do it, or that I would have the opportunity to do it. As a scriptwriter, I would sit on the set when they were doing my scripts and be mystified at everything that was going on around me. It was when I became involved with Rossellini that I truly began to care. He cared deeply. It was intense, more difficult, but more wonderful to live, caring.

I heard a small voice inside me that said, "Yes, you can be a director." Maybe it was always there, but I had never heard it before.

When I was ten, I put on shows on our balcony for children in our neighborhood. The shows were as much like the movies I had seen at the Fulgor Cinema as I could manage, and the children laughed. My mother said I charged admission, but I don't remember this. My sense of money has never been good. If I did, it was a very good idea because I think an audience is suspicious of anything that is free. Even if each child paid only a part of a penny, it meant I was a professional.

One of the reasons I became interested in Jungian psychology is that it attempts to explain our individual actions in collective terms. It furnishes me with an elaborate explanation when I don't already have one. If a journalist had come up to me when I was a child and said, "What is your motive in doing these puppet shows?" I would probably have answered, "I don't know." Now that I am six times older, if not wiser, I can answer, "Because it was in my archetypal collective consciousness," and hold my breath until the bucket falls on my head to cover my pomposity.

Then a scholar will ask me to explain for posterity why I like to drop buckets, and he can write a doctoral dissertation on the subject.

sixteen

BUILDING A SET IS THE
BEST WAY TO TRAVEL

I don't like to travel, because I prefer to travel in my mind. The real thing exhausts me, but if my corporeal being is comfortable in its known setting, I am free of baggage, and it is my mind that can roam. My mind is freed of details like, Did I pack enough undershorts? Did I remember to put the cap on the toothpaste? When I am actually in transit, I want to escape from the confines of the airplane, but my sense of fantasy becomes inhibited by claustrophobia. The airplane and hospital have that in common for me.

When I travel I feel like a suitcase. Only, I am a suitcase with feelings. I don't like to ship myself anywhere. Now, I enjoy hearing about other people's travel. From that I can have the stimulation without the inconvenience. I say, "How interesting," and "How wonderful," and mean it—for them, and I am thinking how glad I am not to be the one in the airport listening to the loudspeaker announcement. I can hardly understand the garbled voice telling about the delay of my flight.

When I was a boy, I wanted to travel and see the world, but then I found Rome and found *my* world. Whenever I was anyplace else, I resented a little that place, because I felt it was taking me away from where I really wanted to be. There were times when I was even superstitious about it. I felt almost invulnerable—as if, as long as I stayed in Rome, I couldn't die. Everywhere else, I felt at risk.

When first I arrived in Rome, I had curiosity, though no expectations. I hoped to be a successful journalist and cartoonist.

There were many places I saw later about which I had been curious, foremost among them the United States. During World War II, I watched beautiful people in beautiful clothes on the movie screens, dancing, going to parties, and especially eating. They always had full Frigidaires. I was fascinated by this wonderful country, America, where everyone was rich and happy, and I longed to visit that country. I made up images about it in my mind, based on all the American movies that were in my head.

When I did visit the United States, my imaginings seemed like foolish little drawings. Everything there was both bigger and smaller than the pictures in my mind. I found the reality was too much in conflict with my fantasy and beyond my comprehension. I knew I would never be able to know and understand it, so I fled, and gradually, the America that survived was the one I made up. The reality of it intruded very little, except when I took the plane and went there.

I have been offered countless opportunities to make films in other countries, especially in the United States. I would not be comfortable making a film anywhere but in Italy, for several reasons. The language problem is not an important consideration for me. I frequently work with actors who are not Italian, and we never have any trouble communicating. In *Satyricon,* for example, because I thought Anglo-Saxon types better fulfilled our expectations of how the ancient Romans looked, I used many English-speaking actors, and they understood me perfectly. I directed them in English. From the standpoint of language, then, I could work in other places, including Hollywood, but there are other, more important considerations.

At Cinecittà, I have total control and total flexibility. I can have any kind of set I want built, and then I can have any changes I might want made later. Since most of my stories are set in Italy, it has rarely been necessary for me to leave for a foreign location. If I did need a foreign setting, as in *Casanova,* the technicians at Cinecittà could easily provide it for me. For *Amerika,* the Kafka film I'm shown planning in *Intervista,* it was easier for me to contemplate a nineteenth-century New York built at Cinecittà than to search for one in New York City itself. When I went to Paris for *The Clowns,* I became even more convinced that I should not leave Rome again. I considered a personal calamity that occurred as a sign. I believe in signs that come to us, especially as warnings, and I try to observe them and give them credence.

I was staying at a hotel in Paris when, in the middle of the night, I woke up and found the room too warm. I went to the window, half asleep, and put my hand through the glass, cutting it. My hand was bleeding badly. I rushed out and took a taxi to a hospital. I was wearing only my bathrobe and pajamas, and in my haste, I forgot my wallet. At the hospital, they asked me to pay in advance. Imagine! They refused to treat me until I paid. Finally, they relented. I took all of this to be an omen which meant I should not work on location in other countries. I believe in heeding premonitions and apparently supernatural symbols, although I do not consider myself to be an extremely superstitious person. Jung calls this "synchronicity," when two logically unrelated events come together in a meaningful way.

My greatest advantage in working at Cinecittà is the freedom I have to direct in my own way. Like a silent-film director, I talk to my actors as they perform their parts in front of the camera. Sometimes the actor doesn't even know what he's supposed to say, or the script has been changed too much at the last minute for him to have learned the lines, so I have to tell him his lines while the camera is rolling. Obviously, in Hollywood with microphones this would be impossible. I would need a telepathic medium to communicate my last-minute instructions to the actors. Antonioni was able to work in London and Hollywood under these conditions, but he is quite different temperamentally from me. He takes Italy with him wherever he goes, so he can be complete anywhere. I feel incomplete anyplace but Rome.

I admire Antonioni very much. What he does, the way he does it, is so different from the way I work, but I respect the integrity and quality of his work. He is a great creator who has made an enormous impression on me. He doesn't compromise, and he has something to say. He has a personal style which is different from everyone else's. Unique. A special eye.

I think I was meant to be a director of silent films. I remember having this discussion with King Vidor, one of the real geniuses of the cinema. I always remember he told me, "I was born at the beginning of the movies." Wonderful. How I would have liked to be born then and to have had the opportunity to begin fresh and invent everything!

Another reason, a personal one, for my preference of Rome over all other production centers is that in the others, I wouldn't know in which restaurants to eat. I've never been particularly interested in trying out many restaurants. Once I discover the one I prefer, I am faithful. It's easier to be faithful to a restaurant than to a woman.

I like to know what the label inside the character's tie is, where the actress bought her underwear, about the shoes an actor wears. Shoes tell a lot about the character. Who ate garlic? I could never know all of this if I worked outside of Italy.

Along with being able to work as a director, the most important element in my happiness in life is freedom. Even as a small boy, my energies were always directed toward struggling against what limited my freedom—home, school, religion, any political control, especially that of fascism, which represented a totality of control, and public opinion to which one had to conform. It was when the fascists censored the comic strips, I realized what bad people they were.

Freedom can be a problem, because being a director of films is a responsibility, and responsibility and freedom are in conflict. The money of the few and the lives of the many are in my hands. Films have such power to influence; that, too, is a responsibility.

Limitations are also very important. Total freedom is too much freedom, and, in effect, it can produce too little freedom. If someone said to me, You can make the picture you want and you can spend eighty million dollars, he would not be giving me a gift, but a burden. I would have to spend all of my time figuring how in the world I could ever spend so much money without making a film that would be so long that we would have to provide pillows for the seats of the theater and rent beds at the ticket booth.

I think I could never have adjusted to the grandiosity of America and its extravagant ways. Everything so big, like America, itself. Unlimited. How terrifying to be told your possibilities are infinite. It must be somewhat frightening for Americans themselves to be told they can do anything, be anything. It is enough to make you freeze in your shoes, paralyzed by the illusion of your own power. And it is, after all, only an illusion. The more money you have to accept, the more strings there are on you, until you reverse Pinocchio's journey to be a boy and you become a marionette. And more money does not necessarily buy a better film.

In *And the Ship Sails On,* I needed a large exterior to paint, so I used the wall of the Pantanella pasta factory. It was where my father, Urbano Fellini, had worked when he passed through Rome on his way back from forced labor in Belgium after World War I. It was while at the pasta factory in 1918 that he met my mother, Ida Barbiani, and carried her off, not on a white charger, but in a third-class coach on the train, with her full consent, away from her home, family, and social class in Rome.

By the time I made *Intervista,* from the perspective of the years that had passed, I had a better understanding of my parents than the view I had in my own youth. I had come to feel close to my father, and I fervently wished I could tell him so. I understood my mother better, too, and I no longer resented our differences. I recognized that life had not given either of them what they wanted, but I tried to give them in retrospect the understanding I gave to the characters in my films.

The deck of the ship in *And the Ship Sails On* was constructed on Stage 5 at Cinecittà. It was supported on hydraulic jacks and rocked realistically. Everyone but me was seasick. It was not because I am such a good sailor, but because I was so intensely involved in what I was doing that I was not aware of the rocking. The sea was created from polyethylene. The obviously artificial painted sunset looked beautiful. The appearance of artificiality is deliberate. At the end, I reveal the set and me behind a camera, the entire magic show.

I wasn't certain about casting Freddie Jones in the role of Orlando. He would be a British type playing an Italian in a Mediterranean setting. Yet there was something about him that appealed to me for the part. After our initial interview, I rode with him to the airport. On the way back to Rome, I was still unsure. Then I saw a bus which had a large sign advertising Orlando ice cream. I took it as a favorable omen and allowed it to make the decision for me. Besides, I didn't really have anyone else in mind.

In the opening, I show the contrast between the rushed confusion of the luxury liner's first-class galley and the slow, stately pace of the dining room. The rich eat very slowly. They never have to worry about shortages. They are more concerned about how they look while chewing.

I was concerned about having lovely food for the people to eat. It had to be photogenic so it would look enticing on the screen. I wanted food that was fresh and deliciously prepared for inspiring the actors. It was important that it smelled good, and we looked forward to eating it afterwards. Maybe everyone did better and there were fewer takes so we could finish before the food got cold.

There is nothing too small for me to do on the set. I move a table, I arrange someone's curl, I pick up a piece of paper from the floor. It is all part of making the film. At home, I cannot make a cup of coffee because I am too impatient to wait for water to boil.

And the Ship Sails On has a great deal to do with opera, a subject I would have avoided in my earlier pictures. It was only in later life that I came to appreciate our Italian operatic tradition. I suppose the reason I said and wrote so much about not liking opera is because every Italian is supposed to love opera, especially every Italian man. My brother, Riccardo, went around the house singing. Love of opera isn't restricted to Italy, of course, but it's more widespread here than in America.

All my life I've had a natural resistance to whatever everyone likes, or wants, or is "supposed" to do. I never was interested in soccer, either to play or to watch, and for a man to admit that in Italy is almost like admitting that you aren't a man at all. I do not like to belong to political parties or to clubs. Partly this is probably in my black-sheep nature, but I think another very real reason is I remember the Black Shirts.

I was a child in a time when we wore the outfits of our school, or we wore the black shirts of fascism, and we were supposed to question nothing. That has made me question everything. I was always suspicious, not wanting to be one of the sheep going to slaughter. So sometimes I may have missed out on a pleasure the sheep enjoyed which I could have had without becoming a lamb chop.

Now I have developed a late interest in opera, but it's difficult to admit you have interest in a subject in which you have vehemently denied having any interest for so long.

And the Ship Sails On required many extras to play the parts of the Yugoslavian refugees, the ship's crew, and the passengers. They were paid according to the time they worked, and the longer it took to shoot the scene, the more they would be paid. I wanted the work to come in on time, even ahead of schedule, within or as close to the budget as possible, but they wanted to make more money.

Some extras playing Italian sailors prodded those extras playing refugees who ambled along at a leisurely pace carrying giggling children. It was more like a picnic in the park. After several halfhearted takes, they would start to do the scene better, but then at the last moment, someone would do something to spoil it.

It didn't go on as long as it might have because I had friends in the group, but it was frustrating. I couldn't imagine how anyone could work on a film and not do it with pride, the best they could. I had always tried to have a good relationship on the set and the support of every person, even the ones doing the smallest jobs. The kind of negative influence I had come to expect, though not to like, was a producer or a producer's emissary hovering near me or furtively talking on the phone somewhere nearby, especially toward the end, while the accountants were counting lire.

I have not seen the film since it was finished, but I wonder how it would seem now in light of what has been happening in Yugoslavia. Would it seem too light, too dated? Or would it speak to audiences more clearly?

The rhinoceros is a distant cousin of the sick zebra I helped to wash when I was a boy and the circus came to Rimini. My theory about why the zebra was sick is that he didn't have any sex in his life. How *could* he feel well? There was, after all, only one zebra in that circus. The rhinoceros is lovesick.

Only one rhinoceros is the same as only one zebra.

When I started to make TV commercials, people said that I had sold my soul to commercial interests. I was deeply hurt. I cannot say that I am so rich I don't want to earn some money, but I have never filmed anything *just* for money. I wouldn't do that. Celebrity doesn't pay the check at Cesarina, but I could never need money so badly that I would do something I didn't believe in. I have been offered fortunes to go and make a picture I didn't feel, in the United States, Brazil, all over. They wanted me to go to Brazil to do a film about Simón Bolívar.

Obviously, I was not paid a fortune to make commercials, but the idea of doing so captured my fancy. Many people said, "How can Fellini make TV commercials after he has criticized them so much, when he hates them?" It was exactly the reason for making one. I was told that I could make a commercial that had artistic integrity. I didn't do it for the money, though I did accept the fee.

To be more exact, I didn't *hate* the existing TV commercials. I didn't *like* them. I had seen so many poor ones on television. Just as I believe television programming doesn't *have* to be inferior in quality just because it's on television, commercials could be miniature artistic endeavors. They should be the best they can be for what they are.

What I hated was having commercials break my films when they were shown on television. They destroyed the rhythm. I strongly oppose the movies being interrupted by commercials. I have been vocal and public on the subject. That doesn't mean I believe there should be no commercials at all. The products are like the movie producers. Somebody has to pay.

Then, the press says, "You have always said you hated having your films interrupted on television for commercials. Now you have made commercials. Have you not betrayed other film directors, as well as yourself?" It's another silly question, often stated in the form of a provocation. Of course, these commercials have not been made to interrupt a film. They can be shown before or after. But if that is not what happens, it's not my fault. I have done the best I can. I don't run the world, or even Italy. What I tried to do was make the commercials as entertaining as possible. This is a subject I never like to talk about. When they ask, "Why did you do a commercial, Mr. Fellini?" I don't answer, because I don't like to listen to myself on the defensive.

Something I personally enjoyed was the idea of instant gratification, like writing an essay, a short story, or an article. I could have an inspiration and then film my idea and see it. It reminded me of when I was writing as a young journalist for magazines and then for radio.

My first TV commercial was for Campari, in 1984.

A bored young woman is looking out of the window of a moving train. A fellow passenger, a man, picks up a remote control device and changes the landscapes seen out of the window, as if it's just a large TV screen. There are various foreign scenes.

The woman shows no interest.

He asks her if she would prefer an Italian scene.

The scene that is now flicked on outside of the window is of a huge bottle of Campari next to the Leaning Tower of Pisa.

At that, the woman becomes happy and animated.

The Barilla pasta commercial I made in 1986 begins on a set which was like the first-class dining room of *And the Ship Sails On.* We see a man and a woman seated at a table. It's obvious they are a couple having an affair. The woman casts suggestive, sensual, provocative glances at her companion.

The waiters are stiffly arrogant. They march in a formal procession. The headwaiter pretentiously tells about the dishes on the menu—in French.

The woman is asked what she wants, and she whispers:

"Rigatoni."

The waiters relax and breathe a sigh of relief. It turns out they are really Italians who had been under orders to pretend to be French. In a chorus, they sing:

"Barilla, Barilla."

Voice-over, an announcer says, "Barilla always makes you feel al dente."

When applied to pasta, "al dente" means firm. Yes, the innuendo is intended. The pleasure of eating and the pleasure of sex are closely linked. For me, anyway.

When I was working for *Marc' Aurelio,* I think about 1937, I wrote a series of articles satirizing advertising claims on radio and in print. In one, a waiter spills a plate of cooked macaroni on a customer in a restaurant. The patron is angry until he finds out what brand of macaroni it is. Then, he's so honored that he orders another plate of it to be spilled on him.

It was a pleasant surprise for me to have people find what I wrote funny. I had never been one to tell jokes, but I made comments based on my perspective on life, a sort of exaggerated truth.

The commercials I made for Campari and Barilla were received with as much attention as feature films. It was announced in the newspaper that a Fellini commercial was going to be shown on TV. Afterwards, each commercial was reviewed and discussed by essayists and critics.

In 1992, I was asked to make a commercial for the Banca di Roma. A few years had passed since I had directed anything at all, so I accepted. Again, as I had for Campari, I chose a railway setting.

I used the effect of a train coming out of a tunnel, as in *City of Women*. As in that film, a passenger awakens from a dream. In the commercial, he realizes that a loan from the bank can make his dreams come true. The solution is more simple than in *City of Women*. The train, like a car, offers the possibility of sitting and watching the moving images from the window, something I have always loved to do.

I was impressed by the books of Carlos Castaneda and wanted to make a film based on them. He was very difficult to contact. After a conversation with a friend [Charlotte Chandler], who had talked with Castaneda's lawyer in California, I decided to go there to meet Castaneda, though he had not yet agreed to a meeting. No one, not even his editor, had ever met the mysterious and ever-elusive author. Only his lawyer who had been receiving the royalty checks from Castaneda's publisher knew him. When I returned to Rome after the peregrination, I told journalists that I met with Castaneda, but that nothing came of it.

The truth is, I never found Castaneda.

When I gave interviews, I told the press answers they wanted to hear, and sometimes I said, "Yes, I met Castaneda." Sometimes I said he was fantastic and more than lived up to my expectations. Other times I said he wasn't at all the way I expected him to be. It seemed a little foolish for me to say we had gone looking for the proverbial wild goose. As it was, the trip used up my interest in Carlos Castaneda, whoever he may be or wherever he may be. It appears he is a person even less social than I. What came out of the trip, besides the experience of the trip itself, was that I never read Castaneda after that. With that trip, I turned the last page, and it was as if I had already made the film.

I was chosen by the Film Society of Lincoln Center to be honored in New York at their 1985 gala. My friend Charlotte Chandler came to Rome to tell me the "good" news.

The honor made me happy—at first. That was my initial reaction. My second was anguish, because no one ever wants to mail me my honor. I have to think about traveling and leaving my work. They were giving me the gift of airplane tickets. So started the dread ambivalence. I began to make the flight in my mind.

Something terribly upsetting for me is the worry that a flight may be canceled. It may seem strange that I dread this occurrence, considering how much I hate to fly, that I would mind so much the cancellation of a flight that I didn't want to take at all. The reason is I've already made up my mind that my destination justifies the unpleasant loss of time. Cancellation means I not only lose more time, but I also have to go through the dreaded anticipation of it again. The anticipation time is much longer than the actual trip. By the time I actually travel, I have already made the flight several times in my head.

As I was born spiritually in Rome, I will die in Rome. A reason I don't travel is I don't want to die somewhere else.

Giulietta went with me to New York, along with Mastroianni, Alberto Sordi, and my publicist, Mario Longardi. Anouk Aimée, as thin as ever, came from Paris and met us in New York. I remember when we were making *La Dolce Vita,* and she came on the set. The fans waiting at the studio gate saw her and they called out, "Feed her! Feed her!" Donald Sutherland had already arrived in New York. Giulietta was always so happy to travel and to have an occasion for a pretty new dress. Ever the actor, Mastroianni hoped it would lead to a good part. Anyway, it led him to Anouk.

At the Lincoln Center gala in my honor, I paid homage to the American cinema and the debt I owed to the Hollywood films I had seen during my Rimini boyhood. When I spoke about Felix the Cat and his influence on me for the audience at Lincoln Center, I never expected people to laugh and respond like that. I didn't know if it was me they loved, or Felix. Both, I hope.

I had always loved New York City, but I never knew if New York would love me. That night it told me it did.

Mastroianni was in the box with me, counting the house. He said, "Look—there are more famous people here tonight in the audience than on the stage!" I don't know if he meant they were more in number or in fame. Then he asked me if I'd noticed Dustin Hoffman whistling enthusiastically when I was presented. No, I hadn't noticed. Mastroianni was used to making live appearances. I was too frozen with fear to be aware of anything except whether my fly was zipped. Often Mastroianni would try to break me up at a nervous moment, to lighten the tension, but this time he knew it was more than his comic talents could achieve. We were *all* taking the event quite seriously.

After the show at Lincoln Center, there was a big party at Tavern on the Green in Central Park. A dinner was served, but I never tasted it. It seems to me I was standing the entire time as hundreds of people came over to meet me and congratulate me. I was worried about not remembering someone I'd met before. I hadn't eaten since early that day because I was too nervous to eat until after I'd given my speech.

I thought we'd go out to eat afterwards, but there was yet another party at a discothèque, far downtown. There were decorations there representing my films, but it was crowded and dark. Giulietta was frightened by the crowd and the darkness, and wanted to leave.

We were all starving, and it was two-thirty A.M. We went uptown, *far* uptown, to a place called Elaine's. Elaine, herself, opened the door. She was more Elaine than anyone could expect her to be. She could have been in one of my films. I would have invited her, but I knew she couldn't leave her restaurant. People who love their restaurants are like film directors on their sets. They can't leave their responsibility. They don't want to. Elaine's restaurant doesn't belong to her; she belongs to it—not only *in* it, but *to* it.

Someone said to us, "That's the table where Woody Allen sits." At that, Alberto Sordi rushed over and kissed the table.

There were a number of invitations to do the talk shows. Against my better judgment, I agreed. I could never be forced to compromise when I was doing my films, but Alberto Grimaldi, the producer, had been nice to me, so I agreed. What I didn't do in Italian, I agreed to do in English. If I made a fool of myself, I hoped the word wouldn't go back to Italy. How would I explain to Italian telejournalists that I had "done the tour" in America when I never would do it with them and always gave as the reason simply that I *never* gave television interviews?

A television interviewer in New York asked me, "Are you a genius?"

What could I say? I was borrowing time in order to figure out what to say. I didn't wish to embarrass either her or myself. So I said, "How nice it would be to think so." That took care of it. And I thought, Indeed! How nice it *would* be to think so!

•   •   •

Going to the movies is a true personal choice to go see one film or another film. The person walks into a dream. When the films ends, he leaves and walks back out into real life. It's different with television.

Television talks to us, at us, when we are defenseless, even unaware. Its message of vulgarity and wrong values is transmitted to people watching while they are on the phone, arguing with each other, even eating conversationless dinners. The best way to watch TV is while you're asleep.

I feel that the all-pervasiveness of TV, with its commercial interests, is a danger to a generation which seems all too willing to let television do their thinking for them and rear their children. In *Ginger and Fred,* if I indulged myself to rave and rant, I would sacrifice my own wish to entertain, and would thus be guilty of the same fault as the thing I'm criticizing. People believe television. It's like a friend talking to them in their houses, joining them at the dinner table, in bed with them.

Television has so taken over that there are people who walk into their homes and turn on the TV sets before they take off their coats. Some of them fall asleep at night with the TV set on, and it stays that way, talking to itself, until it runs out of programming, and the set finally goes to sleep for the night, leaving the glowing screen to light the room. It has relieved us of talking to each other. It can relieve us of thinking, that is, of the internal conversation in which each of us talks only with himself in his own head. The next invasion is of our dreams. At night, in our sleep, each of us can be a contestant on a game show and win a Frigidaire while dreaming. In the morning, everything melts.

People become estranged not only from those closest and dearest to them, but from themselves. I don't think it's my imagination that young people are less articulate now than they were before the advent of television.

The videocassette is between television and the film. I see in it the advantage that you can keep a film you love, the way you can keep a book or a record. You can re-create in a small way on the small screen in your home the cinema situation. I approve, as long as you turn off the lights and do not eat dinner with the film. Eating popcorn, yes. Another crucial difference is that in the movie theater, the chocolate-bar wrapper should be opened and either removed or loosely wrapped around the candy bar to contain it, so warm fingers won't cause it to melt on them. At home watching television, the wrapper need not be removed in advance, except out of consideration for the individual himself or herself, who is viewing and nibbling.

A disadvantage of the videocassette is that something rare and wonderful becomes common currency. I wonder how we would regard gold if it weren't so difficult to obtain. How many times can anyone watch the same film and be moved or entertained?

In the future, very-large-screen, high-definition television pictures will undoubtedly come close to simulating the theater experience in all respects except the communality of shared audience reaction. When this happens, perhaps the conscious choice of choosing one picture over another will be exercised by a visit to the supermarket or a call to the television station instead of attending the theater, in which case there will no longer be any need for theaters. Another harp is lost to the wrecker's ball . . .

Ginger and Fred grew out of an idea of Giulietta's for what was to have been an episode in a TV series. I was to have directed Giulietta's episode. She wanted to do it, and I would have done it for her. It's therefore ironic, because the film attacks vapid, all-pervasive TV, even though it does it with some humor. I made the film because I liked the idea, not because I wanted to attack television. From the beginning, it was intended to be a love story.

There were to have been episodes directed by Antonioni, Zeffirelli, and others. It was a grand plan, but too expensive for television. When the series didn't materialize, Alberto Grimaldi suggested making it into a feature film. Giulietta thought Mastroianni, whom she had known since university theater, would be perfect. The two of them together in a film for the first time would be wonderful, we all agreed.

Of course, he was an overweight Fred. It was actually the fattest moment of Mastroianni's life, but I didn't say this. I know how much he enjoys eating. I sympathize. A fat director is one thing. A fat Fred Astaire is another.

Rather than go on a diet, I thought he would refuse the part, even though he wouldn't like saying no to Giulietta. But far from it. From the first moment, it caught his fancy. It turned out he had always wanted to be Fred Astaire, and he immediately did a little dance for me. He was good, even if when he finished, he was breathing hard.

When Mastroianni said to me that Fred was such a total wreck of a man that he would have to wear Lobb shoes to save his pride, I didn't understand his reasoning, but with Mastroianni, one wouldn't want to try to understand him. Better not to.

He explained that his character would have to wear the best shoes in order to keep up appearances. He said that while not everyone would know the shoes were Lobb, they would see that this was a man who still had his pride, who cared what people thought, and who wanted them to think he was successful. A salesman, he said, would be aware of the importance of his shoes. As a dancer, he would also consider shoes important. It would be good for feeling his character to have the inspiration from the feet up.

Mastroianni is not a Method actor, and usually didn't even insist on a script, let alone want to know the life story and motivations of the character he is playing. So I assumed he wanted a pair of Lobb shoes made to fit him that would be his at the end of the production. It was the least I could do after what I had done to the top of his head.

The greatest friendships are adventures. They are passionate. Sometimes I think that I'm not as good a friend to my friends as I should be. I am too self-centered to be a good friend. I am not self-centered about myself, only about my work. My obsession does not leave room for me to think, How does he or she feel about it? Sometimes I worry that I have been too hard, but I never deliberately test a friendship. I am happy to have it like a gift.

Once I tested, too much, without the intention of doing so. Poor Mastroianni! Old Snaporaz would do anything for me—well, *almost* anything. I don't know if what he did was because of our special friendship or because of his total faith in me as a director, or even because of his consummate professionalism. As friends, we are like schoolboys together. When we work together, he puts himself in my hands, limp, like a trusting doll, prepared with the good spirits to give his all. So what did I do? I acted as Delilah to his Samson, and had him shorn like a lamb.

For *Ginger and Fred*, it was imperative that he not look too good— that he still be somewhat attractive to women, but not *too* attractive.

In the case of Mastroianni, it is quite a feat to minimize his sex appeal. I decided the surest way to deprive him of that sex appeal was to take away some of his hair. Not all of it. Total baldness can be more sexy than thin hair, so the idea was to make it wispy—weak, like mine. Later, he accused me of doing it because I was jealous of him. Of course I was jealous. But it wasn't why I did it. I did it for "Fred," his character. The answer was not the scissors, but the thinning shears. We also used wax. The barber said, "The hair will grow back thicker than ever."

Mastroianni submitted to the barber and his ruthless thinning shears, and the wax, too. He allowed himself to be given an *almost* bald spot in the middle of his head. A few hairs were left to symbolize man clinging to his failing potency. Getting older means everything you took for granted requires greater effort and a little is appreciated more.

When I asked Mastroianni to have his hair thinned, I remembered the day Rossellini asked me to have my hair dyed yellow. The difference was Mastroianni was a star when I asked him.

I had not realized exactly how much difference those thinning shears would make, not just in the character Mastroianni was playing, but to his real self as well. There resulted a deformation of the personality of Old Snaporaz. It was not subtle. His posture was less good. He lost his arrogance. Sometimes, he even seemed ashamed. Wherever he went, he wore his hat at all times, not just outside, but inside, as well, in people's homes, in restaurants, wherever. Sirio Maccione at Le Cirque in New York made an exception for him when he had lunch at this elegant, delicious restaurant, permitting him to wear his hat during all his meals there. During the entire time we were in New York for the Film Society of Lincoln Center gala, Mastroianni removed his hat in public only during the honors, I think—I *hope*—in deference to me. Almost no one mentioned this attachment to his hat, nor could they have guessed why. Some of them thought it was a habit he picked up in *8½*. I suppose they were too embarrassed to say anything. A woman told me he even made love with his hat on, but I have that only as hearsay.

At first, we teased him about it. We expected that his hair would begin growing back soon. Months passed and his hair did not grow back at all. He continued to wear his hat. He was not his carefree self.

One could say he was *almost* morose. He bought more hats. I felt guilty. The barber who said his hair would grow back thicker than ever had disappeared.

More months passed. Then, one day, finally, his hair began to grow back. It grew back thicker than ever. Once again, he was seen everywhere without his hat, and wherever he went, women ran their fingers through his wonderful hair. His playful personality returned.

Mastroianni was asked to make another sacrifice: He was not permitted to dance as well as he could. That hurt. His dream had always been to dance *like* Fred Astaire *with* Ginger Rogers. But if he had danced as well as he really could dance, it would have been inappropriate to the character. And Giulietta would not have liked it if he had danced better than she did.

For the film I was going to make, it was important that I not be sentimental, too sympathetic to the characters, because if I cared too much for them, no one else would. It was also important not to permit them to be *too* self-pitying. Giulietta, particularly, had to keep her upbeat quality. Fred's character was allowed a certain amount of weakness, as long as he didn't overdo it and lose the sympathy of the audience.

Giulietta didn't like the look of her character. She wanted me to make Ginger younger, more attractive. She didn't want to have lines in her face, and she had become concerned with her wardrobe, not just that it was appropriate to her character, but that it was flattering to her. In the beginning, she didn't care how the clothes made her look, as long as they were right for the look of her character, and helped her "feel" her character. She insisted that it was appropriate vanity which the character of Ginger naturally would have. Legitimate, but I think it was Giulietta's vanity, as well. When she was very young, I could have made her look one hundred years old and she wouldn't have cared. She said she still would not have cared if I made her look one hundred years old, but it was that somewhere-in-between that was bothering her.

In the 1930s, Fred Astaire and Ginger Rogers represented the American cinema for Italians. They told us that a joyous life existed. When we began this film, all of us were admirers of Rogers and Astaire, and we saw what we were doing as a kind of homage, a tribute to what they had signified for people all over the world. We were very surprised, shocked, when we heard that Ginger Rogers was suing us. I can't understand what she was thinking.

I had wanted to begin by showing Ginger Rogers dancing on the screen with Fred Astaire, with an Italian audience watching in rapture, but I wasn't permitted to do that. What a shame. It turned out that Ginger Rogers was Marcello's "dream girl." At least she was when we made the film. After the lawsuit, I don't know. Mastroianni and I never talked about it.

Our little picture was about people who worshiped Rogers and Astaire. The title *Ginger and Fred* was meant as a compliment, and I just could not believe it when I was told that Ginger Rogers had reacted with anger and was trying to stop the film from being shown. The damages being asked for were more than the cost of making the film.

I never believed she was the one responsible. She must have listened to other people who said the film ridiculed her. Some critics even said I was making fun of Rogers and Astaire. I never mock what I do. I see what is funny about my subjects, but I never make fun of them. I laugh *with* my characters, not *at* them.

I think it was lawyers and agents who told her whatever story they thought they could use to make money for themselves, and she was fooled. I believe she never saw the film. I could not accept that the Ginger Rogers of the Fulgor Cinema of my boyhood could so betray me. The person who was really hurt was Giulietta, because she had so identified with Ginger, and the movie was really made because of Giulietta. Of course, the case came to nothing, but we who made the picture lost some of our sense of joy, and perhaps the aura of bad feeling brought bad luck. I believe it's essential to create an aura of good feeling, love, around what you do. It's like hanging up a halo. The converse destroys the luck.

In the Italy of the thirties, Ginger and Fred had comforted us, especially those of us who lived in the provinces. In the world of fascism, Fred Astaire and Ginger Rogers showed us that another life was possible, at least in America, that land of unimaginable freedom and opportunity. We knew they were American films, but at the same time, they were ours. Fred and Ginger belonged to us, as did the Marx Brothers, Charlie Chaplin, Mae West, and Gary Cooper. They

were our heritage as well as that of American children. It is not possible to put into words what Hollywood meant in the life of a little
boy in Rimini. Hollywood was America, and America was a dream.
Everyone in Italy wished he could see America. I, too, dreamed that
dream.

My favorite line in the movie—not a message, because I don't like
the idea that a movie preaches a sermon—comes from a monk who
says, "Everything is a miracle. We just have to recognize it."

seventeen

AN OSCAR WITH A PIMPLE
ON YOUR NOSE

I n 1986, I was invited to present an Oscar. I was asked to be a co-presenter with Billy Wilder and Akira Kurosawa. I didn't like to say no because the Oscars have been very good to me and I like to be respectful to them and to these great directors. But I didn't want to say yes, either.

It's a wonderful activity to participate in for someone who lives in Los Angeles and doesn't have to fly from Rome, for someone who doesn't mind speaking live to a billion people in a foreign language, for someone who isn't working at the time, et cetera.

Somehow it's always easier to say yes to a date far ahead. When I say yes, it doesn't seem like the date will ever come, but arrive it always does—well after I have put it out of my mind. There is always pressure by those who are producing my film of the moment to go to America. They say it's because it is an honor, which is obvious, and that it means good promotion, which, I suppose, is also obvious. The reason they don't mention is that they want to make the trip and go to the parties. Producers love film festivals and parties. They love honors. They love the Oscars even more.

Sometimes I give answers like, "I'll try." It's a big mistake. If I leave the door open only a little, there is all that pressure. Often I don't say yes, but people hear yes, because it's what they *want* to hear. They hear my silence, and they interpret it as assent.

At the same time, I admit that I do not like to say no to people. Perhaps it's because I don't like to have anyone say no to me. I don't like to make people unhappy. It's a kind of cowardice on my part. Sometimes I say "Maybe," which is a kind of lie when I know in my heart I want to say no, and I mean no.

Sometimes when I say "Maybe," I pay the price. If you take the time and energy for what you have already done, it is not without a price. I have to do the thing. When I receive any award, I worry. I take the Oscars very seriously, and I had every intention to go in 1986 and be a presenter, but I was walking with Giulietta and tripped and sprained my ankle. My first thought was that they wouldn't believe me. I had a bad reputation for not appearing places after I said I would. My bad reputation probably had been earned. Since I was only one of the presenters, it seemed it wouldn't be so terrible. They had others who wanted to do it. I don't know if they believed me. Was it true? Yes and no. Did I trip? Yes. Did I injure myself? Yes. Did it hurt? Yes. Could I have managed to go to the Oscars and limp onstage for the presentation? Yes. Did I? No.

The week following the Oscar ceremony, I was scheduled to be in New York for the premiere of *Ginger and Fred* by the Film Society of Lincoln Center, which had honored me the previous year. I had a personal relationship there and my ankle was feeling much better. I decided to make that trip. Giulietta wanted to do it, as she had planned to go with me to the Oscars and had been disappointed not to make the trip, and so did the producer of *Ginger and Fred*, Grimaldi, who was with us. In New York, it was a nice surprise to meet Sven Nykvist, the cinematographer for Ingmar Bergman. He had stayed an extra night in New York to be there. I was honored. One of the benefits of success is when people you admire but never expect to meet go out of their way to meet you. I think that because I was in New York the following week, even limping, the people in California never really believed me.

At the reception, I had to sit most of the time, because I still couldn't put any weight, especially my kind of weight, on my ankle. Because I had to sit, Giulietta came and sat in a chair next to me. She is social and genuinely enjoys meeting people, but she has so much sympathy for me that she wouldn't leave me sitting there alone——even though, of course, I was never left alone.

I was trying to hide the pain. Someone advised me not to hide it after missing the Oscars the week before, but rather, I should exaggerate it.

We all like to please. We like best those people who see us the way we want to be seen. The way *I* would best like to be seen and remembered is the way I am when I am directing. When I'm directing, that special energy comes upon me, which surprises me.

I do not have an open set, which I repeatedly say, and I like to have only a few visitors, people I know and trust, or occasionally someone I don't know but who is involved in making films. I always have an extraordinary number of requests to visit the set while I am filming, and I have had a necessary policy of rejecting almost all of these. This is taken care of by my assistant. As to the press, I close my set totally during the first three weeks, until I have made a strong beginning. After that, when someone from the press is present, I never want more than one journalist there at a time. It struck me that I could invite everyone to see what it is like when I am directing by making a film in which I directed myself directing. Television offered me that possibility, to make *Intervista*.

Intervista was originally conceived as a television film to coincide with the fiftieth anniversary of Cinecittà in 1987. Cinecittà would have its own documentary, but my film would be personal, whatever I wanted to say. As usual, I had much more to say than my time or budget or shooting schedule allowed, so my little picture for television became a "filmetto" for theaters. This pleased one of my producers, Ibrahim Moussa, and displeased another, RAI Television. RAI may also have been displeased by my idea at the end, that American Indians carrying TV antennas instead of bows and arrows could attack the film people. My symbolism was less than subtle, but not intended to be bitter.

The idea for the film had actually come to me on a Sunday, all alone at Cinecittà. I like to go there on Sunday. It's quiet, and I can be alone with the ghosts. For making a film, the problem-ghost was Mussolini. How could one tell the story of Cinecittà without mentioning Mussolini, whom Italians prefer to forget? He is so unmentionable that he has come to seem almost a fictitious character for Italians who weren't born until after Il Duce was hung upside down. Vittorio Mussolini ran the studio, and the fascists recognized the importance of films for conveying not just overt propaganda, but covert values and ideas.

As long as Cinecittà exists, I feel comforted. It is my fortress. Like me, it is getting old and dilapidated, but is still there. On Sundays, I would bring food along for the homeless cats who lived there. They were part of the work force, because they caught the rats who tried to eat the cable, or anything else, even actors.

The original idea was for a director to be shooting a documentary about Cinecittà, and I would be that director, shooting my new picture. I thought it would be more interesting if I did an interview with a foreign group that comes to talk with me, in which I would shoot a scene from my new film; then I would remember my first visit to Cinecittà in 1940, and my introduction to Cinecittà, when I was only twenty and had no idea of working in films, much less becoming a director, having gone there as a journalist to do an interview.

I always believe an interview should be conducted in a playful, spontaneous way. My only rule is not to be boring, a difficult rule not to break. I hoped that the film would not be perceived as narcissistic. It shows Cinecittà as it seemed to me the first time I saw it, as well as how it seems to me now.

The actor I chose to play myself at twenty reminded me a great deal of how I looked and acted at that age. He was like me, even to the pimple I had the makeup people put on his nose. I remember going out to Cinecittà to interview an actress, and having the most conspicuous pimple on my nose. It was a sudden pimple, arriving without explanation or excuse. I was certain that everyone was looking at the pimple on my nose, especially the actress. I felt it growing—not my nose, the pimple. Whenever I saw people speaking together, I thought they must be saying, "Look! Look at that pimple on his nose!" I knew how Pinocchio must have felt, although I hadn't told a lie. I was a painfully self-conscious, and at the same time, self-centered young man. Part of being self-conscious is being self-centered.

At one time, I planned to make a film for television about the Fulgor Cinema in Rimini. I may still do it. At one point, it was to be a three-film series, with the first to be about Cinecittà, the second about my impressions of opera, and the third about the Fulgor. The first

At the end of the shooting of *And the Ship Sails On* in 1983, Fellini and Charlotte Chandler pose on the deck of the ship set, which was built on Soundstage 5 at Cinecittà, Rome.

evolved into *Intervista,* which was long enough for the producers to release as a theatrical feature. The series project was abandoned. The Fulgor had appeared in *Amarcord,* but it was a somewhat romanticized version of the one in Rimini. I had it rebuilt at Cinecittà, as the Fulgor appears in my memories. To really know the Fulgor as it was, it would be necessary to spray a theater now with the same bad perfume the Fulgor used then. In those days, a man came around and sprayed cheap perfume to cover over more odious odors. What those might have been are too terrible to discuss. In *Amarcord*, I glamorized the Fulgor. The way I rebuilt it is the way I remember it. I love it, and it's what I would do for a woman I loved.

I wanted to do *Mandrake the Magician* as a film. It was an American comic strip I liked as a child. In the early 1970s, I envisioned Mastroianni as a perfect Mandrake, and Claudia Cardinale as Narda, his girlfriend. I thought she would be perfect, too, but Mastroianni wanted Catherine Deneuve, with whom he was having a real-life affair, as Narda. They had a daughter, as Mandrake and Narda didn't have. Mandrake and Narda never had their life in one of my films. I wonder if it's too late? I have talked many times with Lee Falk, Mandrake's creator, about making the film.

When I was doing *Intervista*, I did accomplish having Mastroianni play Mandrake, if only for a few minutes. I also reunited him with Anita Ekberg, who has been in Rome since *La Dolce Vita*. She loves Rome, especially the food. I rarely see her, but whenever I do, she always "tries out," and makes certain that I know she's available to work.

I am always being tortured by the ray-of-sunshine concept. This is an obsession which mainly afflicts producers. I am most familiar with the Italian producer, but I think this is a universal characteristic. Every producer always wants, at the end of the movie, his ray of sunshine. That's why at the end of *Intervista*, I provide a ray of sunshine coming through the clouds after the rainstorm.

Some years ago, I read a book called *The Free Women of Magliano*, by Mario Tobino. The author was a doctor in a mental hospital, and he wrote about the inmates of this place in a way that was poetic and feeling. He wrote of the mad with a tenderness which affected me, since I personally have always identified with the mad. I have been considered eccentric, strange, but my craziness has been channeled so successfully that it is exalted. How fortunate for me.

In Rimini and in Gambettola, where I spent summers with my grandmother, mental institutions weren't common, and it was not unusual to see the mentally retarded or the mentally ill wandering about or hidden in houses. I felt a fascination for these isolated persons who inhabited separate worlds, outcasts because they couldn't do profitable work and were thus a burden on family and community.

People have deformed ideas about deformity. We are taught to look away from what is deemed ugly, and we are taught through words and by example what we should perceive as ugly.

As a child in Rimini, after World War I, I saw the veterans, the amputees, the ones in wheelchairs. Because there were no places to put those who were considered accidents of nature, the simple-minded, the mentally handicapped, the so-called "freaks," were kept at home, sometimes hidden, by parents who were especially ashamed of them because they were regarded as punishment for evil. In the superstitious world in which I lived, there were many who believed these were bad people, who had been afflicted because they had been cursed or their parents had been cursed. If you had a birth deformity in your family, it was a sign to everyone else that you had been guilty of a wickedness.

Have you ever looked at the "beautiful people," as they are termed? I look around at a film festival. Are they *really* more beautiful?

Giants and dwarves, the fat lady and the bearded lady—these people belong as much to the world as we do. It is our view of them that is handicapped.

In my childhood, I was playing with a group of village children near Gambettola, and exploring a forbidden site, an old convent. We found an idiot child, left there without attention, except to be fed, in the hope that he would soon die, thus saving the bit of food he consumed, and releasing those responsible from the burden, even erasing the disgrace of his birth. It made a profound impression on me. It was a persistent memory, which insisted on appearing in *La Strada*. Once I had told the story in the film, it became Gelsomina's memory rather than mine. I was relieved of remembering the reality and could remember the film.

I had given thought to making a film about the insane, but what I wanted to do remained vague. When I came upon the Tobino book, I thought perhaps this was it, and I prepared a short treatment, but it aroused no interest. Producers would say, "Who wants to see a picture about crazy people?" Only with *Voices of the Moon* did I finally make such a film.

Voices of the Moon presented a special problem for me because it was an adaptation from a novel, *The Poem of Lunatics,* by Ermanno Cavazzoni. This was something I said I would never do, so perhaps that was the reason it tempted me. I have always been tempted by the challenge of doing something different. I had faced somewhat similar problems before with Petronius and to some extent with *Casanova,* but this was unique because it was a contemporary novel, published in 1985. As usual, I solved the problem by doing it totally my own way, but with the approval of the author, who collaborated to some extent.

Film adaptations of books have always seemed to me redundant. The novel, like any art form, is born into its own unique environment and thrives best there. It's like a different syntax, a different language. To transfer something from one art form to another is like asking an actor to play the part of a great man. It's only a façade, an imitation of the real thing.

I am well aware that D. W. Griffith is credited with having invented the feature film by synthesizing the new medium from the stage play and the novel, but I think his contribution is far greater. He understood the potential of cinema to tell a story in a unique way, and he applied his new concepts to translating the novel, and later drama, to what he intuitively understood the screen to be capable of. Film, as he envisioned it, was something new, not something derived from something else. The proof of this is that since the advent of his movies, all forms of storytelling have been dramatically altered by cinematic techniques.

With *Voices of the Moon,* I chose not to adapt the novel to film, but film to the novel. More exactly, I tried to apply my own means of expression to the basic elements of the plot and the needs of the characters.

While I was writing *Voices of the Moon,* I had doubts. I had never had doubts before, not like that, *while* I was writing. Terrible for inspiration. We were working in Pinelli's living room, Pinelli and I, and I would turn to him and say, "Do you really think we should go on with this?" We were working in the same room, at separate tables. He'd given me the bigger desk. He answered, "Yes, of course, we should go on." But I knew I'd never looked for reassurance like that before. Something was wrong, but I didn't know if what was wrong was with the script we were turning out, or with the choice of the project, or if the problem was I'd lost my confidence in myself. I was uncertain how *I* felt about it. How could I bring something to life if I didn't have my own belief in myself, as well as in what I was doing?

Though she didn't say it, I sensed that Giulietta didn't think I'd made a good choice of a project. It was unspoken, but we both realized that it was not a point in my career when I could afford a failure.

A past romance, once it is past, can be a pleasurable memory or a painful one, or even scarcely a memory, but one thing it cannot be is

Federico and Giulietta on holiday during the mid-1980s.

a romance. It is that way for me with a film. I was not entirely surprised that *Voices of the Moon* was unfavorably received by critics and the public. After I had completed the writing and before I began filming, I started to have some misgivings myself. It wasn't that I didn't like it, but I felt uncertain about how an audience would feel. When I asked Pinelli, "Should I withdraw it?" he said no. I think he was right. I feel that once it had been given form, it deserved to have its chance at life.

Now that more of my life is behind me, time seems to race by. There is so little of it left to tell all the stories I feel compelled to tell. Not only does failure make it difficult to find the financing for other pictures, but worse yet, it shakes my confidence in myself. When the world loves what you do, it gives you the approbation that is sustenance for the artist.

It is important to enjoy your success. Performers have been happier in low vaudeville than as headliners in the best theaters. Sometimes I have professional satisfactions. More and more it is only the professional satisfactions that occupy my attention. When I was very young, I used to think about being happy. Happiness is not something I think about now. I know it will not last. And unhappiness will return. But there is a consolation in knowing unhappiness will not last either.

Only one of my films do I consider possibly a failure, or a partial failure, from my own point of view, that is, and this film is *Casanova*. I accepted the project without having read the book, and then was not enthusiastic about what I had taken on. Less than enthusiastic. The result could have been more satisfying, but still I think I made a truthful statement about a despicable character.

With *Voices of the Moon,* I asked the audience to suspend their expectations for a movie, a Fellini movie, and be carried along by the images on the screen. Evidently, they didn't do that. They expected a typical Fellini film, if there is such a thing. Most of its potential audience couldn't even find the film to be disappointed by it.

The novel is, by nature, an intensely subjective medium. The writer is alone with his typewriter, the reader alone with his book. For obvious reasons, conveying subjectivity on the screen, even the television screen, is more difficult. The literal aspect of the images and the sheer number of participants involved in the making of a movie work against subjectivity. Empathy is possible, but empathy is not subjectivity. Personally, I like the sense of objectivity that the cinema conveys, but it's different from the subjective nature of the novel.

In *Voices of the Moon,* the viewpoint is largely that of a harmless lunatic who has just been released from an asylum. He is mad in the romantic sense. He sees things differently from the others. I am a lunatic in that respect, and I can identify with him.

In this film, I must show Ivo's distorted, yet poetic, view of reality without making it too obvious that it is *his* view. The situation is similar to that of *The Cabinet of Dr. Caligari,* except that the resolution of that film was opposed to the director's original intention and imposed on him by his producers. As I understand it, the original ending of *Caligari* revealed the madman as the only sane person in an insane world, but it was changed. In *Voices of the Moon,* the viewpoint remains unchanged. It is for the audience to judge who is sane and who is not.

For audiences unfamiliar with the novel, this was a problem I should have foreseen. Even in Italy, not everyone was familiar with it. The criticism came back to me from the Cannes festival that no one understood my film—obviously an exaggeration. I was supposed to go to Cannes for the black-tie showing, but at the last minute I decided not to go. I had been coerced into agreeing to go when I don't like the film festival situation, and the audience for such an event is not a typical audience, so I didn't feel I could learn anything from their reaction. Their involvement, I feel, is greater with their wardrobe and the event than with the film.

I've been asked if *Voices of the Moon* is an extension of characters I used in *I Vitelloni* and *Amarcord.* There is a resemblance between Marisa, the manicurist, and Gradisca, since both are related to the same memory. And I can identify with Ivo in a symbolic way. But generally the answer is no.

It is very sad for me when Ivo finds that Marisa's shoe fits more than one woman—indeed, many women. It is the message of old age, at any age. It is the birth of cynicism. Romanticism has died within Ivo. He will never be able to hope totally again. He will never be able to trust totally again. There will always be voices in his head asking those little nagging questions that the romantic dares not ask. The very existence of the concept of questions indicates the demise of the romantic spirit.

Roberto Benigni borrows Fellini's viewing lens during the filming of *Voices of the Moon* (1990).

Being old is a lot like being young, but with a less promising future.

Because the world didn't love my film, I must love it more. It is the least my poor creature is entitled to from me.

The failure of your film is a kind of impotence. A failure is embarrassing. To have a few failures destroys your confidence, so that it becomes more difficult to have any future success. Failure, like impotency, can become permanent. You cannot even try. You wish you could blame someone else, but deep down, you know.

I don't like to think of myself as stubborn, because I associate rigidity with a kind of stupidity and irrationality. Yet I know I cannot be pushed, and if anyone attempts to do so, I literally sit down on the ground and refuse to move, in the same way my mother told me I did when I was two years old on the main shopping street of Rimini, and everyone had to walk around me. Finally, I had to be dragged or carried away. My mother was mortified. Knowing and understanding her as I later came to, I'm certain she was. Her life was being concerned with what others thought of her.

It was not so easy for her to assist me toward finding my happiness in life when she had not been able to find her own. I resolved I would not live my life according to the prescriptions of others. I have not. But it doesn't mean I haven't been hurt when I was criticized.

Sometimes I think I acted to the detriment of my own professional well-being because I sensed pressure to do something. In my personal life, I also resisted coercion, though a woman might succeed with subtlety in the soft way women have. Afterwards, however, I resent it if I feel there was trickery. I could never resent anything done in innocence. Giulietta has that innocence. Trickery is foreign to her nature, though she has been known to serve me her special spaghetti at night before asking a difficult question.

A number of people told me that *Voices of the Moon* would not be a success, that it was not the kind of film people expected from Fellini, that it would not be clear for people who hadn't read the novel, that it was too Italian. Perhaps one of the reasons I stayed with the project was just being stubborn.

For the most part, Fellini wore a suit, shirt, tie, and hat when he directed, dressing like a "businessman"— but not always.

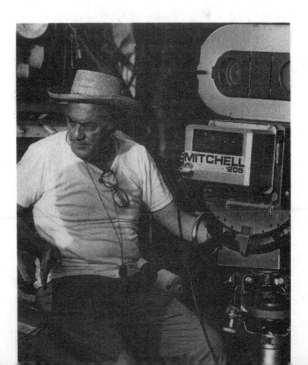

No one likes to hear, over and over, praise for films he made long ago, and always the same films singled out. Every producer really wanted another *La Strada,* or another *La Dolce Vita,* or another *8½.* But especially another *La Dolce Vita,* because it made so much money.

People assume that I am pursued by opportunities to make films. I myself believed that's how it would be. It never happened. Only after *La Dolce Vita* were there choices, but they weren't good ones. Choices matter qualitatively, not quantitatively.

I asked myself what I believe is the important question about creating something. It's simply this: "Is it alive or isn't it?"

For me, the answer for *Voices of the Moon* was yes. It deserved its chance for life. I made the film, and the answer for me is still Yes, it's alive.

If I could choose a film which I would like to have more appreciated, it would be *Voices of the Moon,* because it has been poorly received in the world, like an orphan, even while I am its father, still alive, and because it is my most recent film. It would be nourishing for me to hear, "You were never better, Federico."

I believe that most important to my health is my work. Sometimes I had a temperature when I walked into Cinecittà, and I needed only to arrive there, to be greeted as I entered, and my temperature fled, driven away by the genial welcoming ambiance. When I walk onto the set of a film I am making, immediately I do not have a cold, even if I came in with one.

As long as I have my work, I have my health. Whenever I don't have my work for a while, I get sick. Not everyone understands that, only those who love what they do. My work is a protection, like a suit of armor. It would be an oversimplification to say it's a flow of adrenaline. When I am fulfilling myself, I feel a precious state of well-being.

When *Voices of the Moon* was not well received, and I could not find backing for a next film, I began not to feel as well. I get sick only between films. For me, depression comes when I'm not working. It also comes, though of briefer duration and less intensity, if I'm not working well.

I don't think my films changed much over the years—maybe a little. In the beginning I emphasized plot more. I adhered to story and was more literary than cinematic. Later, I placed more faith in images. I found my films related to painting, discovering for myself that light, rather than dialogue, reveals a character's state of mind, as well as the director's style.

My ideal is to make movies with the freedom of a painter. A painter doesn't have to say what his painting will be. He must be in his studio with his canvas and with his colors. The painting takes shape and fills itself in. If there has been a change in my work, that is it. I have become more free of the plot, letting it develop, going closer to the pictorial.

The motion picture is a synesthetic medium. Synesthesia is the stimulation of senses other than those which would normally be affected by a particular stimulus. A trompe l'oeil still-life painting of attractive food, for example, can stimulate the taste buds as well as the visual sense. An operatic aria can evoke visual images even though it's aimed primarily at the aural sense. Sculpture can stimulate the tactile sense. I frequently feel the impulse to touch the toes of a Roman emperor as I pass one of the statues in Rome. I restrain myself. The emperor may be ticklish. The cinema, I feel, can affect many of the senses simultaneously, and often unintentionally. I try to be aware of this at all times I am working, which means attention to details. When I show people eating a delicious meal, I make sure that the food really *is* good. Sometimes I have to test it before the scene is shot, in order to know what my characters are eating.

The critics write so much about this change in my work, from the earliest days to the later pictures. In the beginning, I was less secure with images and more secure with words. Gradually, my security with images gave me the freedom to allow them to come forth boldly. I realized I could return in the dubbing to give my attention to dialogue. I'm very concerned not just with dialogue, but with sound, sound which is so like image. I am concerned with the totality of sound. The ducks quacking in the background on the farm in *Il Bidone* may have a message to impart that is more important than a line or two of dialogue.

Sometimes a peripheral line of dialogue heard in the background can create an ambiance and make a comment in the under-language which can be more significant than the over-language. An example is the drunken American sailor in the background of one of the night-club scenes in *La Dolce Vita*. As Marcello and his father sit there, the drunken American calling out off-screen, "Play 'Stormy Weather,' " is barely audible. I am told that English-speaking audiences are able to pick that out of the background, and when they do, they find it especially funny, because it's like being "inside" and knowing a secret.

As I gained total control over my work, I was empowered to create totally out of myself and to be able to find myself. There are two kinds of films: those created by the group or committee, and those that pour out of one person. I can say, truthfully, I take total responsibility for what I have done.

There are those who have said, "I will figure out the formula for Fellini's success, and then I will turn out *La Dolce Vita of the 8½-Year-Old Son of Gelsomina*." But of course it doesn't work. They can't figure out a recipe for success because what works once will not work again. I don't have the answer any more than they. Every time I start a picture, I begin my first picture. Each time, before I begin, I feel the same fear, the same self-doubts. Will I ever be able to do it again? More is expected each time. The responsibility grows. The audience has a preconception of a Fellini film. And I have only one source on which I can draw, because it comes from within me.

Michelangelo Antonioni jokes with Fellini on the Cinecittà set of *And the Ship Sails On*.

I don't really want to copy myself, but the strange part of it is I would not know how to make a *La Dolce Vita*–type picture if I wanted to. It's terrifying to realize that I don't have the secret for *La Dolce Vita* any more than anyone else.

What I like to do is to make pictures as different from each other as possible, and I believe it is those which have the greatest potential to be good. The producers are not convinced.

Any success I have as a maker of films is determined by whether I make my visions visible for the audience. To succeed is to be like the magician in a fairy tale who makes something appear that wasn't there before. The magician takes something that didn't exist, or only vaguely existed, and transforms it into something we can see and feel, sometimes to which we can respond.

Critics accuse me of repeating myself. In fact, it's impossible not to do this. The effort to be artificially different, just for the sake of being different, is as false as the opposite. The best comedians did not have a million jokes, but even after we've heard some of them many times, we laugh, maybe harder, because they come from the character, and the underlying humanity that makes them funny is clear to us.

We know that W. C. Fields is a big bluff because he doesn't have any other qualification for survival, so he has to live on his wits, but we identify with him more and more as we see how skillfully he makes something out of absolutely nothing. The Marx Brothers are able to survive happily even though they have been given nothing in life but their wits. I'm talking, of course, about their screen characters. They are infinitely resourceful in their way. The fact that they react to different situations in relatively the same ingenious ways doesn't bother us. It amuses us and even moves us emotionally, because it tells us something about ourselves.

Repetition of ideas with variations is characteristic of all drama. Someone told me about a book on the thirty-nine possible dramatic situations. I think that was the number. He said, "Isn't it amazing that there are so few basic plots?" I'm surprised there are that many!

I am a visual person. Film is images. Later, you can always choose the sound you want, to heighten and improve. For me, the Italian system of dubbing is perfect.

If there had been no dubbing, I would have invented it, to enrich, to give greater precision, to have greater control, and to be sure the

Donald Sutherland, who had starred in *Casanova,* joins Fellini for the Film Society of Lincoln Center tribute in 1985.

faces I have chosen have the right voices. Italian films' being dubbed is a distinct advantage for me. I believe everything can be done better, more expressively, than the original sounds. Trying to get both the right picture and the right sound at the same time imposes a severe limitation. Even after a wrap, I am still making the film. Editing is very important for me, especially the editing of sound. Because of dubbing, I continue to have total control of my picture in all stages of production. I am particularly proud of the polyphonic sound in my films, possible only in postproduction editing. This gives me control of all of the sound, as well as all of the images. I am accused of preferring dubbing because I like to talk while I am directing, to play all the parts. Well, yes; that, too.

I think I can remember the first movie I ever attended, though not its title. I was with my mother in the darkened Fulgor Cinema in Rimini, and there were these enormous heads up on an even larger screen. Two huge women were talking. In my small mind, I couldn't imagine how those people got up there or why they were so big, but I immediately accepted my mother's explanation, which I forgot right away. I do remember wishing I could go up there and get into the screen myself. It looked interesting. But I was also afraid that I wouldn't know how to get out. I could be trapped inside the screen. Perhaps this first remembered encounter with the medium is why I use close-ups only for dramatic effect rather than as a routine narrative device, which is so common nowadays, especially on television. I know the extreme close-up of Oscar's eyes near the end of *Nights of Cabiria* would not be effective if extreme close-ups had been used throughout.

I have always felt that the camera, as the agent of the director, should follow the action, not lead it. I like to think of myself as an observer, not an active, noticeable agent in the narrative. A common mannerism of many directors is to show what they want the spectator to see before the action on the screen dictates it. The audience should *want* to see something before it is shown to them. Of course, when telling a story on the screen, this isn't always possible. I can think of instances when I have thought it necessary to lead an audience, though I hope it wasn't noticeable.

In *Il Bidone,* I remember highlighting a character before he was introduced into the narrative. Augusto and his daughter, Patrizia, enter a theater, and in the foreground I show a man seated in front of them. Later, he will confront Augusto as one of his victims, but the viewer doesn't know this until it happens. I could have just had it happen, without alerting the audience beforehand, but in this case I thought leading the camera was justified. Augusto lives in a world where he always fears detection, and I wished to convey this sense of apprehension to the audience.

Generally, however, I try to cloak my role as director as much as possible. I consciously try to conceal the machinery of the film I am making. The spectator should not be conscious of my camera or my narrative techniques, unless I am making a film about making a film. So I ration obvious devices, like extreme close-ups or rapid cutting or odd camera angles. Style and technique are means to an end, not an end in themselves. In *Toby Dammit,* however, I saw an opportunity to explore these devices more fully, apart from my feature films.

When a director's style becomes a noticeable mannerism, when it becomes more apparent than the story itself, and draws attention away from the spectacle, then it is wrong.

I don't know how to cast my own shadow. I look back over my work and can't recall any movie of mine that is just like another, even when the characters overlap. The character of Cabiria appears in two quite different films, while *Toby Dammit, Satyricon,* and *The Clowns,* made in consecutive years, are so dissimilar they could have been made by three different directors, in my opinion. For me, the only certain failures would be "Gelsomina on a Bicycle" or "Days of Cabiria."

There are two times when it's most difficult to do your work, or that's the way it was for me. One is when you have just had one or more great successes, and it seems to the world you can't fail. That is how it seems to the others, but not to you. They think you know the recipe, when you aren't sure you even know how to cook. The most you achieve is that it is *your own* recipe, not someone else's. But you don't understand yourself why something you have done that was natural to you has been so exalted. An example which comes to mind is all of the writers who still try to imitate Ernest Hemingway; but to *really* steal the way he writes, they would have to steal him.

The other time when it's hard to do your work is when you have been failing. The acclaim is difficult to understand. Its opposite is even more puzzling. Failure is more difficult to understand than is success. You are the same person, but suddenly the world has turned against your progeny. Are they wrong? Are you? One tries not to live in the past. Did your last picture make money, and how much did it make— or lose?

Perhaps one reason I no longer go to see films is, I worry that without realizing it I might copy what somebody else has done. I never want anyone to be able to say I am imitative. Perhaps that's a reason I never go to see my own films. The worst thing that could be said would be "Fellini is imitating himself."

Really, I don't go to see my own films because I always want to remake them. I see a touch here, a touch there . . .

Another reason I never go to see my finished films is a fear I can't even admit to myself—a fear of disappointment. What if I don't love it? What if I feel the need to climb up on the screen and change it? What if . . . ?

Making a film is something along the lines of sending a missile to the moon. It isn't done by chance. The improvisation I practice as a director is to use my eyes and ears, and to be open to everything that

Michelangelo Antonioni, Fellini, and Giulietta chat at a party in Rome during the mid-1980s. Antonioni appreciated Giulietta's talent as an actress, and wanted to cast her in one of his pictures.

is available. The picture is a carefully planned trip, no wandering peregrination. It is on tracks which one must follow, but if you succeed, the end result doesn't seem mechanical. It involves both art and science, but when the picture speaks to you, it is a kind of love talk, spoken in whispers, a subtle hint saying, This little touch will make it better, will help to convey an illusion, will keep the magic. It would indeed be foolish to ignore that in favor of being rigidly bound by a script you wrote months before. In the spontaneity, there is an honesty, which is not improvisation but love, faithfulness to your art. One of the most important aspects for me is that I keep my own alertness and fascination with each film, and that for each film I am a virgin, not just saying, but believing, "You are my first."

Anyone who then sees my mind, my heart, my soul, exposed in all their nakedness, is entitled to his own opinion of my interior reality. They may say how homely Fellini is, referring to my interior, just as many say it about my exterior. Of course, it hurts my feelings, but as I remember Popeye saying, "I am what I am."

There is the implication that a bizarre exterior may indicate a richer inner life. People assume if you are a film director, you are special, different from them, so they expect you to behave in a bizarre fashion and tell absurd stories. If you behave in a normal or mundane way, some of them impute bizarre behavior to you in anything you do or anything you say. They attribute profundity to your sneezes, just as the power of divination was attributed to Trimalchio's belches. More likely, they register obvious disappointment, which they do not bother to hide, because you are only human. If you are nice to them, you are presumed to be worth even less. They hold themselves in such low esteem, they can't respect you if you would know them. Why are some people like that?

The worst thing for me is going to a nice restaurant with people who force you to perform instead of eat. I feel *I* am the entrée, and I'm tempted to look at the menu to see how much I cost. I rarely, if ever, accept an invitation now from someone I don't know.

My address book is closed.

eighteen

INTERVIEWERS WHO JOIN
THE FOREIGN LEGION

I have been asked by publishers about writing my autobiography. Superstition is not the only reason I didn't want to do that. The investment of time in the project was the major reason, time that could be spent developing a film. One of the reasons I was never tempted, and there were quite a few, was that I would have been expected to go back and resee all of my films. I would have had to see the tattered remnants of my work in shreds after years of destruction of the prints. I would have had to see the cuts I was forced to make. These cuts don't exist in my own mind because my memory of the film is of what I shot, of how I visualized it, and of how it grew, of the totality, rather than what it became in the final days of struggle with the producer.

Cutting, even if done by me, was instigated by those who wanted to get in more shows per day, to spend less on prints, or for the benefit of distributors in the United States who wanted longer and more frequent popcorn and candy-bar breaks. The films in my mind are much longer than what most audiences viewing my films have ever seen. They are what I remember shooting, the films of my original intention.

A publisher would expect me to analyze my films and, in so doing, I'd probably prove to be more boring than the most boring of the critics expounding on my films has ever been. I would artificially have to create purpose where none existed. I would have to see significance now in details that I did not see as significant then, except as a story-teller who wants to entertain. If a reviewer said my films are "clown-ish," for me that would a great compliment. So much just happens on a film set, because the film has a life of its own.

I would have to discuss the films with a method more specific and more organized than the way in which I made them. I might need an outline, and possibly I'd have to make a script from the film, a script more carefully adhered to than the one I used to make the film itself. Boring task.

And I would have to be able to see my films from the vantage point of the person I was then, when I was making each film. My own self at the time, though it is part of me, is now something of a stranger to me.

Then I would have to write and rewrite and rewrite until whatever spontaneity of life originally might have been in my words would dis-appear. I would have to justify, to be on the defensive. Let others destroy my pictures, with words as in all the other ways one's films get mutilated. I would rather work to give life to just one more film. And perhaps there is also something of that other factor, that writing one's memoirs does seem something of a closure.

I do not like to give interviews. I do not like to bore myself and others. After all, there is only so much I can say about my life and work, and I've tried to say it in my films. Then sometimes I give in because it is how I began my own professional life, and I remember what it meant to me at the time. I imagine I was not as aggressive as some. I was a bashful interviewer, as inexperienced in the situation of social intercourse as I was in sexual intercourse.

My life is making movies. It is the most exciting thing to do, but it is not exciting to talk about. I could understand why everyone would want to be a film director, but I cannot understand why any-one would want to listen to anyone talking about doing it. When I direct, I don't ever want it to end. But when I'm forced to speak about it, I hear myself speaking, and I sound so boring to myself, and for the interviewer, which is even worse. Then there are the inter-views that vanish into the Great Unknown.

One day you decide to give up some of the time you had put away for yourself because everyone says this is what you must do. Your project can't stand on its own; people have to know about it; publicity and promotion are essential. So you weaken.

You spend your time with someone who brings his machines or makes funny little secretive notes. You look at his face for some clue as to how you are doing, but it is not forthcoming. You try harder, but there is no laughter, no glint in the eye; you have a better chance that the relentlessly marching tape recorder will giggle. You hope at some point he will get tired. But why should he, when you are doing all the work? At some point, you decide: Finished.

You breathe a sigh of relief. The interviewer goes away. But there is always the need for a second interview. No matter what happened in the first, guaranteed, there will be that need for a second one. You have invested so much time and energy, you are locked in. Instead of cutting your losses, you spend more time. Then you wait for some word of the appearance of the interview somewhere in some obscure journal distributed free to ten graduate students at the University of Patagonia, where your pictures don't show. But nothing so wonderful as that.

You hope that what you said will not come out exactly the opposite, that it will have some relationship to what you said and the way you said it, that you will not appear to be more of a fool than you are in reality for having given the interview at all, that someone will read it, and that no one will see it. You almost forget that you gave it.

Then, long after it could have done your film any good, you remember it and wonder about it. Maybe you can tell me the answer. Where do all the interviews go that vanish? Why do people who interview me leave my office and go join the Foreign Legion?

It is absurd to talk about a picture before you have made it. I never meet with the press during the first three weeks. I hope by then to be in control of my film.

Talking about the pictures after they have been made, endlessly analyzing them, kills them. I cannot prevent this form of cinemacide, but I do not wish to preside at the murder of my children. The reason I prefer not to speak about my films is very simply because I don't want to diffuse their emotional impact for the audience.

It's important that I don't weaken the emotions I am experiencing, that they're saved for the film. I like to make films in the same way I live in a dream. It is wonderful in its mystery.

Interviewers are like archaeologists who are looking for some wisdom of the ages inscribed in stone. I found it embarrassing when they came to me expecting gems. I never analyzed what I was going to do the way they analyzed what I did.

I don't consider myself an intellectual, because the way the word is generally used doesn't seem to have much to do with intellect or intelligence. The ones who give that name to themselves are usually people who bore me. They are judges who make pronouncements about other people. I just like to do things. Let the others be judges. I don't like making definitions and labels for my work. Labels are for clothes, for luggage.

I remember one interviewer at the time *8½* opened asked me if "8½" meant the age at which I had my first sexual experience. I said yes. A foolish question like that seemed to merit an equally foolish answer. It was taken seriously, was printed, and was reprinted over the years. I am frequently asked about it. I will never be able to deny it sufficiently. That foolish answer will follow me all the days of my life. I suppose the only way to finish it would be to say, Yes, true— that's what "8½" meant.

In Italy, I am the subject of many theses. The awe of the student is difficult to live up to—and to live with. When you first become aware of it, of course it makes you feel good, but it is embarrassing. Everyone wants to hear the same answers to the same questions, personally, from your own lips. It's a burden. I don't wish to disappoint them.

I don't want to leave behind me more words I have spoken about my work than works I have done. It would be embarrassing to have them say, "Fellini's body of work is talking about his body of work."

Among my friends, I am well known for my exaggerations, embellishments, embroidery of the truth. Some people call that being a liar. I know only that I am more at home with my fantasies.

Anyone who lives, as I do, in the world of fantasy and imagination must make an enormously unnatural effort to be literal in an everyday sense. I've never gotten along well with literal people. You wouldn't invite me to be a witness in court. I was a terrible journalist. I felt compelled to report an event the way *I* saw it, which was seldom the way it really happened from a more objective point of view. I wanted it to be a good story, so in my mind, I fixed it up here and there. The strangest part is that I believe my own version of what I saw, and I find it odd that no one else remembers it the way I saw it. Afterwards I remember better my own embellished version and am my own first believer.

I'm accused of being especially imaginative in the recounting of the story of my own life. It does seem my life is my possession. If I have to live it over again in words, why not arrange details a little to make a better story? I've been accused, for example, of telling several completely different versions of my first love affair. She was worth many! I don't think of myself as a liar. It's a matter of point of view. It's indispensable for a storyteller to enhance his story, to color it, to expand it, to extend its dimensions, depending on how he feels it has to be told in the subjective sense. I do this in life just as I do in my films. Sometimes the reason is I really don't remember.

The cinema is my storytelling medium. No other way of telling a story offers me so much flexibility. It is even better than being a painter, because I can re-create life in movement, emphasizing it, enlarging it, enhancing it, and distilling its true essence. For me, it's closer than music, painting, or even literature to the miraculous creation of life itself. It's actually a new life form, with its own pulse of existence, its own layers of reality, its own perspectives of understanding.

I start from a feeling, not an idea, certainly not an ideology. I am in the service of my story, which wishes to be told, and I have to understand where it wants to go.

Forced by pleading producers to talk to journalists in a festival situation, I get complaints even after having done my best. The journalists don't like the press conference situation. Each one wants to hear every word from me in a private audience. They complain that at a press conference, everyone has the same material. But what do I have to give them but the same material? So I lose a day of my life, which might be the very day that I would have had the best idea I ever had. My sacrifice proves in vain because there is no satisfying the Interviewers from Hell.

What do they say to me afterwards? "Thank you, Mr. Fellini"?

No, not at all. They complain. They say, "You told each of us different stories. Which is true?" They get together and compare notes. What do they expect? That I would tell the same story over and over, always the same, if possible even the very same words? If that was what they wanted, then why couldn't it have been at a press conference?

I have never been able to fathom the expectations of interviewers. I wonder what it was like for Groucho Marx, with people expecting him to say only witty and brilliant things. It is too much pressure performing for strangers who have come to talk with you and want you to say or do something outrageous, so they can tell their friends about it. If you do not give them the right performance, there is that look of disappointment. I feel I am expected to wear a cape and to seem like someone from one of my films. This feeling makes me very uneasy. I become cross and impatient with strangers. I do not want to be asked my opinions, to be "drawn out," to be encouraged, forced to express myself. What I consider the most inopportune is for anyone to expect me to tell about a film I am planning to make. I am there, but I am really not there. I am thinking of what I might be imagining at this moment if I were alone in reverie, of the film I could be seeing in my mind.

Sometimes it occurs to me that there are only two kinds of people involved with films: filmmakers and film unmakers. Whenever someone comes up to me and says, "What is the meaning of your film, Mr. Fellini?" I immediately recognize a film unmaker.

Unmaking films is a much larger industry than making films. Film unmakers don't require rich producers, big studio facilities, or even actors. They don't need to spend years on a project. All they need is the price of admission to a theater and some university education, and then they qualify as film unmakers. They also need a tape recorder, a typewriter, and paper, and maybe an allowance from their families.

Film unmakers can't accept the magic that is cinema without subjecting it to intellectual dissection. It's a biopsy that threatens to become an autopsy. I could understand it if they had to know how the tricks are done, but they have to know what the magician was thinking at the time he was performing the trick and why he's doing it in the first place. Probably he's only wondering if he's going to get another booking, or if the rabbits under the false bottom are still there, or whether he can seduce that buxom blonde in the third row who smiled at him. Or perhaps he's just had an argument with the lady he's about to saw in half.

When a film unmaker comes up to me and asks what I *really* meant when Saraghina, the sardine girl [in *8½*], does her sensual dance in front of the little boys on the beach, I don't know what to say. If I'm very lucky, his dissertation will end up on a library shelf somewhere, sharing the ample dust with other such erudite misappropriations of our valuable and finite natural resources. If I'm unlucky, it will be published as a book, and somebody will read it. If I'm very unlucky, the author will become a professor of film studies in a university or, worst of all, a movie critic. Then people will believe what he writes.

Film unmakers seldom become filmmakers. Someday, however, I predict, exceptional film unmakers will be making documentaries about film unmakers making films about unmaking filmmakers. And it could get worse. There could be unfilm festivals.

The question I hate the most is "Why a rhinoceros?"

There are two questions everyone invariably asks me:

"How do you become a director?" They don't really want to know how *I* became a director, but how *they* can!

The other question is "Are your films autobiographical?" The answer is Yes, but not exactly. They reflect my view of life at a certain point.

It's very difficult to do interviews, because it's a phony situation. One has to ask the questions, and the other tries to please the one who is listening, to appear intelligent, interesting, original, and funny. Whenever I hear that anyone wants to interview me, I try to fly, to escape. I do when I can, because I cannot face the sameness of the tired questions, always the same. I would like to be able to have numbered questions and answers. The interviewer says, "Forty-six." I respond, "Forty-six." We have saved much time.

I am again reminded of that moment in *The Clowns,* when an interviewer asks me, "What is the *message,* Mr. Fellini?" As I start to answer the ponderous question in the pedantic style for which I believe he is hoping, a bucket falls on my head and covers my face, preventing me from speaking. Then another bucket falls over the interviewer's head.

This short scene is my real response to such questions. As I was the director, I could do this. How often I've done it in my mind to interviewers in life asking foolish questions!

Once in a while, I have given a foolish answer to questions such as "Which pictures do you consider the greatest of all time?" I would put in my latest film, especially if it wasn't really a film at all, like *Intervista,* something for TV, an interview. But I quickly learned my lesson. Whatever I said was always taken seriously and put in print forever, just like that. I needed to have a sign which said, "Joke," and underline it.

The other part of making films that I haven't liked is being a beggar. It's the only thing I haven't loved about being a film director, shaking my cup for producers to allow my film to be born. For myself, I never would have begged. I would have died in the street of starvation first. But for my film, I found the strength to sacrifice my pride. For this, I need the strength of my own faith in what I am doing. That is why I find it imperative to have around me only people who bolster me. I need my belief in myself in order to bother people in their homes as I ask for money.

I dislike producers as a group. It's not even natural. I understand their desire to see their money come back to them. As individuals, some have even been good company. So I suppose what I hate about them is their power over me. It reduces me to being a child, not having money of my own, being under the control of others, having to try to please people, even if you don't agree with them—even worse, if you don't have respect for them.

Since I have never cared much for what money buys, it seems strange that the search for it should have come to so dominate my life.

nineteen

MAKING FILMS IS MORE EXCITING THAN SEEING THEM

Once upon a time, I loved seeing movies as much as anyone ever has, and those early childhood films are a part of me. After a certain point, though, I could no longer see the films with the innocence of childhood eyes. In childhood, we have a good balance between real life and the life of fantasy, between the conscious and the unconscious, between being awake and dreaming. Children put themselves honestly and openly into the voyage which is life. Because I changed, the films I was seeing changed for me. I *think* the films changed, but all I can really know is that their effect on me was different. It was when I came to care so deeply about making movies that seeing them was no longer the experience of fanciful escape it had once been. The only movies in which I could really live became the ones I was making. Making films is so much more exciting than seeing them.

One of the reasons I stopped going to movies was they no longer transported me out of myself, only out of the theater, if I could leave without insulting anyone. I cannot imagine how anyone can be a juror for a film festival. I have been invited, and I have declined. After a certain point, I was able to see movies in my own head, and I preferred doing it that way. The span of life is short, and I want to leave as much of a body of work as I can. It is my hope that among those films, there will be images, a vision of the world, that will be immortal, as I cannot be. It is a feeling I do not know how to describe, to have the possibility to share your vision of the world *with* the world.

I am often asked why I don't go to the movies very much anymore, and I've never prepared an intelligent answer to this question. I really ought to think of one—and go to more movies. I rarely get the chance, rarely have the time, but this doesn't seem a satisfactory answer. It seems I could find the time, if that's what I gave the priority to doing. Sometimes I tell Giulietta that I am saving all these decades of movies I have missed seeing, so that we will have something to do in our old age.

My earliest adventures in films as a fan were well before the age of four, perhaps before the age of two, though for the first of those I have to rely on my mother's memory of my being in her lap. My exposure was both to Italian and Hollywood movies. Since all films were dubbed, it would seem we children could have been confused as to which were Italian and which were American, but no such confusion occurred. Those from Hollywood were much better. We children knew the difference, as the adult audience most certainly did.

I didn't know then that I was watching the work of great directors, King Vidor or Josef von Sternberg. I didn't even know that films *had* directors, or what directors were. I think I believed in the beginning that what was happening up there on the screen was actually happening. I seem to remember going back to see a movie with my father that I had already seen with my mother, and I was surprised that the same movie could be happening again. I remember Charlie Chaplin; the comedians were always my favorites. Very much later, when I was grown, I encountered great French films by René Clair, Jean Renoir, Marcel Carné, and Julien Duvivier.

My knowledge of cinema is full of holes and gaps, as is my general education, and my taste is eclectic and eccentric. I saw what came my way, and my list of favorites is my own, a list of what brought me pleasure. I am very familiar with the work of Hal Roach, for example, but I have yet to see a film of Murnau or Eisenstein. For this reason, many do not consider me an intellectual. Not for this reason alone, but for many others, I agree with them.

• • •

It wasn't until I met Orson Welles in the mid-fifties that I went to see *Citizen Kane*. I say this just as a fact. I had seen *The Magnificent Ambersons* years earlier, and was *very* impressed. When I did see *Citizen Kane*, I was as awed as everyone else.

There are many movie directors to whom I owe a debt of gratitude as an audience, if not as a director. I have seen a few of the Bergman pictures, and I like them very much. The films of Ingmar Bergman possess a dark Nordic spirit that is magnificent. Kurosawa is also fantastic, with his singular depiction of the ancient Japanese aristocracy's level of fantasy. What power! And he can make a powerful picture set in contemporary Japan, too. It's impressive that he has that range. When I see a picture and I believe the story, like a Kurosawa picture set in ancient Japan or a Kubrick picture set in outer space, I become an audience, a very naïve audience. That is a kind of paradise. I recover my lost innocence. The death of Kubrick's Hal in *2001* is so sad. I esteem Bergman, Kurosawa, Wilder, and Kubrick because they are capable of making me believe what I see, no matter how fantastic it is.

I cannot say anyone is the greatest, but I can say that no one is greater than Billy Wilder. *Double Indemnity* and *Sunset Boulevard* are part of our lives, a part of our collective consciousness. He is a master. The casting of those films was wonderful. Wilder always had humor, even in melodrama or tragedy. He didn't need anyone to write his lines, and he knew about food. He enjoys eating, which means he is a person who enjoys life. He is very interested in art, not as an artist, but as a collector. Sometimes when you meet famous people, they are not the way you think they will be, but Billy Wilder is just like his films. I made a funny drawing of him. He *is* a drawing.

Kubrick, I think, is a great director who is a visionary and very honest. What I admire especially in Kubrick is his ability to make pictures in any time. He can make a romantic historical drama like *Barry Lyndon*, which was a great picture, a science-fiction picture like *2001*, and a ghost picture like *The Shining*.

Brief Encounter and *Lawrence of Arabia*—David Lean is of the pantheon.

Buñuel is a true maestro, a movie sorcerer.

Among the younger directors whose work I know, I especially like our Italian Giuseppe Tornatore, whose *Cinema Paradiso* has genuine individuality without departing from the great traditions of cinema.

It's a very mature film for a young man to make. For that reason, some people are surprised to find out he *is* so young. Then, because he makes the kinds of films he does, they think he's old-fashioned, which means derivative or imitative. That isn't true. Old or new is not what is important; only what is wonderful is important.

I realize that I am one of the luckiest people who ever lived. I really would not exchange my life with anyone who has ever lived. All I could wish for is more of what I have already enjoyed.

Certainly being a film director has opened the doors of the world to me, and it has brought people I have always wanted to meet to Cinecittà to see *me*. This is wonderful. The little boy from Rimini who lives inside me can hardly believe it.

I remember one day at home I got a phone call in English from someone with what I recognized as an American southern accent. Because of the accent, it was very difficult for me to understand him. He said his name was Tennessee Williams. I thought it was a practical joke. Even as I thought it, I wondered why that kind of joke is called "practical" in English. The voice invited me to lunch. I said I was sorry, but I wasn't going to be in Rome. I had had calls in the past from people who claimed to be someone famous, but who just wanted to talk with me on the phone. Then they didn't appear, while I waited. I had already been fooled, so I wasn't going to be put in that position again.

The phone rang again. It was the same voice. I didn't understand everything he said, but I did hear the name "Anna Magnani," which I picked out in spite of the way he pronounced it. He said that she had given him my number. He again mentioned lunch, but added that Magnani wouldn't be there because she couldn't get up that early.

I understood then that he was familiar with Magnani's habits. She was so nocturnal, she thought three or four in the afternoon was early, and she had to be specially awakened, or she would sleep till five.

Seeing her was never a problem for me, because we would meet, by chance, in a piazza when I was up at six in the morning and went for a walk, and she was on her way home to go to bed, feeding her homeless cats along the way. The restaurants where she ate dinner knew this and packed up the food left over from the plates of their customers, and they gave it to her in a big box when she left.

It really *was* Tennessee Williams, and when I ate lunch with him, I told him that I had not expected him to make the call himself. He told me that he had to use agents to arrange his business, but not his pleasure. Because he was eating lunch with me for pleasure, not to make a film, and because he was calling me at my home, it would have been bad manners to have someone else make the call. He said that he was guilty of everything in the world except bad manners. Then, he laughed. He laughed so loudly at his own joke, everyone in the restaurant of the Grand Hotel turned around to look at us.

I told him that I had rejected the invitation of the first phone call because I thought it was a practical joke, and I mentioned that I found this English phrase a strange one. He said it should be "impractical," at which point he laughed so loudly and so long that once again everyone in the restaurant, or so it seemed to me, turned to stare at us.

Throughout the lunch, he continued to laugh a great deal, but never at anything I said, only at what *he* said.

At the end of lunch, he paid the check. He insisted. In Rome, I always paid the check, except with producers, of course. But he insisted. He said it was bad manners to invite someone to lunch and then leave them with the check. He repeated that he was guilty of many things, but never of bad manners. He laughed even louder and longer, as though the line had grown funnier with the retelling. By this time, no one in the restaurant of the Grand Hotel even looked up from their lunch. He said that I could invite him the next time, and by his paying the check, he ensured that we *would* have another lunch. He was very gracious.

The next time I heard that he was back in Rome, Magnani told me, and I called his hotel. I left word that I would like to invite him to have lunch. I didn't hear from him, so I assumed he hadn't received my message. I called again and left my message again, but when I didn't hear from him, I gave up.

Charles Schulz, who draws *Peanuts,* was someone I enjoyed meeting. It was like Charlie Brown had come to Rome to see me. He drew a *Peanuts* especially for me, then asked if I would make a drawing for him. I did my best, but it was not a fair exchange.

Though I never enjoyed traveling and I never liked film festivals, trips to America, to Moscow, Cannes, and Venice gave me the opportunity to know people I could not have known if I had only stayed in Rome. One of the benefits of being a famous director is the pleasure of meeting some of the great directors one has admired. When I met Ingmar Bergman, I thought there would be an immediate warmth between us, even though his pictures are Nordic and icy.

We were together, talking about the trials of traveling, the weather, mostly subjects neither intellectual nor creative. An eavesdropper would not have known we were film directors.

One never knows which way a conversation will go or how it happens that it takes a particular course.

Somehow, we got on the subject of my childhood puppet theater, and Bergman told me that as a child he had made a theater, too. His, however, was a *film* theater he had made of cardboard, with little seats, an orchestra, and a proscenium. He had a marquee for the front of his theater which featured movies of that time. And he made up stories for his paper-cutout characters, as I had done for my puppet actors. When I described my own puppet theater, it turned out that he had made one like that, too, at about the same time. The difference was, he worked with his sister and some of their friends; I was a loner. His was more technical, more elaborate, with a great emphasis on changes of scenery, elaborate sets, lighting. And frequently he did operas. He didn't charge for performances of his puppet theater the way I did. Whatever business sense I had at twelve, I must have left behind in Rimini.

We each felt that the puppet theater, which had absorbed a great deal of our time and attention as children, was one of the major influences on our lives. As a result of these conversations, Bergman encouraged me to direct for the theater as he does. He assumed I must have had many offers. I do, if not as many as he thought. They are based on the assumption that since I love to work in films, and I would have loved to have worked in the circus, theater is really the same thing.

I hope the reason theatrical producers asked me wasn't just because having me direct a play or even an opera for the first time, they could advertise and sell tickets based on the novelty value. I hope it was because they thought I had potential talent for it.

It was in Rimini that I first discovered the theater. My parents took me to a touring Grand Guignol. I had seen the posters being put up outside the theater, and I knew something marvelous was going to be happening inside. They were doing a mystery.

Inside, the theater itself seemed magnificent to me. The gilded boxes, the velvet, the ornate proscenium. I was more impressed by the grandeur of the setting than I was by the play. I never felt the same about the theater as I did about the movies, but I was so excited after seeing the show that I couldn't sleep all night.

Bergman told me I would find working in the theater intensely satisfying, because I could direct plays "between films." For me, there was no "between films." When I finished one, I started to work on the next. He pointed out that my films were particularly like theater. I must confess that I felt embarrassed when he talked so knowingly about my films. He seemed to have seen so many of mine, and I had seen so few of his. It was apparent to him that I was totally involved in sets and costumes, that I cared about lighting, that acting was something I felt. Why not do both, when it is so much the same thing?

I didn't answer Bergman, who didn't ask it as a question, but spoke rhetorically. He simply stated the case for the film director as stage director. I suppose the answer is that films and theater do *not* seem the same to me. Like opera and ballet, they are compatible, but different. Also, I needed all the time between films to create new ones and, sadly, to look for the money to allow them to exist.

When I met Orson Welles, he told me he was a magician. I have always been interested in magic. I suppose I wanted to *believe* in magic, to feel it was true. I was prepared to fool myself. I tried as a boy to do some tricks, but I was not adept at sleight of hand. My interest in practicing to achieve the illusion wasn't great enough. I've always preferred the spontaneous. I've always rebelled against anything that required discipline, especially if it was someone else's discipline. Welles, on the other hand, liked the mastering of the trick and enjoyed explaining how the trick was done. I liked to believe that magic really was magic.

Mostly, he talked about food. He liked so much to eat, he could have been an Italian. What a marvelous voice he had! When he talked about white beans in olive oil, the sound was so wonderful, he seemed to be reciting poetry. It was actually distracting. It was difficult afterwards to remember what he had said, one was so taken by the sound of it being said.

It was wonderful to meet King Vidor, the director who made *The Crowd* and *The Big Parade*. He was in his seventies, I think, but he wanted to work more than anything. It's terrible that a man of such genius couldn't go on creating because people said he was too old. He told me about the film he was hoping to make, a story about the actor who starred in *The Crowd,* an unknown whom Vidor had discovered. The actor goes from obscurity to momentary world fame only to meet a tragic end because he wasn't prepared to handle big success.

Vidor agreed with me that it was very important to use the non-professional or unknown for certain parts, because there was no way an audience could believe in a movie star, who brought his own identity with him. Vidor saw his actor one day in a crowd of extras leaving the MGM set, and he chose him to be the star of *The Crowd*.

We felt the same way about villains. We didn't like the idea of the all-bad villain. A character can be dishonest or doing something terrible without being all bad. We disagreed on his preference for going out on location. I prefer the studio, where I can have total control of the environment. He did what was good for him; I do what is good for me. I envied the artistic freedom he seemed to enjoy without the financial pressure, and he achieved this within the Hollywood studio system. Irving Thalberg, the head of production at MGM, believed in him. Many of his pictures were daring for their time, even experimental, but they made money. There were advantages to the studio system he said, and I believe it. It must have been like having a patron.

He told wonderful stories about Greta Garbo, who was a close personal friend of his. Ever since I was a child in my mother's lap, I had had a certain resistance to Garbo. King said she walked about her house naked, but only in front of good friends and her servants. She appeared to be oblivious to their watching her, but she was actually quite aware of the attention she was attracting. After that, I saw her films through different eyes.

I thought he had a funny first name, but in his case, he really was a king, so it was all right. When I wrote to him, I drew a crown before his name instead of writing it out. He liked to paint, and he invited me to come to his ranch in California and see his paintings.

He had been attending so many standing ovations at tributes that he thought they might as well just get rid of the chairs. He said, "What you have to watch out for is the time when the postman and the phone bring you invitations to be honored, to be the subject of incessant homages, trips, and lunch invitations, but not offers to make films. One day, the bills and advertisements and the silent phone confirm that you are retired, even when you didn't notice the day it happened."

When we are working on a film, I like to know every person, if I can. Sometimes I make wonderful discoveries that way. I don't really see anyone as "just an extra." Everyone in my film is there to perform his or her part, even those who have no lines, whether they are professional actors or not. I try to put them at ease. Sometimes I ask probing questions of an actress in an effort to expose her very soul, such as "Do you like ice cream?"

I always like to have people around me who are friends, people with whom I get along, people who like me and what I do. So it's said I like only the coterie, the entourage, the yes-men. I suppose it's true. I've always wanted everything pleasant, without arguments. But when they say I'm spoiled by success, that isn't true. I have always been the same.

I have never invited producers to come to my home just because I hope they will produce a film for me. It doesn't mean a producer wouldn't be welcome at my home, but only as a person. It would have to be personal.

I have never liked giving parties any more than I liked going to other people's parties—less. Giulietta liked to invite actors and film and theater people to our house, and they would play charades after lunch or dinner. On these occasions, I frequently excused myself. I could be an actor in a film, but I couldn't bring myself to act in a party game. I'm always much too self-conscious playing myself. Let Giulietta be Charlie Chaplin; I wasn't going to pretend to be Gary Cooper.

I enjoy friends who live with spontaneity. I do not enjoy the company of those who require that you make an appointment to make an appointment. How do I know at what time, or where, I will want to have dinner tomorrow night? The very act of making the commitment has already partly spoiled the occasion for me. I like to act on whim, to pick up the phone and say to a friend, "What are you doing now?" I am a person who does not enjoy making advance reservations for anything. I never make a reservation for a restaurant. I don't even like magazine subscriptions.

I was deeply fond of Nino Rota. He was an important collaborator. He would sit at the piano and I would tell him what I wanted. He would express in notes and tunes what I had said in words. He always understood what I had vaguely in my mind, but couldn't express musically. He thought *La Strada* would make an excellent opera libretto, and perhaps someday it will be one, but regrettably not with his music.

He had a wonderful disposition, and there was never a time with him that I felt like I was working. He was always modest, seeing his music as something secondary to the film, which has to be true for film music.

Attachments in life are made early. As a young man, I had many friends, usually people older than myself. We could sit around and talk for hours. Later, my relationships and the conversations were limited more to professional associations. I had time to know only the people with whom I was working on a film. They became the people I shared a community of interest with. The others had to understand that when I was preparing or making a film, I had no time to be purely social. Many people I knew interpreted this to mean I didn't desire their company. Some of them were right. My work was everything to me. I had time for people only in between films. Only the ones who were working in the film business, too, really understood. I could talk with Francesco Rosi for a few minutes on the phone, and he could understand.

Later, one doesn't make new friends. Not easily, anyway. I made very few. Being a legend, you are set apart. You are no longer trusting and open in friendships. You become guarded, because most people seem to want something. You come to dread the phone ringing, because someone wants something. One day, people say you are in a class by yourself, and that is a lonely place.

It is strange to look back on the important people in your life and realize they do not have the same importance you, at one time, attributed to them. I recognize as childhood foolishness wanting to impress other children whose names I can't even remember now, but there were the others. I think first of my grandmother, who was at one time a unique person in my life, so important that life without her was unimaginable. I felt that if anything happened to her, I would be lost in the world. She was my best friend. Now she comes only very occasionally into my thoughts, and my picture of her is faint. There is also less of her in the image and more of me, as it depends increasingly on my vague and scattered memories.

Sometimes in later years when one person seemed too important to me at a certain moment, I would remember how important my grandmother had been to me in her moment, and that helped me to gain perspective.

I've thought about what I might do if the time comes that I can no longer direct, either because of my physical state, or because no one wants to put their money behind my work.

I could always draw. I haven't had as much time to draw as I might have liked.

I could write, I suppose. I've always thought I might like to write some children's stories. I even made up some stories for a character in a film who wrote children's stories, and then the stories would come to life.

In one there was a small carriage of Parmesan cheese with four wheels of provolone, and the carriage had become stuck in a road of butter. The two horses of ricotta tried to draw the carriage to freedom while the coachman of mascarpone, quivering with fear, cracked his whip, made of strings of mozzarella . . .

I couldn't finish the story, however, because I got too hungry and had to go out and eat.

I destroy almost all of my papers. I do not like to live in the past. There was a time when I saved souvenirs, but that was a long time ago. The years added up, and the papers added up. I've never had much space, so I couldn't find anything anyway. Filing was impossible. When I was busy making films, I didn't have time to look at souvenirs. When I wasn't working, I became depressed, and looking at pictures of the past, when I was making a film, didn't make me feel better.

I've never liked photographs of myself because I never look the way I hope I look. I always believe I look better than in those photographs. I *want* to believe it. Giulietta likes to keep things, like her clothes, so I give her what storage space we have.

People are always asking me for some old script, or article, or letter. This way, I can answer honestly that I don't have it, without having to waste any time looking for it. What I do keep is my photographs of faces which I use for casting because, for me, they are not part of the past, but of the future. They are my starting point. They are hope. I have to remember, though, that the actors age more seriously than the photographs. Sometimes I forget how old some of the photographs are and sometimes actors send me pictures taken years before because they look younger, especially actresses.

I try to throw away everything I can. The test is if I can do without it, that's what I try to do. If it's a contract, and I think someday I may need to find it, I send it to my lawyer. If it's something sentimental I try to throw it away, because the longer I hold on to it, the more sentimental it's likely to become, and thus the more difficult to throw away. This works some of the time, unless Giulietta retrieves it from the wastebasket, and then it can become a permanent possession. If it's something I can't make up my mind about, I give it to Mario [Longardi]. I don't know what he does with it. I don't want to know.

Do I sometimes lose a drawing I value, or a story idea, or even a script? Of course. But the other alternative is to be buried in paper, and I would never be able to find it anyway. I have never been able to afford the space and staff to file everything. I like to come into my office and have everything as clear as possible, the way I wish my mind would be, without clutter. I like to feel reborn each day.

But I do keep the photographs of the hundreds of faces organized in good order where I can find them, so I can begin looking at them the minute I know I am making a picture. As soon as I look at the photographs, my mind begins working faster than I can write. I see a face and say to Fiammetta [Profili], my assistant, "Contact that person." And she responds, "But the address is twenty-seven years old." That probably means the photograph is forty years old.

twenty

"THAT MUST BE HER HUSBAND, FELLINI"

Over the years, whenever anyone said anything against me or in any way committed some wrong against me, it was Giulietta who was angrier than I, who wouldn't forgive them. She took personally in the deepest way any supposed wrong committed against the public person of Fellini, or the more fragile and private Federico.

Whenever we traveled for premieres or festivals, Giulietta was always in great demand. She was not there as Mrs. Fellini, but as Miss Masina or as Giulietta. I was very proud of her career, of her. She worked with other directors and on television, but she was most famous for the pictures she made with me, as Gelsomina and Cabiria. In Italy, outside of Rome, more people recognized her than recognized me. During the time of her television series, *Eleanora,* she was surrounded by people in Milan wanting her autograph. I stood off to the side. I saw a woman point at me and say to her friend, "That must be her husband, Fellini."

She was extremely good in *The Madwoman of Chaillot.* I wasn't working at the time, so I went to France to watch her on the set. Katharine Hepburn was the star, but I didn't really get to know her. I tried to be as invisible as possible because it was generous of the director, Bryan Forbes, to let me be there, and I didn't want him to feel that I was intruding, or that I was secretly directing Giulietta at home. I wasn't, but I have to admit I did give her a few tips.

Highly successful in the television series; she wrote a newspaper column and worked for UNICEF. Giulietta has a special feeling for the family, for those outside who need help, and for children, perhaps because we didn't have any of our own.

Only recently have I realized the important part so many people have played in my life, in the steps that have taken me along the path that made me a film director. Of course, I've always been aware of Giulietta, and if I hadn't been, she was there at my side to remind me. But there were others: my mother and father; my aunt in Rome who let me stay with her; Giulietta's aunt, so important, with whom we lived until we could afford our own place, and that was quite a long time; Aldo Fabrizi; Rossellini; Lattuada . . .

I understood only very late how great an influence and help my mother was. It was not so much what she did, because she did not know exactly what to do. But she never stopped me from being myself. Though my ideas did not coincide with hers, she gave me encouragement and then money to go my own way.

There are words you speak for which you are later sorry, words you can never take back, can never unspeak. Then, there are the sins of omission, those words that you failed to speak. I understand when it's too late that sometimes I let other people down. Sometimes, I let myself down.

I realize now that I had something to give. When I became a successful film director, I wish I had said to my mother, very clearly, in a few sentences, that I was aware of her important, early influence on my life.

My professional artistic independence was bought at the cost of my personal economic independence. My ideal would have been a stipend from a patron to provide for my apartment, food, taxis and phone, a few clothes, and Giulietta's security and happiness. After that, only the money for the current film and next film mattered. I didn't give a thought to my personal economic future, though I can't remember a time when I wasn't thinking in the present about rent or taxes or medical bills or why Giulietta couldn't buy the clothes she liked.

I have never had any talent for money. The opposite. I have a reverse talent for money. I would have made a lot of mistakes in the way I handled it if I had ever had enough to be in the position of making any decisions about the investment of it. I think the reason is I have never had any interest in money. The only time I gave any thought to it was when I first came to Rome and could buy only one meal a day and was a little hungry, or I wanted to buy another coffee, or invite someone to a coffee and had to think about it.

I have never felt the need to buy future security. I don't know if that was because I had so much faith in the future, or so little. I didn't think about money except on the most grandiose scale—the money I needed to pay for making films.

I do not like to collect possessions. I once heard a story about an Argentine gaucho who ate with a knife because he was afraid if he used a fork, he would need a plate, then a table for the plate, a chair to sit at the table, and finally a house to keep it all in.

I am always worried that if I own things, they will own me. I have fought throughout my life the captivity by objects. I suppose to some extent I have done the same thing with people, fighting the inclination to become too emotionally involved, sensing danger when I did.

Because Giulietta, as women do, prefers to have things, we live in a more genteel way than I probably would on my own. In the end, I was owned, after all, by my films.

I've never been very good at deal-making. Somehow, talk of money never suited me. I did not know how to set a specific number on what I was worth. Perhaps I have not been more successful personally in the monetary sense because I have never been able to see numbers as a goal. I did not translate lire into possessions I coveted. The only possession I ever remember wanting was a car, an attractive one, not just for transportation, I admit, but for display. I no longer understand that feeling, but I do remember having it.

I have never been good with big sums of money which seem unreal. I've frequently thrown away that kind of money. In fact, I usually did. The time when I'm likely to be stingy is with small sums of petty cash that don't count. It's for the saving of little bits of money that I'm occasionally likely to go on a deprivation binge.

Taxis are one of the luxuries I most enjoy. One of my economizing attempts was started because I felt I was being overwhelmed by what taxis were costing me while I wasn't working. I saw the money going out and not coming in. There weren't many deprivations I could impose on myself, since I am neither a shopper nor a traveler. I require only adequate shelter. Giulietta cannot give up smoking, and I hate it since I gave it up, after having smoked a great deal myself. So Giulietta needs an extra room in which to smoke. I have told her it is not good for her, but Giulietta does not always listen to me.

The thing I cannot give up is food. If I could cut down somewhat on it, I would do so, not for monetary reasons, but for reasons of girth, so I could pass a full-length mirror without looking away.

I was eating an hors d'oeuvre the other day at a party, and as it was hot, I didn't put the whole thing into my mouth at once. It was crumbly and half of it fell. I was mortified. Had I ruined the white wall-to-wall carpet? Would they need to lift the covering from the entire apartment? Could I stand on the spot, until it was time to leave, and then rush out with the herd of other guests, thus escaping? I looked down. I realized my stomach had caught the uneaten half of the hors d'oeuvre. I didn't know whether to be glad or sad, but I quickly retrieved it and gobbled the evidence.

It is clear that giving up food would not be a way I could save money. In fact, as with any thought I have ever had of diet, famine psychology takes over, and I grow even hungrier and eat more. Thus, I could not afford the expensive thought of giving up food. I decided all that was left to me was transportation. It would not only be an economy, but it would remind me of the wonderful days when, very young, I came to Rome. I was elated to be able to take the public transportation at that time, grateful when I could afford not to have to walk.

But it was not the same. People change. I was not the same. I suppose it lasted for a few months, that resolve of mine. Well, maybe. Though I remember it as a few months, it was more like only one. Then, I hailed a taxi.

Democracy arrived for us in Italy as a sudden freedom from the condition we had lived with for so many centuries. My early life was in the shadow of fascism, but when the Americans came and the Nazis fled, we were the same people of before who knew so little about democracy. We were between the politically corrupt who had apparent good manners and deep, hidden pockets, and the Mafia, who need no explanation. Sometimes I would be approached by the Mafia "laundry," which specialized in dirty linen, but I have never wanted money for a film that badly.

My work may not be priceless in the opinion of some, but I am without a price. I would rather starve than knowingly do something I'm not proud of.

I would have done better if more than one producer had wanted my film. I always had difficulty finding even one, so I didn't have a very strong bargaining position. After my successes, I had offers, especially from Hollywood, to pay me a lot of money, but they wanted me to work there, and they wanted to tell me what film to make. I always wanted to make *my* film.

Several times, rich women, or women with rich fathers, or women with rich, powerful husbands, offered themselves to me for affairs, and they added, incidentally, that they could help me get my films made. I never accepted. I've tried to live as much as possible a life that hasn't been bought.

One time when we were short of cash, I was supposed to entertain some visitors and was worried about the money for the lunch. Sometimes more people come to eat lunch than you are expecting. Giulietta understood about my pride, and she produced an envelope of cash which she said she had hidden and had forgotten about, so I should go and enjoy the lunch and not be worried about getting the check. It was only much later that I learned that she had sold a few pieces of her gold jewelry. They were not of much value and didn't produce much money. I noticed when, after a long time, she had not worn them. She said she didn't care about them, and that someday she would buy some more when we made a lot of money.

I felt terrible. So there was a price. We never made a lot of money, and we never bought more jewelry.

I receive a lot of mail, many fan letters, and I employ a secretary to answer them because I do not like to disappoint people who are waiting for an answer. I answer a few myself, but I cannot do that with very many, or that would be my life, but I do look at all the letters. It is a big job going through the mail, just to see what is important or interesting.

I get many, many letters asking me for money. People send me documents to show their medical problems and to substantiate their cases as the deserving needy. They send pictures of sick children and suffering old people to win my sympathy. And it does. But what can I do? Giulietta and I do not have that kind of money. People imagine that because I am famous, I am rich. They confuse my direction of lavish productions with my having money. It is the same as confusing the actor playing parts with the person he is in real life.

I receive photographs in the mail, some from actors, but many from people who have never acted who would like to be in a Fellini film, and I choose people with or without experience based on their pictures. Very often, the pictures come from parents and are of their children, or someone sends his girlfriend's photo, as if for a beauty contest. These pictures go into the immense files I keep in my office and at Cinecittà. If I were to keep them at home, they would overwhelm our apartment, which isn't very big.

Then there are the scripts. Dozens of screenplays, every week. I prefer not to make films from other people's screenplays. Some of the writers know this and only want my opinions and criticism. Unless I know the person, I always have the scripts returned unopened. In the beginning, I opened the envelopes, but then every time a film of mine came out, I would get letters from lawyers saying I had plagiarized their clients' work. They represented someone who had sent me a script about a Riccardo and I had used the name in my film about someone who could sing, and their Riccardo could sing, and both liked to eat spaghetti, so obviously I had stolen the idea. It didn't matter that I had a brother named Riccardo, who also could sing and eat spaghetti, who appeared in my film as a character named Riccardo. The lawyers would do it for publicity, and maybe they hoped to intimidate me, so I would just give them something to go away. I never did that.

Sometimes the people go to court. They claim to have written my films. There is no limit to how outrageous their claims are. No one has ever won a lira, but it has been a depressing waste of time and energy. Needless to say, now I never, never read a screenplay of anyone who is not a trusted friend.

twenty-one

MAGIC AND PASTA

There are three tenses: the past, the present, and the realm of fantasy.

Clearly, the future tense can be the "What if?" tense. We live in the now but are influenced by the past, which we cannot change except in our own memories. The present is made of the past. It is the tense I like to think of as the eternal present.

The worst prison in which anyone can live is the one of regret. That is the "If only . . ." tense. It is to be avoided, if at all possible, because no one can torture us as we can torture ourselves. When journalists ask me, "What regrets do you have in life?" I always answer, "None." It's the shortest answer I can give and still be polite. Generally, I wish to be polite. But there is a regret I have which I do not generally share. I admitted it to Giuseppe Tornatore. I don't usually give advice, but I wanted to encourage him to do what I wish I had done.

I was the first person to whom he showed his finished print of *Cinema Paradiso*. He screened it for me, all alone, and then he asked me what I thought he should do. I remembered Rossellini, and I was reminded of that time long before when a young, worried hopeful showed his film to a director whose position was much ahead of his at the time. As with *The White Sheik*, this wasn't the final edited version. Rossellini had been there for *me*. I thought of his words, telling me I would someday see the future in someone younger who was at a critical moment in his career.

I liked the film very much, but I also told him that I believed he should cut it, that it was too long. When he asked me what he should cut, I wouldn't tell him. I would never do that. He shouldn't listen to anyone but himself, not even to me.

When his film became a big international success and won an Oscar, I told him he shouldn't make the mistake I made, that of having let so many years go by between films. There are high moments in your life when you are most appreciated. I had that with *La Dolce Vita* and with the Oscars. At those times, the important thing is to work as much as you can.

I believed that it was better not to make a film than to start something I didn't believe in perfectly. But now I have come to think differently. Even from making a bad film you learn something. And perhaps it takes you on a path to something better. I would have done better to work more.

I know now that I am in mourning for all those films I might have done which I never made, which never had their existence.

One of the greatest handicaps is to fear a mistake. You have stopped yourself. You have to move freely into the arena, not just to wait for the perfect situation, the perfect moment. It's what I say now whenever a young director asks me for advice. I said it to Giuseppe when *Cinema Paradiso* won an Oscar:

"This is your moment. Take advantage of it by making as much as you can of it. Don't wait for perfection. Don't wait for anything or anyone.

"When you are young, it seems like the golden moment will last forever, but it is fleeting. You cannot schedule a golden moment at will. These moments have their own life and timing apart from you. The saddest thing is not to notice and appreciate the moment when it's happening, and the next saddest thing is just to savor it without extending it. Make a movie. Make a lot of movies."

If you have to make a mistake, it's better to make a mistake of action than one of inaction. If I had the opportunity again, I would take chances. I would risk making a film that might not turn out as I hoped it would, rather than no film at all. As it is, stories I wanted to tell will die with me.

A film I have always wanted to make is Collodi's *Pinocchio*. It would be different from the Disney version. In my *Pinocchio*, every time the marionette said something untrue to a woman, it would not be his nose that grew.

When I was little, a book seemed to be something to throw at your brother. Books belonged to adults. They were part of school, and school did not seem to be something that opened up the world, but something that closed it, something that interfered with my freedom and imprisoned me for the longest and best part of the day. I didn't see among my teachers anyone I wanted to emulate. I knew very early that I didn't want to be like *them*. Quite the opposite. For me, a book was something that had to do with school and all those people I didn't want to know.

When I was eight or nine years old, I had my first happy meeting with a book that became a good friend to me throughout my life— *Pinocchio*. It's not just a wonderful book, but it's one of the *great* books. I feel that it has had an enormous influence on me. It was the beautiful pictures which first caught my attention. It was the way I wished I could draw.

Through *Pinocchio*, I learned I could love a book, that a book could offer a magical experience, and this was, as it turned out, not just a book for childhood, but one that could be read forever. I have read it several times in my life since my early childhood discovery.

The end of the book is the poorest part because Carlo Collodi, as a nineteenth-century man, moralizes when the puppet becomes a boy. It is sad because, losing his marionettehood, Pinocchio loses his child- hood, the marvelous life of knowing animals and magic, in return for becoming a good, conforming idiot.

Pinocchio was born in Romagna, just like me. I wanted to make the story as Collodi intended it, with live actors, but in the spirit of the great Chiostri illustrations. When I was young, I used to practice drawing by trying to copy those drawings, but I could never achieve what Chiostri did. I had many ideas for showing Pinocchio in the Country of Toys in the film I would make.

I identify not with Pinocchio, but with Gepetto. Creating Pinocchio was like making a film. I could see the relationship between Gepetto's carving out Pinocchio and my carving out a film. Gepetto was making the marionette from a piece of wood, but little did he know that soon he would not be in control. With every chip he carved away, Pinocchio was becoming more. It is exactly the way I feel when I am directing a film, as the film starts to direct me. Gepetto thought he was the one in charge, but the more he carved, the further he got away from it.

Pinocchio was one of my favorite friends. If I could have made the film, with live people as I wanted to do, I would like to have played the part of Gepetto, and there was only one perfect actor to play Pinocchio—Giulietta.

I have always been fascinated by the fairy tales of Charles Perrault and Hans Christian Andersen. Imagine—"Rapunzel," "The Princess and the Pea," "The Little Mermaid"! I would love to bring those fairy tales to the screen. I have this vision of the princess there in her nightdress, so uncomfortable and unable to sleep, on top of a mountain of mattresses, not realizing that it is a pea under the bottom of the first mattress that is the cause of her distress. The scene is so developed in my mind that sometimes I feel I have already made the film. Poor romantic little mermaid who gives all for love, yet we understand, because each of us searches throughout life for love. "The Emperor's New Clothes" is such a profound concept. Fairy tales are one of the greatest expressions of man by men. Another reason I was attracted to Jung was his revealing interpretation of fairy tales as part of our subconscious history.

Life is the combination of magic and pasta, of fantasy and of reality. Films are the magic, and pasta is the reality, or is it the other way around? I have never been very good at distinguishing between what is real and what is not. All artists are dedicated to materializing their fantasies and then to sharing these fantasies. Their creations are fanciful, emotional, irrational, intuitive. I start out directing, but something else takes over. Then, I really believe it's not me who is directing the film; it's the film who's directing me.

Dante's *Inferno* was an idea frequently suggested to me by producers. I had thought of it myself, but never pursued the idea because I believed they had something different in mind from what I would do. I would have treated the entire *Divine Comedy,* but with less emphasis on Vergil and the orgiastic *Inferno* and more on Beatrice in the *Paradiso.* The purity of Beatrice would have been important to me. I wanted to use the style of Hieronymus Bosch, which I found perfect for this work, but the producers wanted only bare tits and naked asses. I could never trivialize Dante by making something commercially sensational out of his work.

Actually, the film I would prefer to make is the life of Dante Alighieri, himself, which was a more fantastic story than *The Divine Comedy* because it really happened. I would treat his peregrinations in the thirteenth century, including some extraordinary battle scenes which Kurosawa might admire.

I have been asked about filming the *Iliad*. When we were children, we read the *Iliad* and memorized it. Then we went out and played *Iliad*, the way American children play cops and robbers. Somehow it seemed presumptuous to me to do "Fellini's Iliad," and I know I could not be bound rigidly. Also, it's difficult to create images for such a story when everyone already has his own images.

A dream of mine was to do *Don Quixote,* with the perfect actor for the part, Jacques Tati. But I could never think of the perfect Sancho Panza. He is almost as important a character as Don Quixote. They are like Laurel and Hardy.

One of the films I hoped to make was the Kafka story *Amerika.* I saw no reason why it couldn't be made at Cinecittà. I'd always admired Kafka, since I read "The Metamorphosis" during the days I worked for *Marc' Aurelio.* Kafka himself had never been in America. I had been there, many times. The picture of America I wanted to show was his, not mine. The novel was not complete, but novels are too long to adapt, and I had what I needed. It's a European's view of America, with something of the spirit of Dickens. Whatever wasn't there allowed some room for my imagination to roam within the episodic structure.

I have always been fascinated by the experience of near-death. I believe in that moment some people learn the secrets of life and death. The price of that knowledge is death, but before the body dies, the truth is imparted to the consciousness of those who die in such a way that there is a lapse of time between their absolute death and their last moment of life, something like a coma.

This was what I envisioned for G. Mastorna. I had long kept secret the story of "The Voyage of G. Mastorna," the film which I had thought to make during several decades of my life. It was conceived early in my career, and I would build on it in my mind, even as I worked on other films. I would never tell the producers much of the idea, which didn't help in getting money for it.

Once, it seemed it was going to happen. We got as far as building the sets. Then I fell ill. I hovered near death for a time. It was in that state that I came even nearer to "G. Mastorna." When I recovered, I couldn't tell what parts of my memories were true and what parts were not. Now I can tell the idea I had for him because I have accepted it is a film I will never make, for many reasons. I have the fortitude left to make it, but I do not have the fortitude left to persuade anyone to produce it. Some of my associates have whispered to each other that Fellini doesn't make the film because he has grown superstitious about it. "Fellini has identified with G. Mastorna," they say, "and he's afraid he will die if he completes the film."

The real reason is I myself have cannibalized "G. Mastorna" while Mastorna waited in the wings. I have borrowed bits and pieces from the idea for all of my films since. Only the main idea is left, and I would have to re-create a new film for him. I planned to utilize certain autobiographical aspects of my own inner life, to draw from my real feelings rather than my real experiences, as I had previously done. My identification with Mastorna has always been intimate, as it was with Guido in *8½*. When I was directing Mastroianni as Guido, sometimes I felt like I was ordering myself around.

For a long time, I refused to talk about the story of G. Mastorna. I believed that if I told the story before I gave it life, I would rob it of its magic. Mastorna could fly, as I frequently did in my dreams. Whenever I flew in a dream, I had that wondrous feeling of freedom. I particularly love flying in dreams. It gives me the same incredible exhilaration I have when I am making a film.

The original inspiration for the story came from my visit to the Cologne cathedral, where I heard about a medieval monk who could fly at will—but not his own will. He could fly when the spirit moved him—only, the spirit that moved him was not his own. He had no control of his *too*-special gift, and was often transported at inappropriate moments to precarious positions from which he was then unable to extricate himself. Also, like me, my character had the problem of being afraid of flying. There was speculation on what the name signified for me. Speculation on the name "Mastorna" became a cottage industry among journalists and film scholars. I found his name in the telephone directory.

Now Mastorna will never fly. I believed it would have been my best film if I could have made it, and now since I know I will not be doing it, I can go on believing it would have been my best film. Alive only in my own mind, it will never disappoint me.

There is a scene I have wanted to use in a film, but I've never been able to find the right film for it. It's seeming to me that I've waited too long, and now I'll be able to see the picture only in my head.

The Palace of Justice was built about seventy years ago. But they didn't allow properly for the weight of the building, and so ever since, it has been sinking into the river. Only recently, it began sinking faster and had to be emptied. Now it's empty, and it has a macabre look. Its best moment was with the rats. The rats are so big that no cats could kill them. The cats, in fact, would be killed.

So, one night—actually, about three in the morning, when there were no people around—they brought the trucks. The trucks were from the zoo, filled with panthers and tigers. They moved the trucks to the tunnel, and then let the tigers and panthers loose, out in the tunnels. Can you imagine in the blackness, the only light was those glowing green eyes . . . !

There was a wonderful film with Mae West in which she tames lions. I would like to have directed that film, Mae West and the lions. It would have been like directing the tigers and the panthers.

The idea of King Kong interested me. I think that noble beast is a great character. The whole conception fascinates me, especially the idea that King Kong represents all men in their total vulnerability to the charms of a woman. I can understand that. King Kong, the romantic. He was deprived of his strength and ultimately destroyed, yet I envy him the immensity of his passion without fear of consequences. Love, hate, rage—how wonderful! I am more of an objective observer in life.

When I told De Laurentiis, after his remake of *King Kong,* that I would have been interested in doing *King Kong,* he said, "Good. How about 'Daughter of King Kong'?"

An idea that came to me in a dream was a variation on the Robinson Crusoe story. A sailor in a small craft is washed up on a South Seas beach. The natives on the island have never seen a European before, so they treat him like a demigod. Since he has no memory of his life

During the filming of *And the Ship Sails On,* producer Aldo Nemni expressed his admiration for Fellini's drawings. The director invited Nemni to have as many of the pictures as he wanted, but Nemni was too courteous to take more than three, a decision he later regretted. These are Fellini's attempts to seek inspiration through drawing.

prior to arriving there, he comes to believe them, entering into their primitive society as a celebrity, like a rock star in our modern civilization. Nearly everyone wants to please him, especially the nubile young maidens, who parade about with their divine bodies and perfect breasts exposed. He has enemies, however, and a plot develops which I unfortunately can't recall, but which held my interest during the course of the dream.

When our hero is about to fall to his enemies, a small seaplane lands in the lagoon, and more Europeans arrive on the scene. Though he doesn't recognize them, they greet him as a friend.

"Federico!" they say, beaming. "You've done it again. You've scouted the perfect location for your Robinson Crusoe film in Polynesia."

I would like to have done a "private eye" picture, a sort of film noir, but in color. I had an offer to do this for television, but it was a series. I don't think I could have sustained my own interest for a series, and if I didn't keep my own interest, how could I keep the attention of the audience? The hour format didn't suit my ideas, either, because I had too many of them.

Many times, over the years, women have said to me, "Why don't you ever make a truly romantic picture?" I never knew how to answer, because I thought I had.

Marcello asked me to think about writing a film we could do together in our old age. He wanted to play a character who was senile. I said, "But what if I'm in my dotage, too?"

No matter how much I said I had lost my foolish optimism, I had not. What I really wanted was to have selective optimism, to know who was real and who was not—who would produce a film. Optimism requires a certain protection, or it grows too fragile. I didn't want to lose my time, or what was left of my hope, but how could I judge? The invitations from all over the world to have lunch only increase. Some days, I could have eaten lunch two or three times with people I didn't want to have lunch with at all.

All the people who want to eat lunch with Fellini when they are passing through Rome! Why not? Putting a canapé into Fellini's mouth is like dropping a coin into the Fountain of Trevi.

Alberto Sordi (left) and Marcello Mastroianni (right) with Fellini at the Lincoln Center tribute. During a party afterward at Elaine's, a Manhattan restaurant, Sordi kissed the empty table at which Woody Allen usually sat.

. . .

I make jokes about Catholicism, and I criticize the faults I see within the organized religion, because sometimes Catholics aren't up to Catholicism. Certainly I am not against Catholicism. I *am* a Catholic.

I am naturally religious. I love mystery, and there is much of it in life. There is even more in death. Since I was a child, I have been interested in everything mystical—the wonders of existence; the unknowable. I love the pageantry of religion, the ritual, the idea of a pope, but especially a code of conduct, of which guilt is an inherent element.

In Italy, what else could one be? The Church was my world before I was old enough to understand. What would I criticize and rebel from if I didn't have this system? I believe a certain religious feeling,

Giulietta Masina with Charlotte Chandler at Cinecittà.

though broadly interpreted, is necessary. I think all of us pray to Someone, Something, Somewhere, even if we call it wishing.

America is a place of endless fascination for Europeans. I am a European Latin, which means I have at least one foot in the past. Probably

Marcello Mastroianni had to dance less well than he actually could in *Ginger and Fred* (1985), so that his and Giulietta Masina's dancing would match. He and Giulietta both loved to dance, had been friends since they were young, and had long wanted to work together.

both. It is not a totally good thing to be an ancient man with thousands of years in one's veins. I have chosen to live in a place where the past is all around me. In Rome, we say, "I'll meet you at the Pantheon for ice cream" or "We'll take the shortcut at the Coliseum." I live in a place where the past is all around us, the ancient past. When you walk around Rome, you cannot help but be affected by the monuments, the ancient walls and ruins of the past, all of that which brings the tourists who take their photographs. *We* do not need photographs. It is part of those of us who live here for most of our lives. It becomes part of the subconscious. I am sure it is part of mine. I think that it affects the way we Romans look at the future. It makes you somewhat indifferent about the future. Deep in my subconscious may be the message, "Nothing is really important. Life comes, and life goes. I am just a small part of it, just a link in a chain." There is some sense of futility in the air of Rome because so many have been breathing it for so long.

When I go to California, some years passing between each of my trips, I notice that I scarcely recognize an area I have visited only a few years before. I do not ask to see any of the ancient monuments because I would probably be shown a gas station. Everything seems to change before you can even make a postcard of it.

Once, when I considered staying there a while, studying film projects, I was offered an office. I said I preferred an old building, in fact, that I *needed* an old building. I didn't think I would be inspired in one of those new glass skyscrapers, and certainly I wouldn't be comfortable in a building with windows that didn't open. They said, "No problem." The next day they told me they had found one they were certain I'd like. Already. Americans are like that. They are so obliging. I went to see the office. It looked new to me. They said, "No, it's old. It's five years old."

America with its innocence and energy. Always looking forward. America is fantastic.

twenty - two

DEATH IS SO
VERY ALIVE

The Oscars have stardust. . . .

When I was a child, I was a little sickly. Nothing too serious—spells of dizziness. I didn't mind. I enjoyed the extra attention. I liked drama. On occasion, I even faked illness or pretended an injury.

As a grown man, I sometimes feigned illness or exaggerated injury as an excuse for not doing something I didn't want to do.

Then, finally, it was too true. When it became real, I was ashamed of sickness and weakness and wanted to hide mine.

In 1992, when I got the phone call from the Motion Picture Academy, telling me that I was to receive the honorary Oscar for lifetime achievement, I was happy, but then I had extremely mixed feelings. A "lifetime achievement" award doesn't necessarily mean that your life is finished, but it may mean that your achievement is finished, or is perceived that way. My first thought was, Would it help me get backing for a new film? My second thought was, How nice! It is certainly an honor being paid to do my work. My third thought was, I wish it were for my last film, which was *Voices of the Moon.* Then I thought, I hope this is not the legendary award given when you have died professionally and are about to die physically, the finishing-off award.

I suppose I could be called superstitious, but I always thought I would receive the Oscar for lifetime achievement—at the end of my life. So I hope this isn't it. I was actually looking forward to receiving it, oh, in perhaps another twenty-five years.

They wanted to give me a first-class, luxury trip. The luxury for me would be not to have to go. Giulietta could go, I thought. She enjoys that kind of thing. She can get a new dress for the occasion. She can get six. Let Mario Longardi go with her. Let Mastroianni go. Anyone but me. I had never liked to travel, and I had come to like it even less. Also, I wasn't feeling well. This time it was not an excuse, and it is very embarrassing to be sick in public. Then, there was the

Intervista reunited Marcello Mastroianni, Anita Ekberg, and Fellini at Ekberg's Rome villa more than twenty-five years after *8½*.

chance that receiving the Oscar wouldn't help as it should. I am always surprised by people's reactions, especially the reactions of producers, whom I never understand. What if they thought my receiving the lifetime achievement Oscar meant that I had retired, or had been retired?

I decided what I would do.

I would make a film of my acceptance speech. I would direct myself, delivering it in Rome, and Giulietta would go to Hollywood and take it there. She would receive the Oscar onstage. Perfect.

I had learned before the Oscars, however, that Giulietta was very ill. It was much worse than she knew. She had some idea, but she didn't want to know. For myself, I would feel the opposite. I would want to know. I've never believed that doctors know everything, but this time I believed, even though I didn't want to. I wanted to do everything I could to make her happy. The truth is, I cannot imagine life without Giulietta.

I had made up my mind I would do everything she ever wanted, to make everything good for her—to always be in a good humor, to pay attention and listen to every word she spoke, to go to parties with her.

One night, Giulietta and I went to a party at the home of friends, and everyone was giving me their unasked-for opinion about why I should go to the Oscars. "Have you changed your mind?" they would ask. "You really *ought* to go to Hollywood to receive your Oscar." How did *they* know what *I* should do?

I didn't say anything, but I wished I had stayed home. I'd gone only to please Giulietta. Then someone said to her, "You must persuade him to go. It's such an honor." The woman gushed on and on and on, and Giulietta said, really only making conversation to be polite, "Maybe he'll change his mind. Maybe he *will* go."

Suddenly I heard a loud, angry retort, and I had spoken it:

"I will *not* go!" I shouted at Giulietta. Everyone had heard. Suddenly, the room was very quiet. Everyone was embarrassed, especially Giulietta. And no one was more embarrassed than I.

What she had said was inoffensive. I suppose my sudden, angry, inappropriate reaction had to do with the weeks I had been resisting all the pressure to change my mind. I couldn't go anywhere without

For their fiftieth anniversary, Federico redrew his wedding card for Giulietta, changing the date to October 30, 1993, and the address to Margutta. In the joined hearts, he wrote 50.

people telling me I had to go—waiters in my favorite restaurants, taxi drivers, people on the street.

Poor Giulietta. She didn't deserve it. I had really gone to the party only because I wanted *her* to have a good time. Why do these things happen? I knew I had embarrassed Giulietta in front of her friends.

I spent the rest of the evening being especially soft with Giulietta. I was as attentive, as solicitous as I could be without seeming foolish. I began to talk too much, nervously, as though a torrent of words could unspeak the words I had spoken. I stayed longer than I had intended. I meant to be among the first to go, but we were the last to go. Probably the hosts wondered if we were ever going, or if we were planning to spend the night. I suppose I wanted to show everyone what a good time I was having. But I could not take back those words and the terrible way I had spoken to Giulietta. Partly, I went to the Oscars to unspeak those words.

Through the years, whenever I had to go onstage to make a speech at the Oscars, I felt just as I had when I was five years old and had

302 / Charlotte Chandler

been called on to recite a poem and monologue at a family gathering. I would go and hide in the bathroom.

Each time as I sat at the Oscars, I had mixed feelings about whether I wanted to win or not, because winning meant I would have to go up onstage and thank all those people. I've always felt that way about every awards ceremony. With the honorary Oscar, there was no possibility that they would change their minds and give the award to someone else. As I waited, I felt five years old again, and I had at least a fleeting desire to go hide in the men's room.

Giulietta is an emotional person, and the Oscars night was a professionally and personally moving occasion for both of us. When Giulietta cried at the Oscars, I suppose that she was crying with joy for everything that was, and with sorrow for everything that wasn't. That moment had the same magic for us that Giulietta and Mastroianni had felt as "Ginger" and "Fred," dancing together again after all those years, together again. Their professional and their personal life was summed up in that moment.

For Giulietta and me, our life together was summed up in that moment at the Oscars.

After the Oscars show, I was relieved and happy. I knew I'd done well. I hadn't let down the taxi drivers of Rome, Giulietta, the Motion Picture Academy, or anyone, even myself. People were congratulating me, but I know you can't trust that. Americans are so polite, they would have been nice even if I had disgraced everyone. I'd been in pain from this terrible arthritis since before I left Rome, but that was nothing compared to the pain of knowing I would be live on television, in English, seen in America, Russia, China, the world— Rome. More than anything, I didn't want to look sick or in pain.

Standing up there, I felt this wave of love from the audience. I even enjoyed it. I couldn't believe it.

When I left the stage, the press was waiting backstage, and there were all the photographers. I've never had so many pictures taken. I was anxious to go back to our hotel, but I wanted to thank the members of the board of governors. They asked me to stay for the dinner party, but I knew I couldn't manage that. The strain was too great. Standing as straight as I could was a great effort. Sophia Loren wanted me to go to Spago for the party there. Mastroianni wanted to go to the parties because he is the total actor, always thinking about his next part, hoping to be seen at one of them and discovered for some great new film. An actor can make a few films in the same amount of time a director needs to prepare just one.

Giulietta was happy. She was crying, but I knew that meant she was happy. She cries when she is happy and also when she is sad, but I have known her long enough to be able to tell the difference.

We all went back to the Hilton, and we had our own private party in the suite—Giulietta, Marcello, Mario [Longardi], Fiammetta [Profili], and I. They could have gone to the parties, but they were very faithful and chose to stay with me. We drank champagne. We were very tired because we were on European time, nine hours' difference. It was already morning in Rome. Giulietta suggested staying another day, so she could shop, but I knew what another day there meant. It would be the press coming, calling. I would be trapped in the hotel all day. Even at lunch, there would be someone from the press to ask me how I felt about getting the Oscar, and other questions, to which I could respond in a trite way while they watched me chew. It was better to get back, better to have the long flight over with, and not to be anticipating it during yet another sleepless night.

The next morning we had to be up very early to pack and to go to the airport.

I love the American breakfast. It so represents that country. Pork sausages for breakfast—imagine! I always say to myself in my head, because I don't talk out loud to myself, When I go back to Rome I'll eat pork sausages for breakfast every day. But I never do, not even one day. The morning after the Oscars, however, I didn't have the appetite for those wonderful sausages, because I was traveling that day, and already my stomach was in transit.

Perhaps there would be producers in Rome who could hardly wait for my return, so they could say to me, "We didn't know how great you are, Federico, until American television said so. Now we know. Forgive us, and please let us back your new film, whatever it is, whatever it costs. Here is a contract, and we can begin right away." I always hope it will be like that. It never is, but I cannot help hoping. In some ways, I suppose I am even more optimistic than Giulietta, but

Fellini, raising his hand in his oath "I swear," with Charlotte Chandler and the "Charlottina" doll made by famed Turin dollmaker LENCI after a caricature by Fellini. It is the morning after Fellini received his lifetime achievement Oscar.

I try not to let people know. I am always disappointed, but I have my two days of hope while I wait for the phone to ring. Of course, the press will be waiting there, too. The Italian press will say, with no more brilliance than the Americans, "Tell us, Mr. Fellini, how does it feel to win an Oscar?"

I say many things smiling, but with sad eyes.

One thing I realized with my honorary Oscar. I never understood how many people love my work, not only in Italy. In America. It makes me very emotional. So many people . . . I don't think I deserve it. So much love and support. So many people caring. So many people concerned about me. Is it because they love my films? It must be.

"Federico and Giulietta." People are saying it now like "Romeo and Juliet." The times in between, the imperfections, have been wiped away. What would have happened to Romeo and Juliet if they had lived to celebrate their fiftieth wedding anniversary? They were teenagers when they met and loved for the first time. Would every minute have been perfect romance? I think it's really been like that for Giulietta and me.

The day of our fiftieth wedding anniversary, the exact day, October 23, 1993, didn't mean to me what it did to Giulietta. She began talking about it a few years in advance. I didn't see that exact day as more important than the day before, or the day after.

If I had chosen the date to celebrate, it would have been the date of the day we met. I do not think there was another woman in the world with whom I could have shared fifty years.

When I say my life began in Rome, that I was born there, and that it is the only place I have wanted to be, almost all of it has been with Giulietta. Giulietta is part of Rome for me, as she is part of my work, part of my life. Giulietta would probably say, "What part?" but one cannot say, because the part is different at different times. However, if something is a part of you, and at times it is your heart, at others your arm, at others your thumb, it does not matter which, only that without it you would be incomplete, not whole.

Before the trip to America, I was working on my next film. At the moment, it's just in my mind. It will be a sort of continuation of *A Director's Notebook*. It's "An Actor's Notebook," and will feature Giulietta and Mastroianni. I want to do something for which the money is easily available from television, because I am anxious to be working. I have many other ideas, but they require finding producers. I believe this will be a nice little film. Giulietta is anxious to work again now without waiting, so also I want to do this for her.

Just before leaving for California to receive my Oscar, I had a dream. I was very thin, as I always am in my dreams, and I had all my hair, more than ever, and it was still very dark, as it was when I was young. I was very lithe, and easily vaulted over the wall of some sort of hospital or prison in which I had been confined. The wall was about twenty feet high, but I had no difficulty because I was so athletic. I felt in wonderful health and full of energy. I had left my arthritis behind me on the other side of the wall.

I looked up, and there was a wonderful sunset in the sky. It was low, so close I felt I could touch it and adjust it a little. I saw that it was made of paper. I wondered how they did that, because I thought I would like to use a sunset like that one in my next film, which I was just about to start, "The Voyage of G. Mastorna." At last. Finally.

It seemed natural that the sunset was paper, because so were the trees and the grass. Perfect, I thought. I had never been a true lover of nature.

I saw my guardian angel was up there, in the sky, and she adjusted the sunset the way I was thinking it should be. She could read my mind. I caught a glimpse of her face, which I had never seen before. She reminded me of my grandmother, only the way my grandmother must have looked when she was young, before she was my grandmother. I wasn't certain. I looked again, but her head was turned away.

I realized I was wearing a Roman toga, but it didn't cause me to trip. It was very comfortable and not at all difficult to run in. I looked down to see if my fly was zipped, only I couldn't find it.

I came to a place where there were two paths and I had to choose. One of them led to a woman cooking. I saw it was Cesarina. That seemed strange, because I never thought that she existed outside of her restaurant. It also seemed a little strange because I knew she had died. But that hadn't affected her cooking. I could smell the white beans in the olive oil. I saw she had a big pot of bollito, just the way I like it. She called out that the scampi were very fresh. "I'll grill them as soon as you sit down to eat. You have to wait for the scampi so the scampi don't wait for you." Of course.

She was going to surprise me. She hadn't even mentioned the fried baby artichokes.

"And for dessert, I have zuppa inglese just the way you always loved it." That was really strange. Because I didn't have zuppa inglese at Cesarina's. It was my favorite when I was little and my grandmother made it. No one ever made it like she did. I wondered how Cesarina got my grandmother's recipe, because my grandmother would never tell anyone the recipe for *her* zuppa inglese. I could smell the alchermes liqueur she had used to moisten the layers of cake. I could smell the freshly grated lemon peel which excited the senses. The concoction had so many layers of cake and custard crème anglaise that I couldn't see the top of it. It just went on and on.

I was about to take that path when I looked in the other direction. I saw a woman with the most beautiful breasts I had ever seen, and she was smiling and offering them to me. She had blond hair and blue eyes, like the ladies who used to come from Germany to take the sun by the sea, summers in Rimini. She said coquettishly, "Come and have lunch here, and then you can eat Cesarina's meal *afterwards*." She underlined the "afterwards," adding, "We'll eat it together." I always enjoyed looking across the table at a beautiful woman while eating a delicious meal.

I'd never cared for making love on the grass. Of course, I'd never tried doing it on paper grass, but suddenly a high bed appeared, covered with a big, soft, white down comforter, and there were the large down pillows of my childhood which were passed through the generations. The young woman, now naked, leaped onto the bed. I did, too, calling back to Cesarina, "Later."

As you can see, in my dream I was very young.

I want to do a picture using my current hospital experience. It would be about sickness and death, but it would not be sad.

I plan to show Death as I have seen Her so many times in my dreams. Death is a woman. She is always the same, a very beautiful woman in Her forties. She is wearing a dress of red satin, trimmed with black lace. Her hair is light, but not yellow blond. She has pearls, not the long strands, only a choker collar around Her long neck. She is tall, slim, graceful, serene, confident. She does not seem concerned about Her looks. She is very intelligent. Her intelligence is Her dominant characteristic. It shows on Her face. It shines through Her eyes. They are not the blank eyes one sees all too often, but there is a kind of light behind them. She sees everything.

Death is so very alive.

twenty-three

THE VEILED LADY
OF THE FULGOR

Y ou tell a story, and while you are doing so, you are living one yourself. I started making a picture many years ago, and I'm still making it. Because I don't go back and see my pictures after I have finished them, they have all come together for me so that they scarcely seemed separated. Students who know the details better than I are always asking me why I did something or other. Sometimes I think they have given me credit for someone else's film. Usually, I cannot tell them, because I cannot remember what I was thinking thirty years ago when I did a particular shot. I can't remember because I haven't seen the film since I made it. Well—there are a few exceptions. When they are shown at a festival like Venice or Moscow, I can't escape, and it would look peculiar if I closed my eyes. All I know is that for a long time, it seemed to me I was making just one long film, that all I could wish is that it be longer, that it was all I ever wanted to do, the greatest happiness to which I had ever aspired.

There is nothing that shocks me more than to see my age in print. Or to have Giulietta say to me, "How would you like to spend your seventy-second birthday?" Or to have a journalist say, "How does it feel to be seventy-two?" I think, "How would I know? What does that have to do with me?"

Seventy-two isn't a number you look forward to. The time it looks good is from the perspective of eighty, when you are looking back at it.

I have never been very conscious of the passage of time. Time did not really exist for me. I have never cared about watches or clocks, only what was imposed on me. Deadlines. Overtime. Not making people wait. I think I would be unaware of it if others did not remind me. I still feel the same way I felt when I was the dark-haired, skinny boy who dreamed of Rome and found it. My life has gone by so fast. It seems to me like one long, uncut Fellini film.

I was always the youngest in my group of friends, because I was attracted by people older than myself. They had broader experiences on which I could draw. I could learn from them; thus, whether they were or were not more intelligent, they seemed so.

It was very strange for me when I noticed that I was being invited to birthday parties of people I knew, and suddenly they were all younger than I. It seemed to happen overnight. It was even more shocking when I realized that among the people I had known in my life, the dead outnumbered the living.

Where do you go next?

It has always been my belief that whatever you do should lead to something else. No matter how successful anything I did was, there was never that line around the block of all those producers asking for a meeting, on their knees begging for my next film. No. There was never that constant ring of the telephone, not even after *La Dolce Vita*. Not even after the Oscars. Perhaps it was like with the beautiful girl no one calls because they are certain she will be too busy for them, that she is overwhelmed by far greater offers than theirs, with endless, unimaginable choice, so the beautiful girl stays home on Saturday night while the homelier ones have dates. Giulietta and I have spent many Saturday nights at home alone.

People said I was good at pitching my projects, the way I played all the parts and brought them to life. I do not think so. They were happy to see Fellini stand on his head, but when it came time to put their money into my next film, they brought in the committee of accountants who would never approve what I did.

I was naïve. I believed every time. They would say, "Let's eat lunch." I could never believe they just wanted to eat lunch with Fellini. But after the lunch, they would disappear. Finally, in my mind when they said, "Let's have lunch," I heard the unspoken rest of the sentence: "and that's all."

Then, I no longer believed at all. My naïveté had given me protection, so when I stopped believing in everyone, I began believing in no one. Thus, I closed the door on myself. Probably there were lunches I should have eaten, but I had no way to determine which ones. For me, eating is such a great pleasure, I always wanted to share meals with friends. I've never understood the idea of why they, especially the Americans, like the "business lunch." Is it because of the charge account? Or is it because they know you can't get up and leave during the middle of your spaghetti? I see in my mind the picture of a little naked Fellini, all tied up, wrapped in chains of spaghetti.

There is a certain kind of carefree that returns to you in old age, different from the carefree of youth when you didn't know any better. It's more like being free of caring. It isn't joyous at all, as it was in youth, but it is a kind of freedom, and all kinds of freedom are precious in some way.

The struggle muscles inside relax. They are released from trying so hard, that struggle of the middle years. You lack the energy to go on, the fortitude to face another disappointment.

You relax, like in a hot bath. You lie there and yield, knowing all the while the water will soon be cold.

Now people tell me Rome is cracking. I try not to notice, but of course one sees it. Everyone notices it even more when a famous beauty shows the wrinkles of time.

Rome is aging much faster now, and differently, in a way that is graceless. It has less to do with "antique" and more to do with decay. They give reasons like the smog, but I think it is an attitude, a loss of optimism and pride which permeates even the statuary. Rome looks older to me now. Perhaps it's just because I'm getting older.

I would like to die knowing I am just about to start my next film, knowing exactly what it will be, the general idea, with all of the money raised by a producer who says, "You do what you want, Federico. Spend what you need. I trust you." And maybe looking for faces—actors to express what I want. I wouldn't want to die in the middle of a film, because I would feel I was abandoning it, leaving my helpless creature. . . .

The end of a film is not for me a happy time, like the end of a love affair—the many telltale good-byes, the clear signs that passion is winding down, when the people who have worked together have sworn eternal friendship because of their bond, and now each is going his own way, having perhaps lost the slips of paper with the names and addresses of the never-to-be-forgotten others.

If I am Il Mago, as they call me, then, when I make a film, the magician and the virgin get together. My film is a virgin, and at the end, when she's complete, I no longer feel the same way, and I desert her.

Old age commences when life becomes repetitious, when everything you do is something you have done before, more times than you can or would even wish to remember. The limits of a human being are only the boundaries of his imagination. Because a new creation can make one feel new, the price a person will pay to experience the discovery of life as it was before it became repetitious, with the consequent surcease from boredom, is less only than one's soul.

The Fulgor. Sometimes I feel my life began in that little theater, that dilapidated old picture palace, suffocatingly hot in the summer, uncomfortable in all seasons, but once the film began, I was transported to other places, other times.

Then, I would go and sit on the beach, and make up stories. I would imagine them being acted out on the screen of the Fulgor.

I fantasized about the veiled lady who sat in the Fulgor, smoking her cigarette. The veil reached just short of her lips. I was afraid she might catch fire. As long as I live, I will remember those wonderful eyes resolutely fixed on the screen, while several teenage boys felt up her skirt. The expression on her face never changed, even when she stayed through the film a second or even a third time. My fantasy was to be one of those boys. Sometimes, I claimed to be one of them. The truth of the matter was, whatever I did was done only in my mind, as was so much of my activity in those days.

In those days, I would never have believed that one day a photograph of me would hang in the minuscule foyer of the Fulgor. If I ever had any doubts that I had made it . . . ! I can imagine little boys like I once was going by the picture and saying, "Who is that? He doesn't look like a movie star." Their parents tell them that I am probably the owner of the theater, and they blame me if that day they saw a film they didn't like.

I've always regarded the movie palace as a sacred shrine, a place to have respect. Recently, I went into a theater in Rome, and there was only one person there. He had his feet propped up on the back of the chair in front of him, and while he was watching the picture, he was listening to his Walkman. He was wearing roller skates.

When I am between pictures, I have to face my real problems— God, money, Giulietta, money, taxes, money. It's no wonder I look for escape to the playground of Cinecittà.

The place of the Fulgor Cinema in Rimini was taken in my adult life by Cinecittà. I have spent many years of my life at Cinecittà, and the hours have added up.

It's a great thrill for me to stand on Stage 5 of Cinecittà even when it's empty and I'm all alone. The emotion is impossible to convey.

When I first set foot there, I had exactly the same strange sensation that I remembered having as a little boy when I was taken for the first time to see the circus, when I knew I was expected there.

Circus people are never surprised by things that happen to them. I admire that. The obvious implication is that anything, everything is possible. It is the opposite of the rationality of the learning forced on us, which tells us to impose limitations on ourselves, and also to always feel guilty.

I think of my life as a series of films. These films represent me more than any other part of my life. They aren't just films for me; they are the story of my life. So it seems that finally I did, after all, as I'd always wanted to do as a little boy sitting in the audience, get up there and go right into the screen of the Fulgor. At that time, I didn't know what a director was, so being an actor seemed more fun. In the beginning, I didn't really even understand what an actor did. I believed the people were really up there living those lives.

My generation was shaped by the idealized picture of that wonderful life in America as presented by the American films. The western hero, detective, whatever, the individual was everything in American stories. I could identify with that. I *wanted* to identify with that. The individual was the winner, the noble figure. I think I first really began to hate fascism when it cut us off from America and everything I loved—American movies and American comic strips.

It was nice in those American movies. There were always rich, happy people. It seemed natural at the time that anyone who was rich would be happy. A given. They were beautiful and danced well.

Dancing seemed to me inextricably linked to being rich, and thus happy. I, personally, could never master dancing well. I always had two right feet. Those Americans in their nice world always seemed to be dancing on the roofs of skyscrapers. And when they weren't dancing, they were eating. Or they were speaking on their white telephones. My passion for cinema began there.

Work became more important to me as I grew older. When you are very young, there are many competing pleasures. Maybe you need less to make yourself happy because everything is new to you. The world of old age is a shrinking world. Smaller things are magnified. It's like childhood. Few people are important to you, but they are *very* important. Little things get bigger. Food becomes more important. It is your work that makes you feel young, not your love affairs. After a certain point, your love affairs make you feel older.

When I was very young, I thought about what old age would be like. It didn't seem very real. I assumed I would be exactly the same as I was then, except that I might have a long white beard like Father Christmas and not ever have to shave. I planned to eat whatever I wanted—mozzarella, pasta, rich desserts—and I would travel and see the museums I never had the time to see before.

One day I looked into my shaving mirror and thought, "Where did that old man come from?" Then I realized he was me, and all I wanted to do was work.

There were interests of mine which I have had all my life, but which I saved for the late years when I might not be working. The major thing I wanted to do was to go to all the great museums of the world and see as much art as I could. I've always had a feeling for art. Art moved me. I never had that kind of interest, for example, in music. I would like to have seen everything by Rubens. He liked to paint the same kind of women I drew in my funny little pictures. Then there was Botticelli, all those pink-and-white innocents in large sizes. Hieronymus Bosch impressed me very much, too. There is a wonderful Munch museum in Norway I would like to have seen. Even in Italy I haven't seen much. I've been intending to see again some paintings in the church on the Piazza del Popolo, a few blocks from where I live. I'll probably do that. Perhaps I'll show them to a visitor, so that I see them again.

Time is rushing by now. I remember how slowly a day went in Rimini. I walked along the beach. I worked on my puppet theater. I drew pictures. Now, I don't know where the days go, have gone, moving not singly but in multiples. The greatest luxury of youth is not being conscious of time.

I've thought of making a film about it. In childhood, the film would move along slowly, and as the child reached adulthood, the pace of the action would accelerate. The end would be almost a blur.

I once read a Fredric Brown story in *Playboy* magazine in which a man discovers the secret of immortality. The only trouble is, the pace of the world keeps speeding up around him, so that he starts to see the sun and moon racing faster and faster across the heavens each day. Finally, he becomes part of an exhibit in a museum, seated at his desk, with a pen in his hand, apparently frozen in the middle of writing a manuscript. It's explained by the museum guide that he's still alive, but moving so slowly you can't know it. He's in the middle of writing about what has happened to him, but probably won't finish for centuries.

I think sometimes as I near the end of my life, It has gone so fast. Where did the time go? How did it pass so quickly?

It's strange to realize that people are talking about you who don't know you, whom you don't know. Waiters, taxicab drivers, people whom you've talked with sometime, that's one thing; but people who don't know you at all . . . ?

What is really embarrassing is to have your internal physical problems talked about on television. Terrible!

I always wanted to be handsome and powerful, physically the kind of man women love and men envy, like those muscular young athletes who practiced Greco-Roman wrestling on the Rimini beach. At least, I would like to keep what little I have and not look old—even if I am. Once I had some hope that a fountain of youth had been found.

A friend of mine told me about a place in Romania, I don't remember the name, where you could go for special secret treatments. I think you were blindfolded and ate sheep glands. You entered at the age of seventy, and it took until you were seventy-one before you got out, but when you did, you didn't look seventy-one anymore. You looked sixty-nine.

So, when I passed seventy, I asked my friend, who was a few years older than I and who had been there, where the clinic was. But he couldn't remember.

As a boy, I would feign sickness to get extra attention. As a young man, I simulated illnesses to escape Mussolini's army. As a man of middle age, I used not feeling well to avoid honors and festivals, for which I could imagine no other excuse. Finally, in old age, my infirmities became real, and I will now do anything not to have people know the truth, because I am embarrassed by and ashamed of my weakness.

A sign of growing old is when interviewers start asking you, "What would you do differently if you had your life to live over again?" I give some sort of answer because I don't wish to be rude, but I don't tell them the image that comes into my mind because they would think it vain and frivolous, and no one wants to be a subject for ridicule.

I see myself as a tall, skinny Fellini, vigorously lifting weights. That's what I would do differently. I would lift weights.

I've never felt good about my body. First, I felt too thin. I didn't want anyone to see me in a bathing suit, so even though I lived by the sea and loved the sea, I didn't learn to swim.

Later, I felt too fat. Always I felt too soft. I was planning to make some time to build up my body, but I was always too busy or too lazy.

It's difficult to be a good lover if you feel ashamed of your body.

I was a skinny youth who couldn't gain weight. Inside, I still feel like that. Sometimes I start to run up a flight of stairs, and I am surprised to find I can't do it a few steps at a time, the way I did it then. I am shocked to find myself puffing and out of breath, almost from just the thought of exertion.

I live in the present. I've never been able to worry seriously about the future. The future has a kind of science-fiction unreality for me. I have never been able to imagine myself growing old, even as I've already become old. I see myself in my mind as still young, but it's not how I see myself in my shaving mirror. For this reason, I don't really look at myself when I shave, so I cut myself a lot. It's unfortunate I don't look well with a beard. The discrepancy between the reality and the picture in my mind is why I still draw myself young and thin, the way I still feel inside.

. . .

The man who could fly is a theme that has fascinated me since my youth. Even as a boy, I thought about being able to fly.

I was always dreaming that I could fly. When I did, in my dreams, I felt very light. I loved those dreams. My flying dreams were exhilarating.

Sometimes I had giant wings, which could be seen by everyone, wings so big that they were even unwieldy. Other times, I didn't need wings, I just took off, propelled by a power within me. Sometimes I had a destination. Sometimes I was just exploring.

It's strange, because there is nothing I hate more than flying in an airplane. The only way I have ever wanted to fly was *without* a plane.

I would be asked by colleagues and collaborators, Why did I want to make a film about a man who could fly? They knew I hated being in an airplane. I'd answer, "It's a metaphor." That kept them quiet.

At a certain point in my middle age, some might call it early old age, I began to dream that I could no longer fly. I was someone who had been able to fly. The implication was clear. Once, I had known how to do it and had been in total control of my own power. But now I was deprived.

It was terrible. Terrible. To have lost such a gift. I, who had had the gift, knew better than others the wonder of the experience.

I decided the reason I couldn't get off the ground was I was too fat. The answer was simple—to go on a diet. Simple answers, though, are often not as simple as they seem. It's always "simple" to go on a diet. I had done it hundreds of times. I always began my diet in my mind. That was where it always began and where it always ended. That was also where I did exercises, the gymnastics that would give me a body I was proud of. My diet would always last until my next meal. Then I ate more than ever. Thinking about dieting always made me very hungry. It was the fear of being deprived, a kind of famine psychology. Thus for me, dieting was very fattening.

I know I have to face that G. Mastorna may never fly—he who was the companion of so much of my life. Now I understand that I really *did* fly. I flew when I was directing films.

A gift is a blessing only if it is appreciated and enjoyed. I believe the greatest gift I have been given in life is my visual imagination. It is the source of my dreams. It enabled me to draw. It shapes my films.

The films are fixed in time, but I am not. When I am put in a position where I catch a glimpse of one of my films made thirty years ago, it makes me more conscious of that.

Someone says, "Imagine, you did that thirty-five years ago!" For some reason, they always make it longer ago than it was. No, I for one, cannot "imagine" it. For me, it seems like yesterday.

When I was younger, if someone had asked me what old age meant, I would have said, "Old age means canceling a late-afternoon orgy."

I can go on as long as I believe I am going to do another picture. At some point, it won't be true. I will have been retired, but I won't know it. It's important not to know the moment it happens.

I don't think about feeling young or old, but I think about health. That is what's important. I would like to live on only as long as I am healthy.

When you live with another person for fifty years, all of your memories are invested in that person, like a bank account of shared memories. It's not that you refer to them constantly. In fact, for people who do not live in the past, you almost never say, "Do you remember that night that we . . . ?" But you don't have to. That is the best of all. You *know* that the other person *does* remember. Thus, the past is part of the present as long as the other person lives. It is better than any scrapbook, because you are both living scrapbooks. The past may be more important for people who do not have children and who do not see themselves in the future as their genes living on in the persons of their children and grandchildren. That is why the thought of how the films we made will be remembered or viewed in the future is more important to both of us.

When I speak of "our" films, I don't mean just those of mine in which Giulietta starred. She was always there for me, during all of them, so even when she didn't come to the set and stayed at home, she cared about me, and she cared for me. I called her frequently on the phone. She would be there and cook supper for me, at whatever hour, and she was really my first assistant. I often showed her what I had written before anyone else saw it.

I never showed anything to anyone, even Giulietta, until it was thoroughly set for me. It was important that I had it well constructed in my own mind before I told it. If not, others might say, "You could do this," or "You could do that," and I wouldn't be firm because the characters wouldn't yet have their existence in my own mind. Once they have their own existence, each character lives. Once I know each character intimately, I know what he or she thinks, what each will do, and I could never betray one of them.

My life's work hasn't been real work, just a long vacation. My work and my hobby are the same. My work is filmmaking. My hobby is filmmaking, and filmmaking is my life.

Somehow my hand and my mind were linked for inspiration and creativity. I might have an idea without a pencil, but it was really only with a pencil in my hand that my imagination was stirred. Always having good pencils around was very important to me. In my dreams, of course, I didn't need a pencil, but it was essential that when I woke up, I recorded the pictures of my dream imagination, so that I kept a visual record of the story in my dream books.

For me, inspiration means making direct contact between your unconscious and your rational mind. An artistic creation has its own needs, which present themselves to the author as indispensable. All genuine details come from inspiration. Congeniality and good feeling are good for the spontaneity necessary.

As soon as I work on one idea, an outpouring of other ideas comes, often unrelated to the first, and all of the ideas compete, saying, "Me. Me. I want to be born." Each tries to be the strongest.

When I tell Giulietta not to smoke, people think it's because I miss smoking, because I was a smoker who long ago gave it up. That's not the reason. I gave up smoking when my chest began to hurt. After that, I didn't like for Giulietta to smoke, especially the way she did, which was all the time. It's not a coincidence that her characters on the screen smoke so much. I didn't think it was good for her, and I knew it wasn't good for me. The smell of the smoke had come to annoy me, and I couldn't understand why I had ever enjoyed it.

I think Giulietta believed she would get fat if she stopped smoking. She looked at me as the living proof of that, even though I gave up smoking *after* I got fat. It became such a source of dissension between us that we not only had to get her a separate smoking room for our apartment, but whenever we traveled, she had to have a separate room attached to our hotel suite, into which she could go and smoke.

• • •

I don't know how to be "politically correct." I heard this phrase when I was in America. I don't know what is currently "politically correct," and moreover, I would not want to know. I speak for myself, even though I know I must be wrong some of the time, especially since I have such limited information about everything. I certainly don't believe what I read just because it's in print. I think that television too often makes news rather than reporting it, because of the opinions of those doing it and because of the false impression of reality created by so much repetition. I have never been interested in belonging to clubs or political parties, or reciting "party-speak."

I lived with the illusion for a long time that death was something that happened to other people. As I draw closer to what is the average life span of man, I know that my own future is limited. I have thrown away most of my papers, leaving nothing to embarrass Giulietta or me. I have no children to worry about providing for. I have my films to represent me in the future, or I hope they will do so.

I often hear people say that the best death is to live a very long time and then to just close your eyes one night and die as you sleep. Sudden death. *That* is the death I do not choose.

I would like, near the end of my life, in that period of coma so close to death, to have a dream vision which reveals to me the mysteries of the universe. And then to wake up well enough to make a film about it.

I fear sickness and physical infirmity, which would keep me from working. I don't look forward to death, but I have never feared it in the way I fear old age and physical decadence. I don't want to live to be a hundred.

A sickly child, I would feel dizzy, and I suffered from fainting, which the doctor said was an imperfection in my heart. He said it probably meant I would have a short life expectancy. Some time ago, I had already lived long enough to have proven him wrong. Being regarded as sickly when I was a child won me a lot of special attention. It didn't worry me at all. It made me feel special. Death had a romantic mystery about it.

Now I feel differently. If I were to fall ill and not be able to work, for me that would be a living death. The idea of physical decadence troubles me. Not to make love eight times in a night.

Well, maybe seven.

When I was a child, my little friends would often say, "When I grow up, I'm going to be . . ." I never said that. I couldn't picture myself in the future. I wasn't concerned. I really couldn't imagine myself as one of those big people around who were grown up.

Perhaps that's why I've grown old without growing up.

Federico Fellini died in Rome on October 31, 1993.

I first met Federico Fellini in the spring of 1980 at the hotel in Fregene, about an hour from Rome, near what was then his weekend house. The meeting had been arranged by our mutual friend Mario de Vecchi, an Italian producer. Until that moment, I had never spoken with Fellini, not even on the telephone. Unable to judge exactly how long it would take me to travel from Rome to Fregene, and not wanting to be late, I had arrived forty minutes early.

I was sitting there, contemplating my second cappuccino a bit forlornly, because Fellini was late enough for me to begin to wonder whether he was coming at all. Fortunately, I wasn't wearing a watch, so I didn't realize exactly how late it really was. Fellini was notorious for making appointments and then not keeping them, but I couldn't believe he'd do that to me. It was not consistent with the image of the person I had perceived from his work. I had made the trip to Rome in perfect faith, specifically to talk with him and to write about him.

On that sunny Sunday, the Conchiglia bar was deserted, except for the occasional appearance of a waiter glancing in my direction to see if I might want yet a third cappuccino. Everyone was out enjoying the spring weather. The book I'd brought for the trip didn't hold my attention anymore, so I just looked through the picture window. I couldn't see one square foot—or in this case, one square meter—of beach that wasn't covered by bodies. The number of sun-worshipers seemed to be exceeded only by the number of automobiles, though it was unlikely anyone had driven two. Fellini's Fregene was obviously an extremely popular weekend place to be.

Behind me, I heard the sound of footsteps approaching my table. Turning, I recognized Fellini, who sat down beside me. He was a big man, six feet tall, but with a larger aspect—that of being bigger than his physical size would indicate. It was not only his height, but his broad shoulders and chest that gave this impression. He seemed about to outgrow his clothes.

His voice was softer than might be expected from such a large man, and it caused you to draw closer in order to hear every word. If that didn't bring you close enough, he would draw you closer by taking your arm, touching your hand, or putting his arm around you. There was a lot of physical contact. His voice seemed to me to have the quality of a caress. It gave a kind of intimacy to whatever he said.

He apologized for being late, and then explained that he wasn't *really* late. He, too, had arrived early, just before me, and had taken a seat in the next room. I hadn't thought to look because I believed *I* was so early.

Feigning melodrama, he said, "We have lost forty-five minutes in our life together which we can never make up, but we must try!"

As dramatically as I could manage, I said, "I hope we never catch up but always try."

During the next fourteen years, for my part we never did catch up because the end of every visit always came too soon. The tone remained for the most part light, with a sense of banter, even when the subjects were serious—*especially* when they were serious.

Fellini's conversation was often highly animated, ranging from expressive looks to the rich repertory of Italian gestures that tell all— and a bit more. In high mood, Fellini would act out all the characters in one of his anecdotes.

Fellini entered into the daily game of life with a playful spirit. He told me at our first meeting that "playful" interviews are the best— not only more fun, but more revealing. When I asked him how we could achieve that kind of interview, he said there were no rules; we would have to find our own way. He compared it to the ambiance he liked on his sets, saying, "I strive for flexibility, so no one is forced into a mold. It should be impulsive, exploratory fun—like the games of childhood."

It was, of course, a privileged childhood to which he referred, one with money, power, and freedom. He admitted that people had accused him of behaving like a willful child accustomed to getting only his own way on the set, and he confirmed that they were right. He suggested that he was influenced by his childhood interest in being a puppeteer, and that he came to see his actors as puppets. He said that as the director, he could not say, "I think, maybe, perhaps," but only "I want." As the director, he had to be determined and confident, and thus he could seem to some to be arrogant.

For our first meeting, already having had all the cappuccino I could drink while awaiting his arrival, I ordered *spremuta di arance rosse,* the Italian orange juice, which is as dark red as tomato juice. Fellini told me that if blood oranges weren't in season at the moment he would paint the oranges red for me. Outside the picture window, it was suddenly cloudy. Fellini asked if I was aware that he could also bring out the sun. Without waiting for my answer, he waved his hand. The clouds passed and the sun shone brightly. It was an auspicious beginning.

The orange juice arrived, dark red. I commented that he had painted the oranges exactly the right color and was indeed "an artist." He invited me to visit his office to see his drawings.

At the end of our first meeting, Fellini rode away on his bicycle. He wasn't watching where he was going, but where he had been, exactly the opposite of what he had just said he did when making films. He looked back at me, waving first one arm and then the other, and then both at the same time. With Fellini's big frame impeccably attired in a blue silk Sunday suit with white shirt and blue tie, the bicycle seemed absurdly undersized and was only partially visible beneath him as he pedaled off.

The next day I went to his office on Rome's Corso d'Italia. The attractive 1920s façade saved the best for inside, in the private way that Italian buildings have of keeping their secrets. Behind the wall was the garden, intended not to be shown off, but to show in. I went up a few steps to the ground-floor studio, an apartment serving as his office.

Inside, the high-ceilinged room reflected its occupant. It looked just like Fellini. It was tall and sunny; tidy, but rumpled; masculine and comfortably worn. It was a room without fussy possessions, a state that, Fellini explained to me, he had achieved only through the greatest exercise of will, keeping very little, avoiding clutter. With the years, he had found that his interests had not expanded, but instead contracted, till in their shrunken state they had come to represent what he felt had become his tunnel vision. The tunnel was his work. The light at the end of the tunnel was his completed film. When he reached that light, it was his signal to enter a new tunnel.

"My work is my life," he told me. "Even more, it's my happiness. A vacation is my punishment."

He continued: "Artistic creation is humanity's dream activity. The most important aspect of creative work is to establish contact with your inner self and to bring out the themes within you.

"A person's fantasy is more sacred to him than his reality. The test is, if you laugh at a person's reality, he may forgive you, but he'll never forgive you if you laugh at his fantasy."

He led me to an already broken-in leather sofa that felt like an Italian glove. In the style characteristic of a man who didn't do anything in a small way, Fellini strode to one of the bookshelves filled with bound volumes of his work. He carefully removed one of the oversize scrapbooks. The outside had the well-used look of all his possessions. One could not have imagined anything new in the room. If Fellini brought anything new to his office, it seemed the article would age on the way there. He sat on the sofa next to me, holding the heavy book in his lap out of consideration for my pleated white skirt.

"The dream books of my drawings are very dusty," he said. "I don't look back much."

The drawings he showed me represented not his sleeping dreams, but his mind "playing" at night. "These are really visions, not dreams. A man's subconscious creates the dream, but his vision is his subconscious idealization.

"Here is one where I am lying naked on the railroad tracks," he said, opening the book to the first page. "I suppose it's because in sexual relationships and in life I feel vulnerable and am aware of the risks." He sighed. "Yes, life with women is very dangerous."

He turned to the next page. On it was a thin young man being overwhelmed by an abundantly endowed, typically Felliniesque woman. "In my drawings," he explained, "Fellini is this poor naked little fellow. He is very thin. Skinny. In my dreams, I am never fat. And I had more hair then. He's about to be smothered with love by this larger-than-life, mountainous creature of sexuality. He thinks he is going to make love to her. But she is too much for him, and he will be swallowed up. Poor fellow. He is lost, the victim of his own libido. But he will die happily.

"I draw myself at about twenty. That is because I haven't changed inside. That is still the way I feel inside, the way I see myself."

I asked him about a picture of a telephone which had two pictures of the same woman's face, one ecstatic, one angry.

"It is the woman I am speaking with at the other end of the telephone," he told me. "She is bitterly jealous because she believes there are other women in my life. She is right, but she doesn't know, she only suspects. Women fight over me—in my dreams."

He showed me a picture inspired by a dream he had had just before one of his films was going to open.

"I am the little man in the small boat. The waves are very high, and there are sharks all around. You can see how afraid I am. The little boat is being pitched about by the waves, and I don't have any oars.

"In my dream, I saved myself. Sitting in the boat, I looked down and noticed I had a prick as big as a tree. So I used it to row first to one side and then to the other, swinging my prick from one side to another. Using it as my oar, my prick rowed me to safety."

He turned the page to another drawing.

"The next one is a dream about my childhood. You see that young boy standing in the middle of the street, completely naked? That is me. I have gone out into the traffic. The little cars are whizzing all around. There is so much traffic and no traffic lights, and I am directing the traffic with my prick.

"As you can see, I'm never sexually impotent in my dreams. I can do anything I want. That is why dreams are so superior to reality. I can make love twenty times a night.

"Man is quite fragile—sexually, that is—and the least thing can upset him and throw him off his stride.

"Woman is much stronger than man. Often man is conquered by women, who use him, even though he thinks of himself as a conqueror. Man is very naïve."

He continued turning the pages. "In one of my drawings, I'm in a basket in the sky. But my basket is missing. I'm floating high in the air in my basket. You can see the clouds.

"In this one, I am with the Pope. I am about fifteen years old. I really had met the Pope, who called me Fefe.

"Here, I am with God. You can see God as the great maker and destroyer of clouds. In my drawing, God is a woman. She is nude and voluptuous.

"And this one," he said, turning to another page. "Do you know what the naked woman is saying to me as she holds up the big key over the water closet? She says to me, 'This is your key. We'll put it in the water closet and flush it down.' She has a mind to have a new life with me, and she wants to cut off all my past. She doesn't want me to even remember any other woman." He turned the page again, revealing another nude woman.

"This is a dancing girl who has taken off all her clothes. She wants to get to know me better. She will do anything to entice me because she wants me so badly."

I could barely see what was on the next page, because he flipped past it so quickly, saying, "Look away, *bambina*. This one is too obscene for you." The next one was only a little less obscene. It featured another amply endowed nude woman with Fellini.

"This one is so big and beautiful, isn't she? I've lost something, you see, and I'm looking for it in her vagina." He paused, then said: "You're blushing. You want to stop this interview?"

Visits with Fellini had some element of the ceremonial or ritual, but visits to Cesarina, his favorite restaurant, had an air of the sacred. On our first visit, Fellini cautioned me to behave decorously in the presence of the patroness, whose name the restaurant bore.

I was admonished to exercise great care in anything I might say to Cesarina, to be reverent but not obsequious. He explained that some might consider her rude simply because she treated her restaurant as if it were her home, and had to pass on everyone who ate there. He warned me that she didn't like women, but there wasn't much I could do about that.

He added in mock seriousness, "She exists only in the restaurant, you know. There are people like that. They and their place are symbiotic. She is never seen arriving in the restaurant or leaving it, only in it. She is one of those people in the world that I most admire, because she exemplifies what I respect—genius in your chosen field and total dedication to it."

Though he was the favorite of the grande dame, "almost an adopted son," he said, he never took his status for granted, believing that at any moment, on a whim, she could change, like Caligula. For him to live in Rome and be deprived of Cesarina would have been a punishment too horrible to contemplate.

He liked best to order many dishes and taste some of each. He encouraged me to order lavishly, not parsimoniously, more than I could eat, and dishes different from those he ordered. I learned that this was for his benefit as much as for mine. He was thus able to sample everything. He would eat as much from my plate as from his own, carrying the idea of the Chinese restaurant to the Italian. He said we had to order a great deal of food because we were only two taking up a table, even when it was only a table for two. He loved having a taste of this and a taste of that—the luxury of eating in a restaurant, he pointed out, rather than at home.

After most of the food had somehow been eaten, he would say to me, "Save room for the dessert. There is a wonderful cake."

Many of our conversations were accompanied by food. Fellini was aware that the word "companion" was derived from the Latin words for "with bread."

He told me, "Food is love. There is a great significance in the amount of love that is put into the preparation of food. It is more than just pride. Love should be listed as an ingredient.

"So much that is good in life happens with shared food. A world that is based on things being fast and convenient worries me. A TV dinner represents for me an uncaring world, a world of solitude."

The people Fellini told me he would most like to have met were Groucho Marx, Mae West, and Laurel and Hardy. I had known Groucho well in the last years of his life and had written a book about him. I'd known Mae West and had written about her. He liked to talk with me about Groucho and Mae. He had never heard their real voices, because foreign films in Italy were dubbed into Italian by other voices.

I had brought with me a T-shirt with a picture of Groucho Marx on it—a souvenir of my first book, *Hello, I Must Be Going,* which was about Groucho. The T-shirt said "Hello" on the front, and "I Must Be Going" on the back. I told Fellini I had brought extra-large, but he didn't *have* to wear it.

Fellini responded, "But I *want* to wear it. You may think of me wearing it. But I'll wear it only with nothing else on," he said, holding it up against his chest and posing, "not even my undershorts. Do you like that?"

I asked if I could have a photograph. He said, "Of course." But it never arrived.

An evening in Rome with Fellini that I have always remembered was typical of his efforts to be polite and his dislike of saying no. It was an evening to which he had committed himself, but to which he looked forward with no joy.

We were on our way by taxi to the home of a journalist and his wife, a graduate student writing her doctoral dissertation on Federico Fellini. The dissertation was even more specific: It was on the writings of Fellini for *Marc' Aurelio,* the work of his youth.

The material Fellini wrote for *Marc' Aurelio* influenced Fellini himself throughout his life, and he continued to draw on it for ideas and vignettes. His job with the most famous humor magazine in Italy forced him to think, to put his thoughts on paper, and to find his own style from his natural talent. Even more important, his basic concepts and philosophy of living were formulated and articulated.

Marc' Aurelio was Fellini's university. He developed a trade, a profession, and an art, and he came into contact with some of the best creative minds in the country, who inspired him, taught him, and later provided a network of connections. Their recognition of his special talents, which some perceived as genius, provided a wonderfully nurturing environment and gave him confidence. Fellini believed he wouldn't have had the necessary perseverance to go ahead if he hadn't seen his work published. He reflected throughout his life on the extent to which he had been shown generosity, without jealousy, by guides who were older and more experienced than he. He was forced to write every day to live. Knowing he was going to be paid and published gave him the incentive and energy to work so hard. Though he referred to a certain "laziness" on his part, throughout his life his productivity was impressive. He estimated roughly that he might have done about a thousand pieces for *Marc' Aurelio,* including sketches and drawings with captions, as well as long stories and continuing episodic tales. As he recalled it, he was not able to remember a single instance in which something he wrote was not printed, a remarkably stimulating and satisfying kind of approbation for a young man.

Fellini could have found a polite excuse and declined the young woman's invitation, but she had been writing to him for such a long time, and was now about to present her thesis at the university. Since Fellini was not making a film at that moment, he had accepted, and then found it difficult to cancel the meeting, though he had considered doing so. He didn't want to disappoint her, and besides, he'd lost the phone number.

That evening, we left the taxi at the point where the streets become too narrow for it to pass. The driver, who had recognized Fellini, promised to wait for us.

We walked through the narrow, winding streets of Trastevere, the old section on the outskirts of Rome, on our way to an address scribbled on a tiny piece of paper that Fellini had almost lost twice during our taxi trip from the center of the city. On our way, we stopped at a café for cappuccino and cake, because Fellini said there probably wouldn't be anything much to eat. He felt we should fortify ourselves. The stop offered a brief postponement of the inevitable, the forthcoming ordeal, and there was a particularly tempting cake in a window we happened to pass.

Entering the building, Fellini had to bend over, almost in half, to enter the low door. In the extremely low-ceilinged apartment, we were stunned by a sumptuous array of food that indicated days of planning, shopping, and preparation. The wine was too expensive. The young woman's elaborately coiffed hair represented half a day at the beauty salon, and she served in a black cocktail dress and stiletto heels. For the occasion, the finish had virtually been polished off the furniture, which was the kind that had grown very old without ever becoming antique.

After the dinner, with obvious pride and anticipation, she presented Fellini with her completed doctoral dissertation. The document was contained in two thick volumes. Politely, Fellini leafed through the pages and nodded with approval whenever he observed her observing him. As she watched him, she scarcely breathed, or so it seemed. He would open the thesis to a page, look at it, and say, "Wonderful." Then he would skip a hundred pages or so and read something. "Interesting," he would comment.

He stayed much longer than he needed to stay, perhaps partly from inertia, but partly because he saw how thrilled the people were. He had clearly given them a gift—a memory, which is one of the best gifts anyone can give. He understood that it was a gift he had within his power to bestow.

Fellini hadn't really enjoyed the idea of being a thesis. When he saw the work, which had taken several years, he was stunned just by its physical size. Whatever the quality, the weight was impressive. Leaving the apartment in Trastevere, Fellini said to me, "So many pages. Imagine, more than three years of her life! And it isn't even about my films. It's about my days with the *Marc' Aurelio* magazine. She said she read over five hundred of my pieces. It was all more than forty years ago. Forty years ago!"

But I knew he was truly pleased with what she had done, or he would never have stayed so long.

It was after four A.M. when we left. The small, winding streets were virtually black. There was almost no light and there was no one around. We were lost and couldn't even find our way back to the apartment building we had just left. Our whispers to each other seemed loud, indeed.

"Do you think it's safe here?" I asked him.

Without a second's hesitation, he answered, "No."

I was sorry I had asked. He reminded me that he'd told me not to carry a purse with money and my passport in it. I had taken his advice, but it wasn't my purse I was thinking about.

Fellini told me, "Once I could have walked anywhere in Rome with no thought—absolutely anywhere. I had a special immunity. It was like being a sheriff. Now there are a lot of strangers around, new people from all over. We have imported muggers. These new ones, they won't recognize Fellini. If they do, they won't care."

Then we realized we were not alone.

We heard voices—male voices—though we didn't see anyone. From around a corner appeared six well-built young men, all wearing black leather jackets and talking loudly. They moved in close behind us.

Fellini instructed me not to look as if I were afraid, but the night was so dark, it seemed brave expressions would be wasted. He said we couldn't be far from where our taxi was waiting, if it was still waiting after all those hours.

The leather-jacketed group drew closer, forming a semicircle around us. They had stopped talking. No one was smiling. Then, one of them moved out in front of the others, closer to us. He stared at Fellini. Fellini stared back. Then, even in the near darkness, we saw the young man's white smiling teeth. The figures relaxed. The one who had stepped forward, apparently the leader, greeted Fellini:

"Buona sera, Federico!"

A few words were exchanged. We were escorted to where our taxi was still waiting. Then the group went on its way, to whatever its destination might have been.

"They were the ones I know," Fellini said.

I had noticed.

The taxi had waited all those hours for us. The driver was sleeping peacefully. He had had no doubt that eventually Fellini would return.

At one of our first meetings, Fellini had said:

"I would like to have a nice little conversation with you, but it shouldn't be carefully planned and measured. The little conversations are the best ones, and they should be spontaneous when you feel them, when they happen. I feel one must put oneself honestly and openly into the voyage which is life."

He didn't like advance appointments. He didn't like to do anything that required specific commitment. Fellini preferred everything he did, except making films, to seem casual and spontaneous. He liked riding around Rome best when we had no itinerary, saying to me:

"I love to wander without a fixed destination. Going to a particular place has never pleased me in the way just riding around has. The images that file continuously past the window of my car, just like a film, are among the most provocative of my life."

He felt the same way about walking around Rome, and he never tired of it. I wore flat shoes, the only possibility when having dinner with Fellini, who might say, "It's good to walk home after dinner," without mentioning that it was a forty-minute walk. When my soles wore out, Rome was a good place to shop for shoes with thicker soles.

Wherever we went, Fellini would make up mini-dramas about people at another table in a restaurant, or he would discuss character types he saw in the street. As we rode by, or as we walked along, someone might have an interesting face or a certain quality which inspired him. He was always person-observing, especially liking to look at the people who were looking into the shop windows on the Via Condotti. Everyone in Rome who could afford it would shop, or if they couldn't afford it, at least window-shop, on the fashionable street. Because the Via Condotti was closed to all traffic except pedestrian, we walked in the middle of it. Fellini pointed out several fashionably dressed couples carrying the handsome shopping bags and ribboned packages from Valentino, Armani, and Bulgari. On the Via Condotti, women carry their purchases with pride, the contents being light in weight but heavy in value. Fellini indicated a beautiful young woman with an older man. "He's certainly *not* her grandfather," he said. "She's a 'trophy mistress.' See how proud he is of her?"

Fellini continued: "In the afternoon, one can walk along the Via Condotti and see the rich men living their 'five-to-seven' lives. If they are *very* rich it might be 'four to eight.' They are taking their afternoon strolls with their 'second wives.' They shop with their mistresses, then take their packages and stop for a vermouth or a Cinzano. After that, they go to the 'nest,' and the man is finished in time to arrive at home for dinner with his wife and children."

We heard the sounds of shouting around the corner on a side street, out of sight. Fellini turned to me and said, with a perfectly straight face, "Charlottina, do you hear all that? Do you know what that noise is? It's a protest demonstration against Fellini. It's all the people I don't see, everyone I don't give interviews to. They see me with you, and they say, 'Why is he doing it with this American instead of us?' "

He noticed a handsome pair of shoes in the Gucci window. "They look comfortable, don't they?" he said, speaking rhetorically. They looked more than comfortable. Farther down the street, a bordeaux cashmere scarf in the window of Hermès attracted him. Before I left Rome, I bought the scarf and gave it to him. Though he always denied both caring about material possessions and being a sentimental person, when I was in Rome and the weather was cool enough, it was frequently *that* bordeaux scarf he wore.

Fellini was a regular window-shopper only on the Via della Croce, where a chocolate cake in a window might cause him to hesitate, or the smell of a cheese might entice him. While he had been amazed and impressed by the size and scope of a Los Angeles–style supermarket, he did not place his faith in stores that purported to be "experts" in everything. He said that only a "food sensitive" could discern the best mozzarella and also the best Parmesan, and certainly the same person could not be expected to look into the heart of a melon and know if it was crying out to be eaten now, in its prime moment, or if it was begging for another two days to ripen properly.

As I was about to leave Rome in that spring of 1980, after several weeks of talking with Fellini, he told me that he wanted to draw a picture of me. I hoped he would do it while I was in Rome.

"No," he explained, "I can see you better after you've gone. In my mind's eye, I'll draw my memory of you."

The drawing reached me in London a few days later. With it was a somewhat apologetic note, terming the picture of "Charlottina" "one of my funny, unflattering little caricatures." I loved it. Fellini had seen me as I saw myself, with one exception: He had drawn me wearing gold Gypsy earrings. I wasn't wearing earrings like that when I was with him—nor, indeed, had I ever worn any.

I called to thank him and to say I loved the picture. Then I asked why he had drawn me wearing gold earrings.

"You wear them on the inside," he said.

I went right out and bought a pair.

During my next visit to Rome, on the way to meet Fellini, I walked past his favorite bakery, and a cake in the window intrigued me, especially after I inquired and found out it was a *torta di polenta*. On impulse, I bought it.

When I gave it to him, Fellini commented that polenta torte sounded like "something from the macrobiotic vegetarian restaurant." Then he ate it with gusto. I was pleased that I had been able to introduce Fellini to something in Rome. I asked him if when he came to New York he would introduce me to something there. He said he would be coming to New York, and added, "I already have the idea in my mind."

We often ate breakfast, lunch, tea, or dinner at the Grand Hotel. It was the place he chose to celebrate whenever I was in Rome around the time of his birthday, January 20. The birthday party was always a teatime celebration, and added to the patisserie of the Grand Hotel was the birthday "cake" that had become our tradition. I brought it from New York, and in reality it was not a cake at all, but brownies from Madison Avenue's E.A.T. It represented Fellini's discovery of the American brownie, which I also brought at all times other than his birthday.

The Grand Hotel provided us with plates and silver forks with which to eat our brownies, while guests stared at us, either at Fellini or at the brownies. A few of them tried to order the brownies and had to be informed that they had come from "outside." Fellini had privileges everywhere.

Even on his birthday and with only coffee and cake, he would never permit me to pay the check, even when I gave the money in advance to the maître d' or claimed that my publisher would reimburse me.

Believing Fellini when he said that "To truly know me, you must see me doing what I do," that he was "really alive" only when directing, I called from New York in 1982 to ask him whether I might come to Rome to observe him directing his new film, *And the Ship Sails On.* Until then, it had always seemed to me better to visit during weeks when he wasn't working, in order to share his free time, time when he didn't feel any pressure. Fellini said, "Why do you ask? I would never say no to you about anything." He told me that he would send someone to the airport "to fetch me," because he was shooting and couldn't come himself. On my arrival, I was taken directly from the airport to Stage 5 of Cinecittà.

As I walked onto the pitching ship's deck which had been built on the soundstage, Fellini greeted me warmly: "I am happy you are here, Charlottina."

I said, "You told me that if I only knew you talking, without seeing you working, I didn't really know you. So I've come to see you directing."

Fellini leaned forward and, putting his hand up to hide what he was saying (thus drawing everyone's attention to it), he whispered into my ear, "Then you have to know me in bed."

I did my best to play my part and look as embarrassed as possible.

No one heard what Fellini said, but the crowd of technicians, actors, and extras standing about allowed their imaginations free reign, and my arrival was thus a lighthearted and playful break in the day's work. It also brought me into the situation in a sympathetic and funny way that made me totally accepted on the set. No one questioned my presence.

Becoming serious, Fellini said, "Welcome, Charlottina, to Cinecittà, my *real* home."

Then he introduced me to those who had gathered around: "This is Charlotte Chandler. She has written a wonderful book about clowns, the Marx Brothers, especially about a great clown, Groucho. Having written about clowns, she is going on, writing about me." (Fellini had told me that while others saw him as a circus ringmaster, his own view of himself was, "I am now a clown, and the movies are my circus.")

In one of our earliest conversations, Fellini said:

"For working closely with people, a long or even a short collaboration, I need an atmosphere of congeniality and complicity. I need to work with people who are close friends. The friendships should build. We should have adventures together. And then, we should have memories together."

It certainly was true for me. Any time I saw Fellini, it was likely to be a memory in the making. I was never bored for one minute, and there was never a time when I wasn't sorry to have the experience come to an end.

On the set, Fellini would walk over to me between takes; he might whisper into my ear, well aware that many eyes were upon him.

"We'll go to Morocco tomorrow," he would say to me, playfully.

"Oh, yes," I would answer, enthusiastically.

The next week, he would ask, "Would you like to go to Istanbul tomorrow with me?"

"Of course," I would reply without a second's hesitation.

In this game, the trips began with his question and ended with my answer. I never assumed more, and I was never disappointed. I was sharing Rome with Fellini, and that was what I wanted. I was surprised, though, to see how many broken hearts there were because of Fellini's supposedly broken "promises." If Fellini had asked me about going to the moon with him, I would have said yes.

"Nonsense often makes the most sense," he told me.

On the Cinecittà set of *And the Ship Sails On,* I watched Fellini trying unsuccessfully to get a certain effect from one of his actors, who
just could not seem to achieve the desired reaction.

The actor was supposed to register stunned surprise on glimpsing
the pale and fragile ingenue, who was crouching on the deck, hidden
by a great gray cloak and hood. Fellini called for a break while he
talked individually with each of the actors.

On the next take, the cloaked figure turned to look up at the actor,
who, this time, registered exactly the right expression.

Unbeknownst to the actor, Fellini had replaced the young actress
with the oldest man he could find.

It was a highly practical joke, because that was the take that took.

On the set, Fellini talked and explained continuously. He kept up
a constant flow of directions and conversation, and he tried to recognize everyone and to maintain maximum rapport. He might come on
the set and ask, "Did anyone have any good dreams last night?" He
coached, cajoled, comforted, acted out all the parts, including those
of the women. "I can be a wonderful nymphomaniac," he told everyone. Off the set, however, he never talked as much as he did for his
larger audience. He could be quite a good listener. In a conversation
with one person, he was often very quiet, and in the most cherished
friendships, he could be silent, too.

Fellini had told me that when I saw him directing on the set, he
would be so dynamically transformed that I should be prepared not
even to recognize him. Though I did see the difference that he had
predicted, I recognized him. The change was not as great as he
believed. I realized that what was different was the way he felt.

From those on the set, there was total respect, even reverence.
Everyone seemed thrilled to be in a Fellini film, from the stars to the
extras. Even the producer's representative and the union overseers,
who were there to watch over and protect their own interests, were
fascinated by the legendary director.

At lunch, away from Cinecittà, when Fellini knew there were no
longer eyes watching, then, he would slump a little, physically and
verbally. Almost every day, however, he ate with the entire group,
playing the part of director through the meal, with conversational
flourish and physical antics, stylishly directing the food, considerately
making certain everyone had a place to sit.

Through the long hours on the set, Fellini was always in action, always keeping the verbal bond with actors and technicians, but it seemed to me he was alone. The private person inside him was both protected and occupied, imagining and drawing his film in his own mind.

Aldo Nemni, a successful businessman who loved films and whose first venture as a producer was *And the Ship Sails On,* came from Milan as frequently as possible to watch the genius of Fellini at work and to say good-bye to his money. He told me that Fellini was the total artist, in love with his work, transported by the creative process.

On faith, Nemni had put his money into the venture because of the unique opportunity to do a picture with Fellini, who presented the project with intelligence, wit, even a certain modesty. Then, behind the camera, Nemni noted, Fellini became a man suddenly transformed by his passion, living only for and in what he was doing, "totally obsessed, like a man in love—everything else disappeared."

With Nemni, Fellini felt an instant rapport, and he hoped he had found a producer for life, as well as a friend. Since Nemni was refined, intellectual, and ethical, Fellini could accept that he didn't like to eat quite as much as he did.

Fellini did not like to work on location, so it was necessary not only to build the ship at Cinecittà, but also to reconstruct the sea. The artificial sea had to undulate with the perfect irregularity of real waves, but hydraulically generated, "whatever the cost."

Even when Fellini was offered the opportunity to save money in a rapidly rising budget, anywhere from hundreds of thousands of dollars to millions of dollars, he was just as cavalier with his own money as with that of the producers. Any respect he had for money disappeared; only the film mattered. The start date was changed when, according to Nemni, Fellini, who was surprisingly superstitious and concerned with signs, suddenly announced that it was not a propitious moment, that he felt a sense of foreboding. The date was changed, either for that reason or because he wasn't quite ready.

Nemni decided to limit his profits in return for limiting his risk. "I lost a little money," he told me, "but I had a unique and unforgettable experience which I remember happily. Producing a Fellini film was my calling card in the film business, and I profited in so many indirect ways from knowing Federico." So many of us did.

Nemni was Giulietta's escort at the premiere of the ballet of *La Strada* at Milan's La Scala. He and Fellini remained friends, though he never produced another Fellini film.

From where I sat, on what was supposed to be the upper deck of *And the Ship Sails On,* I could feel the constant pitching of the vessel as the technicians rocked the set. My chair was placed there each day, and I sat alone, unless Fellini came over to explain something or to chat, or unless Marcello Mastroianni, Sergio Leone, Robin Williams, Paul Newman, Michelangelo Antonioni, or other visiting celebrities or friends dropped by the closed set. Once in a while, a second chair would be placed there, waiting. That indicated Giulietta Masina would be arriving. She didn't come often.

Chicly dressed in an Italian suit and petite even in high heels, she would be greeted by Fellini. Everyone on the set knew her, not just as Fellini's wife, but for her own lustrous career. She was professionally respected and personally liked. She never stayed long, as though she didn't want to intrude.

She greeted me warmly. I had first met Giulietta in New York City when she was on her way back to Rome from the San Francisco Film Festival, where she had been honored. She was thrilled by the enthusiasm of the reception given her there. Fellini had called from Rome to tell me that Giulietta was coming through New York. He asked if I could see her and spend some time with her, because she wasn't accustomed to traveling alone. I invited her to Le Cirque for lunch, where she was recognized as soon as she entered. Several times during the next year, Federico tried to repay me for whatever I had spent when Giulietta was in New York.

During the filming of the sinking of the ship in *And the Ship Sails On,* I was given a white surgical mask to wear because the fumes and smoke were so bad. Fellini and everyone not on camera wore the little masks, which seemed mostly decorative since they weren't really adequate to protect anyone from anything from which anyone needed protecting.

On the set, Giulietta sometimes whispered to me, and I would see Federico look in our direction. I worried that we would be singled out and reprimanded. He did scold her once, but it was when she was speaking with someone else while he was directing a scene. She didn't take it seriously, as I would have. I didn't know what to do, because I didn't want to be rude to her, and I didn't want to be rude to him.

The first time she visited the set when I was there, she invited me to have tea with her. She said she was feeling seasick from sitting on the pitching deck. We were gone a long time. I returned alone. She had gone back to their Margutta apartment, to which Fellini would return late every night. The next day, when she again invited me to have tea, I was concerned that Fellini might feel I was more interested in tea than in the reason for which I had come to Rome, to see him work. So I declined that day.

When we were together, Giulietta recalled her first meeting with Fellini. Though she was attractive and popular in school, the object of a great deal of masculine attention in her classes and theater activities, she said she was utterly dazzled by the young Federico. "He was not like anyone else. After I met him, no one else could compare, and that has remained true all these years. If anything, Federico has become even more himself."

In the early days of their courtship, Giulietta felt that she, more than anyone else, "understood" Fellini. In 1983, as we sat on the deck of the ship that was to sail on, she mused wryly, "I was very innocent. Certainly no one ever totally understands a man as complex as Federico, not I and least of all Federico, himself.

"He told me that he couldn't understand me, but that was because he was always looking for the complicated instead of the simple. In our daily life, he likes everything as uncomplicated as possible because he is creating the complications in his own head.

"Our courtship was romantic and intense, because there was a war on, and Federico had to hide from the fascists who wanted to take him away for military service. He had to stay in my aunt's apartment, hidden away, as much as possible, so we were together most of the time.

"I was going to school, and I liked school, but nothing could compete with Federico. He was my first and only love. He still is.

"Federico was so very funny. He made me laugh, but it's difficult to remember specific examples. It wasn't so much *what* he said as *how* he said it. But I do remember when he called to ask me to meet him and have lunch. I knew his name, but I had never met him. All I knew was that he was the author of the radio show in which I had been given the leading part, so I was already intrigued. The show was called *Cico e Pallina,* and I was Pallina. The show was about a young married couple.

"Federico's voice was so wonderful. It would have been difficult to say no to anything he asked, just because of his voice—soft, warm, especially when he is speaking with a woman on the phone. In later years, I could always tell when it was a woman he was speaking with. I was an actress and had been in many plays, and had worked all the time with actors, but nobody sounded like Federico.

"He said, 'Hello, Giulietta. My name is Fellini.' He said Fellini, not Federico. And then he said something like, 'I am fed up with life, but before I leave this world, I must see you, if only once, to see what my heroine looks like.'

"I knew he must be joking, but I wanted to see what he looked like, too. Maybe, deep down, I already knew intuitively that he was going to be my hero."

Cico e Pallina was drawn from stories he had written a few years earlier for *Marc' Aurelio.* At the time, Giulietta hadn't realized that the character she played was based on Fellini's first romantic involvement. When she did find out, she didn't mind. The stories were largely imaginary, he told her.

It seemed to her only yesterday that she had met Federico. "Well, last month," she said, adding wistfully, "but I think to Federico it seems much longer ago." She recalled that at their first lunch he was more concerned with the food than she was, a pattern that continued throughout their life together.

"Recently when I mentioned our first meeting to him, he didn't remember it as I did, but there was one thing he did remember much better than I did: He could name everything we had for lunch that day; not just what he ate, but what I ate, too."

She paused, then added, "Federico always had a wonderful food memory."

Giulietta believed that her portrayal of Gelsomina had brought whimsy and sympathy to the character. She considered that to be her contribution, beyond what the script provided. The original script had called for Gelsomina to seem retarded or even insane, with less humanity. Giulietta felt that with this approach she would not have had the audience's sympathy, but rather its pity. The audience has to share with Gelsomina what it means to be painfully lonely. She is pathetically in love with the brutal, thoughtless Zampanò.

"Someone wanted to make a Gelsomina doll," she told me. "I wanted to have one, but Federico hated the idea, so it never happened. He didn't like the people and thought they were trying to cheat us."

Giulietta was social, but reserved. Fellini claimed to be shy, but Giulietta's shyness was more apparent, while his was more deeply felt. Giulietta was usually quiet when she was with Federico, but she talked freely when he wasn't there.

"I love parties, dinner parties, being with friends," she explained, "but I am happy just being there without the need to say much. When I am with Federico, I feel I am in his shadow, but I don't mind it, because it is a wonderful shadow. I believe people would rather hear what Federico has to say."

She paused, then said, "I've always wondered what Federico is like with other women. I only know how Federico is with me.

"Federico never needed much sleep, just a few hours a night, so he always had more time than other people to get into trouble. People ask me why I am so understanding about Federico's peccadilloes. I'm not. Of course, I don't know what he really does. I and everyone else know what he puts up there on the screen, and what he says in interviews. He is an Italian man, and they *have* to talk about their sexual exploits in order to have the respect of other Italian men. I suppose the truth is somewhere between what he tells the world and what he tells me. Federico tells me that none of it means anything. He never says that none of it is true, or that none of it ever happened, only that none of it ever meant anything. He always returned home to me because I am a part of him.

"Federico never volunteered any information. If I asked him questions about whether there were other women in his life, he told me approximately what I wanted to hear. If I accused him of lying, he agreed with me. He tells me nothing he does affects what we have between us, that I am his life's companion, that we have shared our lives and now we share our memories."

Sophia Loren was to have been the star of Fellini's "Journey with Anita," the film he hoped would follow *The Nights of Cabiria.* Publicly, Fellini said he dropped the film because of Sophia Loren's unavailability in Italy at that time, which was true. Privately, he had another reason.

Giulietta believed that the amorous adventure of the married protagonist was based on an actual infidelity of Fellini's. In real life, she
believed "Anita" could have been anyone except Anita Ekberg or
Sophia Loren. Fellini denied this, but didn't look for another actress
to play the part, because, as he told me, "There was only one Sophia,
and besides, Giulietta was right." In the story, Giulietta's character,
the wife of an unfaithful husband, was complaisant. The real Giulietta
was far from that.

"People say Italian wives are different," Giulietta said, "that they are
so much more tolerant. It isn't that Italian wives are different. It's that
Italian husbands are different. What choice do we have? So I try to
look the other way, because where could I find another man like Federico? Nowhere. He is unique, my Federico—a genius. I suppose
genius has privileges."

Giulietta told me about working with her husband, the director. The
greatest problem she had faced with *Juliet of the Spirits* was her awe of
working again with the legendary Fellini. As a young director, he had
launched her career as an actress. At the time of *Juliet of the Spirits,*
Fellini was her husband of more than twenty years; but with Fellini
the director, she was an actress being directed by a living legend, and
she felt inhibited.

Giulietta personally identified with the character of Juliet; Fellini
had created the film specifically for her, and he said the character was
inspired by the real person who was his wife. The film was conceived
after a certain amount of personal turmoil in their own lives. He had
been rumored to be involved with other women; even worse, at
times, another *woman,* and Giulietta believed he was. Since she considered Federico the most attractive and exciting man in the world,
she found it natural that all women would want him. That he would
want some of them was also only natural, but Giulietta couldn't adjust
to what she believed was the truth in the rumors.

If she could have gone back in time, she said, she would have
asserted herself even more strongly in order to change Federico's
mind about the concept of *Juliet of the Spirits.* She believed the film
was a turning point for them professionally. At that moment, he was
at the pinnacle of his career, following *La Dolce Vita* and *8½. Juliet*
wasn't a failure, but it wasn't the kind of success, critically or com-

mercially, that the two preceding films had been. After *Juliet of the Spirits,* the element of financial risk always inherent in producing a Fellini film was perceived as greater, especially in light of the con-stantly mounting cost of making a film. Giulietta had believed from the beginning that the conception of her character was wrong; it did not reflect a woman's point of view, but a man's. She had been stopped by her husband's myth. She knew he was a genius. The world had recognized and confirmed this. How could she tell *him* what to do—especially when he wouldn't listen?

Giulietta remembered with great warmth a night in New York City which she characterized as one of the most wonderful of her life. It happened in 1965 at the Fifth Avenue apartment of Jacqueline Kennedy. Mrs. Kennedy gave a dinner party in honor of Fellini and Masina on the occasion of the U.S. premiere in New York of *Juliet of the Spirits.*

"We had such great hopes for the film," Giulietta recalled, "and there had been some disappointments over the way it had been received, but that night was perfectly wonderful! The Fifth Avenue apartment faced Central Park, and Jackie's walk-in closet for her clothes was the biggest I had ever seen. I could never have imagined having so many dresses all at once, but I thought it would be very nice. In all of my life, I had not owned as many dresses as she had in that one closet. And I think she had more closets. It was a very big apartment, with a wonderful view. The food seemed perfect, but I was too excited to remember what I ate. Probably Federico remembers the food. What I remember is that everything was perfect, especially Jackie herself. It's a night I have remembered all my life."

Giulietta regretted not having acted in more films, without waiting for Federico's. "The time went by so fast, and then it was all gone."

The sympathetic prostitute portrayed by Shirley MacLaine in the film *Sweet Charity* was drawn from Giulietta's Cabiria character in *The White Sheik* and *The Nights of Cabiria*. When MacLaine was honored by the Film Society of Lincoln Center in 1995, she talked with me about her Charity Hope Valentine and Giulietta's Cabiria:

"I wanted to get to the underbelly of the character. I saw *Nights of Cabiria* to study Giulietta Masina's conception. Cabiria is tough, unsentimental, but she's also childlike and proud. She's always look-ing for something, not really understanding what she wants. She looks for it in her lovers, in a home, in religion, even in trying to improve her professional status as a prostitute.

"For me, the key to her character is the money she keeps in a coffee can in her house. It's her hope chest. No matter what happens to her, she never loses hope. Even at the end when she's lost everything except her life, she smiles through the tears.

"My friend Bob Fosse was the director, and he was a great fan of Fellini's. After I'd done the film, I met Fellini and Giulietta when they were in California. I noticed she was so quiet in the presence of her husband. She let him do all the talking."

Michelangelo Antonioni recalled for me an example of the personality and humor of Fellini. Antonioni had been away from Italy for about a year and a half, making *Zabriskie Point* (1970) in Hollywood. On his way home, he stopped over in London because he was interested in the Carnaby Street life of that moment and in the hippie scene. As he was going through customs, the police found some marijuana in one of his shoes. It was a big scandal. The newspapers everywhere played up the story.

On Antonioni's return to Italy, Francesco Rosi and his wife, Giancarla, gave a dinner party at their house in Fregene to welcome him. Of course, everyone there had read about Antonioni and the marijuana. Among the guests were Fellini and Giulietta.

There was a lot of tension. People were feeling rather awkward. They talked about everything in the world except the marijuana episode. Giancarla took Fellini aside and said, "This is terrible. What are we going to do to break the ice?"

Fellini walked over to Antonioni. He bent down, took off one of his own shoes, and held it out to him, saying:

"Have a smoke?"

Everyone laughed and there wasn't any more tension.

Roberto Rossellini talked with me about his estrangement from Fellini. Our conversation began as a discussion of the American Friends of the Cinémathèque Française. Mary Meerson of the Cinémathèque had introduced us, and as we discussed the meaning of the word *friend,* he recalled his relationship with Fellini:

"We were going to have dinner one night, but in the afternoon Federico called me and said he couldn't, because he'd told someone else he was having dinner with *him* that night, and had forgotten. He said he had to do the other because he'd already broken several dates with the other person, who it turned out was an absolute enemy of mine. I wasn't pleased. I'd been offered no choice. I'd been given no apology. I did not understand why Federico would eat with a person like that, a man I knew Federico found, at the very least, boring.

"The next day Federico called to see about our getting together. I asked him about the dinner he'd had the night before. He said it was boring, as I knew it had to be, tedious. Then he added, 'In a way, you *were* at the dinner.' He paused. I would not have asked him a question about it. I knew the person would have nothing good to say about me. He went on. 'You were the main subject of conversation. He said terrible things about you all evening.'

"I did not care *what* the man had said about me, but the question I asked was, 'When he said those terrible things about me, what did you say?'

"Federico answered, 'Nothing. It wouldn't have been any use. He loathes you. I couldn't have changed his mind.'

"He was right. He was right for him—but wrong for me. Federico's response was pragmatic, logical. And he'd been honest with me. He could have lied and said he spoke up for me, but that was not Federico's way. He didn't feel he had done anything wrong. To me, however, it seemed wrong of him not to say something on my behalf. In his place, I would have instantly said to the man, 'Federico is my friend. If you say another word on the subject, I'll leave.' That is, if I had been in Federico's place. But I wouldn't have been in his place, because I wouldn't have accepted an invitation from one of *his* enemies.

"When Federico wanted to reschedule our dinner date, I told him I was busy that week, and that I would call him. But I didn't. I certainly intended to do so, but I put it off. Our warm, easy camaraderie was gone. Life took us in different directions, as it tends to do if we allow it to.

"Federico is a genius, and I am proud that I was one of the first to give him the opportunity to work at what was his destiny."

In 1993, Alberto Sordi was at work directing and acting in a film in which he played an old coach driver who was trying desperately to save the life of his faithful old horse. Sordi had known Fellini and

Giulietta since World War II, when they exchanged jokes to lighten the tension in Rome.

"We were both about twenty," he told me. "We met in a place where writers for *Marc' Aurelio* often went for a coffee and cake. Fellini looked like a haunted hippie."

Sordi commented on the difference between the kind of woman Federico was always talking about, the kind of woman Federico seemed to have as an ideal—and Giulietta:

"Federico remained a little boy, with the images of a little boy—the big woman with huge breasts. Your mother looks big to you. He had an obsession with big breasts. Giulietta was the opposite of the women he talked about. She was like a little girl. It was so amusing when they stood together. The contrast in the size of each of them! But he was able to be the protector of this little girl, even though he remained a boy.

"He and Giulietta were very complementary. Most people I have known changed if they became successful. Never Federico. We were friends from the time he first arrived from Rimini, very provincial, and he found Giulietta. She took him to her home and gave life to that poor, thin boy. She took care of him and her family adopted him. He needed taking care of—regular meals, his clothes looked after.

"After their honeymoon, we would go to a little restaurant where we paid only for spaghetti; but the cook was a friend of mine, and underneath the spaghetti, he would hide a piece of meat."

For Tullio Pinelli, Fellini's longtime writing collaborator, it was apparent from his first meetings with young Federico that Fellini had a special destiny:

"Federico was in his mid-twenties. I was thirty-eight. He was tall, slim, young, and had very much hair. He was from Rimini. I was from the Piedmont. We were from different worlds, and when we stood together, we were like one head on top of the other; but immediately, we got along, because we shared a great love of life.

"Fellini was charismatic. He knew exactly what he wanted, and he couldn't be deterred. A born director. He was firm. No compromises. He was so young, but he was all ready to be a director.

"One early incident sums it up for me. Back in the time of World War Two, we were in the Grand Hotel of Trieste, a fabulous nineteenth-century hotel. After the bombs, there were few standing buildings in Trieste. This great hotel had a suite named the Emperor's Suite, so called because the Austrian emperor had slept there. Federico was only an unknown scriptwriter, but he saw that suite, and he just *had* to have it. He wanted that suite. I said to him, 'Are you crazy?'

"The next time I saw him, he was moving his things into the Emperor's Suite.

"I saw Federico for the last time just before he left for Switzerland to have heart surgery. I drove him around Rome. We rode past an arcade that once had been full of cats, where we used to go and feed them ham and cheese."

Tennessee Williams asked me if I had noticed when I met Fellini how alike they were. I admitted that the resemblance hadn't occurred to me.

"But didn't you notice," Williams went on, "how tall he is and how short I am? Didn't you notice that he always wears a tie by choice, while I would rather wear chains if I am given the choice? Haven't you noticed that I have been frequently involved with men, while Fellini is totally absorbed by an interest in women? I like women, too, but I am more likely to love one in a million, and he is more likely to find all but one in a million of interest.

"The bigger the world is, the happier I am. Fellini likes a small world. I am always searching for my place. He has found his. My dear friend, Frankie [Frank Merlo], had a Spanish expression he had heard somewhere: 'El mundo es un pañuelo,' which means 'The world is a handkerchief.' Fellini's world is a *small* handkerchief. He is happiest to never leave Rome. He even has his few places—restaurants, neighborhoods—in Rome. I'm not ridiculing it. Perhaps I envy it. I, myself, am always looking for my own personal home of the heart, *the* place where I belong. Fellini found his in Rome. I'm still searching.

"So how are we alike? We both love our work more than anything else, and our second interest is sex. We both began submitting our writing when we were very young, and sold stories to magazines when we were in our teens. Also, we are both very intelligent. So you can see, we are really quite alike.

"He has a younger brother and sister, just as I do, and a strong mother, and a father who was a traveling salesman, just as mine was.

His father was also an unfaithful husband who believed he was a good father and husband, just as mine did. But his mother wasn't crazy like mine. As children, we were both sickly. When he was young, his mother was told by a doctor that his heart was bad and he shouldn't expect to live a very long or active life. My mother was told the same thing about me, and we both outlived a lot of doctors.

"I told him about American southern food. He is immensely interested in food. He enjoys talking about it. I only enjoy eating it."

Tennessee laughed his signature laugh, which always carried throughout any theater in which his plays were being performed, beyond the voices of the actors on the stage.

"I went to the men's room, and when I came back Fellini was drawing on the napkin. I wish I could do that wherever, whenever. I need to be set up in exactly my environment, the right time of day for the light, a canvas, paint, and brushes. Of course, I get ideas for pictures, just as I do for plays. I always mean to carry a pad and write them down, because my ideas come so fast and so many that I can't remember them all. But I forget the pad, and I forget the ideas. The only time the ideas don't come like that is when I sit down and deliberately try to make them come.

"To be creative you have to feel pain. It's for sensitive people, those who care, and thus are doomed to be disappointed. I consider myself to be that kind of creative person. Fellini and I are both men of pride, laughing on the outside, but feeling the pain for those dreams which, for one reason or another, we fail to bring to life, and for those we bring to life which are then unappreciated or even scorned, treated like sickly children, a shriveling experience.

"I said, 'Call me Tom,' and he said, 'Call me Fefe.' Well, obviously I couldn't call him that. I couldn't say a word like 'Fefe' without feeling foolish, so we didn't call each other anything. In fact, come to think of it, we didn't call each other. I wonder how that happened? He was one of the greatest people I ever met. I wanted him to direct something I had written. *Anything* I had written.

"We talked about doing something together. I told him about some of my short stories. He liked the idea of making a film of three of my short stories. That format really suited him. I had thought about expanding one of the stories, or even writing something new specially for him, but he said just to send him the short stories when I got back.

"Well, I couldn't wait to do it. I instituted a search for everything I'd written. I did try a few new story ideas which I thought were particularly suited to his directorial style and which I thought left room for his wonderful imagination to play with. I directed my assistant to have some unpublished manuscripts retyped. I had only one copy of some of my books, so I ordered an immediate search of bookstores by some service that did that. We got a tremendous amount of material together to send to Rome. Then, I waited for Fellini's response.

"I never heard anything. Well, I thought, 'That's how those Italians are.' So, I made up my mind not to give it another thought. I would just shut it out of my mind. But still, for a long time, I watched the mail.

"One day, about a year later, I tripped over a pile of rare copies of my books and plays that I didn't even remember owning. I started reading, and then I realized how they happened to be there. I wonder if Fellini would have answered if I'd mailed the package. I thought of doing it then, but I knew the moment had passed. Life is often like that.

"There is an oft-quoted, more often paraphrased line of mine which I believe I am entitled to take the liberty of paraphrasing:

"Fellini and I tell life the way it *ought* to be.

"We are both called liars. But that is false. It is simply that truth is not our primary concern. We are more concerned with heightened expression, which sometimes reveals itself as fantasy. But which is the greater truth? That which is imposed on us from outside and represents the truths of others, or is it the unending scenario transpiring on the stage in our minds? There is no greater reality than the one in your own head, and that is what the artist has to share.

"I remember going with my sister, Rose, to see Fellini's film *Amarcord*. This was, of course, long after her lobotomy. Rose watched the film delightedly, though there were some scenes of far-out comic erotica which I thought might shock her. Not at all.

"When her visit was over and it was time for her to go back to the place where they took care of her, I asked her what she had enjoyed most during her visit with me. I thought she might refer to her new dresses, or to those devilishly delicious fudge sundaes in which we had indulged. Instead, she responded without a second's hesitation, 'That wonderful movie.'

"Rose, you see, had declined tea with the Queen of England when I had suggested the possibility, because *she* was the Queen of England—in her mind, that is, and though this film does not need any more critical quotes, Fellini is welcome to that one from the self-proclaimed ruler of the British Empire."

At lunch in Paris, Roman Polanski talked with me about his first meeting with Fellini:

"In 1963, I had gone to Cannes, hoping to see as many films as possible and to meet potential producers. At that time, I thought *Citizen Kane* was the greatest picture ever made, but when I saw *8½*, which was shown out of competition, I was emotionally moved, and I thought it was equally a masterpiece. It was all I'd ever dreamed of seeing on the screen. I haven't seen it for a long time, but if I saw it now, I believe I'd feel the same way.

"My film *Knife in the Water* was nominated for an Oscar in the best-foreign-film category, and in 1964 I was invited to go to California. This was an honor. It meant I would meet some producers, and also it meant I would eat regularly at the expense of the Academy of Motion Picture Arts and Sciences.

"On my arrival, a treat was planned for me—Disneyland. The real treat was that a part of our little tour group was Federico Fellini, whose *8½* was competing against *Knife in the Water*. I knew I didn't have a chance, but I was happy. I met Snow White and Giulietta Masina.

"I remember Fellini liked Disneyland, or I think he did. He called it 'La Dolce Vita for kids,' and he said he'd like to make a documentary about it. I couldn't understand why anyone who could make *8½* would want to do that. I remember that Fellini said what he *really* wanted to do in Los Angeles was to meet Mae West and Groucho Marx.

"I couldn't help daydreaming about what it would be like to be standing up there and receive the Oscar, but my reverie was disturbed because I knew nothing could compete against *8½*. At the Oscar ceremony, I was seated next to Fellini and Giulietta, who was tearful. 'Why are you crying, Giulietta?' Fellini asked her. 'I haven't lost yet.'

"When the winner was announced, Fellini bounded up to the stage. And Giulietta cried harder, a flood of tears. *She* was crying when *I* was the one who should have been crying! I can't say that I didn't feel some disappointment, even though I thought I was prepared. One is always better prepared for winning. But I also felt proud. My film was one of only four which had competed against one of the best pictures of all time.

"Later, Fellini mentioned in an offhand manner that he hadn't really cared all that much if he won or lost. I didn't say anything, but I saw what he felt just before the names were announced, and I could feel the wave of feeling he experienced. That was what was real. I was sitting next to him. He couldn't tell me he didn't feel anything."

In Tokyo, Fellini was entertained by Akira Kurosawa, to whom he said, "I like Japan very much, including the cuisine." For Fellini, however, most memorable on this occasion was the company. "Imagine," he told me, "I was eating with Kurosawa!" As rarely happened, Fellini could not remember what he ate—especially since the courses had Japanese names.

"When I saw my first Fellini film," Paul Mazursky told me, "I'd never been out of Brooklyn, but I *knew* the young men in *I Vitelloni.* 'Felliniesque' is a vision of humanity that is funny, sad, but hopeful.

"I wrote a screenplay, *Alex in Wonderland* [1970], and I wrote into it a part for a film director; not *any* film director, but Fellini. He didn't know me, but I sent a telegram to him in Rome. He answered, saying no. 'I'm not an actor.' He added, 'If you come to Rome, please call me.' The next day, I flew to Rome.

"Fellini agreed to meet me and have lunch the next day in the Grand Hotel. At lunch, he agreed to play the director in my film. I flew back to Hollywood and shot the film, everything but Federico's part.

"Then Mario Longardi called and told me that Federico wasn't going to be able to do the part. I didn't say anything. I pretended I hadn't heard well. The next day I flew to Rome.

"Mario said to me, 'Didn't you understand what I told you? Federico said no.' I said it wasn't a good connection and that I wanted to talk with Federico. Mario told me he was having lunch at Cesarina. I went there. Fellini was eating spaghetti. I walked up to his table. He looked up from the spaghetti, and just said:

" 'Okay. I'll do it.' "

• • •

In 1985, Fellini was honored with a gala tribute held by the Film Society of Lincoln Center in New York City. A few days before the black-tie event, he was invited to a party in his honor in Connecticut. I was among the guests, which included film-society board members and staff, and the visiting guests and celebrities who had come to New York to participate in the tribute.

Fellini, as guest of honor, arrived early, and he and I took a walk around the grounds. The land outside the house was as cared-for as the interior—old trees and new flowers—but there was something else, an intruder. Obviously he had no invitation and had lived, or rather died, to regret crashing that party. He was an extremely large, dark gray, very dead rat.

I averted my eyes and tried to ignore the unignorable. But Fellini was not about to permit that. He said, "Look!" taking my arm and turning me toward the large, immobile mound. "Isn't that wonderful!"

The dead rat was situated on a stone step. Other guests had begun to arrive, and Fellini drew me to the foot of the steps, off to the side. "We'll watch from here," he announced. "Look at their feet," he told me, as assorted guests descended.

The pirouettes accomplished by the large men's shoes and the daintier high heels of the women were something I supposed I might one day see incorporated into a Fellini film.

"This rat reminds me of one I met once in Rimini," he confided, "but of course that one was alive."

He told me to wait while he went to get someone. "Are you going to leave me here with *him*?" I asked, but Fellini was gone. He returned quickly with Marcello Mastroianni, accompanied by Anouk Aimée, who was looking very *la dolce vita*. They were happily reunited.

Mastroianni had a nine-year-old look on his face. Fellini's expression was only a few months more mature. Like schoolboy chums with a secret, they led the way. Just before they reached the dead rat, Fellini and Mastroianni stepped apart, Marcello indicating to Anouk the rodent corpse. With Mastroianni-esque chivalry, he stood poised to catch her should she plunge forward. She didn't, but her *Vogue* cover aspect completely disappeared, her cool poise crumbling.

She and Marcello went back inside, but Fellini said he would like to remain and watch the guests' reactions. Most tried to pretend they hadn't seen the rat, but were unsuccessful.

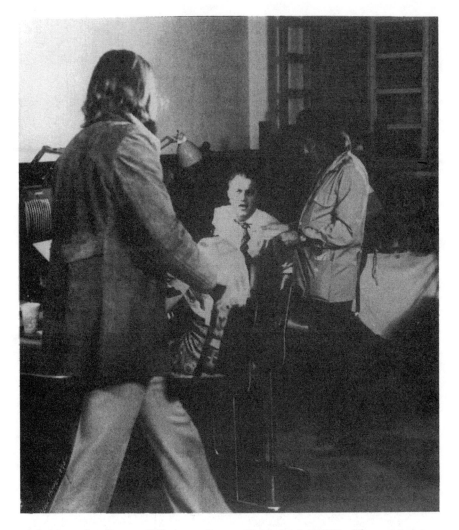

Paul Mazursky directs Fellini in *Alex in Wonderland* (1972). The setting is a Cinecittà editing room, and the star of the film, Donald Sutherland, appears in the foreground.

Fellini asked me how long I thought the rat would be there. I supposed, with numerous servants about, his stay on the steps would be relatively limited. Fellini bet that the cadaver would still be in place when the party ended. I bade *adieu* to it, and Fellini said "*À bientôt*," and we went back into the house to join in the festivities.

As the party ended, once more I accompanied Fellini to the garden. I didn't need to go very far to see that he had won his bet. He said

In 1973, Fellini welcomed a new friend to Rome, an aspiring young film director who would himself go on to become a legend at an early age: Steven Spielberg.

to me, "I knew it would still be there, because there was no one specifically employed as a remover of dead rats."

The night of the film society tribute, Fellini told the Lincoln Center audience:

"The Fulgor had seats and standing room for five hundred. From the American movies of the 1930s, I discovered there existed another way of life, a country of wide-open spaces, of fantastic cities that were a cross between Babylon and Mars."

Mastroianni, in New York for the Fellini tribute, continuously wore his hat, even inside—*especially* inside. No invitation to take it off prevailed as long as there were strangers present. When we were left alone with only Fellini and Anouk Aimée, he finally took it off, revealing some wispy, thin hair and a prominent bald spot on top of his head. Extremely self-conscious, Mastroianni pointed an accusing finger at Fellini and said, "*He* did this to me!"

Mastroianni was referring to the sacrifice he had made for *Ginger and Fred*. Mastroianni kept touching his hair self-consciously, apparently in unending disbelief, as well as to check to see if any had grown that day. Until the barber readied him for the role of Fred, he had taken his hair for granted. Now it was a constant source of preoccupation.

"It is strange," he told me, "to hear everyone in Rome saying, 'Poor Mastroianni—look at him. He has aged overnight.' It is terrible. I never knew what it was to be the object of pity before."

The story has a happy postscript. About six months later, I saw Mastroianni in New York, arriving for lunch at Le Cirque. As I walked toward him, we didn't say anything. I just reached up and ran my fingers through his thick curls. He smiled and said, "Real."

Mastroianni said of his relationship with Fellini, "A friendship and rapport like the one between Federico and me is so special it should be homosexual to be normal.

"Federico is my friend and my favorite film director. Our relationship is totally natural. When we are together, we never have to be guarded. We have similar interests. We both like sex and food. We prefer beautiful women and good cheese to politics."

"Seeing the fading of Cinecittà," Fellini told me, "has made me feel old. It makes me suddenly feel older than anything else ever has."

The 1992 auction of the props and other property of Cinecittà was, for Fellini, like a death knell for the place he considered as much his home as he did the Rome apartment he and Giulietta had shared for so many years.

The ruin into which Cinecittà had fallen was a sign of hard times for the Italian film industry. The future was most bleak for the largest of the stages, Number 5, where Fellini had made his films. A stage that size had become a dinosaur. Only Number 5 had been big enough to contain the imagination of the director referred to as Il Mago. Even Fellini, however, was not enough of a magician to support the great Italian studio with its world disappearing around it. Not only had the United States and the rest of the world stopped going to Italian films, so had the Italians. The Americans were no longer making films in Italy, which had gone from being one of the cheapest to being one of the most expensive places to work. Finally, the sudden collapse of the government, with leading politicians and businessmen going to prison, had done nothing to enhance the attractiveness of Cinecittà as a mecca for moviemaking.

Over the years, Fellini had enjoyed going to Cinecittà on Sundays because he found the atmosphere inspiring and he loved the luxury of being alone, an impossibility on the other days of the week. In later years, sadly, it was all too easy to be alone there, any day.

The props and costumes of Cinecittà were sold at auction for bargain-basement prices. Fellini understood that all these resources would never be available to a director again. He found it heartbreaking that the roles these props and costumes had played in films that were everyone's heritage had not made them more valuable. No one cared in which films they had played their part, or who had worn a particular coat or dress. Far from bidding the steep sums Americans were ready to pay for the ruby-red slippers in which Dorothy had followed the Yellow Brick Road or the sled that said "Rosebud," customers at the Cinecittà auction found themselves at something more closely resembling a giant rummage sale. They carted away tables rescued from the junk heap without their attached memories, to face an uncertain future in which they would function somewhere merely as tables.

"Imagine, not for collectors, but for bargain hunters," Fellini told me. "The price of life is death. The price of success is failure.

"We are dying together, Cinecittà and I. They auctioned off its parts. Mine aren't in demand."

In his last years, Fellini had innumerable honors but few opportunities to make films. "It's very flattering to get an Oscar and have tributes, but all I want to do is work." He mourned the pictures he might have made—"The Voyage of G. Mastorna," "Don Quixote," "Pinocchio" . . .

The last years, spending all of his time and energy trying to sell his work, had broken his heart. "And now I have to have the doctor fix it," he told me, touching his heart. At that moment, I didn't understand the full implication of what he was saying.

Even while film festivals honored him, and invitations to appear came from around the world, Fellini was in Rome, wondering whom he could call at six or seven A.M., who might still be awake at midnight, making as many as a hundred phone calls in a week, trying to raise money for his next film. In spite of his legendary status—even because of it—producers were not inclined to put their money behind his work.

Any suggestion of going to lunch in Rome with a stranger who had brought a "deal" was certain to incur Fellini's wrath. He had been disappointed too many times. He became exceedingly distrustful of foreign visitors who said they wanted to eat lunch with him to discuss a film project. He was worried that he had become a kind of tourist attraction for people in the film business who were passing through Rome anyway. Strangers came from everywhere, but especially from the United States, making extravagant promises and then, as he described it, "walking into the sunset, followed by 'The End.' " Fellini grew increasingly convinced that he couldn't work outside Italy because "I wouldn't know the labels inside my characters' clothes or where they bought their ties."

Fellini contrasted his youthful expectations of old age with the reality:

"There is a difference in the powers of the imagination. When I was a child, I could easily imagine myself as a grown man, or even as an old one. Now that I am an old one, I would like to imagine myself as a young one, but it's not that easy."

Fellini felt he still had within himself the creative power, "but the world was saying no, not a sudden no, but a lingering no, like a sickness. It's only after years of futility that you understand the moment at which it happened, at which you have been retired."

On the set of And the Ship Sails On, Fellini had said to me, "Put in your book that if this film isn't a blockbuster, the next time I'll have to announce that I'm fatally ill! Better yet, I will announce, 'No, I am *not* fatally ill!' If I deny it, everyone will believe it's true. Then I'll hide in my apartment for a while so that producers will want to make Fellini's last film.

"But even that won't work because they will be afraid I'll die during the film, and they won't have sufficient insurance to make a profit."

In 1993, the Academy of Motion Picture Arts and Sciences voted to honor Federico Fellini with the honorary Oscar. It would be Fellini's fifth Academy Award. The other four were awarded for *La Strada* (1954), *The Nights of Cabiria* (1957), *8½* (1963), and *Amarcord* (1973).

On behalf of the board of governors of the Academy, then-president Robert Rehme called Fellini long distance from Los Angeles; Giulietta answered in Rome. He told her that Federico was to be awarded an Oscar, but he told her in English. Giulietta had some understanding of English, but she was frozen, as she usually was when she heard English being spoken to her on the phone. Rehme, unsure what Giulietta had understood, said he would call back.

It was morning in Los Angeles, and by coincidence Rehme's next appointment was with Ibrahim Moussa, one of the producers of Fellini's *Intervista*. So Moussa spoke with Giulietta, who then called Fellini to the phone to hear the news, which made him happy until he hung up and began to have second and third thoughts, producing the travel scenario in his head, contemplating the dreaded acceptance speech he would be called on to deliver.

He was reluctant to make the trip to Los Angeles, but not because he didn't fully appreciate the honor. Fellini understood he would be joining the list of such directors as Charlie Chaplin, King Vidor, and Alfred Hitchcock, all of whom had received this award.

He never traveled well, and at seventy-three he had very real physical problems. Giulietta, herself not well, but always eager to travel and loving the honor, agreed to receive the Oscar in his place.

At the last minute, Fellini changed his mind. He told me it was really the Rome taxi drivers who had convinced him he had to go. Whenever he took a cab and he was alone, he sat in the front seat, where he and the driver talked. ("They tell me how to make films, but I don't tell them how to drive.")

"They made my appearance at the Oscars seem a matter of national pride," he explained. "I am not only letting them down, but betraying

"Charlottina," the caricature Fellini drew of Charlotte Chandler. The flower represents her writer's pen.

my country. I cannot go to any of my favorite restaurants without being greeted by the waiters, asking, 'Are you going to the Oscars?' When I say no, I am given free of charge their unwanted advice that I 'must' go."

The real reason Fellini changed his mind was infinitely more serious. Even before the award, he had known that, no matter how much Giulietta denied it, no matter how much he did not want to accept it, she wasn't well. He understood that this Oscar meant a great deal to her, as did his being there to receive it. The reason he had hesitated was his own illness—painful, crippling arthritis.

"It's very embarrassing to be ill in public," Fellini told me. What he feared most was not being able to perform well at the Oscars. He didn't want his infirmity to be noticed.

On the Academy Awards show, however, before an estimated one billion viewers, his appearance was memorable. After Marcello Mastroianni introduced him, there was a standing ovation, and Fellini said to the audience:

"Please. Sit down, be comfortable. If one here is to feel a bit uncomfortable, that's only me."

Sophia Loren, who was holding the Oscar, said, "To Federico Fellini, in appreciation of one of the screen's master storytellers: Congratulations!"

In response to Fellini's thanks, she asked, "Can I give you a kiss?"

"Yes, I want it," he responded with enthusiasm.

"Okay," she said, and kissed him.

"*Grazie,*" Fellini said.

"Thank you very much," Sophia said.

Fellini shook Mastroianni's hand, then faced the audience. He spoke in a voice that gave no hint of illness or nervousness:

"I would like to have the voice of Domingo to say a long, long thanks. What I can say? Well, I really did not expect it, or perhaps I did. But not before another twenty-five years.

"I come from a country, and I belong to a generation for which America and movies were almost the same thing. And now, to be here with you, my dear Americans, makes me feel at home. I want to thank all of you for making me feel this way.

"In these circumstances, it's easy to be generous and to thank everybody. I would like, naturally, first of all, to thank all the people that have worked with me. I cannot name everyone, only one name, of an actress who is also my wife. Thank you, dearest Giulietta.

"And please stop crying!"

The camera cut to Giulietta in the audience, weeping.

Then it returned to Fellini, who said, "*Grazie*." And it was over.

This was the most touching and dramatic moment of the evening for those watching in the theater as well as for television viewers around the world. The vast TV audience saw a radiance, a relationship, Giulietta's tears of joy. They did not know, of course, that both Federico and Giulietta were ill.

"Don't cry, Giulietta" has become a popular phrase in Italy. It is frequently said when Fellini's name is mentioned by people who don't speak English.

The long plane ride, the acceptance speech in English before a world audience, standing straight when he was suffering from arthritis and didn't want anyone to realize he had problems—the experience had been an excruciating ordeal. When Fellini was healthy, he hadn't hesitated to say he was sick, to use the smallest ailment or injury as an excuse not to travel; but when he really was sick, he didn't want anyone to know. He didn't relish sympathy. He feared not being believed because he knew he had cried wolf too many times. Then, too, any rumors of physical frailty could hurt his chances of obtaining money for a new film.

Fellini's presence was in great demand at every party that night. Parties, however, held no appeal for him. The Rome–to–Los Angeles flight had proved a great strain, and he had insisted on making the long journey with no stopover, so anxious was he to have it all over. Away from Rome he felt like a plant uprooted.

Though he wanted to go back to the Beverly Hilton directly after being photographed holding his Oscar in the press room backstage, he also wished to be courteous to the Academy's board of governors, who had voted for him. He waited long enough to thank them, but did not stay for the dinner honoring the winners and nominees.

He was pleased finally to be back at the hotel that night, the first time in months he could truly relax. The world imagined how happy Fellini had to be receiving his Oscar; however, he really enjoyed it only when it had ended. He told me there was nothing he found more tiring than indecision. He hated being confronted by a dilemma, and subsequently making the same decision over and over. After months of nervous anticipation and dread of both the travel and the television appearance, after the energy expended on the dilemma of whether to go or not, and with all their worry about illness, he, Giulietta, Mastroianni, Mario Longardi, and Fiammetta Profili celebrated with champagne in his hotel suite.

Marcello would have liked to attend every party. Sophia Loren wanted him to go with her, and Catherine Deneuve, the mother of one of his daughters, was in Los Angeles that night because her film *Indochine* had been nominated for the foreign-film Oscar. Giulietta was wearing her Oscar dress, and it was *her* night, too, but she chose to stay with Federico, as did Mastroianni and the others.

On the morning after the Oscars, I was with Fellini at his hotel. He was preparing to go back to Rome on the next flight from Los Angeles. He came out of the elevator and walked toward me, with obvious difficulty. We sat in the back of the lobby, beyond the invisible inhibition barrier that the gathering of fans and media was not supposed to approach.

Fellini was happy with my assurances, and reassurances, that he had been wonderful on the Oscar show, that his posture was straight, that he hadn't looked sick or seemed unduly nervous, that everyone could understand his English, that he didn't look fat, that his hair didn't seem thin.

"At the moment I was actually standing up there," he said, "it was very exciting, thrilling. Afterwards, I didn't remember it very well."

He was pleased that at the Directors Guild reception in his honor he had been able to speak for a few minutes with Billy Wilder, though he hadn't felt well enough to make the scheduled stage appearance. "Billy used to be older than I am," he said, "but now he seems younger."

Paul Mazursky, who had been Fellini's friend for many years, was also at the reception. "Paulino always wants to take me to Farmers Market and to Venice. Venice, California. Someday I will go with him, but not this time."

We were interrupted by a teenage girl who asked for an autograph. "Do you know who I am?" he asked her.

"Fellini," she answered unhesitatingly.

She didn't have paper and pen, so he traced his name on her forehead with his finger. When he had finished, she giggled and seemed satisfied. Even if she couldn't paste the signature in her autograph book, she could keep it in her memory.

After she left, Fellini said, "Yesterday I asked someone who wanted my autograph if she knew who I was, and she said, 'Yes, Mr. Filmini.'"

We sat and talked for a long time that seemed a short time. "I don't know exactly what is wrong," he said, "but I know my relationship with my body has changed. I no longer take it for granted. It lets me know that it is there, and not in the old way—for pleasure. It sends me little messages, or bigger messages. It no longer serves me, paying attention to my commands. It shrieks, 'I'm the boss!'

"I don't look forward to sleep now because I no longer have those wonderful dreams in which my mind plays, or if I do, I cannot remember them. I could adjust to a certain amount of damage to my body as long as my fantasies are intact. Even more than dying, I fear the death of my imagination.

"It's strange how, as you grow old, you wake up earlier and earlier, when you have nothing to get up for. No reason to get up at all. Perhaps it's because you have grown greedy for life, not wanting a single minute to get away from you, once life is speeding by. I always awakened early, but now that the day holds less promise, my body seems to be more eager for it, to clutch at the daylight.

"I remember wondering why old people, as their lives grow less worth living, grow more frightened of flying, and now it has happened to me. I never liked it, and a near escape made me more certain that even G. Mastorna wasn't meant to fly. Now, I find that taking a flight worries me more than ever, because I worry in anticipation; I have really made the flight several times by the time I arrive at my destination. Worse yet, the physical pain I feel now doesn't allow me a moment's escape. It makes me fully conscious of every moment on the plane. I can no longer escape some of the journey, as I used to in my mind. It seems I cannot find a place for myself.

"Heart trouble and strokes run in my family. My mother's brother had a stroke and couldn't speak. My father's brother, my own brother, Riccardo—all of them died of these problems, and my mother was told my heartbeat was irregular when I was a child.

"During the trip here, I was remembering my father's funeral where I saw, standing far in the back, far from my mother at graveside, a number of buxom women my mother and I didn't know. They were all crying, pools of tears. It turned out they were saleslady clients to whom my father had offered his conserves and confections—and something more. My father was not really so different from me. I was wondering who will attend my funeral."

In a lighter tone, he added, "Don't be sad, Charlottina. Remember, at its best, life is homemade *semi-freddo* [soft ice cream] with dark hot chocolate."

He left me to go back upstairs, and as he entered the elevator, he turned and, with some effort, raised his arm, waving to me. I remembered by contrast the graceful image of Fellini on his bicycle, jauntily riding away from me the day I first met him, in Fregene fourteen years before.

From the moment Fellini returned to Rome from Los Angeles, leaving the day after the awards ceremony and arriving April 1, 1993, there was little time to enjoy his new Oscar. Besides the suffering imposed by his arthritis, Fellini had to decide whether or not to have heart surgery. Uneasily, he made the decision, and though still uncertain about it, in June he went to Switzerland to have a bypass operation.

Fellini had said many times that places with mountains frightened him. He never knew why. He said that in his dreams, whenever there were mountains, bad things happened. Recovering in Zurich after the operation, he was desperately unhappy. As always, he longed to be in only one place, Rome, and then there were those ubiquitous and, for him, ominous Swiss mountains in view . . .

He carried on his usual flirtatious banter with the Swiss nurses, but they were too serious to appreciate it. The Swiss hospital food was not to his taste. There was muesli when he would have preferred risotto. Almost as soon as he awakened from the anesthesia, Fellini decided he was ready to leave. He said he had been dreaming about food and was anxious to return to where they had some.

The doctors advised him to remain in the hospital. If he insisted on leaving too soon, at the very least he should move to a Zurich hotel and stay near the hospital. He was resolute—"stubborn," they called it. The compromise effected was that Fellini would be permitted to go, not to Rome, but to recuperate in the peaceful resort of Rimini, his childhood home, a town on the Adriatic coast about a hundred miles south of Venice.

This wasn't what Fellini wanted to do, to return to Rimini; the contrast with the place in his memory and the contemporary reality was always disconcerting for him. He found himself expecting to see in the street his mother's little dog, Titina.

"I think of the circus which passed through town when I was a child. It probably was a little circus, though it seemed great to me. That was when I thought all adults were tall. It is so important, the moment in your life at which you discover something. Maybe my love of films, discovered at the Fulgor, where the Marx Brothers became my real family, has something to do with a refusal to grow up."

The temptation of a suite at the Grand Hotel, however, offered the local admiration he found nourishing in small portions—and, of course, there was the room service.

After a short stay in Rimini, Giulietta returned to Rome to take care of bills, mail, and other matters that called for immediate attention. Also, she had to see her own doctors. Fellini wanted to go with her, but the trip to Rome had been forbidden by his doctors. Fellini was persuaded to stay and wait in Rimini because he didn't want to be seen in Rome by producers who might decide he was too sick to work, or by the ever-waiting photographers.

Giulietta was certain that, no matter what he said when he was trying to get what he wanted, once Federico was back in Rome he would refuse to return to Rimini. She believed that Fellini always had a selective memory about promises made when he was trying to be persuasive.

Giulietta's trip was meant to last only a few days. Sadly, it came at the wrong moment. All at once, everything was going wrong for Federico and Giulietta.

When he was a boy, a suite at the Grand Hotel had represented for Fellini the unattainable, the unimaginable. He never would have believed that one day he would be living there, an honored and acclaimed guest, and that the hotel would feel privileged to entertain him. He remembered, as a boy, being chased away by the concierge. He certainly would not have believed that his stay would be totally joyless because he was a prisoner of illness. Even room service, which had always excited him, held no glamour.

While Giulietta was away, Fellini, in his hotel suite, suffered a stroke. He collapsed, too weak to call for help, too far from the phone. He never totally lost consciousness, but he was alone for forty-five minutes before the hotel maid entered to turn down the bed and found him lying on the floor.

Fellini was rushed to the hospital in Rimini where, once again, he made jokes for the benefit of the nurses, of the press, and of himself. Privately, he saw the stroke as an especially terrifying omen, because it happened close to where his brother, Riccardo, had only a short time before suffered a fatal stroke.

In the hospital, Fellini took the Last Rites.

The stroke was considered serious, but it was not perceived to be life-threatening. Fellini was told that, with time and therapy, complete recovery was possible. Even if the worst came to pass and the use of one arm and one leg was impaired, and even if he had to use a wheelchair, the doctors said he could lead a full life. He didn't feel that way. His first reaction was he would rather die than live as an incomplete man, without his pride. He was advised to go to Ferrara where "the great stroke hospital," the Ospedale San Giorgio, was located, where Michelangelo Antonioni had been sent in 1985.

Fellini consented, though Ferrara did not seem to him to be on the way to Rome. He believed his only chance to live and recover and work again would be in Rome.

At the hospital in Ferrara, Fellini underwent therapy, and his spirits improved when he was allowed to have a telephone. Though he had never really liked speaking on the phone, from the hospital in Ferrara it now provided a lifeline to Rome. He did the boring exercises the doctors prescribed. He ate the dull, "healthy" food. He even watched television.

Fellini didn't feel free to go out into the garden after a photographer was discovered hiding in a tree, poised to get a photograph of him in his wheelchair. He said that for him it was impossible to imagine facing a life of "the chair."

"It's terrible when the mind is going as fast as ever, faster, and the body will no longer take orders from it. It's like being trapped in someone else's body. Now I understand I am a missing person. I've lost myself."

In a phone call from the hospital during a period when Fellini believed he would recover sufficiently to work, I sensed in his voice a certain release from tension. He said he felt a kind of freedom—the freedom one has when the most terrible thing that could happen has already happened. He cautioned me, though it was certainly unnecessary, not to tell anyone where he was.

Giulietta wasn't in Ferrara with him, but not by choice: She was secretly hospitalized in Rome. An announcement was released to the press that she was suffering from nervous exhaustion caused by the strain, but the truth was the doctors had said she had cancer, an inoperable brain tumor.

In 1993, at the Beverly Hilton Hotel, the morning after the Oscars, Fellini said to me, "I can't imagine life without Giulietta."

Giulietta told the doctors specifically that if their news was bad, she preferred not to hear it. Deeply religious, she preferred to pray for the best.

When Fellini learned how critical Giulietta's condition was, and that she was aware of it, he announced that he *had* to go to Rome to see her in the hospital. He was absolutely determined.

The trip was to be a well-kept secret. Only Mario Longardi, a few friends, and a few doctors were to know. The press was not supposed to find out, but they did. The reporters were waiting. Fellini spent a day and a night and part of the next day with Giulietta at the hospital in Rome, and then returned by ambulance to Ferrara.

Back at the hospital in Ferrara, he was frustrated because there seemed to be no change in his ability to use his hand or to walk. He was told that improvement would take time. It already had. No one was able to guarantee total recovery. Fellini saw in the doctors' eyes disbelief that he was going to make that total recovery. He tried to resign himself. What else was there to do? The only hope was work. If he could just go back to making films, then he could help Giulietta, too, by being with her. He *had* to be with her.

The answer was Rome, even if he had to be in a hospital in Rome. Fellini succeeded in convincing the doctors that he would recover more rapidly there. He left Rimini again—this time to stay in Rome, as it turned out, for the remainder of his life.

The date of his and Giulietta's fiftieth wedding anniversary was drawing near. For all the past years, Fellini had joked with Giulietta that it was *her* anniversary, not his. Giulietta had never found this comment funny.

Giulietta had been permitted to leave the clinic, and Fellini was dedicated to making their fiftieth anniversary everything she had wanted it to be. The anniversary had become extremely important to him, too. He had drawn a card for her. On one side, he had reproduced the one he drew for her on the day they were married, and on the opposite side he drew the same card with only the date changed, 1993 instead of 1943, and the address of their home changed from Lutezia to Margutta.

Fellini considered various plans. He didn't want a party, but they could have a wonderful dinner. Giulietta had suggested dinner with a few friends; she would cook her special spaghetti. He said they should be alone together, in a great restaurant.

Meanwhile, Fellini persuaded his doctors at the Ospedale Umberto I to let him have a brief excursion, even in the dreaded chair. He wanted to visit a bookstore. He was told that books could be purchased for him, but that wasn't at all what he wanted. He missed the personal pleasure of selecting for himself.

For Fellini, making the purchase in the store gave the books not only their own life, but the life of the experience of buying them. The bookstore salespeople recognized him and chatted about films; one clerk asked Fellini to read the script he had written. Fellini invited him to drop it off at the hospital. Customers joined in, and everyone expressed wishes for Fellini's rapid recovery.

At other times, Fellini hadn't enjoyed being the recipient of this much attention while shopping. It made shopping take a long time, and everyone watched you, observing what you purchased. Usually he didn't enjoy shopping, except of course for buying food on the Via della Croce. But anything that took him away from the hospital seemed cheerful. To be there in the bookstore in the presence of all those healthy people, and among his fans, was pleasing.

On the way there and back, it was thrilling just to breathe deeply the air of Rome, which he believed he could actually distinguish from air anywhere else in the same way a French authority on perfume, called a nose, can do with scents. Inside the hospital, where he was supposed to remain for some days longer, it was difficult to realize that he was in Rome, because hospitals are hospitals wherever they are. Still, he was back in Rome, and for Fellini, that meant that everything was going to be all right.

Fellini was stimulated by having been out in the streets he loved so much. If he could go out to buy books, then why couldn't he take Giulietta to a restaurant on Sunday for lunch? The two of them could have a brief respite from illness. They could plan their anniversary celebration. He who had been embarrassed by any public display of the celebration of something so personal as a wedding anniversary was now committed to making the day special. Fellini defined a wonderful marriage as "one that both people think is wonderful." Now he remembered the distant past, their youth together. It was more vivid in his memory than their later struggles at compromise. He wanted to redeem himself for any of his "bad behavior" over the years. He wanted to make Giulietta as happy as possible.

He was so totally caught up in the project, as he always was in anything which he did with his whole heart, that he was even willing to admit to the number fifty. Though he understood he was too famous to keep his age a secret, he didn't like to say the exact number, as though saying it made it more real. Admitting to a fiftieth wedding anniversary was admitting to being of a certain age. Federico was more sensitive about his age than Giulietta was about hers.

Despite some trepidation, the doctors in the Rome hospital were won over by the arguments of the ever-persuasive Fellini. Seeing how those few hours outside the hospital had bolstered his morale, they consented to his leaving for a Sunday lunch with Giulietta, who had already returned home to their apartment. Federico hoped soon to join her there. Believing that she was even more ill than he, he suggested they have a pre-celebration, a kind of rehearsal of their anniversary, which was only two weeks away.

After more than half a century of sharing meals, that Sunday lunch was to be their last, though neither of them knew it.

Fellini wanted to go to Cesarina, but on Sunday it was closed. Cesarina herself had died some years before, but her restaurant had remained his favorite. He chose another nearby, but found it also closed. His third choice was open and welcomed them.

Giulietta was always hopeful, and now Fellini felt that way. A good meal was important to his mood.

Eating with abandon and talking animatedly, Fellini suddenly began choking. The cause was a piece of mozzarella. The stroke had affected his ability to swallow, but in the pleasure of the moment, he had forgotten. It was a disturbing moment, but it passed and didn't seem to be of any great consequence.

After lunch, he took Giulietta home, and then he went on with the young man who had been driving them to look at a possible new office he contemplated renting. Fellini had liked the location when he had looked at the plans from his hospital bed. On visiting the office, he pronounced it perfect. He wanted to sign the lease the next day, indicating that once again he was looking forward to preparing a new film. He would have signed that very day, except it was Sunday. He planned immediately to begin working on his new idea, a story about two old vaudeville performers who haven't seen each other in years, but meet at the hospital in Ferrara after each has had a stroke. Built around illness, the hospital, and the fantasies induced by a stroke, including a near-death experience; it was a variation on "Mastorna." He planned to use the Rimini-Ferrara-Rome hospital experience constructively, to make a film about what had happened to him. He told me, "In that way, I can make my illness into a positive experience instead of a negative one. By making films of my memories, my memories are replaced by memories of the films I make of them."

During a serious illness a quarter of a century before, Fellini had had the same thought: "The first time I experienced a brush with death, when I realized how close it had been, once I was able to stop struggling just to be able to breathe, I thought: If I had died, I would have been *really* angry about it.

"Deprived. I would have been deprived of making so many films. My films would have finished in the mid-sixties. Now I can't be angry, not with the life I've had. Disappointed, perhaps, because I'd like to make one more film, just one more, oh, and just one more after that . . ."

The previous time, however, as soon as Fellini had left the hospital, he found he was happy to forget the entire experience. He characterized his response as "shaking it off," as a dog does. Fellini said to me, "Now I am planning my script, but when I am back home, I probably will want to shake the memory off again and make a film about a different subject."

Sadly, Fellini never returned home.

That Sunday evening at the hospital, following his last lunch with Giulietta, Fellini suffered a massive stroke, lapsed into a coma, and was rushed to intensive care. This time the doctors held out no hope for his recovery, though Giulietta and his family and friends still hoped. Against the advice of the doctors, Giulietta insisted on visiting her husband in intensive care, though he did not seem to be aware of her presence. In the unfeeling terminology of medicine, he was pronounced brain-dead.

As Fellini lay in a coma, the Italian paparazzi were outside the hospital in force, waiting.

Two weeks later, one day after his and Giulietta's fiftieth wedding anniversary, without recovering consciousness, Federico Fellini died.

The report of Fellini's death went out on television before anyone told Giulietta. It was from television that she learned of his death. Mario Longardi rushed to her side, to comfort her as much as one could and to meet the press, which would be converging on the Via Margutta. As it turned out, reporters had already arrived, totally filling the narrow street.

At the hospital, the press, especially the photographers, had been gathered day and night. Undoubtedly for a price, someone with inside information told one of the paparazzi that Fellini had just died. The photographer somehow managed to get into the intensive-care unit, where he pulled back the sheet and pushed away the tubes in order to take an unobstructed shot of Fellini in death. The assumption was that the photographer wore hospital whites and passed through pretending to be an attendant. The scene was reminiscent of the moment in *La Dolce Vita* when Paparazzo begs Marcello to take him into the apartment with him for just one shot of Steiner's body.

The photographer rushed the picture of Fellini to one of the television stations, which then showed it on the news. The public outcry was instantaneous. The station was besieged by phone calls, unanimously registering outrage. Advertisers threatened to cancel their ads. The public was appalled, and the picture elicited the reaction it deserved as the ultimate invasion of the privacy of Italy's beloved Fellini. All other stations rejected the photo, as did every newspaper and magazine, including the scandal tabloids. It wasn't known whether they did so because they had human feeling, or because they learned of the negative reaction to the first showing of the photograph.

Only during the last months of Fellini's life, though neither of us knew they were to be the last months, did I notice a lingering sadness in his tone, which did not allow for much playfulness on my part. I understood that his health had failed, that he felt physically threatened. He found the thought of being an invalid more terrible than any fear of death. He was immensely sad about the films he hadn't made, no longer believing that he had much future as a director.

He was feeling uncertain even about what he termed a "limited film," that being one the very limitations of which enhanced its potential for happening, and happening soon. Before he became so ill, he had promised Giulietta that he would make another film for her. It was to be a fiftieth-anniversary gift. She wanted to act in one more film of his, and, looking back to *A Director's Notebook*, he had thought of doing "An Actor's Notebook." It was the least ambitious of the projects to which he aspired, with a relatively low budget, and it would reunite Giulietta and Mastroianni.

When I heard that Federico had died, I believed that whatever the apparent cause, it was really of a broken heart. The boy, Federico, and the man and director, Federico Fellini, died—but the legend, Fellini, lives on.

Now, with Federico Fellini gone, his films have found new life. They are traveling to theaters from New York to New Delhi, from São Paolo to Singapore, and newspapers in many languages feature glowing stories about Fellini. In Italy, the total fame that had eluded Fellini in his lifetime was his in death. While he remained in a coma, television, radio, and the newspapers gave constant reports of his condition. There were innumerable clips from his films on television, as well as showings of the complete films. Suddenly, Fellini was in everyone's home in Italy. People who had never seen one of his films thought of him as a friend. He had become the most famous man in the country. Fellini was more famous in death than he had been in life. When he died, all Italians thought they knew him and each felt the loss.

Banners were hung out of windows in Rome saying, "Ciao, Federico." Restaurants he had patronized put black ribbons over his photograph. The ribbons remained for several weeks. Then they were taken away—and Fellini belonged to forever.

At his Cinecittà memorial tribute, the huge backdrop of the sky which had been used in *Intervista* served as the background for Fellini's coffin. Appropriately, it was a cyclorama of make-believe sky—*his* reality.

No one spoke as the procession filed by the coffin. The sound of the silence was total. As the mourners passed the bier, they paused briefly, some leaving flowers, gifts, and notes.

Fellini and Antonioni had known each other and had mutual respect for each other's work, but they had never been close friends. In late 1992, when Antonioni was decorated by the president of Italy at the

Quirinale Palace, Fellini had attended. "Of course, Michi had a chair," Antonioni's wife, Enrica, recalled, "but absolutely everyone else had to stand." A stroke suffered several years earlier had made it difficult for Antonioni to remain standing through such a long ceremony.

It was generally known that Fellini was suffering from arthritis, but he stood during the entire program, locked in a vise of pain which must have made the event seem interminable.

Fellini had faced a Hobson's choice: to attend and suffer, or to stay away and suffer. His absence would have been more noticeable than his presence. It would have seemed that either he wasn't properly honoring a great colleague or that he, himself, was sick. Neither alternative was acceptable for Fellini.

Despite his own illness, Antonioni was there with Enrica, among the many filing by the coffin on Stage 5, to pay homage to Fellini.

Alberto Lattuada and his wife, Carla Del Poggio, who had made *Without Pity* and *Variety Lights* with the very young Federico and Giulietta, were at the funeral. Lattuada had given Fellini his first co-directorial credit in *Variety Lights*. "He started his career next to me," he told me. "I discovered he had something to say to the world." Lattuada had also given Giulietta her first screen role in *Without Pity*.

"Giulietta was relatively composed," Lattuada told me. "But when she saw us, she started crying. She said, 'We were together, all four of us, when we were young and happy. It seems such a short time ago.'"

Mastroianni was the only one who spoke out critically after the Cinecittà tribute, one of the greatest in Italy in modern times. Asked by the press to comment about his friend, Mastroianni said, "They are honoring him when he is dead instead of making it easier for him to make the films when he was alive. Now everyone is declaring what a genius he was, but no one seriously offered to help him in all these recent years. More reflection is needed to understand how great the man was."

Sophia Loren, who only months before had shared the stage with Mastroianni and Fellini at the Academy Award ceremonies, said, "A great light has gone out, and now we are all in the dark. The world will be much sadder without his imagination."

Lina Wertmüller, who began her career as Fellini's assistant on *8½*, attended the memorial tribute at Cinecittà wearing her trademark white-rimmed tinted glasses and limping on crutches. While picking fruit, she had fallen out of a tree.

"I have been asked a thousand times," she told me, "about what I learned from Fellini.

"I was ten years old when I listened to his radio show. I read his work and admired his drawings. I loved his drawings. I saw his first movies. I met him.

"A glimpse from his alive eyes. His eyebrows. He was so curious. He loved freedom. He had a lot of fun, which you shared with him. When you were with him, you were at the core of a whirlwind. If you could only follow him. He said, 'Follow me, and jump.' One had to have faith and not hesitate. You could be injured if you were afraid and hesitated.

"I've thought about what most attracted me, and I know what it was. It was that he talked to my imagination.

"Federico never forgot the comical, ironic side. He always looked for freshness and avoided the frozen. I knew Federico the man, the director, the artist, the scoundrel.

"Being close to him as his assistant, I understood how important choice was to him. He wanted the world of choice, but then he wanted to eliminate what he decided not to use. He wanted to get rid of all the papers that didn't get used. I said, 'No, don't tear those up,' but he didn't listen to me. Tearing up was a positive act because it eliminated something he no longer had to carry around in his mind.

"Knowing Federico was like opening a window on a larger landscape. The time after World War Two was exceptionally vital and alive. There was so much creative energy. It was a golden period. I was lucky to be around then, beginning. Federico is the most 'artist' of anyone I ever knew, and if he heard me saying this, it would make him angry.

"It's so big a gift to have had Federico in my life. He taught me so much when I worked with him. And when I wanted to leave before the film was made, because I had the opportunity to make a film of my own, he wasn't angry. He was happy for me, and he even helped me get some of the last financing for *The Lizards*.

"Before I started work on it, I went to Fregene to see Federico. The sea was rough, and it was very cloudy. He said to me, 'Tell your story as if you were talking to a friend.' "

While Wertmüller was working for Fellini, she was given a photograph of a face, "the size of a postage stamp," and sent around Italy to look for an unknown girl who looked like Claudia Cardinale.

"Federico wanted Claudia Cardinale for a part, but he didn't believe her husband, who was a rich producer, would permit it, so we ran ads in the newspapers describing the actress we wanted. We were specific. 'Do you have the right-size hips?' we asked in our notices. 'Do you recognize in yourself this kind of beauty? If so, come to this place.' "

Hundreds of girls everywhere turned out for the call. A general description had been put into the newspaper notices, but many of the "girls" who showed up were not girls at all, but old enough to be the mother of the character, and some of them weighed enough to be two of her.

"I remember how that square was filled with women, every kind of woman. They ranged in age from twelve to eighty. They were as totally different from the description we had circulated as was possible. There was no limit to the differences. Many were far from beautiful. It was a zoo. We were Gypsies searching for a renaissance beauty, and a humpbacked woman and a one-eyed one turned up in the group. For me, the outstanding characteristic of the gathering was its amazing optimism. They were all so incredibly optimistic.

"There were hundreds to choose from. I selected the five finalists. They were all good, but one of them stood out from all the others. She was perfect. She looked more like Cardinale than Cardinale, even younger. I knew Federico would love her.

"Meanwhile, he happened to meet Cardinale and mention the part to her, and she immediately said she wanted it.

"The poor girl I had selected didn't get it.

"I was his assistant director for three months. It was a great time in my life. I've never been happier. I was in love with him. Every woman who ever met Federico was in love with him.

"People are saying now how sad it is for Giulietta. How terrible to lose him. Of course it is. But when I saw her at the funeral, I thought, 'How lucky she was to love a man like that for fifty years!'

"Poor Giulietta, to lose Federico, but lucky Giulietta, to have had him for so long."

Anthony Quinn, who starred as Zampanò, the mentally weak strongman loved by Giulietta's Gelsomina in *La Strada*, told me:

"My life started over again with *La Strada*. It opened all doors for me. When he showed me the script, it was only four pages long, but the character he wanted me to play was a beautiful one. I had already worked with his wife, and she had told me about the story.

"I didn't speak much Italian when I met Fellini. I spoke Spanish with him. I didn't know if I should speak English, Italian, or Spanish for the film. He said, 'It doesn't matter. Just say numbers. Your facial expression, the character, is what matters. Don't lose the character speaking while trying to concentrate on remembering lines.'

"Fellini didn't like to analyze. When he directed an actor, he liked to see the personality emerging. That's because he was an artist, and he was used to seeing a personality emerge from his drawing.

"I could identify with Fellini because I live with my *duende*. That's a Spanish word for the spirit inside you that drives you. I could feel the drive in him when he was directing me for *La Strada*. I *was* Zampanò! I knew Fellini would never quit. He would have worked seven days a week.

"My father was a Hollywood cameraman in 1926. When sound came in, they didn't know what to do. Does the camera tell a story or does the writer? James Wong Howe said you never cut to a close-up unless you have a secret. On TV today, everything is a secret. Federico saved his close-ups so they meant something.

"One day I was giving an interview with a journalist. I'm always very serious when I do this. When it was over, Federico came up to me and said, 'Tony, why did you tell them the truth, which was ordinary, stupid? You told them your mother was a Mexican Indian. Why didn't you tell them she was an Indian princess?'

"Fellini had his dream world. Like Cervantes—Don Quixote and Sancho Panza. Or Shakespeare. Fantasy is the richness of life, and that is what Fellini dealt with. Reality isn't cinema. Cinema is imagination. He had a passion for what he did. There are very few artists in the movies. Fellini was one.

"Federico had an amazing characteristic which I call his infant quality. He was so open. He was naïve in the best sense of the word. He learned from every person. He was an emotional sponge. But he had an attention to detail that was very adult, personal, and meticulous.

"Giulietta was wonderful to work with—Gelsomina, the sweet, lost girl. I thought Giulietta would have a big career. She didn't make as many movies as I thought she would, but she had wonderful talent, and she and Fellini worked very well together.

"I'm sorry Federico and I never spent more time together, more special time. For me, special time is the time you spend alone with another person. I look for people who are different from me. I think most people look for people who are like themselves. Fellini wasn't like anyone."

Nadia Gray told me that she learned a great deal from Fellini, just watching him direct. "The bad directors arrive late, unshaven, and they yell. They yell because they don't know what they want to do. They think if they yell at somebody, people will think the temperament means they are gifted.

"Mr. Fellini came on the set always on time, with a tie, smiling, discussing everything with the actors, the technicians, including everybody. He was like that because he knew what he wanted. He improvised, but he knew. He never came on with a scream.

"Sometimes we would ride back to Rome together and talk. He didn't talk about the film, but about me. He would show concern for my problems at the time. It's sad to imagine the world without him."

Talking with me shortly after Fellini's death, Gore Vidal said:

"He called me Gorino, and I called him Fred. He called me Gorino first; he never commented about how he felt about my calling him Fred, but he always responded to it. He was a great man and very funny, but he had a Sistine Chapel complex.

"We would sit at cafés with lots of food, and talk about subjects of importance, like *Myra Breckenridge*. Movies are the lingua franca of our culture. Fred wanted to know about Mae West. He never tired of hearing about her. He didn't believe me when I told him how long it took me to realize Myra was a man. I told him I thought the fun of writing books instead of making films was writing a book is serendipitous. He said that for him making films was serendipitous, and I suppose it was.

American director John Landis had seen *Toby Dammit* and loved it, but his real discovery of Fellini came, as he tells it, with *Satyricon*:

"I was eighteen years old and working in Yugoslavia as a gofer on the film *Kelly's Heroes*. My friend and I had gone to Trieste to buy cheap sweaters at Upims. I saw a theater that was playing *Fellini Satyricon*. I didn't think about it until after I bought my ticket and sat down in the theater, but of course there weren't any subtitles.

"A year later, I was in Geneva, and I saw that *Satyricon* was playing there. On the marquee it plainly said *Fellini Satyricon,* with subtitles. I bought my ticket and, of course, the subtitles were in French and German!

"Watching the film for a third time, in Los Angeles with English subtitles, I realized that Fellini was a painter, an artist who used the camera as painters use a brush.

"I have no answer to the eternal dilemma of art versus commerce. All filmmakers have been through the humiliation of having to beg for money. The Italians probably have had over fifty governments since World War Two, but only one Fellini, and his work will be remembered long after the producers and financiers who said he was irresponsible are forgotten.

"I first met Fellini because of a werewolf. I was in Rome promoting *An American Werewolf in London,* and Mario Longardi, who always worked with Fellini, was the publicist. Mario introduced my wife, Deborah, and me to Federico, and we had a long and very funny lunch together.

"Deborah was hugely pregnant with our daughter Rachel, and Federico held her hand all through lunch. To this day, at the mere mention of his name, Deborah will always proclaim, 'He's a genius!'

"Federico and I would trade jokes. He was always extremely funny. Now, every once in a while I hear a joke, and I think, 'I wish I could tell that one to Fellini.' "

Spike Lee thought about the inspiration Fellini had been in his life and about his meeting in Rome with the great director. He had first seen a Fellini film when he was in high school. "It showed me what you can do and that there are no limits. It was my dream to meet him, and after I became a director, I had the chance to have dinner with him in Rome.

"We talked about our problems in dealing with producers and studios. At that moment, I was having trouble in my professional life and in my personal life, with the studio and with my girlfriend. I'd just had a quarrel with my girlfriend, who'd left me and wasn't speaking to me, and I wanted her to come back. I was having a lot of trouble getting the final cut on my film. Fellini told me, 'You have to fight for the final cut. You must have it. You are right to fight for it.' Of course, he was in a better position to have others give in to his demands than I was.

"I said, 'But what about my girlfriend? She's left me and isn't speaking.' I don't know why I thought that because he knew how to make great films, he understood women.

"He didn't say a word. He just picked up a paper napkin from the restaurant and began drawing on it. He drew a picture of me on my knees pleading, and over my head he made a comic-strip balloon which said, 'Please forgive me.' He said, 'Give this to your girlfriend.'

"So when I went back, I did. She took the napkin and she liked it. She was so impressed she kept it, but still she didn't speak to me. We didn't get back together.

"Well, I met someone else, someone I cared about, and I knew the other was a mistake—a double mistake, because she wouldn't give me back the drawing. I wish I knew how to get back Fellini's picture of me."

When Universal sent Steven Spielberg to Rome in 1973 to promote *Duel,* he was anxious to use the opportunity to meet Federico Fellini. Not making a picture at the moment, Fellini met the young director, who was just starting out on a career that could never have been foreseen by Fellini, or even imagined by Spielberg himself.

Mario Longardi remembers the meeting as jolly, and young Steven as shy and respectful. Fellini liked him and ate one of his long, leisurely lunches. At the end of the meal, Spielberg produced a small, inexpensive camera and asked politely, if a little nervously, would Fellini mind having his picture taken with him? Fellini didn't mind at all, even when it turned out to be not just one shot.

Some time later, Spielberg wrote to Fellini saying that he kept the photograph in his office and that it had brought him luck.

In 1993, Spielberg was being honored with the Golden Lion at the Venice Film Festival at the same time that Fellini was recovering from a stroke in the hospital in Ferrara. Despite his own problems, Fellini wrote a note congratulating Spielberg.

In a letter dated September 10, 1993, Spielberg answered Fellini, who he and everyone else believed was recovering:

"As you read this, I hope you are feeling a lot better. I have been a fan of yours ever since I could see. . . . It is an additional thrill to know I've been awarded the same honor you received for the body of your work recognized and saluted a few years back.

"Your films have been a great source of inspiration for me. They have contributed more than most other movies in defining film as art. I'm sorry I didn't get a chance to see you in Venice, but I'm sure our paths will cross in the future."

He closed by saying, "All my best, as I continue to look at your films and gain more and more inspiration."

It was the last letter Fellini ever read.

The tribute to Fellini at Cinecittà was followed the next day by the religious service at the Santa Maria degli Angeli church. The service was attended by the families of Federico and Giulietta, and by their friends. In attendance were not only the members of the film community, but also the president of the republic and the leaders of government. Premier Carlo Ciampi said that Italy had lost its "great national poet."

The streets were lined for blocks around by fans of Fellini—people he didn't know at all, but who knew him. Among them were the waiters and taxicab drivers of Rome. Large numbers of taxi drivers had driven their cabs as near to the church as they could, creating an additional traffic jam. The thousands in the crowds who hadn't known Fellini personally were mourning along with the millions who watched the television news.

Giulietta had told family and friends that they did not need to wear black: "Federico wouldn't like it." She wore dark glasses to hide her eyes, which were red and nearly closed from her tears of grief. She wore a turban to conceal the loss of her hair from radiation treatments, which she had successfully kept secret.

Throughout the church ceremony, Giulietta clutched her rosary. In the most poignant moment, at the very end of the service, she raised her arm with the rosary held high, and waved good-bye to Federico.

"Ciao, amore," she whispered.

There was the implication that Giulietta felt she would be with him soon. The few people who were close to Federico and Giulietta were aware that she was not likely to outlive him by much, and that she knew it.

The coffin with Fellini's body was escorted to Rimini by his sister, Maddalena, and her daughter, Francesca.

Giulietta did not make the trip to Rimini, but rather stayed in Rome. The reason given was that her sorrow, her anguish, was too great to permit her to make the trip. That was true. It was also true that she was too ill. She returned to the Margutta apartment, heartbroken.

I remembered her words to me of several years before: "My most important role has been being Federico Fellini's wife."

Then she added, "But when two people are married for as many years as we have been, roles shift, even within a day, and there were times when I was Zampanò and he was Gelsomina." Without the unique presence of Fellini, their home seemed empty. As she battled for her own life, Giulietta struggled through the loss of her husband of fifty years, her great director and closest friend.

Her family—her brother and sister, Mario and Mariolina, and her niece, Simonetta—tried to comfort her. Simonetta is the daughter of Giulietta's sister Eugenia, only a year younger than she, who had died a few years before. Simonetta remembered her mother holding her as they waited at the airport for Uncle Federico and Aunt Giulietta, who were returning from the Academy Awards in Hollywood. *La Strada* had won the Oscar as best foreign film, and her aunt and uncle had been recognized as world-famous artists and celebrities. All of this was beyond the little girl, who knew only it was a moment of great happiness. As Uncle Federico and Aunt Giulietta descended from the plane, it was Giulietta who was holding the Oscar. Seeing Eugenia and Simonetta, she waved it proudly.

Giulietta's family sat with her as she read the cables and letters of tribute and condolence from around the world from heads of state— Boris Yeltsin, François Mitterrand, Emperor Akihito of Japan, as well as from old friends and fans who had no other way to express their sense of loss.

Each morning, Giulietta would go into the kitchen, where she would automatically turn on the radio, as she had for so many years, and she would listen to all the words about Fellini. It was difficult for her to bring herself to go into their living room, which Fellini had called his thinking room.

Giulietta received offers of film parts, letters from festivals and museums, suggestions for projects, and events. There was the possibility of a Broadway musical of *Juliet of the Spirits,* a project with which she particularly identified. Marvin Hamlisch was interested in doing the music, and Fellini and she had talked about the changes they would like to make, to have the character conform more to Giulietta's conception.

Giulietta was in great demand all over the world. Suddenly, Federico was no longer there to invite that year, or the next, or the one after that, and everyone wanted Giulietta. There were opportunities for the travel she loved. She had enjoyed appearing at festivals with the Fellini films in which she had acted, and was immensely proud of them. They were, after all, her children, too.

After the death of her husband, however, Giulietta's health took a devastating downturn. The strength of spirit with which she had resisted her illness while he was alive seemed to be all used up. Her illness had brought an end to her public life. Private life was what remained, and that barely, as her travels became limited to trips from the Via Margutta to the hospital.

She spent as much as she could of her brief remaining life at home, but she was hospitalized more and more. During her last months, she grew too weak to go home anymore.

Her family was advised to prepare themselves. It was suggested that they think about funeral arrangements. Giulietta continued to cling to life.

The strength of her will to live, even without Federico, impressed the doctors, but their sad expressions revealed the truth.

With the spirit of Gelsomina and Cabiria, and of Giulietta herself, she stopped the doctors from telling her what she did not want to hear, as she had done throughout her illness. In her heart, of course, she knew, but the articulating of the words made death seem more real, more imminent.

"Why tell me what I can't do anything about?" she said to the doctors. "I don't want to hear anything bad. I want to have as much time as I have left to live in the best way I can."

These were words her character might have spoken in a Fellini film.

Giulietta Masina survived only five months after the death of Fellini. She died in Rome on March 23, 1994.

It was only one week short of a year since she had sat there in Hollywood in the audience, watching her husband of almost fifty years receive his Oscar. She had shared that lifetime of achievement both personally and professionally, and as the tears had filled her eyes and streamed down her cheeks, Fellini, from the stage, had lovingly admonished her not to cry. It was one of the most moving moments in Oscar history. Neither Fellini nor Giulietta would be alive when the next Oscars were presented. At that moment, however, she had been worried about getting tear stains on the white spangled jacket she had given so much time to selecting.

There would be no more tears of joy for Giulietta, no more of the grief that had followed the illness and death of Federico.

She was dressed in the long black skirt she had chosen for the Oscar ceremony because she believed it made her appear taller and slimmer. At the Oscars, her hair had been short and soft, but after her death, it was necessary to add a white turban to hide the ravages of the treatments she had endured. In one hand was her treasured pearl rosary, with which she had said her recent farewell to Federico, and a red rose. In her other hand, near her heart, she held a small photograph of Federico.

The death of Giulietta so soon after Fellini was not a shock to those who knew and worked with them. It had been believed by many friends and co-workers that neither would live long without the other.

Giulietta was taken to Rimini, to be with Federico.

Even in happy years, Easter had been a sad holiday for Giulietta, reminding her of the Easter death of their baby. She never spoke of it, because she did not wish to spoil the holiday for others. Only Federico knew how she felt. In 1994, almost fifty years after the death of their infant son, just before Easter, Giulietta died.

Giulietta's last words were "I am going to spend Easter with Federico."

Films are listed in the order in which they were made. Asterisks indicate previously uncredited participation in films. Original titles, usually in Italian, are listed first. American (or English) titles appear in parentheses.

ABBREVIATIONS

FF: Federico Fellini
S: screenplay
D: director
AD: assistant director
A: art direction
C: costumes
P: photography (cinematography)
E: editor
M: music
Chor: choreography
Sd: sound
GO: general organization
EP: executive producer

PM: production manager
Prod: producer
O: country/countries of origin (if other than Italy)[1]
L: length of final print (may vary from country to country)

Fellini as Writer and/or Actor

1939

Imputato, alzatevi! (Defendant, On Your Feet!)
D: Mario Mattoli; S: Vittorio Metz, Mattoli; gag writer: *FF
Cast: Erminio Marcario

Lo vedi come sei? (See How You Are?)
D: Mario Mattoli; S: Vittorio Metz, Mattoli, Steno; gag writer: *FF
Cast: Erminio Marcario, Carlo Campanini

1940

No me lo dire! (Don't Tell Me!)
D: Mario Mattoli; S: Vittorio Metz, Marcello Marchesi, Mattoli, Steno; gag writer: *FF
Cast: Erminio Marcario

Il pirata sono io! (The Pirate Is I!)
D: Mario Mattoli; S: Vittorio Metz, Marcello Marchesi, Mattoli, Steno; gag writer: *FF
Cast: Erminio Marcario

1941/42

Documento Z-3 (Document Z-3)
D: Alfredo Guarini; S: Sandro De Feo, Guarini, Ercoli Patti; gag writer: *FF
Cast: Isa Miranda, Claudio Gora

Also as *gag writer: *Bentornato Signor Gai, Sette poveri in automobile, I predoni in Sahara*

---

[1]Country of origin usually denotes sources of backing, not actual shooting locations.

1942

Avanti c'è posto (*There's Room Up Ahead*)
D: Mario Bonnard; S: Aldo Fabrizi, Cesare Zavattini, and Piero Tellini, *from a story idea by FF
Cast: Aldo Fabrizi, Andrea Checchi

Quarta pagina (*The Fourth Page*)
D: Nicola Manzari; story by Piero Tellini and FF; S: Tellini, FF, Edoardo Anton, Ugo Betti, Nicola Manzari, Spiro Manzari, Giuseppe Marotta, Gianni Puccini, Steno, Cesare Zavattini (seven episodes by different writers)
Cast: Paola Barbara, Gino Cervi

1943

Campo de' fiori (*The Peddler and the Lady*)
D: Mario Bonnard; S: Marino Girolami, Aldo Fabrizi, Piero Tellini, and FF, from a story by Bonnard
Cast: Aldo Fabrizi, Anna Magnani, Peppino De Filippo

L'ultima carrozzella (*The Last Carriage*)
D: Mario Mattoli; S: FF, from a story idea by Aldo Fabrizi and FF
Cast: Aldo Fabrizi, Anna Magnani, Enzo Fiermonte, Paolo Stoppa

Chi l'ha visto? (*Who's Seen Him?*; released in 1945)
D: Goffredo Alessandrini; S: Piero Tellini and FF, from their story
Cast: Virgilio Riento, Valentina Cortese[2]

Gli ultimi Tuareg (*The Last Tuaregs*; never released)
D: Gino Talamo; S: FF and unidentified collaborators

1944

Apparizione (*Apparition*)
D: Jean de Limur; S: Piero Tellini, Lucio De Caro, Giuseppe Amato, *FF
Cast: Alida Valli, Amedeo Nazzari

---

[2]In Hollywood, Cortesa.

1945

Tutta la città canta (*The Whole City Is Singing*)
D: Riccardo Fredo; S: Vittorio Metz, Marcello Marchesi, Steno, *FF

Roma città aperta (*Open City*)
D: Roberto Rossellini; AD: FF; S: Sergio Amidei, FF, and Rossellini, from a story by Amidei and Alberto Consiglio; L: 105 minutes
Cast: Aldo Fabrizi, Anna Magnani, Maria Michi, Marcello Pagliero

1946

Paisà (*Paisan*)
D: Roberto Rossellini; S: Klaus Mann, Alfred Hayes, Marcello Pagliero, Sergio Amidei, Rossellini, and FF, from a treatment by Amidei and Mann
Cast: Carmela Sazio, Robert van Loon, John Kitzmiller, Maria Michi, Marcello Pagliero, Harriet White; L: 120 minutes

1947

Il Passatore (*A Bullet for Stefano*)
D: Duilio Coletti; S: *FF, Tullio Pinelli
Cast: Rossano Brazzi, Valentina Cortese, Carlo Ninchi

Il delitto di Giovanni Episcopo (*The Crime of Giovanni Episcopo/Flesh Will Surrender*)
D: Alberto Lattuada; S: Suso Cecchi d'Amico, Aldo Fabrizi, Piero Tellini, FF, and Lattuada, from a novel by Gabriele D'Annunzio; P: Aldo Tonti; A: Guido Fiorini; C: Gino C. Sensani; E: Raffaelle Barba; M: Felice Lattuada and Nino Rota; Prod: Marcello D'Amico, PAO-Lux Film; L: 94 minutes
Cast: Aldo Fabrizi (Giovanni Episcopo), Yvonne Sanson (Ginevra), Roldano Lupi (Wanzer), Ave Ninchi (Ginevra's mother), Nando Bruno (Antonio), Amedeo Fabrizi (Ciro), Alberto Sordi, Gina Lollobrigida, Silvana Mangano, Gino Cavalieri, Gina Luca Cortese, Francesco De Marco, Farrante Alvaro De Torres, Maria Gonelli, Lia Grani, Folco Lulli, Giorgio Moser, Gilberto Severi, Marco Tulli

Senza pietà (*Without Pity*)
D: Alberto Lattuada; AD: *FF; S: FF, Tullio Pinelli, and Lattuada, from a novel by Ettore Maria Margadonna; P: Aldo Tonti; E: Mario Bonotti; M: Nino Rota; Prod: Carlo Ponti; L: 94 minutes

Cast: Carla Del Poggio (Angela), John Kitzmiller (Jerry), Giulietta Masina (Marcella), Folco Lulli (Jack), Perre Claudé (Pierluigi), Daniel Jones (Richard), Enzo Giovine (Sister Gertrude), Otello Fava (the deaf one), Lando Muzio (the captain), Romano Villi (the bandit), Max Lancia (Cesare), Armando Libianchi, Mario Perrone

L'ebreo errante (*The Wandering Jew*)
D: Goffredo Alessandrini; S collaborator: *FF
Cast: Vittorio Gassman, Valentina Cortese, Rossano Brazzi

1948

L'amore (*Ways of Love*): Part 1, *Una voce umana;* Part 2, *Il miracolo* (Part 2 released in U.S.A. as *The Miracle*)
D: Roberto Rossellini; AD: *FF (*The Miracle*); S: (1) Roberto Rossellini, from *La voix humaine* by Jean Cocteau; (2) Tullio Pinelli and FF, from a story idea by FF
Cast: (in Part 1) Anna Magnani; (in Part 2) Anna Magnani (the goatherd), FF (the wanderer)

In nome della legge (*In the Name of the Law*)
D: Pietro Germi; S: Giuseppe Mangione, Germi, FF, and Mario Monicelli, from a book by Giuseppe Guido Loschiavo
Cast: Massimo Girotti, Charles Vanel, Saro Urzi, Camillo Mastrocinque

Il mulino del Po (*The Mill on the Po*)
D: Alberto Lattuada; S: FF and Tullio Pinelli, from a novel by Riccardo Bacchelli, adapted by Bacchelli, Mario Bonfantini, Luigi Comencini, Carlo Musso, and Sergio Romano; P: Aldo Tonti; A: Aldo Buzzi; C: Maria De Matteis; E: Mario Bonotti; M: Ildebrando Pizzetti; Prod: Carlo Ponti; L: 107 minutes
Cast: Carla Del Poggio (Berta Scacerni), Jacques Sernas (Orbino Verginesi), Isabella Riva (Cecilia Scacerni), Giacomo Giuradel (Princivalle), Leda Gloria (Sniza), Domenico Viglione Borghese (Luca Verginesi), Anna Carena (Argia), Nino Pavese (Raibolini), Giulio Cali (Smarazzacucco), Mario Besesti (Clapasson), Edith Bleber, Pina Gallini, Rina Perna, Dina Sassoli, Giulio Spaggiari

Città dolente (*Sad City*)
D: Mario Bonnard; S collaborator: FF
Cast: Luigi Tosi, Barbara Costanova

1950

Il cammino della speranza (The Path of Hope)
D: Pietro Germi; S: FF and Tullio Pinelli, from a story by Germi, Pinelli, and FF
Cast: Raf Vallone, Elena Varzi, Saro Urzi

Francesco giullare di dio (The Flowers of St. Francis)
D: Roberto Rossellini; S: Rossellini, FF, Felix Morlion, and Antonio Lisandrini, from the legends surrounding St. Francis of Assisi
Cast: Aldo Fabrizi, Arabella Lemaitre, Alberto Plebani

1951

Persiane chiuse (Behind Closed Shutters)
D: Luigi Comencini; S: Massimo Mida, Gianni Puccini, Franco Solinas, Sergio Sollima, and *FF
Cast: Massimo Girotti, Giulietta Masina, Eleonora Rossi Drago

La città si difende (Passport to Hell/The City Defends Itself)
D: Pietro Germi; AD: FF; S: FF, Tullio Pinelli, Germi, and Giuseppe Mangione, from a story by Luigi Comencini, Pinelli, and FF
Cast: Gina Lollobrigida, Paul Muller, Fausto Tozzi, Renato Baldini, Enzo Maggio

Cameriera bella presenza offresi (Attractive Maid Available)
D: Giorgio Pastina; S: FF and Tullio Pinelli, from a story by Nicola Manzari
Cast: Aldo Fabrizi, Vittorio de Sica, Alberto Sordi, Giulietta Masina

Il brigante di tacca del Lupo (The Brigand of Tacca del Lupo)
D: Pietro Germi; AD: FF; S: FF, Tullio Pinelli, and Germi
Cast: Amedeo Nazzari, Saro Urzi

Europa '51 (The Greatest Love)
D: Roberto Rossellini; S: Rossellini, Sandro da Feo, Mario Pannunzio, Ivo Perilli, Brunello Rondi, Diego Fabbri, Antonio Pietrangeli, and FF
Cast: Ingrid Bergman, Alexander Knox, Giulietta Masina

1957

Fortunella
D: Eduardo De Filippo; S: FF, Enno Flaiano, and Tullio Pinelli
Cast: Giulietta Masina, Paul Douglas, Alberto Sordi

1972

Alex in Wonderland
D: Paul Mazursky; S: Mazursky and Larry Tucker; P: Laszlo Kovacs
Cast: Donald Sutherland, Ellen Burstyn, Meg Mazursky, Paul Mazursky, FF (as himself)

1974

C'eravamo tanto amati (*We All Loved Each Other So Much*)
D: Ettore Scola
Cast: Nino Manfredi, Vittorio Gassman, Stefania Sandrelli, Marcello Mastroianni, Vittorio de Sica, Aldo Fabrizi, FF (as himself)

1979

Viaggio con Anita (*Voyage with Anita/Lovers and Liars*)
D: Mario Monicelli; S: Tullio Pinelli, *FF
Cast: Giancarlo Giannini, Goldie Hawn

1983

Il tassinaro (*The Taxi Driver*)
D: Alberto Sordi
Cast: Alberto Sordi, Giulio Andreotti, Silvana Pampanini, FF (as a taxi passenger)

Fellini also appears as himself in four of his own films, and he narrates or is heard, voice-over, in several others (see below).

Fellini as Director

1950

Luci del varietà (*Variety Lights*)
D: Alberto Lattuada and FF; AD: Angelo D'Alessandro; S: Lattuada, FF, and Tullio Pinelli, with the collaboration of Ennio Fla-

iano, from a story by FF; P: Otello Martelli; A and C: Aldo Buzzi; E: Mario Bonotti; M: Felice Lattuada; PM: Bianca Lattuada, GO: Mario Ingrami; Prod: Lattuada and FF, Capitolium Film; L: 100 minutes.

Cast: Carla Del Poggio (Liliana "Lilly" Antonelli), Peppino De Filippo (Checco Dalmonte), Giulietta Masina (Melina Amour), Folco Lulli (Adelmo Conti), Franca Valeri (Hungarian choreographer), Carlo Romano (Enzo La Rosa, lawyer), John Kitzmiller (John), Dante Maggio (Remo, the master of ceremonies), Alberto Bonucci and Vittorio Caprioli (theatrical duet), Giulio Cali (fakir), Silvio Bagolini (Bruno Antonini, the reporter), Checco Durante (theater owner) Giacomo Furia (Duke), Alberto Lattuada (theater menial), Mario De Angelis (maestro), Joe Fallotta (Bill), Renato Malavasi (innkeeper), Fanny Marchiò (soubrette), Gina Mascetti (Valeria Del Sole), Vanja Orico (Gypsy singer), Enrico Piergentili (Melina's father), Marco Tulli (spectator), Nando Bruno

1952

Lo sceicco bianco (The White Sheik)
D: FF; S: FF and Tullio Pinelli, with the collaboration of Ennio Flaiano, from a story idea by Michelangelo Antonioni; P: Arturo Gallea; A: Raffaello Tolfo; E: Rolando Benedetti; M: Nino Rota; PM: Enzo Provenzali; Prod: Luigi Rovere, P.D.C.–O.F.I; L: 85 minutes
Cast: Alberto Sordi (Fernando Rivoli, the White Sheik), Brunella Bovo (Wanda Giardino), Leopoldo Trieste (Ivan Cavalli), Giulietta Masina (Cabiria), Lilia Landi (Felga), Ernesto Almirante (the director), Enzo Maggio (the hotel doorman), Ettore M. Margadonna (Ivan's uncle), Fanny Marchiò (Marilena Vellardi), Gina Mascetti (Fernando's wife)

1953

I vitelloni (I Vitelloni; released as The Spivs in the U.K.)
D: FF; S: FF, Ennio Flaiano and Tullio Pinelli, based on a story idea by Pinelli and a story by FF, Flaiano, and Pinelli; P: Otello Martelli, Luciano Trasatti, and Carlo Carlini; A: Mario Chiari; C: M. Marinari Bomarzi; E: Rolando Benedetti; M: Nino Rota; PM: Luigi Giacosi; Prod: Lorenzo Pegoraro, Peg Film/Cité Film; O: Italy-France; L: 103 minutes

Cast: Franco Interlenghi (Moraldo), Alberto Sordi (Alberto), Franco Fabrizi (Fausto), Leopoldo Trieste (Leopoldo), Riccardo Fellini (Riccardo), Eleonora Ruffo (Sandra), Enrico Viarisio and Paola Borboni (Moraldo and Sandra's parents), Carlo Romano (Michele, the antiques dealer), Lida Baarova (his wife), Claude Farell (Alberto's sister), Jean Brochard (Fausto's father), Arlette Sauvage (unknown woman in movie theater), Vira Silenti (usher), Maja Nipora (lead dancer); Achille Majeroni (Natali, the old actor), Silvio Bagolini (idiot), *FF (unseen narrator)

L'amore in città (*Love in the City;* fourth episode: *Un giornalista racconta agenzia matrimoniale* [*A Matrimonial Agency,* also known as *Marriage Bureau*]. Directors of the other episodes: Michelangelo Antonioni, Alberto Lattuada, Carlo Lizzani, Francesco Maselli, Dino Risi, Cesare Zavattini)
D: FF; S: FF and Tullio Pinelli, from a story idea by FF; P: Gianni Di Venanzo; A: Gianni Polidori; E: Eraldo da Roma; M: Mario Nascimbene; PM: Luigi Giacosi; Prod: Cesare Zavattini, Faro Film; L: 32 minutes
Cast: Antonio Cifariello (reporter), Livia Venturini (marriage candidate)

1954

La strada (*La Strada*)
D: FF; S: FF and Tullio Pinelli, with the collaboration of Ennio Flaiano, from a story by FF and Pinelli, dialogue by Pinelli, and the artistic collaboration of Brunello Rondi; P: Otello Martelli; A: Mario Ravasco; C: Margherita Marinari Bomarzi; E: Leo Catozzo; M: Nino Rota; PM: Luigi Giacosi; Prod: Dino de Laurentiis, Carlo Ponti; L: 115 minutes
Cast: Anthony Quinn (Zampanò), Giulietta Masina (Gelsomina), Richard Basehart (Fool), Aldo Silvani (Signor Giraffa), Marcella Rovere (widow), Livia Venturini (nun), Mario Passante, Yami Kamedeva, Anna Primula

1955

Il bidone (*The Swindle*)
D: FF; S: FF, Ennio Flaiano, and Tullio Pinelli, from their story, with

the artistic collaboration of Brunello Rondi; P: Otello Martelli; A and C: Dario Cecchi; E: Mario Serandrei, Giuseppe Vari; M: Nino Rota; PM: Giuseppe Colizzi; Prod: Titanus/S.G.C.; O: Italy-France; L: 104 minutes

Cast: Broderick Crawford (Augusto), Richard Basehart (Picasso), Franco Fabrizi (Roberto), Giulietta Masina (Iris), Giacomo Gabrielli ("Baron" Vargas), Alberto De Amicis (Rinaldo), Lorella De Luca (Patrizia), Sue Ellen Blake (Susanna), Mara Werlen (showgirl), Irene Cefaro (Marisa), Alberto Plebani, Riccardo Garrone, Paul Grenter, Emilio Manfredi, Lucetta Muratori, Xenla Valderi, Mario Passante, Sara Simoni, Mario Zanoli, Ettore Bevilacqua

1957

Le notti di Cabiria (The Nights of Cabiria)
D: FF; S: FF, Ennio Flaiano, and Tullio Pinelli, from their story, with dialogue collaboration by Pier Paolo Pasolini; P: Aldo Tonti; A and C: Piero Gherardi; E: Leo Catozzo and Giuseppe Vari; M: Nino Rota; PM: Luigi de Laurentiis; Prod: Dino de Laurentiis, Les Films Marceau; O: Italy-France; L: 110 minutes

Cast: Giulietta Masina (Cabiria), François Périer (Oscar D'Onofrio), Franca Marzi (Wanda), Dorian Gray (Jessy), Amedeo Nazzari (Alberto Lazzari), Aldo Silvani (fakir), Mario Passante (lame man), Pina Gualandri (Matilde), Polidor (friar), Ennio Girolami (pimp), *Franco Fabrizi (Cabiria's first lover), *Riccardo Fellini

1960

La dolce vita (La Dolce Vita)
D: FF; S: FF, Ennio Flaiano, and Tullio Pinelli, from their story, with dialogue collaboration by Brunello Rondi; P: Otello Martelli; A and C: Piero Gherardi; E: Leo Catozzi; Sd: Agostino Moretti; M: Nino Rota; Prod: Giuseppe Amato, Angelo Rizzoli, Riama Film/Pathé Consortium Cinéma; O: Italy-France; L: 178 minutes

Cast: Marcello Mastroianni (Marcello Rubini), Walter Santesso (Paparazzo), Yvonne Furneaux (Emma), Anouk Aimée (Maddalena), Adriana Moneta (prostitute), Anita Ekberg (Sylvia), Lex Barker (Robert), Alan Dijon (Frankie Stout), Alain Cuny (Steiner), Renée Longarini (Signora Steiner), Valeria Ciangottini (Paola), Annibale Ninchi (Marcello's father), Magali Noël (Fanny), Nadia

Gray (Nadia), Laura Betti (Laura), Jacques Sernas (star), Riccardo Garrone (Riccardo), Ferdinando Brofferio (Maddalena's lover), Alex Messoyedoff (priest), Rina Franchetti (children's mother), Aurelio Nardi (children's uncle), Iris Tree (poetess), Leonida Rapaci (writer), Audrey MacDonald (Sonia), Polidor (clown), Franca Pasutt (feathered girl), Giulio Paradisi, Enzo Cerusico, and Enzo Doria (photographers), Vadim Wolkonsky (Prince Mascalchi), Prince Eugenio Ruspoli (Father Mascalchi), Alberto Plebani (coroner), Gio Staiano (effeminate youth), Giaromo Gabrielli (Maddalena's father), Harriet White (Sylvia's secretary)

1962

Boccaccio '70 (Second episode: *Le tentazioni de Dottor Antonio* [*The Temptation of Dr. Antonio*]. Directors of the other episodes: Mario Monicelli, Luchino Visconti, Vittorio de Sica)
D: FF; S: FF, Tullio Pinelli, and Ennio Flaiano, from a story idea by FF, with dialogue collaboration by Brunello Rondi and Goffredo Parise; P: Otello Martelli; A: Piero Zuffi; E: Leo Catozzo; M: Nino Rota; Prod: Carlo Ponti, Concordia C.C., Cineriz/Francinex-Gray Film; O: Italy-France; L: 60 minutes
Cast: Peppino De Filippo (Dr. Antonio Mazzuolo), Anita Ekberg (Anita, the woman on the poster), Antonio Acqua (Commander La Pappa), Eleonora Nagy (little girl), Donatella Della Nora, Dante Maggio (Dr. Antonio's sisters), Giacomo Furia, Mario Passante, Giulio Paradisi, Polidor

1963

Otto e mezzo (*8½*)
D: FF; S: FF, Ennio Flaiano, Tullio Pinelli, and Brunello Rondi, from a story by FF and Flaiano; P: Gianni Di Venanzo; A and C: Piero Gherardi; E: Leo Catozzo; M: Nino Rota; GO: Clemente Fracassi and Alessandro Von Norman; Prod: FF, Angelo Rizzoli, Cineriz/Francinex; O: Italy-France; L: 135 minutes
Cast: Marcello Mastroianni (Guido Anselmi), Anouk Aimée (Luisa Anselmi), Sandra Milo (Carla), Claudia Cardinale (Claudia), Rossella Falk (Rossella), Barbara Steele (Gloria), Ian Dallas (Maurice, the magician), Mary Indovino (mind reader), Eugene Walter (American journalist), Gilda Dahlberg (his wife), Vadim Wolkonsky (hotel

manager), Marco Gemini (young Guido), Riccardo Guglielmi (Guido as small child), Georgia Simmons (his grandmother), Yvonne Casadei (Jacqueline Bonbon), Mino Doro (Claudia's agent), Giuditta Rissone (Guido's mother), Annibale Ninchi (Guido's father), Guido Alberti (Pace, the producer), Jean Rougeul (Carini), Tito Masini (the cardinal), Edra Gale (La Saraghina), Madeleine Lebeau (French actress), Neil Robertson (her agent), Mario Pisu (Mario Mezzabotta), Rossella Como (friend of Luisa's), Mario Tedeschi (headmaster), Elisabetta Catalano (Luisa's sister), Mark Herron (Luisa's suitor), Polidor (clown), Nandine Sanders (stewardess), Hazel Rogers (black dancer), Elisabetta Cini (cardinal stand-in)

1965

Giulietta degli spiriti (*Juliet of the Spirits*)
D: FF; S: FF, Tullio Pinelli, and Ennio Flaiano, with collaboration by Brunello Rondi, from a story by FF and Pinelli; P: Gianni Di Venanzo; A and C: Piero Gherardi; E: Ruggero Mastroianni; Sd: Mario Faraoni, Mario Morici; M: Nino Rota; GO: Clemente Fracassi; Prod: Angelo Rizzòli, Federiz/Francoriz; O: Italy-France-Germany; L: 148 minutes
Cast: Giulietta Masina (Giulietta Boldrini), Mario Pisu (Giorgio), Valentina Cortese (Valentina), Caterina Boratto (Giulietta's mother), Sylva Koscina (Sylva), Luisa Della Noce (Adele), José Luis de Villalonga (José), Silvana Jachino (Dolores), Elsabetta Gray (Giulietta's maid), Milena Vukotic (Giulietta's maid and the saint), Sandra Milo (Susy, Iris, Fanny), Alessandra Mannoukine (Susy's mother), Ina Alexejeva (Susy's grandmother), Eugenio Mastropietro (Genius), Alberto Plebani (private detective Lynx-Eyes/priestly apparition), Lou Gilbert (Giuletta's grandfather), Valeska Gert (Bhishma), Fred Williams (Arabian prince), Edoardo Torricella (Russian teacher), Alba Cancellieri (Giulietta as a child), Dany Paris (suicidal girl), Federico Valli (Psychologist), Felice Fulchignoni (Don Raffaele), Friedrich von Ledebur (headmaster), Guido Albertu, Maria Tedeschi

1968

Tre passi nel delirio (*Spirits of the Dead;* third episode: *Toby Dammit* [*Toby Dammit*]. Directors of the other episodes: Roger Vadim, Louis Malle)

D: FF; S: FF and Bernardino Zapponi, from the story "Never Bet the Devil Your Head" by Edgar Allan Poe; P: Giuseppe Rotunno; A and C: Piero Tosi; E: Ruggero Mastroianni; M: Nino Rota; GO: Enzo Provenzali; Prod: Alberto Grimaldi, Raymond Eger, PEA/Les films Marceau/Cocinor; O: Italy-France; L: 37 minutes

Cast: Terence Stamp (Toby Dammit), Salvo Randone (Father Spagna), Polidor (aged actor), Antonia Pietrosi (actress), Anne Tonietti (TV commentator), Fabrizio Angeli and Ernesto Colli (directors), Aleardo Ward and Paul Cooper (interviewers), Marina Yaru (the devil as little girl with ball)

1969

Block-notes di un regista (Fellini: A Director's Notebook; TV documentary)

D: FF; S: FF and Bernardino Zapponi; P: Pasquale De Santis; E: Ruggero Mastroianni; GO: Lamberto Pippia; M: Nino Rota; Prod: Peter Goldfarb, NBC-TV; O: USA; L: 60 minutes

Cast: Marcello Mastroianni, FF, Giulietta Masina, Maria Ceratto, Gasperino, Bernardino Zapponi, Eugenio Mastropietro, Caterina Boratto, Marina Boratto, Cesarino Miceli Picardi, Lina Alberti, David Mauhsell, Martin Potter

Fellini Satyricon (Fellini Satyricon)

D: FF; S: FF and Bernardino Zapponi, based on *Satyricon* by Titus Petronius; P: Giuseppe Rotunno; A: Danilo Donati and Luigi Scaccianoce; C: Danilo Donati; E: Ruggero Mastroianni; M: Nino Rota with Ilhan Mimaroglu, Tod Dockstader, and Andrew Rubin; historical adviser: Luca Canali; GO: Enzo Provenzali; Prod: Alberto Grimaldi, PEA/Les Productions Artistes Associés; O: Italy; L: 138 minutes

Cast: Martin Potter (Encolpio), Hiram Keller (Ascilto), Max Born (Gitone), Salvo Randone (Eumolpo), Fanfulla (Vernacchio), Gordon Mitchell (robber), Mario Romagnoli (Trimalcione), Magali Noël (Fortunata), Capucine (Trifena), Alain Cuny (Lica), Danika La Loggia (Scintilla), Giuseppe Sanvitale (Abinna), Eugenio Mastropietro (Cinedo), Joseph Wheeler (patrician), Lucia Bosé (his wife), Donyale Luna (young Enotea), Elisa Mainardi (Arianna), Marcello Di Falco (proconsul), Gennero Sabatino (ferryman), Hylette Adolphe (slave girl), Maria Antonietta Beluzzi (old Enotea), Tanya

Lopert (young emperor), Sibilla Sedat (nymphomaniac), Luigi Zerbantini (her slave), Lorenzo Piani (her husband), Pasquale Baldassare (hermaphrodite), Antonia Petrosi (widow of Ephesus), Wolfgang Hiller (soldier at tomb), Luigi Montefiori (minotaur), Salvo Randone (Eumolpo), Silvio Belusci (dwarf), Pasquale Fasciano (magician), Patricia Hartley (his assistant), Giuseppe San Vitale (Habinnas), Carlo Giordana (captain)

1970

I clowns (The Clowns)

D: FF; S: FF and Bernardino Zapponi, from their story; P: Dario Di Palma; A: Renzo Gronchi; C: Danilo Donati; E: Ruggero Mastroianni; M: Nino Rota; PM: Lamberto Pippia; Prod: Elio Scardamaglia, Ugo Guerra, RAI/ORTF/Bavaria Film/Compagnia Leone Cinematografica; O: Italy-France-Germany; L: 93 minutes

Cast: FF, Maya Morin (secretary), Alvaro Vitali (sound technician), Lina Alberto (assistant), Gasperino (cameraman), Carlo Rizzo (manager), Tino Scotti (notary public), Nino Terzo, Dante Maggio, and Gaetano Sbarra (technicians), Fanfulla (white clown), Giacomo Furia, and (as themselves) Liana, Rinaldo, and Nando Orfei, Anita Ekberg, Franco Migliorini, Tristan Rémy, Pierre Etaix, Victor Fratellini, Victoria Chaplin, Baptiste; French clowns: Alex, Maiss, Bario, Père Loriot, Ludo, Nino, Charlie Rivel; Italian clowns: Riccardo, Billi, Tino Scotti, Carlo Rizzo, Freddo Pistoni, The Colombaioni, Merli, Valdemaro Bevilacqua, Janigro, Vingelli, Fumagalli, Carini, Sorentino, The Martanas

1972

Fellini Roma (Fellini's Roma)

D: FF; S: FF and Bernardino Zapponi, from their story; P: Giuseppe Rotunno; A and C: Danilo Donati; E: Ruggero Mastroianni; M: Nino Rota; Chor: Gino Landi; GO: Danilo Marciani; PM: Lamberto Pippia; Prod: Ultra Film, Les Productions Artistes Associés; O: Italy-France; L: 128 minutes

Cast: Peter Gonzales (young Fellini), Francesco Di Giacomo (his bearded friend), Fiona Florence (Dolores), Anna Maria Pescatori (prostitute), Galliano Sbarra, Alfredo Adani, and Mario Del Vago (three comics), Veriano Ginesi (fat lady), Alvaro Vitali (dancer), Libero Frissi (performer), Loredana Martinez (singer), Pia de Doses (princess), Mario Giovannioli (cardinal), Guglielmo Guasta (Pope), Marne Maitland (guide to the catacombs), Gore Vidal, John Francis Lane, and Anna Magnani (as themselves), FF (as himself and the voice of the camera); Italian version only: Marcello Mastroianni, Alberto Sordi

1973

Amarcord (Amarcord)

D: FF; S: FF and Tonino Guerra, from their story; P: Giuseppe Rotunno; A and C: Danilo Donati; E: Ruggero Mastroianni; Sd: Oscar De Arcangelis; M: Nino Rota; PM: Lamberto Pippia; Prod: Franco Cristaldi, Federico C. Produzioni, PEC Federico; O: Italy-France; L: 127 minutes

Cast: Bruno Zanin (Titta Biondi), Pupella Maggio (his mother), Armando Brancia (Aurelio, his father), Stefano Proietti (Oliva, his brother), Peppino Ianigro (his grandfather), Nandino Orfei (Patacca), Carla Mora (maid), Ciccio Ingrassia (Uncle Teo), Aristide Caporale (Giudizio), Luigi Rossi (lawyer), Magali Noël (Ninola/Gradisca), Marina Trovalusci (Gradisca's sister when small), Fiorella Magalotti (Gradisca's grown sister), Josiane Tanzilli (Volpina), Antonino Faà di Bruno (Conte di Lovignano), Gian Filippo Carcano (Father Balosa), Armando Villella (Professor Fighetta), Mario Liberati (owner of the Fulgor Cinema), Marcello di Falco (prince), Gennaro Ombra (Biscein), Gianfranco Marrocco (Conte Poltavo), Alvaro Vitali (Naso), Bruno Scagnetti (Ovo), Bruno Lenzi (Gigliozzi), Francesco Puntieri (lunatic), Vincenzo Caldarola (Emir-beggar), Maria Antonietta Beluzzi (tobacconist), Domenico Pertica (blind singer), Fides Stegni (art-history teacher), Giovanni Attansio (bald fascist), Francesco Maselli (physics teacher), Ferrucio Brembilla (fascist leader), Franco Magno (headmaster), Mauro Misul (philosophy teacher), Dina Adorni (math teacher), Mario Silvestri (Italian teacher), Marcello Borini Olas (gym teacher), Fernando De Felici (Ciccio), Francesca Vona (Candela), Donatella Gambini (Aldina Cordini), Fausto Signoretti (coachman), Fredo Pistoni (Colonia), Mario Nebolini (town clerk), Milo Mario (photographer), Antonio Spaccatini (federale), Bruno Bartocci (Gradisca's bridegroom)

1976

Il Casanova di Federico Fellini (*Casanova;* also known as *Fellini's Casanova*)

D: FF; S: FF and Bernardino Zapponi, freely adapted from *The History of My Life,* by Giovanni Giacomo Casanova; P: Giuseppe Rotunno; A and C: Danilo Donati; E: Ruggero Mastroianni; Chor: Gino Landi; Sd: Oscar De Arcangelis; M: Nino Rota; PM: Lamberto Pippia; Prod: Alberto Grimaldi, PEA; L: 170 minutes

Cast: Donald Sutherland (Casanova), Margareth Clementi (Sister Maddalena), Cicely Browne (Madame d'Urfé), Clara Algranti (Marcolina), Tina Aumont (Henriette), Daniel Emilfork Berenstein (Du Bois), Clarissa Roll (Annamaria), Mariano Brancaccio (Gianbruno), Carmen Scarpitta and Diane Kourys (the mother and daughter Charpillon), Daniela Gatti (Giselda), Reggie Nalder (Faulkircher), Dan van Husen (Viderol), Sandra Elaine Allen (giantess), Antonio De Martino (her companion), Sergio Dolce and Antonio De Martino (her assistants), Veronica Nava (Romana), Olimpia Carlisi (Isabella), Marika Riviera (Astrodi), Mario Cencelli (Dr. Mobius), Silvana Fusacchia (Silvana), Chesty Morgan (Barberina), Luigi Zerbinati (Pope), Alfonso Nappo (Dr. Righellini), Adele Angela Lojodice (the mechanical doll), Marie Marquet (Casanova's mother), Dudley Sutton (Duke of Württemberg), Marjorie Bell (Countess of Waldenstein), Francesco De Rosa (Casanova's servant), John Karlsen (Lord Talou), Mario Gaglardo (Righetto), Angelica Hansen (hunchbacked actress), Susanna Nielsen, Alfredo Sivoli, Gennero Ombra

1979

Prova d'orchestra (*Orchestra Rehearsal*)

D: FF; S: FF, from his story idea, with the collaboration of Brunello Rondi; P: Giuseppe Rotunno; A: Dante Ferretti; C: Gabriella Pescucci; E: Ruggero Mastroianni; M: Nino Rota; GO: Lamberto Pippia; Prod: Daime Cinematografica, RAI Uno, Albatros Produktion; O: Italy-Germany; L: 72 minutes

Cast: Baldwin Bass (conductor), Umberto Zuanelli (copyist), Clara Colosimo (harpist), Elisabeth Labi (pianist), Fernando Villella (cellist), Ronaldo Bonacchi (contrabassoonist), Giovanni Javarone (tubist), David Mauhsell (concertmaster), Heinz Krueger and

Angelica Hansen (violinists), Francesco Aluigi (principal second violin), Franco Mazzieri (trumpeter), Daniele Pagani (trombonist), Andy Miller (oboist), Sibyl Mostert (flutist), Claudio Ciocca (union representative), Filippo Trincia (union representative), FF (voice of the camera)

1980

La città delle donne (*City of Women*)
D: FF; S: FF and Bernardino Zapponi, from their story, with the collaboration of Brunello Rondi; P: Giuseppe Rotunno; A: Dante Ferretti; C: Gabriella Pescucci; Sd: Tommaso Quattrini, Pierre Paul Marie Lorrain; E: Ruggero Mastroianni; M: Luis Bacalov; Ballet: Mirella Aguiaro; Chor: Leonetta Bentivoglio; EP: Franco Rossellini; PM: Francesco Orefici; Prod: Opera Film/Gaumont; O: Italy-France; L: 145 minutes
Cast: Marcello Mastroianni (Snaporaz), Bernice Stegers (unknown woman on train), Iole Silvani (motorcycle girl), Donatella Damiani (Donatella), Ettore Manni (Dr. Sante Katzone), Anna Prucnal (Elena), Rosaria Tafuri and Edith Diaz (ballerinas), Fiammetta Baralla (Olio), Alessandra Panelli (housewife with child), Gabriella Giorgelli, Maria Simmons and Carla Terlizzi (feminists), Mara Ciukleva (elderly woman), Katren Gebelein (Signora Small), Pietro Fumagalli, Armando Parracino and Umberto Zuanelli (three men on the slide), Bentley Boseo (policewoman), Agnes Kalpagos (prostitute), Silvana Fusacchia (roller skater), Karin Mallach (feminist journalist), Liliana Paganini, Marcello Di Falco, Bobby Rhodes, Franco Diogene

1983

E la nave va (*And the Ship Sails On*)
D: FF; S: FF and Tonino Guerra, from their story; Opera Texts: Andrea Zanzotto; P: Giuseppe Rotunno; A: Dante Ferretti; C: Maurizio Millenotti; Chor: Leonetta Bentivoglio; E: Ruggero Mastroianni; M: Gianfranco Plenizio; GO: Pietro Notarianni; EP: Franco Cristaldi; Prod: Aldo Nemni, RAI Uno, Vides/Gaumont; O: Italy-France; L: 132 minutes
Cast: Freddie Jones (Orlando), Peter Cellier (Sir Reginald Dongby), Norma West (Violet Dongby), Victor Poletti (Aureliano Fuciletto),

Fiorenzo Serra (Archduke of Herzog), Pina Bausch (Princess Lherimia), Barbara Jefford (Ildebranda Cuffari), Elisa Mainardi (Teresa Valegnani), Paolo Paoloni (Maestro Albertini), Pasquale Zito (Conte di Bassano), Janet Suzman (Edmea Tetua), Jonathan Cecil (Ricotin), Philip Locke (prime minister), FF (as himself)

1984

Bitter Campari (TV commercial)
D and S: FF; P: Ennio Guarnieri; A: Dante Ferretti; E: Ugo De Rossi; M: "La rumbetta del trenino" by Nicola Piovani; Prod: Giulio Romieri, Brw & partners; L: 60 seconds

1985

Ginger e Fred (*Ginger and Fred*)
D: FF; S: FF, Tonino Guerra, and Tullio Pinelli, based on a story by FF and Guerra; P: Tonino Delli Colli and Ennio Guarnieri; A: Dante Ferreti; C: Danilo Donati; Chor: Tony Ventura; E: Nino Baragli, Ugo De Rossi, and Ruggero Mastroianni; M: Nicola Piovani; GO: Luigi Millozza; Prod: Alberto Grimaldi, PEA/Revcom Films, in association with Les Films Arianne, FR3, Stella Film Anthea, RAI Uno; O: Italy-France; L: 126 minutes
Cast: Giulietta Masina (Ginger), Marcello Mastroianni (Fred), Augusto Poderosi (transsexual), Friedrich von Ledebur (Admiral), Toto Mignone (Toto), Franco Fabrizi (master of ceremonies), Gianfranco Alpestre (lawyer), Martin Maria Blau (assistant director), Jacques Henri Lartigue (the flying friar), Ezio Mariano (intellectual), Barbara Scoppa (journalist), Ginestra Spinola (clairvoyant), Francesco Casale (gangster), Isabelle La Porte (TV hostess), Pippo Negri (panties inventor), Luciano Lombardo (defrocked priest)

1986

Alta Società Rigatoni Barilla (TV commercial)
D and S: FF; P: Ennio Guarnieri; A: Danilo Donati; E: Ugo De Rossi and Anna Amedei; M: Nino Rota, arranged by Nicola Piovani; Prod: Fabrizio Capucci, International Cbn; L: 60 seconds
Cast: Greta Vaian, Maurizio Mauri

1987

Intervista

D: FF; S: FF, with the collaboration of Gianfranco Angelucci, based on a story idea by FF; P: Tonino Delli Colli; A and C: Danilo Donati; E: Nino Baragli; M: Nicola Piovani; EP: Pietro Notarianni; Prod: Ibrahim Moussa, Alijosha Productions, in collaboration with Cinecittà and RAI Uno; O: Italy-France; L: 113 minutes

Cast: FF (as himself), Sergio Rubini (reporter, young Fellini), Paola Liguori (the star), Nadia Gambacorta (Nadia, the Vestal Virgin), Antonella Ponziani (blond girl), Pietro Notarianni (fascist leader), Lara Wendel (bride), Antonio Cantafora (groom), Maurizio Mein (assistant director), Anita Ekberg, Marcello Mastroianni, Danilo Donati, Tonino Delli Colli (as themselves), Nadia Ottaviani (Cinecittà archivist)

1990

La voce della luna (Voices of the Moon)

D: FF; S: FF, with the collaboration of Tullio Pinelli and Ermanno Cavazzoni; based on Cavazzoni's novel *Il poema dei lunatici;* P: Tonino Delli Colli; A: Dante Ferretti; C: Maurizio Millenotti; E: Nino Baragli; Chor: Mirella Aguyaro; M: Nicola Piovani; Sd: Tommaso Quattrini; PM: Roberto Mannoni; GO: Pietro Notarianni and Maurizio Pastrovich; Prod: Mario and Vittorio Cecchi Gori, Tiger Cinematographica, Cinemax; O: Italy-France; L: 118 minutes

Cast: Roberto Benigni (Ivo Salvini), Paolo Villaggio (the prefect Gonnella), Nadia Ottaviani (Aldina Ferruzzi), Susy Blady (Aldina's sister), Dario Ghirardi (reporter), Marisa Tomasi (Marisa), Angelo Orlando (Nestore), Dominique Chevalier (Tazio Mecheluzzi), Niger Harris (Giuanin Micheluzzi), Eraldo Turra (lawyer), Giordano Falzoni (professor), Ferruccio Brambilla (doctor), Giovanni Javarone (gravedigger), Lorose Keller (the duchess), Patrizia Roversi (daughter of Gonnella), Uta Schmidt

1992

Banca di Roma (three TV commercials)

D and S: FF; P: Giuseppe Rotunno; A: Antonello Geleng; E: Nino Baragli; M: Nicola Piovani; Prod: Roberto Mannoni, Film Master; L: 120 seconds each

Cast: Paolo Villaggio, Fernando Rey, Anna Falchi, Ellen Rossi Stuart

Fellini's Awards

1953

I vitelloni (I Vitelloni)
Venice: Silver Lion (no Golden Lion awarded)

1956

La strada (La Strada)
Hollywood: Academy Award: Best Foreign Film
New York: New York Film Critics Circle Award: Best Foreign-Language Film
Venice: Silver Lion

1957

Le notti di Cabiria (The Nights of Cabiria)
Hollywood: Academy Award: Best Foreign Film

1960, 1961

La dolce vita (La Dolce Vita)
Cannes: Golden Palm, 1960
Acupulco: FIPRESCI Award, 1960
New York: New York Film Critics Circle Award: Best Foreign-Language Film, 1961

1963, 1964

Otto e mezzo (8½)
Hollywood: Academy Awards: Best Foreign Film; Costumes (Piero Gherardi), 1963
New York: New York Film Critics Circle Award: Best Foreign-Language Film, 1963
Moscow: Moscow Film Festival Grand Prize, 1963
West Berlin: Berlin International Film Festival Jury's Special Award, 1964

1965

Giulietta degli spiriti (Juliet of the Spirits)
New York: New York Film Critics Circle Award: Best Foreign-Language Film

1974

Amarcord (Amarcord)
Hollywood: Academy Award: Best Foreign Film
New York: New York Film Critics Circle Award: Best Foreign-Language Film

1976

Il Casanova di Federico Fellini (Casanova)
Hollywood: Academy Award: Costumes (Danilo Donati)

1985

Venice: Golden Lion for life's work

1993

Hollywood: Honorary Academy Award

index

CHARLOTTE CHANDLER wrote *Hello, I Must Be Going,* the bestseller about Groucho Marx, and *The Ultimate Seduction,* conversations with great figures of the twentieth century. She has written for films, television, radio, magazines, newspapers, and the theater, and is a member of the board of the Film Society of Lincoln Center.